LONDON, NEW YORK, MUNICH, MELBOURNE, DELHI

Senior Editor Alastair Laing
Senior Art Editor Sara Robin
Managing Editor Esther Ripley
Managing Art Editor Alison Donovan
Editors Sharon Amos, Emma Callery
Designers Tina Vaughan, Kathy Gammon,
Vanessa Hamilton, Vicky Read
Illustrator Andy Crisp
Photographer Peter Anderson
Production Editor Ben Marcus
Production Controller Man Fai Lau
Picture Researcher Jenny Faithfull
Publisher Mary-Clare Jerram
Art Director Peter Luff

First published in Great Britain in 2010 by
Dorling Kindersley Limited
80 Strand, London WC2R 0RL

A Penguin Company

2 4 6 8 10 9 7 5 3 1

A CIP catalogue record for this book is
available from the British Library

ISBN: 978 1 4053 4441 8

Colour reproduction by Alta Images, London
Printed and bound by Hung Hing, China

IMPORTANT NOTICE

Neither the authors nor the publishers take any responsibility
for any injury or damage resulting from the use of techniques
shown or described in this book. The reader is advised to
seek appropriate expert advice before undertaking electrical
work. For all construction work the reader is advised to wear
protective clothing and follow instructions carefully
throughout. Advice on natural remedies in this book is not
intended as a substitute for medical advice and use of them
is entirely at the reader's own risk.

Discover more at
www.dk.com

DICK & JAMES STRAWBRIDGE

PRACTICAL SELF SUFFICIENCY

THE COMPLETE GUIDE TO SUSTAINABLE LIVING

Contents

AUTHORS' INTRODUCTION

We are lucky enough to live on a smallholding in a beautiful part of Cornwall in our own valley and half a mile from the sea. Our move to Newhouse Farm was documented in the BBC TV series *It's Not Easy Being Green*, but it was not inspired by television; it was a family decision that was the culmination of years of experimenting and dreaming about the good life.

We have always had an interest in self-sufficiency. Some of Dick's earliest memories are of helping his father in the garden, or collecting mushrooms with his mother; quality time that produced the tasty vegetables he remembers from his childhood. While James has always been involved with nature and the garden, going for walks collecting berries or digging over the gardens of the many houses we've lived in. Now we both write and work in television. There is still a mortgage to pay so we have to spend time away from Newhouse Farm, but returning is always calming and makes us smile; it reminds us why we have our smallholding.

This book is aimed at everyone who has a desire to be a bit more self-sufficient or to live life more sustainably. There is absolutely no reason not to start today. It doesn't matter where you are living there is something in this book for you. You can reduce your energy bills, make cheese in any kitchen, grow herbs and tomatoes on any windowsill, and learn more about sustainable living and apply it to your situation. This book is a collection of the information that we have been amassing for years. We don't expect you to jump in and do it all at once, but no matter what stage in your life you are at, we are sure there will be something in here for you.

Don't forget to have fun – if you are not smiling you are doing it wrong!

Dick & James

SAFETY WARNINGS

While we want you to feel empowered to try many of the things included in this book, we don't want you to take risks, cut corners, or get out of your depth. We use a wide range of sharp implements and power tools in our projects. Make sure you familiarize yourself with them at the outset and feel competent to use them before you start work. Also read through the advice and cautions included here.

Renewable energy options

■ We've focused on what is possible on a range of sites and showed you the nuts and bolts of our own solutions, but before you consider putting any of this into practice on your own plot, check what permissions are needed from your local authority. Seek advice from and work with a qualified electrician and your energy supplier at all times.

Biofuels and anaerobic digestion

■ We've shown how we made our reactor and a digester from an assortment of oddments to prove that you don't need expensive custom-built kit. However, we're able to fall back on years of engineering experience and if you have any doubts about your own competence, get some expert help. When dealing with chemicals, heat, and gas, you can't be too careful.

Animal husbandry

■ Some advice about hygiene: if you have a young family insist on scrupulous hand-washing after children come into contact with livestock to reduce the risk of e-coli infection. Lambing-time is especially risky for pregnant women as contact with newborn lambs or any of the by-products of the birth carries a risk of infection that can cause miscarriages. Partners attending lambing ewes should wear protective clothing and gloves and wash thoroughly to remove potential contamination.

Dairy produce

■ Keep everything you use and your kitchen environment scrupulously clean while you make dairy produce. And if you are pregnant avoid using unpasteurized milk, as products may harbour listeria or campylobacter bacteria.

Making natural remedies

■ It's always best to seek proper medical advice before you self-treat with home remedies, especially if you are suffering from recurring symptoms or have a serious or long-standing illness. When using tinctures try small amounts first; also test our salves and creams on a small area of skin before using to check for allergic reactions. Be especially cautious if you are pregnant or breastfeeding, as some herbs are contraindicated during these times.

What are the basics for life?

We're lucky that life in the 21st century is easier than it has ever been at any other time in history, but convenience can come at a price, and many people now want to get back to basics. So, what are the basics for life? Food and shelter is the simplest answer, but we are looking for a good quality of life, too, and for that we need comfortable shelter, quality food, and a good amount of pleasure.

Turning dreams into reality

Most people have a dream where their life is very different from how they live now. There are so many things that we would like to do, but time and/or money tends to be the main stumbling block. So work is partly the problem and partly the solution. Should we live to work or work to live? A few of us are able to say that our work is fun, fulfilling, and we would choose to do it even if we weren't being paid. However, the vast majority of us have yet to find a way of living our dream. So what's stopping us?

We've always been struck by John Seymour's idea that he was writing for "dreamers and realists", and we're keen to help dreamers turn their dreams into reality – hopefully sooner rather than later.

Living the dream

Rushing around in our modern world, it's tempting to put convenience before quality. But we have very firm views on what we call "quality" food, and living on our smallholding at Newhouse Farm, growing our own fruit and vegetables, and rearing our own meat, we put this ahead of convenience every time.

Everyone here cooks, and we're lucky that we're all quite good at it. Time spent in our large farmhouse kitchen preparing meals is very sociable; we look in the fridge, see what needs harvesting outside, and then create a menu. There's nothing quite like fresh, quality (there's that word again) produce, enjoyed just after it's been picked and prepared. It may be old-fashioned, but we also still sit down around the table for lunch and supper, which allows everyone to catch up and talk.

Even without the produce of a smallholding at your fingertips, quality food is achievable. As you will see in this book, everyone can grow something that they can eat.

Rediscovering local food

Modern transport systems keep the supermarkets stocked with an abundance of foods, and it's easy

1

2

3

4

to forget what is seasonal and local. Consumers have demanded variety at a reasonable price and the supermarkets have responded; or have supermarkets led and we have followed? Either way, it now seems acceptable for food to travel halfway round the world and then to be stored and distributed in the supermarket chain before we get a chance to eat it.

When we buy food, our first choice is local, seasonal, organic produce. If what we need doesn't fit all these criteria we go for local and seasonal, or seasonal and organic. We have been known to deviate from our principles, but let's not forget Douglas Bader's words: "Rules are for the obedience of fools and the guidance of wise men."

Gimme shelter
Our homes come in many shapes and sizes, and offer comfortable shelter, but we question the definition of "comfort". We've been "ecovating" our old farmhouse for years, aiming for a home that's warm and cosy, and generates very few bills, so that as we grow old we won't have to worry about the escalating cost of water and energy. We believe that to be truly comfortable you need to know you can live within your means, even in an uncertain future.

There are many ways to achieve this. The simplest is to concentrate on reducing the amount of fuel and water you use, and then to find ways of providing the utilities you need. This approach is valid for any home; in fact, we would go further and say it's essential for every home.

The pleasure principle
The final requirement for a good quality of life is enjoyment. We're all different and we find happiness, peace, harmony – call it what you will – in our individual ways. We've tried many aspects of sustainable living; some we've really enjoyed, others we haven't. Our philosophy is that you should try as many different things as you can and then continue to do those that suit you.

It's important to remember, too, that you don't have to wait until you've bought your ideal property to embark on a more sustainable lifestyle. Have a go now! The experiences you gain and the fun you have may be the catalyst you need to fulfil your dream of a better life.

1. Using an aqueduct to divert part of our stream allows us to harness the energy in the water. **2. The farmhouse** in winter is warm and well-insulated, and the energy is sourced in a variety of sustainable ways. **3. Seasonal crops,** such as strawberries, harvested when they are ripe, taste a hundred times better than early forced crops. **4. We have fun** mixing clay for an earth oven. **5. Local produce** has a low carbon footprint and helps generate income for smallholders like us. **6. Wind turbines** are a dependable source of energy if you live in an exposed area. **7. Learning new skills** like basketry is fun and creative. **8. Home baking** is one job we really enjoy on cold winter days, when the smell of fresh bread lifts the spirits.

5

6

7

8

Self-sufficiency vs sustainability

A sustainable lifestyle takes planning, preparation, and practice, but to be truly self-sufficient and live off the land, means an even bigger commitment. There may be many reasons why you can't fully adopt the good life immediately, but there's nothing to prevent you from pursuing part of that dream right now, regardless or where you live or the size of your plot.

ESSENTIAL CONSIDERATIONS

How much time do you have to spend working?

Time spent sitting behind a desk to pay the bills is time that you're not on your plot enjoying your chosen lifestyle. However, you have to go into things with your eyes open and accept that to provide sufficient funding for, say, a smallholding or larger plot, it may be necessary to postpone your full commitment to the paradise you have planned.

Where should you live?

Many of us need to be near a workplace, perhaps in an urban setting, for part of our life. If you have no choice where to live, it's important to make the best use of your environment to try out all those things you want to do later. If you're taking the plunge and moving to the country, it's easier and cheaper to find a smallholding in a remote place away from the modern world, but that also limits your opportunities for paid employment, and usually means you have a very small choice of facilities close by. We liked the idea of being part of a community and felt we needed some of the trappings of 21st-century living, such as good rail and road links, broadband, and mobile phone coverage.

How much support do you need to fulfil your dream?

On a smallholding, there's always more to do than you have time for. Nature is always keen to reclaim any land, so there's an ongoing struggle, which depends on the size of your chosen battlefield. In a rural community you will find lots of local expertise, but that can cost money if you want more than a bit of advice. It's important to assess how fit you are and what you are capable of. One thing's for sure – you'll get fitter.

What do we mean by self-sufficiency?

For us, self-sufficiency is a way of life where you endeavour to produce all you need from the resources that are available to you. In the past, such a lifestyle was essential for subsistence farmers; the communication infrastructures we take for granted didn't exist and people had to live on what they could obtain within a few miles of their homes. Communities formed where natural resources were concentrated and people traded their skills and produce to ensure everyone had all they needed to live. It was often a matter of trying to survive rather than having a good quality of life. In many countries this is still the case, but in the developed world today we don't need to do everything ourselves or within the local community. That has some positive benefits, but reaching outside the community, especially across the continents, can have a serious impact on the planet.

What do we mean by a sustainable lifestyle?

Living a sustainable lifestyle means using no more than our fair share of the planet's resources to meet our needs. In the future we can expect energy and food to increase in price as resources become scarcer, and consequently, a degree of self-sufficiency will become essential.

Self-sufficiency automatically leads to a sustainable lifestyle, as you try to produce everything you need, but sustainability is achievable without being entirely self-sufficient, if you make sure you are acting as a conscientious consumer.

A better way of doing things

Until a couple of years ago all books on living sustainably would start by having to justify the need to do it; now, few people won't acknowledge that we're living beyond the planet's means. The eco-warrior's mantra of "Reduce, Reuse, Recycle" is the best way we can all contribute. Put simply, we have to cut down on the resources that we're using, and stop throwing so much away.

Whether you live on a farm or in an urban flat, you can make your lifestyle more sustainable. Reducing what you use in all aspects of your life also makes sense financially – from saving energy in the home to minimizing unused food that's thrown away, and mending old clothes instead of discarding them. Identifying areas where you can cut down will help you to realize what really is important and what you simply won't miss. Sign up to your local Freecycle website and use it to dispose of items you don't need and acquire things that still have a useful life in them, rather than buying new.

1. Friends and family help to make light work of a construction job. **2. Smoke from our woodburner** floats above the cold air in the valley on an autumn morning. **3. Hard physical work** is part of our lifestyle, but keeps us fit and feels better than going to the gym. **4. The good life** is not all hard work: elderflower champagne is one of the pleasures. **5. Onions** and our intrepid mouse hunter enjoy the warmth of a polytunnel.

How much land do you need?

When we first started out, we were in rented army accommodation with small plots, so we know what it's like to have very little land. We then moved to our own terraced house, a semi-detached house, and finally into a smallholding with space. We may have been the neighbours from hell, but we tried everything we could think of in each of our plots, from keeping bees to building smokers.

Make the most of what you have

We all wish we had more land, whatever our plot size. We'd love to have space for livestock, woodlands, and even for some natural meadows, but we know that our first priority is to make full use of what we've got. You can have a really productive plot, even in a tiny urban garden, and if you're out at work all day, this may be as much as you can handle in your spare time.

Living in a "normal" house can mean space is an issue if you want to be self-sufficient; but it should not be a major problem if you are aspiring to a sustainable lifestyle. Suburban living doesn't have to be about immaculate lawns and washing the car every weekend – you can be very productive on an average urban or suburban plot: your veggie patch, cloches, greenhouse, polytunnel, beehive, and chickens can go a long way to help you achieve a degree of self-sufficiency. In fact, your garden may even make you the envy of your friends and neighbours.

If you live in the city or suburbs the good public transport links mean you don't need a car, so you can reduce your demand on finite fuel reserves. There are plenty of shops, too, where you can buy local, environmentally sound produce and products. Taking all this into account, you may end up with a lower-impact lifestyle than those with a similar-sized rural plot.

Where to acquire more land

If you are using your available space to the full, and you have time and energy to take on more land, the next problem is how to get hold of some. The odds are that your local land is expensive, or you may find your ideal plot has been sold, but persevere. Most landowners are not keen to sell, so see if you can rent a fallow or unproductive area from a farmer, and after years – yes, years – of softening him up with boxes of produce, he may give in and decide to sell.

Allotments

Britain has an allotment scheme where local councils have a duty to provide land for residents to grow their own fruit and vegetables. The origins of allotments can be traced back over centuries but the system as we know it came into practice in the late 19th century, when philanthropic Victorians were keen to provide poor people with the chance to grow their own produce, and to stop them from getting drunk in their leisure time.

Allotments are no longer the place where men retreat to their sheds or grow prize onions. Many are worked by women and whole families. In our village some allotments have three generations sharing the labour and the bounty.

In Britain, allotments are governed by local bye-laws. On some plots it may be possible to keep hens, bees, pigeons, rabbits, and even pigs. But you can expect restrictions on planting trees, erecting fencing, subletting, digging a pond, or using the plot for business purposes. If you are lucky enough to acquire an allotment, always ask to see a copy of the rules before you get carried away.

Community gardens

Land for cultivation also comes in the form of community gardens, which are on the increase. They tend to be in urban areas, often on reclaimed wasteland, where they provide a valuable space for local people to grow their own food. Generally run by volunteers, they are also a great way of bringing people together.

Councils and local authorities are increasingly making unused land available for community gardens. These schemes take a lot of effort to get off the ground and organize, but if there is one near you they are well worth joining.

Landshare schemes

Landsharing may seem altruistic, but it is practical and many people are happy to allow others to cultivate some of their land. A national UK landshare database shows you what is on offer in your area. Alternatively, there is a very good chance that someone will know who could do

with a hand; for example, an elderly person who can no longer cope with a large garden and would appreciate a box of veg in return for use of a plot, or a farmer with some fallow land.

With any luck you'll end up with the extra growing space you need, while landowners benefit from a productively cultivated plot and some produce to sample into the bargain.

1. Allotments are much sought after in cities and suburbs, but it is still worth joining the waiting lists at a few sites.
2. A productive urban garden can be as beautiful as it is bountiful with some flowering fruit and vegetables. **3. Large areas of farmland** are rarely up for sale, but you may be able to rent fallow land from a local farmer or landowner.
4. If you want cattle you will need a few acres of good pasture, and possibly space for a shed for them in winter.
5. Fruit trees that have been grafted on to dwarf rooting stocks are ideal for growing in pots in a small courtyard garden **6. Allotments have rules** but some allow you to keep animals, such as pigs, hens, and bees. Find out what is allowed before buying any animals.

5

6

The cycle of the seasons

We moved to rural Cornwall to live closer to nature, and every day we learn more about the seasons and the nuances of living in our valley. No matter where you live, there is a real opportunity to make the most of each season, to appreciate the variety of local produce on offer, observe different wildlife, and to enjoy the changeable weather, come rain or shine.

Enjoying seasonal food

With fresh strawberries in summer, warming squash soups over winter, and a turkey at Christmas, we really enjoy the fruits of our labour. Each one offers a real treat and marks the passing of the seasons.

It's equally frustrating, though, to realise that it's May and oysters are out of season until September (the wild ones, not the farmed variety). Or that it's September and yet again we have failed to get our fly rods out and missed the wild trout.

Nothing compares to the taste of local produce in season. Although we're not fully self-sufficient – some things, such as flour, rice, and sugar cane, we can't or won't produce ourselves – we eat extremely well. We grow our food, rear it, harvest it, kill it, forage for it, hunt it, prepare it, cook it – and enjoy every mouthful.

Getting back to nature

We get in touch with our roots in many different ways – we know that sounds a bit "new age", but it is a fair description. Most involve being up close and personal with nature. In autumn, for example, there's nothing more impressive than watching a murmuration of starlings gathering before dusk on a clear evening. Seeing wildlife at different times of year outside your front door is very special, so don't miss out. Go for walks or enjoy some feathered company while you work on your plot.

Adjusting to the climate

We live in a changing world and the seasons appear to be changing, too. They still follow one another, but global warming seems to be playing havoc. We get hail in June, floods in July, and long periods of sunshine in January. Nature is responding too – birds nest before their food sources are available, and plants flower early and are then killed by frost.

We've tried to choose the best time of year for certain projects in this book based on our experience, but year on year we are having to adjust to fit in with changes in our Cornish microclimate, as well as globally.

Even though it feels small, Britain has significant natural variations in climate. It is drier in the east than in the west, much colder in the north than in the south, windy at the coast and on mountains, where it is also colder. Valleys have frost pockets and mountains create rain shadows.

Our experience and advice from Cornwall is definitely not "one size fits all". It takes years to learn about the conditions specific to a given geographical location, and you will need to adjust your dates and activities to suit the microclimate in the area you call home.

The seasons at Newhouse Farm

No matter what time of year it is or whatever the weather, we always find something to enjoy in our valley.

Winter We tend to rely on our stored harvest in winter and supplement outdoor veggies with crops from the greenhouse, geodesic dome, and polytunnel. We put the chickens in the polytunnel to feed on the pests and leftover soft fruit. We plant trees in unfrozen soil and leave the potatoes to chit in the potting shed. We maintain our tools, practise indoor crafts, plan projects or study, experiment and research.

Spring At the spring equinox, when the sun is higher, we prepare the vegetable beds and harden off plants we sowed earlier under cover. They can be transplanted when the risk of frost has passed. We also incubate eggs, and hatch and raise chicks, ducklings, and goslings.

Summer The vegetable beds are in full production, giving us time off "to smell the roses" and go to the nearby seaside. We buy in five-week-old turkeys to fatten for Christmas and spend time preserving and storing – late summer is filled with making jams, chutneys, and cider.

Autumn This is when we harvest crops and clear the land. As turkeys and geese fatten up, we kill and process our pigs to ensure the freezer is full and that new salamis and air-dried hams are hanging for next year.

1. In early summer the runner beans are in flower and squashes are scrambling over the raised beds . **2. Late summer** is a bountiful time when we can sell some of our produce. **3. Winter stores** of apples provide delicious treats months after the harvest. **4. Fattening up the turkeys** in summer and autumn reminds us of the pleasures yet to come. **5. In late winter** it's too cold to plant seed outside, but we can chit potatoes indoors for an early crop. **6. Spring** is a busy time, as we hatch eggs and rear goslings, ducks, and chicks.

Urban opportunities

In the UK more people live in urban areas than in the countryside, and whether you see living in the city as a necessary stage before moving to your rural idyll or you're a confirmed city dweller, you'll be amazed how easy it is to reduce your carbon footprint. A few small steps – from growing your own salads to reducing the amount of waste you put in your dustbin – can make a big difference.

Make the most of city life

It may come as a surprise but a sustainable lifestyle can be easier to achieve in an urban setting than in the country. Mass public transport systems mean you don't need a car, while densely packed housing tends to be very energy efficient.

A car uses masses of energy, from the embodied energy used to manufacture it to the fuel to run it, so using public transport is one of the greenest things you can do.

Urban houses tend to be smaller and typically built in terraces. Your neighbours' homes serve as a direct form of insulation to reduce heating bills, and smaller spaces require less energy to heat them in the first place.

Energy and waste in the city

Add to your home's energy advantage by insulating your loft and hanging thick curtains to keep heat in. Reduce electricity bills by choosing energy-efficient appliances when it's time to replace a fridge or freezer, and replace light bulbs with energy-saving types. You can also do some research and switch to a green energy supplier.

Trying renewables

If you are aspiring to the rural idyll, an urban house or apartment is a long way from your destination, but that doesn't mean that it can't be "en route" to your final dream home. It may be easier to be sustainable in an urban setting where the infrastructure, if selectively used, can reduce the amount of energy needed to support a person or family. That said, it's near impossible to be self-sufficient in an urban setting, although there are many things you can do and learn while living in the city.

Saving energy should be your priority, but there may also be scope to try out a couple of renewable options. If you live in a house, check out your roof. If it has a south-facing slope, consider installing a solar thermal system to heat water. Of all the renewables this would be our top priority; it can pay for itself very quickly and even in winter it will capture enough solar energy to pre-heat your water.

Household waste

Composting prevents waste going to landfill sites and produces the perfect soil improver for raised beds and containers. In a small garden or on a patio the most compact option is a wormery; it produces great compost, plus a potent liquid fertilizer (see page 127). A bokashi tub (see page 104) will compost cooked food and dairy waste.

For other items, check out recycling facilities offered by your local council so that you put only the bare minimum into landfill each week.

Save water

Reducing the amount of water you use makes environmental sense and can save you money. Aerated taps, dual-flush loos, water-saving showers, dishwashers, and washing machines, all use less water. If you have a patio or garden, connect a water butt to the gutter on the house to catch rainwater and use it to water the garden and indoor plants.

Growing your own

In a city, outdoor space is always at a premium. You may only have a balcony or windowsill, but however small the area, use it to capacity. FIll window boxes, both outside and inside, with herbs, salad leaves, cherry tomatoes, or chillies.

If you don't have anywhere to grow your own produce, put your name down for an allotment or look out for community gardens where your neighbours get together to grow food on spare local authority land (see pages 16–17).

If you can't grow your own at all, you can still shop seasonally at farmers markets and buy produce with few associated food miles.

City foraging

Gathering wild foods is easier than you think. Look out for hedgerow berries along canal banks, public footpaths, and parks. Nettles are common on wasteland; pick them to brew beer (see page 255).

In the kitchen

Try being a bit more self-sufficient in the kitchen too. How about baking your own bread (see pages 232–235), and making chutney with the green tomatoes left on your patio plants (see pages 236–237)? Churning your own butter or making cheese is fun (see pages 226–229) and gives you a real sense of achievement.

1. **Making preserves** to stock up the pantry is something we can all do, wherever we live. 2. **Start off plants** in trays before planting out in pots or raised beds. 3. **Hanging baskets** are ideal for growing strawberries. Suspend them with copper wire to deter slugs and snails; the wire gives the pests a mild electric shock. 4. **A wormery** transforms kitchen waste into compost, takes up minimal space, and you can even grow a courgette on top. 5. **Grow your herbs** in pots on a patio or on a windowsill. 6. **Use a garden irrigation system** to water plants in containers. 7. **Small solar PV panels** may provide useful energy around the garden. 8. **Tomato plants** can be grown in large pots and baskets.

5

6

7

8

The urban plot

There are lots of different ways to maximize your use of space, however tiny your plot. Think vertically: grow climbing beans up walls, tie in a grapevine along a trellis, and train fruit trees as space-saving espaliers. Tuck a wormery into a corner and catch rainwater in a butt. Don't forget wildlife, even in the city. Plant nectar-rich flowers in among vegetables to attract pollinating insects and keep a bird table well stocked to encourage birds into your plot that will munch their way through insect pests. If you want to keep livestock, you don't need much space for a couple of chickens in a moveable ark, and you'll have the satisfaction of eating your own eggs for breakfast.

Espalier apple trees (2) *take up very little space and training them increases the harvest.*

KEY TO PLOT

1. **Tool and potting shed** *(pp.130–131)*
2. **Espalier fruit trees** *(pp.154–155)*
3. **Small lean-to greenhouse** *(pp.112–115)*
4. **Solar panel for irrigation** *(pp.110–111)*
5. **Wall pots for edibles** *(pp.124–125)*
6. **Bee B&B** *(p.123)*
7. **Herb and vegetable bed** *(pp.140–147)*
8. **Cold frame for protection** *(pp.116–117)*
9. **Raised bed for vegetables** *(p.126)*
10. **Climbing plants, such as beans**
11. **Potato bag**
12. **Loft insulation** *(pp.42–43)*
13. **Solar thermal panels** *(pp.62–63)*
14. **Edibles in windowboxes** *(pp.124–125)*
15. **Bokashi bin** *(p.104)*
16. **Recycling bins** *(pp.92–93)*
17. **Solar dryer** *(pp.244–245)*
18. **Water butt** *(p.78)*
19. **Seating area**
20. **Herbs in pots** *(pp.156–157)*
21. **Flowers to attract pollinating insects**
22. **Trellis for climbing plants**
23. **Hanging baskets for edibles** *(pp.124–125)*
24. **Wormery** *(p.127)*
25. **Compost bins** *(pp.104–106)*
26. **Bed for salads** *(p.143)*
27. **Fig tree for fruit and shade**
28. **Salad and vegetable bed** *(pp.140–147)*
29. **Small wildlife pond** *(p.123)*
30. **Grapevine** *(p.149)*
31. **Chicken run for fresh eggs** *(pp.188–195)*
32. **Bird table close to water supply** *(p.122)*

A solar dryer (17) *uses the sun's energy to preserve foods, such as tomatoes and apple slices, by drying out all the moisture.*

A bee B&B (6) *provides shelter for solitary bees, which are vital for pollinating plants and ensuring a crop.*

A bokashi bin (15) *converts cooked food and dairy scraps into compost – with no unpleasant smells.*

Potato bags (11) *allow you to grow your own spuds anywhere – even on a balcony.*

A cold frame (8) *is like a mini greenhouse, while* **raised beds (9)** *are ideal for city gardens where there is no soil. Put up some trellis at the back for* **climbing plants (10)** *such as runner beans.*

Solar thermal panels (13) *warm up water efficiently. Use them to supply a shower in an extension with a south-facing roof.*

Plant windowboxes (14) *with herbs, salad leaves, and tomatoes. Cut-and-come-again salads will keep producing all summer long.*

Suburban expansion

Gardens in the suburbs tend to be larger than city plots, offering greater opportunities to become self-sufficient. In fact, we believe that a well-designed suburban garden can be more productive than a larger plot that's difficult to manage efficiently. A house and garden with hens, fruit trees, a polytunnel, and some renewable technologies can provide you with almost everything you need.

Becoming energy efficient

Wherever you live, your top priority should be to reduce the amount of energy you use. In the suburbs you may be able to take this a step further with "microgeneration technologies", which generate power from the sun, wind, and other renewable sources on a domestic scale. Combine these with energy-saving ideas and there is absolutely no reason why you shouldn't become completely self-sufficient in electricity.

Assessing the possibilities

To find out if your site is suitable for the microgeneration of energy, start by assessing the possibilities offered by your roof (see renewable energy options, pages 58–59).

One practical option could be solar photovoltaic panels (see pages 60–61), which make electricity from sunshine. However, the panels must be positioned on a south-facing roof to operate efficiently.

Heating your home

Using woodburning stoves to heat part or all of your house is feasible in a suburban area where smoke control regulations are not too restrictive (see pages 82–83). Regulations do vary, however, so you'll need to check with your local authority first. Solar thermal panels use the sun's energy to heat water (see pages 62–63). Like photovoltaic panels, they need to be installed on a south-facing roof.

Saving and collecting water

Dual-flush toilets, aerated showers, and low-water-usage washing machines are all essential if you want to reduce water consumption, and a water butt is a must for any urban and suburban garden.

You can also expand the ways in which you collect rainwater and how you use it. For example, you could install a rainwater harvesting system, which stores the run-off from the roof in an underground tank (see pages 76–79). You could then use this water to supply toilets, showers, and other household appliances.

Converting your garage

We have never actually kept our car in the garage: the space is far too valuable. Like many people, we use it as a workshop and a store. For more information about equipping a workshop, see pages 52–53.

It is also possible to turn a corner of your garage or any outbuilding into a biodiesel plant to produce fuel from waste vegetable oil – we find making fuel for our car very empowering (see pages 84–87).

The shed can become more than storage space for tools. Add a lean-to and turn it into a smokehouse for curing foods, or a store room for air-dried hams, pumpkins, and home-made beer and wine.

Making the most of your garden

If your garden has enough space for either a greenhouse or a small polytunnel, you can greatly extend your growing season. They not only protect young plants from frost, enabling you to start crops earlier in the year, but they also allow you to grow salads and herbs over winter.

Improve the productivity of your greenhouse or polytunnel by installing a heat sink (see pages 118–119) to keep it frost-free in winter.

In larger gardens you'll have room to plant some fruit and nut trees (see pages 150–153). Trees take little tending and, when established, can produce large crops.

Attracting friendly wildlife

Extra space in the average suburban plot means more room for wildlife too. Dig a shallow pond to encourage frogs – they eat slugs. Attract bees, which pollinate fruit and veg, with a patch of wildflowers and bee-friendly plants like lavender (see pages 120–123). A beehive, sited away from busy paths and seating areas, is also possible (see pages 212–213).

Expanding your flock

Hens are easy to keep in the suburbs. You will need space for a dedicated area in spring and summer, and can then allow them to roam freely in autumn and winter when the garden is at its least productive (see pages 188–195). Unless you have a large pond, ducks are not an option, and you'll be unpopular with the neighbours if you keep geese – they're too noisy.

1. **Biodegradable seed pots** are easy to make from recycled cardboard tubes. 2. **Chickens** are simple to keep if you have a large garden. 3. **Start your crops early** by sowing seed in a greenhouse in late winter for an early summer harvest. 4. **Raised beds** provide productive spaces for growing rows of your chosen herbs and other plants.

The suburban plot

The garden of a typical suburban semi-detached or detached house can be turned into a very productive plot, with a good-sized vegetable patch, greenhouse and fruit trees, and plenty of room to house a flock of chickens and to try your hand at keeping bees. There's also space to experiment with making your own biodiesel to fuel your car, and to install a combination of renewable energy systems to reduce your electricity bills.

Composting bins (2) *are best placed in a shady, secluded spot close to the kitchen garden.*

KEY TO PLOT

1. **Beds for crop rotation** *(pp.108–109)*
2. **Compost bins** *(pp.104–106)*
3. **Willow trees** *(pp.278–279)*
4. **Compact fruit trees** *(pp.150–155)*
5. **Beehives** *(pp.212–213)*
6. **Polytunnel for early crops** *(pp.114–115)*
7. **Trained fruit trees** *(pp.150–155)*
8. **Shed and smokehouse** *(p.130, p.248)*
9. **Smoker for smoked food** *(pp.250–251)*
10. **Bed of medicinal plants** *(pp.264–265)*
11. **Herb spiral** *(pp.158–159)*
12. **Chicken enclosure** *(pp.188–195)*
13. **Roof-mounted wind turbine** *(pp.64–67)*
14. **Bird box and wildlife area** *(pp.120–123)*
15. **Woodstore** *(p.82)*
16. **Windowboxes for herbs** *(pp.124–125)*
17. **Solar photovoltaic panels** *(pp.60–61)*
18. **Solar thermal panel** *(pp.62–63)*
19. **Rainwater storage tank** *(pp.78–79)*
20. **Biodiesel reactor** *(pp.84–87)*
21. **Straw-bale extension** *(pp.50–51)*
22. **Air-source heat pump**
23. **Bokashi bin for meat and dairy** *(p.104)*
24. **Household recycling bins** *(pp.92–93)*
25. **Water butt to collect rainwater** *(p.78)*
26. **Pots of herbs and salads** *(pp.124–125)*
27. **Greenhouse plus heat sink** *(pp.118–119)*
28. **Wormery for kitchen waste** *(p.127)*
29. **Automated irrigation system** *(p.110)*
30. **Wildlife pond** *(p.123)*
31. **Earth oven** *(pp.252–253)*
32. **Pumpkin patch** *(p.141)*
33. **Mushroom logs** *(pp.160–161)*
34. **Wildflower garden** *(pp.120–122)*
35. **Living willow hut** *(pp.278–279)*
36. **Solar dryer** *(pp.244–245)*
37. **Seating area**

A wildlife pond (30) *attracts frogs and toads, your allies in the war on slugs.*

A large greenhouse (27) *has space for exotic plants, from melons to tomatillos, as well as room to start off seedlings under cover.*

Plan vegetable beds (1) *carefully to crop over a long season.*

A herb spiral (11) *is a decorative stone-edged bed. Choose a sunny site for your herbs.*

The chicken coop (12) *should be situated close to the house so it is easy to collect eggs and check on the health of your birds. Close proximity to the home will also deter predators.*

Full-size solar photovoltaic panels (17) *on a south-facing roof will generate energy to heat water and part of your home.*

Biodiesel reactor (20) *Build your own in a corner of an outbuilding and produce fuel for your car from waste cooking oil.*

Rural adventure

If you're planning to make the move to a smallholding, the possibilities are enormous, from growing most of your own food to selling your electricity back to the national grid. But do it with your eyes open. You'll find that every day brings different challenges, and stamina and a sense of humour come in handy. Life on a smallholding is hard work but rewarding, and enormous fun.

Making the most of the land

When you're looking for a smallholding, the physical features of the land will determine what you can do with it. The orientation of the plot reflects what you can grow: check to see how much land is facing south and is thereby sunny and warm with lots of potential; for example, a south-facing slope is ideal for planting grapevines (see page 149). If there's a stream running through the plot, then using water power to generate electricity will be an option (see pages 68–73). Other beneficial features to look for are woodland to manage for fuel and fencing (see pages 182–183), and a field to graze sheep or cattle (see pages 204–211).

The human factor

If you have enough space, time, money, and motivation, you can achieve anything on a smallholding, from growing most of your own fruit and vegetables, to rearing your own bacon. Even now, years after we bought ours, we still talk about using the potential of our land and we're still excited about it.

Earning enough money to live means you must plan projects carefully, but you have to be flexible. Priorities are overridden on a daily basis – all it takes is the rain to get in where it shouldn't, or an animal to look off colour. But the work makes us smile: it's satisfying and we're here because we want to be.

Watch out for red tape

In the UK there are a huge number of regulations that may dampen your enthusiasm, from paying an abstraction fee for diverting a stream to applying for planning permission to erect a wind turbine. Thankfully a large number of local councils now have an enlightened approach to environmentally friendly projects, but expect some hurdles if you live in a building that is listed for historical reasons, or if your plot is in an Area of Outstanding Natural Beauty (AONB).

Maximizing energy production

Even in a suburban garden it is possible to generate enough energy to power a home; on a smallholding you may also be in a position to sell some back to the national grid. Analyze your plot to work out which options to go for. Take wind speed readings, measure water flow, and note south-facing roofs on barns and outbuildings as well as on the house (see pages 56–73).

We were keen to experiment with water power so six months after we moved in, our waterwheel was up and running, generating enough electricity to light our home.

Heating

Solar thermal panels for hot water are one of the best investments you can make. In winter, boost their effect by using a wood-fired back boiler to heat up the water to a more comfortable temperature (see pages 62–63 and 82–83).

Wood-burning stoves are the sensible option in a rural area, especially if your smallholding has woodland which you can coppice for a free supply of carbon-neutral fuel.

Dealing with waste water

Most rural properties rely on a septic tank to collect waste water. You can take this one step further and install a reed bed system to treat effluent naturally (see pages 80–81). The best human waste management, though, has to be a compost toilet (see page 77). You will save masses of water used to flush a conventional toilet, and the waste decomposes into a useful compost to be used on fruit and nut trees – not the lettuce!

Increasing your livestock

You need a good few acres to keep cattle and sheep, but goats can be kept in smaller spaces – we once had a pair in a large back garden. Pigs need space to run around and can earn their keep by clearing and manuring uncultivated land (see pages 200–209).

Growing fodder for animals

Once you have a few chickens, goats, and a pig or two, it's easy to run up a sizeable feed bill. Reduce it by growing animal fodder crops (see pages 176–179). As well as maize, kale, and fodder beet, try sunflowers. Feed pigs the leaves and stems, and you can enjoy the seeds.

1. **Install a waterwheel** if you have a fast-running stream on your land.
2. **Pigs rotovate the ground** for you as well as making bacon. 3. **Geese** make great burglar alarms. 4. **A woodburning stove** supplies free heat if you have a woodland to supply the fuel. 5. **Large vegetable beds** and fruit trees can cut food bills dramatically.

The smallholding

With more space to play with you can keep a wide range of animals, and grow the crops to feed them. Growing crops under cover on a large scale, combined with successional sowing and crop-storage systems mean you can grow and eat your own food nearly all year round. And you'll have scope for various renewable technologies.

KEY TO PLOT

1 Bamboo for garden canes *(p.178)*
2 Ram pump to supply water tank *(pp.74–75)*
3 Grapevines, tea, and hops *(p.149, p.179)*
4 Spring plus dual-powered pump *(p.79)*
5 Duck enclosure with pond *(pp.198–199)*
6 Netted strawberries *(p.150)*
7 Compost bins *(pp.104–106)*
8 Water tank to supply polytunnel *(pp.114–115)*
9 Cold frame *(pp.116–117)*
10 Greenhouse with heat sink *(pp.118–119)*
11 Fruit cages *(p.152)*
12 Beds for crop rotation *(pp.108–109)*
13 Pig enclosure *(pp.200–203)*
14 Waterwheel and aqueduct *(pp.72–73)*
15 Fodder crops *(pp.176–179)*
16 Turkey enclosure *(pp.196–197)*
17 Woodland *(pp.182–183)*
18 Beehives *(pp.212–213)*
19 Mushroom logs *(pp.160–161)*
20 Goose enclosure *(pp.198–199)*
21 Fruit and nut orchard *(pp.150–155)*
22 Grid-linked wind turbine *(pp.64–67)*
23 Geodesic dome *(p.114)*
24 Medicinal garden and wildlife area *(p.265)*
25 Sheep and cattle area *(pp.204–211)*
26 Pollarded willows *(pp.278–279)*
27 Chicken enclosure *(pp.188–195)*
28 Solar dryer and raised bed *(p.244, p.126)*
29 Woodstore *(p.82)*
30 Recycling bins and wormery *(pp.92–93, p.127)*
31 Herb spiral *(p.158–159)*
32 Earth oven and smoker *(p.252, p.250)*
33 Reed bed system *(pp.80–81)*
34 Rainwater storage tank *(pp.78–79)*
35 Solar thermal panels on roof *(pp.62–63)*
36 Ground-source heat pump
37 Grid-linked solar PV panels *(pp.60–61)*
38 Workshop and hay shed *(pp.52–53, p.180)*
39 Biodiesel reactor in outbuilding *(pp.84–87)*
40 Compost toilet *(p.77)*
41 Root cellar *(p.181)*

Ducks (5) *such as these Indian Runners must have access to a large pond.*

A geodesic dome (23) *is the perfect undercover environment for growing plants.*

Cattle (25) *require a few acres of good pasture to graze, and some types may need a winter shelter.*

A polytunnel (8) *extends the growing season so that you can pick salad leaves in winter and start off artichoke seedlings ready to plant out for an early crop.*

Pigs (13) *will clear uncultivated land, but they need a sty to sleep in at night.*

Geese (20) *help to keep the grass short, make good intruder alarms, and are good birds for the table.*

Beekeeping (18) *is seasonal work. In summer, keep a regular eye on your bees – it only takes an hour a week– and harvest the honey.*

31

IN THE HOUSE No matter what sort of a house you live in – be it terraced, semi-detached, or detached; in town or countryside – you'll find it's possible to reduce your energy usage and save a lot of money in the process. Whether you plan to build your dream home or simply want to renovate an existing property, this chapter will help you understand how your home actually works and suggest possible ways to make it more energy efficient. We'll also fire your imagination with some more radical options for green builds...

Taking stock

Most homes were designed before the idea of sustainable living was even thought of, and only the newest homes built over the last few years are designed to truly conserve energy. However new or old, by making a few changes to your lifestyle you can make your house more environmentally friendly and save lots of cash by reducing your use of gas, electricity, and water.

TAKE AN ENERGY AUDIT

Assess your energy consumption and bills by taking an audit of different areas in your house, using this checklist. Then read this chapter and see where savings can be made.

EXTERNAL AND BUILDING INFRASTRUCTURE
- Lights
- Taps
- Roof and loft
- Windows and doors
- Chimneys
- Guttering and rainwater
- South-facing walls, roof, and windows

SITTING, DINING AND BEDROOMS
- Energy usage
- Standby usage
- Lights
- Windows and curtains
- Doors
- Radiators

BATHROOM
- Energy usage
- Standby usage
- Lights
- Windows and curtains
- Doors
- Taps
- Toilets
- Showers
- Bath
- Hot water
- Grey water
- Radiators

KITCHEN
- Appliance energy usage
- Standby usage
- Lights
- Windows and curtains
- Doors
- Taps
- Fridge and freezer
- Extraction
- Hot water
- Grey water
- Radiators

Making the most of your house

If you are about to build a new property, ensure the performance of the structure is super-efficient. For the rest of us, it's a matter of getting the best from the house we have.

Our farmhouse is hundreds of years old and was made from materials that were available at the time, but it was built to last and in places our walls are over 1.2m (4ft) thick, so it has some amazing insulation properties.

Your most important, and free, source of energy is the sun, so it's worth checking where it rises and sets, and for how long it falls on windows, walls, and patio doors, as well as the garden. You will then know where to install solar panels and thermal systems, or make windows larger to capture more of this free heat (see pages 60–63).

Reducing your consumption

Your best starting point is to get out all your utility bills to see where you are haemorrhaging cash. Draw up a simple chart, noting the cost of each quarterly or monthly bill for heating, electricity, water, and transport, as well as the unit price. This will then highlight how much money you are paying, and areas where savings can be made. Reducing your consumption is always the first step, before you start any big "green" projects.

The following ideas will instantly reduce bills and energy consumption.

Heating Turn it down one degree and reduce your bill by ten per cent. Pull the curtains at night and use draught excluders on doors. Turn the heating off for a period before you go to bed; a well-insulated house will stay warm. Install reflectors behind your radiators so that they heat the room, not the walls. Make them by sticking foil to pieces of cardboard.

Electricity Use low-energy bulbs and turn lights off when not in use. Turn off your computer, TV, and other equipment at the wall – never leave them on standby, which costs as much as leaving a couple of light bulbs on all night. Switch to a green electricity tariff that will supply your needs from renewable sources.

Household tasks Only use your washing machine and dishwasher when you have a full load, and dry clothes outside for free. Use pressure cookers – they're fast, very energy efficient, and economical.

Water Take showers rather than baths, but don't use power showers that use lots of water. Install a "hippo" in the toilet cistern (see page 76).

Lifestyle Use public transport or walk when you can. When shopping, think about the miles your purchases have travelled and what they are made from. Look for local, seasonal, organic products, or those labelled "fair trade", which help to protect workers in poorer countries.

1. Sunlight entering your windows can be harnessed and used to heat areas of the house. **2. Solar PV panels** on south-facing roofs can provide power for your home. **3. Hang washing outside** to dry – it's free and makes clothes smell really fresh. **4. Don't leave taps running** when washing; fill the basin instead. **5. Locally produced goods** reduce transport costs and pollution, and help support small businesses.

Conserving energy at home

We depend on a huge range of appliances in our homes, from essential items like fridges and washing machines to laptops and sound systems, and they all need electricity. In addition, most of us use lots of energy to keep our homes warm in winter. But adopting energy-saving strategies makes good financial and ecological sense, whatever your house size or lifestyle.

Don't waste heat

Heating or cooling your home takes a lot of energy. It pays to have an efficient system, but even more fundamental is to ensure you don't waste the heat you are using.

One way is to ensure your house is draught-proof. You wouldn't have the heating on and the windows open, and it makes equally little sense to let all the heat escape through lots of gaps. Minimize this loss by fitting draught excluders to doors and windows – there are even systems to reduce the wind rattling through old sash windows. You also don't need to pay for new double glazing to achieve

a draught-free, warmer home; thick curtains that you can close every evening are really effective.

Remember, too, that not all the house needs to be heated to the same temperature. Thermostatic valves on radiators ensure you don't overheat bedrooms or rooms that are seldom in use.

Energy-efficient appliances

If you want to save money on your electricity bill, make sure you buy an energy-efficient product when you replace any household appliance. Look at the manufacturer's label (see box opposite) to check a product's

efficiency. It often pays to spend more for an efficient appliance, such as a freezer, that over its lifetime will generate significant energy savings, without compromising performance.

Comparing running costs

To calculate the running costs of an appliance, multiply its consumption (given in kWh on a label stuck on the side somewhere) by the price you pay for your electricity, and then multiply again by the number of hours you use the appliance.

A plug-in monitor is a handy device when working out running costs. Then, when you go shopping

1. Fit a draught-excluding strip to all external doors to keep your home warm.   **2. Draught-proof your letterbox** with brush strips.   **3. Thermostatic radiator valves** allow you to heat rooms to different temperatures.   **4. Low-energy bulbs** are available in options to suit all fittings.   **5. Lag pipes** in an insulated loft to reduce heat loss.

for a new electrical appliance, such as a fridge or washing machine, you can make a proper comparison.

■ **The manufacturer's energy label** on a new appliance shows how much electricity it uses under standard operating conditions. It's measured in kWh per year for fridges and freezers or in kWh per cycle for washing machines and dishwashers.

■ **Laundry and dishwasher labels** also have ratings for washing, spin and/or drying performance. The A-G ratings are similar to the main energy-efficiency ratings, and are based on standard industry testing. Remember, an A rating is the most efficient.

Choose low-energy light bulbs

At Newhouse Farm our lighting circuit is powered by the waterwheel, but that doesn't mean we aren't careful about conserving our own energy. We were amazed by the difference it made when we switched to using low-energy light bulbs rather than old-fashioned incandescent ones.

Many modern homes have halogen ceiling-mounted lights because they look good – but they still give off heat like incandescent bulbs. And any light bulb that emits heat is wasting lots of energy doing this, rather than creating light.

There are now low-energy compact fluorescent lamps (CFLs) that fit into any light socket; some of these are even compatible with dimmer switches. Replacing just one 100W incandescent bulb with a CFL that provides the same light for just 20W will reduce the energy usage of that light fitting by 80 per cent.

LED savings

Light emitting diodes (LEDs) are the most energy-efficient option. An LED light bulb uses about 4W to produce as much light as a 50W halogen bulb. What's more, they can last for as long as 25 years. Check out the sums:

■ 10 lights fitted with halogen bulbs in a kitchen use 50W each. If they're on for three hours in the morning and five in the evening, they're using electricity for 8 hours every day.

■ 500W for 8 hours is 4kWh units of electricity a day. (A kWh is a kilowatt hour, or 1,000 watts for an hour.)

■ If you pay 15p per kWh, you are spending 60p per day, or £219 per year to light the kitchen.

■ Replacing them with LEDs at approximately 4W each means they are using 40W for 8 hours, or 0.32 kWh per day.

■ That means you will pay just under 5p per day, or £17.52 per year.

Replacing your halogen light bulbs with LEDs will therefore save you more than £200 per year – and that's just in the kitchen!

ENERGY LABELS

Energy labels rate products in terms of energy efficiency. They show how much electricity is used under standard operating conditions. By law, in the UK, the label must be shown on all refrigeration and laundry appliances, as well as on dishwashers, electric ovens, and light-bulb packaging.

In Australia, *energy labels feature a star rating for quick assessment and also show annual energy consumption based on average usage.*

In the USA *the Energy Star label means that a product has met, or has even exceeded, the government's stringent energy-efficiency requirements.*

In the EU, *energy labels are used to rate products from A★ (the most efficient and least energy used), down to G (the least efficient and most energy used).*

QUICK FIXES

These ideas don't cost much to instigate, but will make a sizeable difference to your bills.

■ Install **thermostatic radiator valves** and zone the heat.
■ Change **incandescant bulbs** to low-energy bulbs, CFLs, or LEDs.
■ Buy a **wireless electricity monitor** to keep track of how much energy you are using. They provide an exact reading and show you where savings can be made.

■ **Lagging** your hot-water tank, and the pipes around it, will pay for itself in a couple of months – thereafter you are saving oodles.
■ If your boiler is more than 15 years old, replacing it with a **new efficient boiler** can generate significant energy savings for you. In the UK, building regulations state that all newly installed gas and oil-fired boilers must be condensing models, which save energy by extracting heat from the exhaust gases.

Using passive solar gain

The sun is a fantastic source of free heat that can be harnessed very simply to warm our homes, using a technique called "passive solar gain". We refer to it as passive because there are no moving parts, switches, motors, or control systems; we let nature do all the work. The idea is to collect and store heat when the sun is shining, and to radiate it back after the sun has gone down.

Collecting the heat

The sun's heat energy passes easily through glass and warms the room beyond, which means windows make ideal solar collectors. For maximum capture of solar energy, a house needs large south-facing windows. In a new build this is easy to achieve by siting the house accordingly. Even if it can't be oriented precisely north-south, you can still harness a good percentage of the sun's energy (see box below).

If you want to adapt an existing house, there are several options. You can install bigger windows on south-facing walls, or replace the glass in existing windows (see box opposite), and consider laying a stone floor in south-facing rooms. A black floor is the most efficient at absorbing and storing heat, but any solid floor can act as the main heat sink – the material that stores warmth.

Warm air rises because it is less dense. By using this effect – thermo-siphoning – and installing a system of vents, you can move air warmed by the sun around your house. The most efficient way to do this is with a Heat

Capturing the sun's heat

Using solar energy is a constant balancing act between capturing enough heat during the day and preventing it from escaping at night, while ensuring the house doesn't overheat in summer.

Capturing the sun's energy
This diagram shows houses facing southeast; the same percentages hold true for houses facing southwest.

Sun's rays

67.5 degrees 36% gain

45 degrees 70% gain

0 degrees 100% gain

22.5 degrees 92% gain

N

The ideal house faces due south

Houses facing south receive sun year round; by harnessing solar gain you can reduce your heating costs.

Seasonal variation
As the earth tilts towards the sun in summer, the sun climbs higher in the sky and rises and sets well to the north of east and west. In winter, the earth tilts away and the sun sinks lower in the sky, rising and setting well to the south.

Summer solstice

Spring and vernal equinox

Winter solstice

The ideal position for passive solar gain

A house that faces due south will be most efficient at capturing the sun's energy. But even if your house is 45° off south you will still be able to harness 70 per cent of the possible solar gain.

Keeping cool in summer

A roof overhang shades windows in summer but doesn't affect heat gain in winter when the sun is lower in the sky. Deciduous trees similarly allow light through in winter and block out summer sun.

Recovery Ventilation (HRV) system (see pages 42–45), though it's not strictly passive as it uses a pump.

Optimize your windows

The type of glass in your windows determines how efficiently you can capture solar energy, and it is assessed in two ways:

■ **Solar control** refers to how much of the sun's energy passes through the glass and into the room. The Solar Heat Gain Coefficient (SHGC) compares the total amount of energy that passes through the glass to the amount of solar energy actually striking the glass. An SHGC of 0.86 means that 86 per cent of the solar energy hitting the window enters the room. The lower the SHGC, the less energy entering the house.

■ **Thermal control** refers to the insulating value of glass. It measures the rate at which heat is lost from a warm room to the cool air outside. Up to 60 per cent of heat loss in a well-insulated home is through the windows, but thermal control can be improved by coating the surface of the glass with a microscopic layer of metal or metallic oxide. This is known as a "low-emissivity coating" (see box below). The disadvantage is that the coating reduces the SHGC of the glass, so that less energy is absorbed in the first place.

Connect a conservatory to an HRV system to pump air warmed by the sun round the house during the day. Create a heat sink with a dark stone floor, and it will move the stored heat in the evening too.

Storing the heat

The materials for a heat sink range from concrete or masonry walls and floors to tanks of water (see page 118). In the average room, the heat sink will be the floor. Walls are a less likely option, unless your house has solid stone walls or eco-walls designed to store heat (see page 48). A material's capacity to store heat is known as its "thermal mass"; the more heat your heat sink stores, the bigger its thermal mass.

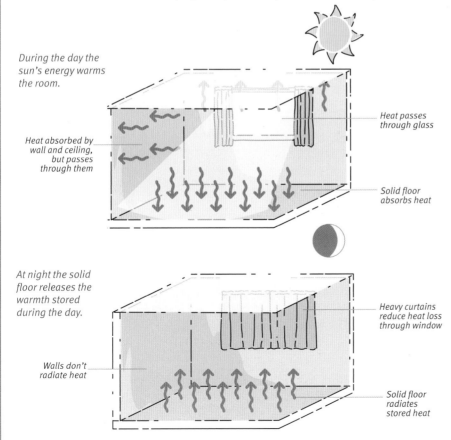

During the day the sun's energy warms the room.

Heat passes through glass

Heat absorbed by wall and ceiling, but passes through them

Solid floor absorbs heat

At night the solid floor releases the warmth stored during the day.

Walls don't radiate heat

Heavy curtains reduce heat loss through window

Solid floor radiates stored heat

KEEPING HEAT IN

For windows that capture heat in the winter and retain heat inside the house as the air outside cools, you need a low-emissivity coating on the inside pane of glass in a double-glazed unit.

Daytime   Night-time

Low-emissivity coating allows 66–75 per cent of heat energy to enter during the day, then reflects back 90 per cent of the heat that would be lost through the glass at night.

Improving home infrastructure

Our houses vary hugely in design, size, and the materials they are made from. In the UK some of the housing stock is ancient and, in many cases, the buildings are a long way from being efficient to run and heat. That said, they have stood the test of time and it is usually much greener to slightly modify an older building than sinking lots of energy into a new build.

Improving thermal properties

Harnessing the potential of your home so you can live as sustainably as possible means using what you have to the best of your ability. Not surprisingly, the first thing to do is reduce the amount of energy it takes to run your home. Improving its thermal properties is the logical solution to reducing energy consumption. There are two main areas: insulating, with the minimum amount of thermal bridging; and improved air tightness – draughts mean lost heat.

Thermal bridging

The purpose of insulation is to slow down the movement of heat; the higher the conductivity of a material, the more quickly heat can move through it. Insulation materials are rated by their resistance to heat transfer, the R value. The higher the R value, the lower the heat transfer.

When different materials with different thermal conductivities make up a wall or ceiling, then the heat will flow through the different materials at different rates. Areas that have poor insulation or where the materials allow lots of heat to flow through them are called "thermal bridges".

The loft hatch tends to be a thermal bridge. Walls and, more specifically, the junctions between walls and the ceiling need to be carefully thought about, to ensure they are airtight.

If you decide you need to add more insulation, you must sort out all the thermal bridges and draughts or your investment will be wasted.

Remember that the first layer of insulation is the most effective. The law of diminishing returns dictates that each additional layer of insulation is less effective than the previous layer.

Superinsulation

It is possible to insulate a property so that you should not need to provide heating at any time of the year. All the warmth you require can be produced by other sources in the house. For example, humans produce about 100 watts of heat per day. Even your cat and dog give off heat – and how about the surplus heat given off every time you boil the kettle?

If you want to go down the path of superinsulation, heating your property predominantly by sources of intrinsic heat (that is, waste heat generated by

INSULATION MATERIALS

It is fair to say that any insulation is good insulation. However, there is a big difference in the raw materials used to make it and this difference is reflected in the price, with eco-friendly options at the top of the scale.

If you can afford the more expensive, environmentally friendly insulation, that's great. But if you are put off by the price, we would encourage you to get whatever you can afford and install it as soon as you can. Any insulation is better than no insulation. Of all the eco-projects you can possibly undertake at home, insulating provides the best return and it will save you the most energy.

Insulation options
Recycled materials that can be turned into insulation include plastic bottles spun into fleece, recycled denim, newspaper waste, and sheep's wool that is too coarse for knitting and weaving. Wool is naturally fire-resistant (no chemical treatment necessary), won't go mouldy, and is completely safe to handle – no masks or gloves needed – making it much more suitable for DIY.

Insulation for every situation *From left, expanded foam for pipework, recycled plastic fleece, a jacket for a hotwater tank, foil reflectors for radiators, and a large roll of sheep's wool loft insulation.*

appliances and the body heat of the occupants), with very small amounts of back-up heat, you must address every area that could possibly be losing heat. Solutions include:

- Very thick insulation under floors, on walls and inside the roof space.
- Detailed insulation where walls meet roofs, foundations, or other walls in the property.
- Airtight construction, especially around doors and windows.
- A heat recovery system to provide fresh air (see page 44).
- No large windows.

Fitting superinsulation to an older house may involve building new exterior walls to allow more space for insulation. You must install a vapour barrier to prevent condensation and possible mould and mildew. A vapour barrier should be no further out than a third of the R value of the insulated portion of the wall. This way, the vapour barrier will not usually fall below the dew point, and condensation will be minimized. Alternatively, an interior retrofit will preserve the external look of the building but room sizes will suffer.

Air tightness

It's surprising how draughty the majority of homes are. Unless houses have been built to exacting standards and tested, there is a very good chance the air tightness will be less than desirable. The "build tight – ventilate right" concept has been promoted in the UK since the 1980s and there are now standards set for new builds that specify maximum air permeability to prevent uncontrolled air leakage. See the box for how to assess your home, and likely areas that will need draughtproofing.

Assessing air tightness

Reducing air permeability is a cost-effective way of improving energy efficiency. You can book a specialist company to run a controlled building air-permeability test to measure the performance of your home, but you probably have a good idea where the problem areas are. Fortunately, they can easily be resolved with simple, inexpensive forms of draughtproofing. Here are the main weak spots in a house.

Air leakage not only wastes energy, it allows warm moist air to flow into cooler areas, resulting in condensation.

Draughtproof crucial areas
Use brush strips and foam-backed tape to seal windows and doors. Make sure holes are filled where pipes and cables pass through the walls.

Gaps in buildings tend to occur during construction, for example between floors and walls.

Gaps around ceiling light fittings

Vents and chimneys leak air

Air escapes through hollow walls into the roof

Gap where ceiling and wall join the eaves

Draughty windows

Air escapes through floor and ceiling voids

Gaps where cables and pipework enter house

Specialist tests use pressurized air, smoke tracers, and thermal imaging to locate leaks.

Draughty front door

Junction of floors and walls

43

The principles of heat recovery

The idea behind the heat recovery ventilation (HRV) system is very simple. Your house has warm areas, warm wet areas, and cooler areas. All you have to do is get rid of the moisture and take some of the heat from the warm bits and pass it to the cold bits. You may not find it as warm as central heating, but the temperature should be comfortable.

How it works

A system of ducts connects the extractor vents from the warm areas to a heat recovery unit. A roof vent draws in fresh air, which is warmed and forced through another set of pipes to supply warmed fresh air to the cooler areas. Meanwhile, the stale air is vented to the outside. Heat recovery is very efficient: well over 90 per cent of the heat should be kept in the house.

A heat recovery unit *installed in a loft. The pipes running to and from the unit are lagged to prevent heat loss.*

Fresh outdoor air is drawn into the HRV system. It passes through a filtration system to remove the pollen and dust.

Heat recovery unit in loft

Stale air passes out under the eaves, taking with it condensation from poorly ventilated rooms and any smells.

Fresh air in

Stale air out

Air removed from warm steamy bathroom

BATHROOM   **BEDROOM**   **BEDROOM**

Warmed-up fresh air is piped to cooler rooms

Air removed from warm kitchen, along with cooking smells

KITCHEN   **LIVING ROOM**

Air removed from warm room, such as a living room with woodburner

How warm is warm?

Hundreds of years ago the people who lived in our farmhouse would not have expected it to be warm, but this is the 21st century and we want to be comfortable. There's an ongoing battle at Newhouse Farm as to the exact, technical definition of "comfortable".

MOVING HEAT AROUND THE HOUSE

At Newhouse Farm we have four woodburners downstairs. Extraction vents and pipes distribute their heat upstairs to the bedrooms. But a system can work using other sources; for example, the heat generated in a busy kitchen to warm a sitting room.

Traditional homes

Living in a historic building has its pluses and minuses. Newhouse Farm has lots of character and we are very aware of being custodians of our heritage but we are also restricted about how much we can disrupt the fabric of the building. The historical preservation orders on the building mean we need permission to make changes, which affects how we can improve the building's thermal properties.

Air tightness vs breathing

Air tightness as a way of conserving energy appears contrary to an old building's need to "breathe" to prevent damp. And when we arrived at Newhouse Farm damp was certainly an issue. Somehow an earlier owner had managed to install double glazing, so the rattling sash windows you would expect in an old building – and that would have provided some ventilation – were nearly all missing. (We are gradually replacing the plastic PVC windows with wooden, double-glazed ones, with special sash seals to reduce the draughts.)

So our method of letting the house breathe, without losing heat, was to install a whole house ventilation and heat recovery system, which has been a triumph (see box opposite). The vital air-flow system stops damp building up, while the heat recovery unit minimizes heat loss and actually distributes heat from warm rooms to cooler areas of the building.

Accepting what you've got

With an old building it is necessary to just accept it for what it is. Stone and slate have been used as building materials for centuries, and trying to calculate their R value can be meaningless. A thick rubble wall will have very good insulation value, provided it is solid. However, all old

Traditional buildings across the globe were built from local materials, with a low environmental impact. **1. Wooden shingles** on a house in New England, USA. **2. Stone cottages** in a Cotswold village, UK. **3. Timber framing** in Alsace, France. **4. Wooden** colonial houses in the Philippines.

SETTING RENOVATION PRIORITIES

Anyone renovating a home faces a lot of decisions. Here's how we prioritize.

Draw up a list of jobs and rate them as urgent or important. Arrange them using this diagram, to work out which jobs are both urgent and important – a leaky roof falls into this category. Do those jobs now to the best of your ability. Then tackle important tasks before they become urgent. If you let them drag on until they're in the top corner, you spend your time firefighting rather than working to a plan.

IMPORTANT ↑	DO WELL ENOUGH TO SATISFY YOU NOW	DO NOW TO THE BEST OF YOUR ABILITY
	DON'T WORRY AND DON'T FEEL GUILTY ABOUT IGNORING	MAKE A PLAN AND DO PROPERLY AS SOON AS YOU CAN
		URGENT →

rubble-stone walls have voids and it's by no means certain what material is inside the core. Even if you were permitted to improve the performance of the walls on the outside, you would undoubtedly change the character of the building. As the rooms of many older, not frightfully grand, buildings are so small, it is not really viable to insulate on the inside. Sometimes it is best to accept that older buildings were not meant to be so warm you can walk around in your underwear.

Green buildings
If you decide to build a sustainable home we reckon the only limitations you have are your imagination, money, and local planners. Each of these will

be an issue, so you may as well reconcile yourself to that fact.

As the earth's resources become scarcer it is important to re-assess the ways that we use energy and materials. Environmental impact and, very importantly, running costs will soon be critical factors in designing new buildings.

We can learn from traditional methods. Do we have to build from materials that have been shipped halfway round the world, using large amounts of energy in the process? Or could we take the trouble to find locally produced materials that could do the job as well, if not better? Here are some ideas:

▪ **Use wood** from trees grown locally, or at least responsibly.

▪ **Source natural materials** that do not rely on high-energy processing. For example, try UK-manufactured sheep's wool insulation.

▪ **Avoid timber preservatives** and certain paints, removing the need for additives made from toxic chemicals.

▪ **Specify durable timber** that does not need decorating – rather than re-painting every few years.

▪ **Consider a green roof** (see box opposite). It is insulating, attractive, and reduces your carbon footprint.

We are wary of statistics, but it is obvious that learning to build and live sustainably is becoming more of an issue and it has been shown that buildings consume some 40 per cent of the world's total energy and about 16 per cent of our water.

Designing for efficiency
In new construction, the cost of extra insulation and the wall framing needed to contain it can be offset by removing the need for a dedicated central heating system, for example.

But there is a more fundamental calculation required. Whole-life costs also need to be taken into account. If you have a choice of two similar-sized properties and one has bills that will consume about 5–10 per cent of your net income (this will obviously fluctuate from year to year due to supply problems, natural disasters, or geopolitical events), and the other has negligible bills, which one would you rather live in? We have an aversion to giving lots of our hard-earned cash to the utility companies, so that question is a no-brainer!

Think about shapes
We've become very used to houses being boxes. Why? The obvious reason is they're easy to build. But for an object to have the smallest surface area – which will minimize heat loss – it should be spherical.

1. The first environmentally friendly housing development in the UK – Beddington Zero Energy Development (BedZED). Homes are made from reclaimed or natural materials. **2. Earth shelters** in New Mexico, USA, are made from rammed earth and car tyres (see pages 48–49). **3. A zero-carbon house** in Kent, UK, needs no fossil fuels for heating. Its vault shape gives it high thermal mass.

SEDUM ROOFS

Green roofs have been standard practice in many countries for thousands of years. Their insulating properties are used in the cold climates of Scandinavia to help retain heat and in African countries to keep buildings cool.

What you should know

Sedum roofs are a mixture of flowering dwarf succulent plants grown on matting for easy installation. They are low maintenance, not no maintenance, and should be checked at least once a year in spring, when you can give them a dose of fertilizer. The orientation of your roof will affect the plants' growth rate – they need four hours of sun a day– and if you have a south-facing roof they might need an irrigation system. Consider these points before installing a green roof:

■ Your existing roof should be sound and watertight, with no guttering leading onto it.
■ Running water will erode the sedum matting and standing water will kill the plants.
■ The roof surface must be smooth to avoid creating air pockets under the sedum matting.
■ The building will have to be strong enough to support the weight – a sedum roof can weigh more than 40kg per sq m (88lb per sq yd). You may find your roof will need reinforcing.
■ The roof will be a lot heavier after snow or rain and any subsequent flexing of the building could cause windows to break.
■ Consult an architect or structural engineer if in any doubt.

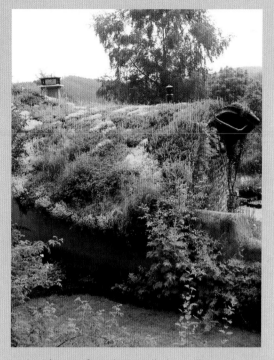

A sedum roof *can be installed on a flat or sloping roof, but the incline should ideally be less than 25°. You'll need access to the roof from time to time to weed it and water if necessary in dry spells.*

We are not suggesting everyone try living in an igloo, but maybe boxes are not the way ahead? There are many creative architects out there – it's all a matter of deciding what you are prepared to live in.

Materials are now available to enable you to build any shape of property you fancy. It's slightly more problematic getting a kitchen fitted, but that's a minor issue. If you are truly starting with a blank piece of paper you can get as close to nature as you want. But, even if you are only considering building an energy-efficient extension, you can still explore all sorts of less popular materials – straw bales for example (see pages 50–51), car tyres, or an earth shelter (see pages 48–49).

Then you can turn your attention to the interior of your home. One area where there is a readily available, eco-friendly choice, is paint.

Eco-friendly decorating

Conventional paints can release compounds into the air that are known to harm human health and the environment. There is an alternative. Eco-paints do not contain toxic chemicals such as benzene, toluene, formaldehyde, and mercury. They are completely free from volatile organic compounds (VOCs) – the solvents that carry the pigment and then evaporate as the paint dries, and which can cause headaches, sore throats, and eye irritation.

Another advantage is that they are "breathable", and allow moisture to evaporate from walls. Combined with a natural breathable plaster on the walls, this can reduce condensation and high humidity levels.

It may feel odd buying "organic" paints but they have real benefits. Even the production process has a smaller carbon footprint.

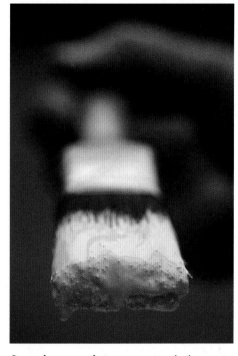

Organic eco-paints use natural pigments for colour and natural solvents such as citrus oil to carry the pigment. Other eco-paints use casein, which is a milk protein, and come in powder form so you just add water and stir.

Building an earth shelter

Earth shelters are buildings that use earth stacked against the external walls to provide an effective thermal mass – that will conserve heat when it is cold and keep the temperature cool in warm summers. This is a sustainable form of construction that relies on well-designed passive solar systems (see pages 40–41) and often uses renewable materials for the fabric of the building.

Could you live in one?

Let's tackle the perceived problems with living in an earth shelter right up front. The question on many people's lips is: are they damp and cold? It's a fair cop: some below-ground designs could be damp, like a basement. The answer is to put in a damp-proof course and drainage, and the sun's energy will keep the shelter warm. Passive solar gain can be used to heat all the rooms with the help of a Whole House Ventilation and Heat Recovery system (see page 44).

Construction types

In its most basic form an earth shelter could be a cave in a hillside. But we're not suggesting going back in time and living like cavemen; building practice has evolved so that designs now incorporate many forms of modern sustainable architecture in an efficient, earth-covered shell. Like any new building, earth shelters need planning permission. And if you aren't an experienced builder, you will need help with construction.

The earthship

In this design the majority of the living space is below ground, with a bank of windows along one wall

Off-grid earthship

This is our favourite style of earth shelter. It has to be built into a south-facing hill or slope, so that the northern side of the house is highly insulated by the natural shape of the earth and the south side acts as a great source of solar energy (vice versa if you're in the southern hemisphere). Many designs are completely off-grid; that is, self-sufficient in electricity and water.

TYRE WALLS

Old tyres are easy to come by and make solid walls with great load-bearing qualities. They're weather-proof and fire-resistant.

■ **Shovel earth** into the tyre one scoop at a time. Pack it in by bashing it with a sledgehammer. Keep adding more earth, working evenly round the tyre. Do this in situ, as you build up the tyre wall.

■ **Stagger the tyres** like bricks. Fill the gaps between them with earth.

South-facing slope is excavated to house the earthship.

Grow root crops on slope and sedum on roof to prevent erosion

Chimney for woodburner

Solar thermal tubes heat water

The main part of the structure is built from old car tyres (see box left), including a retaining wall for the slope behind and damp-proof course.

French drains filled with sand and gravel

Internal walls built from bottles have thermal mass, storing heat during the day and releasing it at night.

Timber framing supports roof

Underground tank to store rainwater

Using the soil's assets
The soil's density keeps the temperature inside the shelter at a constant 8°C (46°F) or so. That's a bit too cool to be comfortable, which is why you need passive solar heating. Earth also has excellent sound-proofing properties.

(see below). Its earth roof means you don't lose any growing space on your plot: planting up your roof can even help prevent erosion.

Earth berming

Earth berming involves heaping earth against a building's external walls and sloping it away from the house.

You can't simply add earth berms to a conventional house. Typically, you'd need a purpose-built heavy-duty timber-framed structure or stonework, stacked with thick layers of soil. Imagine a giant molehill with a cavity of rooms within it. The roof can either be covered completely with earth or heavily insulated with your chosen material, from sheep's wool to rock wool or composite insulation. With this type of earth shelter there's less risk of damp, compared to building below ground level, and there's little digging apart from foundations. Neither are you confined to a specific landscape.

Going underground

An underground home is a major project, usually for people living in very hot climates. It involves excavating a central courtyard area, often called an atrium, to supply adequate ventilation and light to the rooms leading off. Unless the ground is really hard, internal structural supports will be a crucial element of the construction.

DESIGN FACTORS

■ **The topography** of the land will decide what you build. An earthship must have a south-facing slope; earth berms and underground homes are suitable for flat sites.

■ **Find the natural water table**. If you dig down below it, not only will you have damp problems, you may end up with flooding.

■ **The soil** around the shelter should ideally contain plenty of sand and gravel for drainage. It's a good idea to install French drains – effectively ditches filled with gravel and sometimes pipes – to channel water away from the foundations.

■ **With the huge weight** of earth resting on the building, it's crucial that the initial structure is strong enough to support it.

Passive vent for heat recovery ventilation system, page 44

Wind turbine to generate electricity

Roof lights illuminate rear rooms

Solar PV panels produce electricity

Large south-facing windows for solar gain

Overhanging roof gives shade in summer, without blocking the low-angled sunlight in winter.

Reedbed water treatment sytem

Clean water flows into the pond

By working with the landscape *to build an earthship you end up with a structure that blends comfortably into the surrounding area, as well as one that has a smaller ecological footprint.*

Earth berms *can be incorporated into more familiar houses. These traditional Icelandic homes have stone foundations, timber framing, and a covering of thick turf for insulation, and can be built on the flat.*

49

Building with straw bales

Straw bales are among the most ecologically sound building materials available, and using them for construction is a highly sustainable option. They have great load-bearing strength, are non-flammable, have effective insulation properties, and they look good too. As well as these benefits, the building process is simple, satisfying, and forgiving, as well as being creative and fun.

Why build with straw?

Building structures with straw bales is empowering because you can create a structure even if you are inexperienced or unfamiliar with many conventional building techniques. Bales are also cost-effective per unit when compared to bricks and mortar, and ecologically sound – the buildings can be composted at the end of their life, which can be over 100 years.

Of course, there are disadvantages. Splash-back from rain bouncing up from the surrounding ground onto the base of the walls may cause damp problems, but can be avoided by raising the first straw bales above ground level. High humidity can also be a serious issue in wet regions and in exposed sites where straw bales benefit from an outer skin of wooden cladding to protect the walls from wind-driven rain and water damage. However, we feel the positive factors far outweigh the negative points.

Materials

Straw is made from the dead plant stems of grain crops like wheat, barley, rye, or oats. Bales are fairly easy to find, and are often available at local farm shops. They should be dry when you buy them and must be kept under cover if there is a risk of rain. The bales should be well compressed, too; if it is difficult to get your fingers under the string around them, then it is tight enough. Due to their density and the lack of air in them, bales are non-flammable when built, but it's still wise to make the storage area a fire-free zone.

Performance

The thermal insulation properties of straw bales are excellent; indeed, they are better than the current building regulations require. So straw bales could keep your new home or extension nice and cosy and working efficiently, but only if you make sure you insulate the floors and any gaps in the walls too. They also have superb sound-proofing qualities.

Principles of building

Straw bales can be used to build anything from two-storey houses and barns to small house extensions. Straw bale building is divided loosely into two methods, which aren't mutually incompatible.

■ **For load-bearing walls** that can withstand the weight of the roof, bales are placed on top of each other like giant building blocks. They are pinned together with coppiced hazel, and windows and doors are placed inside wooden structural box frames. The flexibility of this style makes it fun to try curved and circular walls.

■ **Infill** involves first building wooden frames for the walls and the roof to provide structural support. The wall spaces are then filled in with bales. The benefit of this method is that you can store the bales beneath the roof out of the rain while you are working. Infill is the best option for creating large open spaces such as warehouses or industrial units, but requires good carpentry skills.

DESIGN FACTORS

■ **Aim to make the walls** the length of a number of whole bales with no areas smaller than half the length of a bale, especially by windows and doors.
■ **Position doors and windows** at least one bale length away from load-bearing corners.
■ **Build the foundations** so they are the width of the walls.
■ **Avoid using metal pins** in the walls as it may encourage condensation from the warm moisture-laden air inside the house.
■ **Use a breathable** limewash or lime-based paint to finish your building and help protect it against the weather.

1. Load-bearing walls have excellent lateral strength to protect them from wind damage and even earthquakes.
2. Wooden wall frames are expensive but provide greater stability for windows and doors than load-bearing walls.

The structure of a straw bale wall

Before starting to build with straw bales, you need to create a solid and stable base that distributes weight evenly over the ground beneath. The base does not need the same degree of solidity as foundations for bricks and mortar as straw weighs about 60 per cent less. We recommend self-draining foundations made of rubble, stone, or tyres, which could then be reused if the building is dismantled.

Working with bales

It is good practice to "dress" a bale before positioning it. Tighten the strings if they are loose and make the ends squarer with a hammer claw, dragging it along either side of the string. Then pull and tease the straw until the end looks square. If you need to customize bales to the right length, restring both halves of a bale before cutting the original strings. Use a baling needle, which is a giant needle with two holes at one end for the two strings to be threaded through the bale. To curve a bale, simply place one end on a log and jump on top of it until you have your desired curve; but make sure that the string stays in place.

A wooden frame *built with bale-sized spaces between the uprights is the perfect support.*

Walls built from straw bales *are remarkably straightforward structures. Wooden pins and lime render continue the use of natural materials.*

A wooden roof plate spreads floor and roof loads across the width of the walls

When building the roof, add a slight overhang to protect the walls from rain

Once the wall is four bales high, pin them with more hazel stubs; for corners, use hazel hoops or staples

Build the bales in layers like you would bricks

Wooden wall pins wrapped in hessian add strength to the structure; to position them, hack out a groove with a claw hammer, drive in the pins, and cut flush with the sides

Lime render is a weatherproofing finish; the walls remain breathable, so last longer

Cut 30-cm (1-ft) hazel stubs and sharpen with a billhook; drive into the foundations and place the first layer of bales on top

To avoid splashback, raise the first layer from the ground; sleepers work well

Galvanized nails fix the wooden wall pins to the sleepers

Build the foundations – or base plate – from rubble, stone, or tyres filled with rammed earth

LIME RENDER

Lime render is one part quicklime powder to three parts damp sand (or 1:2 for the first coat, so it is stickier) and is best made two months in advance of using. Mix with a shovel and wear goggles. It gets very warm, so mix it regularly.

■ **Before applying,** trim the walls, ironing out unwanted bumps.

■ **Apply a thin coat** by hand, wearing thick gloves, and rub it in well. Leave for 1–2 days to dry.

■ **Wet the walls** with a mister and apply two more coats, preferably mixed with chopped straw. Rework over cracks, misting and squishing it firmly into any gaps. Protect from direct sunlight, heavy rain, and frost until it has dried.

Lime render *can be coloured with pigment powders or painted.*

Setting up a workshop

A workshop can save you money. You'll be able to make things instead of buying them and repair objects yourself, rather than sending them away to be fixed at great expense. As well as standard hand tools, we reckon every smallholder needs a cordless power drill, an angle grinder, a collection of hammers, and some welding equipment. We also recommend setting up a charging station for cordless power-tool batteries, with clearly labelled areas for "charged" and "charging". This extra bit of organization means you can always find a fully charged battery when you need one.

KEY TO WORKSHOP

1. Dustpan and brush
2. Overalls
3. Leather apron
4. Paper towels
5. Selection of rawlplugs
6. Power points
7. Eye irrigation kit and Steristrips
8. Nails
9. First-aid box
10. Screws
11. Pens/pencils
12. Window for natural light
13. Voltmeter
14. Big battery charger
15. Power-tool chargers
16. Power tools
17. Cutting disks
18. Goggles
19. Radio
20. Vertical bench drill
21. Portable work bench
22. Bin
23. Plumbing parts
24. Lathe
25. Bench metal grinder
26. Painting/decorating equipment
27. Drill bits and screws
28. Charged batteries
29. Ammo boxes for hand tools
30. Strong vice
31. Compressor
32. Drawers for small items
33. Welding mask
34. Welder
35. Wire brush

Wear a sparkproof leather apron to stop your clothing catching alight when welding

You can't have too many power points: the more you have the quicker you get a job done

Keep an eye irrigation kit to wash out grit or dust

Keep the workshop floor clean with the wire brush and dustpan and brush

A compressor is useful for inflating tyres, blowing dust out of old engines and for putting in rivets

The main work bench *is the heart of a workshop. We try to keep ours as clear as possible, so we always have space to work. It helps to have pens, pencils, and a tape measure within reach.*

Generous floor space *gives you room to work under cover.*

Use a voltmeter to check whether batteries are fully charged

Keep a range of cutting disks for metal and wood

A couple of charged batteries provides portable power whenever you need it

Hard hats and welding masks (33) and dust masks and goggles (18) *must be in good condition for them to be effective. Properly fitting goggles are vital for metalwork, as a tiny shard of metal in your eye is excruciating and damaging.*

Wall-mounted hooks *make tools easy to find, especially if you allocate specific areas for different types of tool.*

Army ammo boxes (29) *make great store-and-carry boxes for hand tools; they're tough enough to take outside.*

Shallow drawers (32) *are useful for storing small items such as staples and fastenings. Make sure you label them clearly.*

53

ENERGY AND WASTE Having reduced the amount of energy you are using, why not start generating your own? Any investment you make now will help future-proof you against price rises that you have no control over – and all the hard-earned cash that used to go to the utility companies will be yours to spend on the good life. Even the most technology-phobic will discover there is something very empowering about not being reliant upon others for your energy, water, and waste-disposal needs.

Understanding electricity

Before you decide what renewable energy systems you are going to install, it's definitely worth getting an overview of the basic science governing electricity. So here's the techie bit – this isn't an excuse to skip ahead! Have a go at reading these pages. They will help you to work out what your needs are and what renewable options are possible on your plot.

KEY TERMS

■ **Amps** The flow of electrons forming an electric current is measured in Amps.
■ **Conductors** Materials such as metals, where atoms have loosely bound electrons so there is little resistance, make good conductors.
■ **Insulators** Materials such as rubber that don't readily conduct electricity because their electrons are not easily displaced.
■ **Power** A measurement of how much energy you are using each second, measured in Watts.
■ **Volts** The "potential difference" between two points on a conductor.

Generating power

You can use renewable technologies to generate electricity in one of two ways. One option is to generate alternating current (AC) electricity mechanically by moving magnets past wires (see below) – this is what a wind turbine or the axle of a water wheel does. Another method that we use on a domestic scale absorbs energy from the sun into solar photovoltaic (PV) panels, generating direct current (DC) electricity. The energy can be used immediately, for example, to light your home or run a pump, or can be stored In batteries.

Storing energy

In a battery, a chemical reaction occurs and then electrons travel through a wire from one terminal to the other, and the result is direct current (DC) electricity (see below). Batteries are particularly useful for off-grid systems as they are fairly cheap and power can be stored and used when needed. If you wish to store electricity that you have generated in a battery bank, use leisure or "deep cycle" batteries – the sort used on caravans or boats, or to power electric fences. They are designed to deliver less current for

THE ESSENCE OF ELECTRICITY

At the centre of every atom is a nucleus, which is divided into even smaller particles called protons and neutrons. Around the nucleus, electrons orbit.

Nucleus

Electron

The protons within the nucleus have a positive charge and the orbiting electrons are negative. When there is a balance between the two, the atom is neutral.

Usually atoms have fixed numbers of electrons, which cannot be moved away from the atom. But if there is an excess of free electrons on some atoms in one site (for example, in one of

the silicon-based layers of a solar panel), and a deficiency of electrons on other atoms in a neighbouring site (such as the adjoining layer of the solar cell), and there is a route between them, then the electrons will start to move from one location to the other. This flow of electrons is called a current. The "potential difference" between the two sites is known as voltage and the electricity generated is measured in volts.

Direct current (DC) electricity

When a battery is connected to a circuit, some of the material in the battery starts to dissolve and some of the atoms lose electrons. This means there is a deficiency of electrons at one of the terminals. This potential difference sets the electrons in motion and the current flowing. The current that

Battery *Fan*

Elecron flow

Direct current *can be used for small appliances that are often associated with camping, such as a 12V kettle or a fan.*

a battery produces is called direct current, or DC – this is easy to remember because DC electricity travels from one battery terminal *directly* to the other terminal.

Alternating current (AC) electricity

AC is what the mains supply provides and so it's good to be able to produce it at home, either to sell back to the national grid or to feed into the existing electrical circuits in your house.

a longer period of time. Once flat, they're intended to be recharged. They cost about the same as car batteries, but the latter are unsuitable for most renewable applications as they aren't meant to be fully discharged then recharged once flat.

AC/DC conversions

You might imagine that one form of power would work for everything, but there are good reasons for having the capability to switch from AC to DC and vice versa. Rectifiers and inverters are devices that enable such conversions.

Rectifiers change an AC supply into DC. We use a rectifier to charge up a set of batteries using the AC current produced by our spinning water wheel. We can then store the energy that the wheel generates in batteries that can be drawn upon in the evening when we use the most indoor lighting.

Inverters work the other way to rectifiers, converting DC to AC. They are pretty well essential if you want to continue to enjoy a 21st-century lifestyle while making full use of green technology.

There are a number of inverters available, with significant differences in quality. It has to be said that some inverters can cause lights to flicker and have been known to destroy complex electronic equipment such as computers.

So it's worth opting for the more expensive, most useful version. This is the pure sine wave inverter, which ensures the electricity you produce matches the electricity distributed in the national grid.

When choosing an inverter, you need to know what sort of appliances you want to power from it. Ask the installer and, if in doubt, check the details with your electrician.

1. Our grid-linked wind turbine allows us to sell any excess electricity we create back to the national grid. **2. The energy created** by these solar PV panels is stored in leisure batteries for such things as pumping water from our spring to powering our greenhouse heat sink.

To understand AC electricity, it helps if you think back to school as you may well remember a diagram of a magnet with lines of flux linking the two poles (see right). These lines of flux illustrate the invisible power in a magnet. Now imagine moving a magnet near a coil of copper wire. The magnetic field passing through the wire will cause the electrons to move in the coil and so generate a current. The stronger the magnets, the more lines of flux cut the copper coil, and the more electricity you generate. You can make more electricity either by moving the magnets past the coil faster or by bringing them closer to the wire.

Mount a set of magnets on a rotating disc and you have a system that makes AC (see right). All you have to do to create the electricity is put in energy to

make the magnets spin. In this way you could harness the power running in a stream or the energy contained in a breeze blowing over an exposed hill

Lines of flux *between the north and south ends of a magnet are invisible.*

Magnets *rotating past a coil of copper wire generate alternating current (AC).*

GRID LINKING

You must use the skills of a certified electrician to ensure you are set up correctly so that you can be linked to the national grid. The systems must have a safety mode that switches them off if the grid connection fails. It's easy to imagine what would happen if you were gaily putting electricity into the grid while a maintenance team were working on a problem with their mains supply switched off. Also, renewable energy systems must synchronize to the grid. If they are not in synch, the combined effect will produce dirty AC.

Renewable energy options

Before you start harnessing the elements to heat and light your home it's worth considering your motivation as it will determine what systems are best for you. You will also need to assess your site as you may not have suitable resources. Finally, you should decide on how self-reliant you want to be. Do you want to remain connected to the national infrastructure as a safety blanket?

Why do you want to use renewable energy?

If you simply wish to reduce your impact on the planet and money is not an issue, then all you need to ensure is that the energy it takes to set up your renewable energy technology, known as the "embodied energy", will be less than the energy you save during its lifetime.

However, for the majority of us, financial savings tend to be just as important as environmental savings – so, the systems you choose must make financial sense now and for the future, as well as helping the planet. When doing your sums, you may be concerned about the length of the payback time, but remember that your investment can also future-proof you against energy price rises and possible shortages. So add peace of mind into your calculations.

There is also the advantage that well-chosen renewable energy systems will add to the value of your property, making them a better investment than many interior refurbishments.

What are your resources?

Your opportunities depend on different factors that relate to your plot. Carry out a site survey and ask yourself some key questions before hiring a certified installer to put in an expensive system. For example:
- Do you have **south-facing roofs** or surfaces on which to place solar thermal systems or solar PV panels?
- Do you get **winter sun**?
- Can you **use the wind**? To decide this you will need to know: where are the prevailing winds? What is the average wind speed? And will your local planning authority give you permission to erect a turbine?

- Do you have a **water source**? If so, how far will you have to move the water for it to be useful? Is there sufficient flow/drop to harness the water energy to turn it into electricity? (See pages 68–73.) You will also need to apply to DEFRA for a licence to abstract water.

When you are considering what is possible on your plot you should also think about what you would really *like* to do. If you have always wanted a wind turbine or a water wheel and either or both will work on your site, then go for it. Better that than to take the kiddie in the sweetshop approach and opt for it all. You need to prioritize because ultimately cost will dictate what you can achieve.

How self-reliant should you be?

There are some big advantages to using the national grid as a buffer for your renewable projects. You have something to fall back on if any of your systems fail and you can sell any surplus to the grid. There is also something comfortingly mainstream and normal about still being connected to the rest of the country.

That said, grid connection does mean you won't have a truly independent system and unless you are disciplined and use no more than you produce, you will still be facing regular bills and price rises when energy costs increase.

1. The water wheel at Newhouse Farm generates enough electricity to light our house. **2. The grid-linked turbine** is positioned as high as possible to take advantage of the wind.

Our renewable energy systems

Here at Newhouse Farm we decided to remain connected to the grid, but not to be fully dependent upon it, so we have some systems that are grid-linked and others that are stand-alone.

The stand-alone wind turbine works with solar PV panels to charge batteries. These power the pump that brings water from the spring to our house

Underground cable links to circuits in the power house

Aqueduct and water wheel powers the lighting circuits and is independent of the grid

The solar PV panels are grid-linked so we can sell the surplus energy that is generated on sunny afternoons

Underground water pipe

Solar thermal tubes harness the sun's rays to heat the water used inside the house

Grid-linked wind turbine puts excess energy into the grid on windy nights

Underground cable

The powerhouse

HRV system distributes heat around the house (see pages 44–45)

Biofuels in woodburner

Conservatory for solar gain

If you wish to break free and come off-grid, you won't be able to use the infrastructure that currently exists for electricity, gas, or water as a back-up to your own systems. You will be taking full responsibility for your own energy and water supplies, and although that is a heady prospect, the reliability of the systems you are putting in place will become a key issue. Start by addressing a series of "what ifs?". What if…

- it's not sunny for days/weeks?
- it's not windy for days/weeks?
- it's neither sunny nor windy for days/weeks?
- the water flow from your source reduces during the summer?
- you have to take a system out of service for planned maintenance?
- something malfunctions in a system and you need to fix it?
- your stored/harvested water is not replenished for a day/week/month?

A huge storage capacity for excess energy may seem the answer, but providing masses of storage that you may only use occasionally is a very expensive option. Instead, focus on what you consider to be essential and then be prepared to compromise if nature temporarily leaves you a bit short. For example, you may consider that it's essential to flush the toilet but that baths are a luxury. So if your rainwater tank starts to get low, you will choose to limit baths and use the shower instead.

There are plenty of other examples that demonstrate that limiting your energy usage is not necessarily a hardship. How about limiting the amount of time the television is on each day; or using the kettle on the woodburner rather than switching on the electric kettle? You can also give up the tumble dryer and use a washing line instead.

CALCULATE YOUR ENERGY USAGE

Before you invest in a renewable energy system, you need to work out how much energy you use so you can calculate how much you need to make. To find out the amount of energy an appliance uses, multiply its power by the number of hours it is turned on for, or use a plug-in energy monitor. The standard unit to measure this is kilowatt hours (kWh) – a kilowatt is 1,000 watts – and it is the unit of electricity you get billed for.

- A 2kW heater that is run for 1 hour will use 2kWh of energy.
- A 100W light running for 5 hours will use 0.5kWh.
- A 3kW electric oven run for 3 hours will use 9kWh.

If your ambitions lie firmly in the realms of living "off-grid", using only home-generated power, it's important to first reduce the amount of energy you are using (see pages 36–39).

Using solar PV panels

Whenever the sun shines, it offers us a powerful source of energy in the form of photon rays that can be converted instantly to direct current (DC) electricity by photovoltaic (PV) cells. These can be used for all sorts of jobs, from powering low-voltage water pumps to charging a mobile phone. Solar panels can be fitted to most roofs and are often the best-value systems to link to the national grid.

Improved efficiency

In the past, solar panels were considered to be expensive and inefficient, but recent technology breakthroughs have increased their efficiency to as high as 80 per cent and reduced the price per kilowatt of power. The increased effficiency means a small area of roof can provide enough power to be useful for an average home.

The life of a solar PV system is impressive as there are no moving parts to convert the solar energy into electricity, and the glass is self cleaning. Our system is guaranteed to supply at least 80 per cent of the 3kW peak (see right) for the next 25 years. Indeed some of the earliest PV panels are still making electricity after 40 years of service.

How solar panels work

Each solar panel is an remarkable lattice of layers of silicon-based cells. When the sun's photons hit a layer of silicon that has free outer electrons around the atoms, these move to the layer beneath, which comprises atoms with electrons missing. The resulting flow causes a small current, but because there are many cells linked together, the whole panel produces a useable voltage of DC electricity. This current is then changed to AC through an inverter if it is being grid-linked (see page 57), or remains as DC current if it is going straight into a battery.

Power capability

As a rough guide, a south-facing solar panel installation in the UK with a 3kW peak capability should provide enough energy over the year to meet the estimated average household demand of 3,300kW.

Solar PV systems are specified as having a "peak power capability", because they depend on how much sun shines on the panels. Surprisingly, the systems do still make electricity on overcast days, though obviously less than on sunny days. However, it

SITE CHECKLIST

■ How much **electricity** do you use in your house? Can you reduce it?
■ Do you have a **south-facing roof**?
■ Does your roof get **winter sun**?
■ If you are hoping to install panels on the roof of your house, have you checked with the **local authority** if planning permission is needed?
■ Are there any **grants** available in your area?
■ Size does matter – **how much space** do you have for your panels?
■ What is the **peak output** in kW of the system you have been quoted (see opposite)? How long is the predicted **payback**?
■ Have you considered a **combined system** for operating a small off-grid energy solution?

1. **Solar PV panels** on the roof of our barn. 2. **Adjustable ground-mounted panels** enable you to track the sun during the day. 3. **A small panel** powers the fan in our greenhouse heat sink (see pages 118–119).

is also worth mentioning that your specific microclimate is key when making any decisions about power capability. After all, a solar panel simply might not be the right option if you live in a shady valley.

Stand-alone systems

Solar PV panels are extremely useful for charging batteries and so are ideal for powering a stand-alone system that is remote from a mains supply, such as a pump for a watering system. For a stand-alone system, it is important to be sure that your solar panel can provide enough energy to power whatever you intend to use it for. If you are using your pump for two hours a day, work out how much power you will use (see right) and install enough panels to supply it. As long as your panels are a suitable size and you have sufficient batteries, you should seldom have an occasion when there is not enough power to work the pump because you will

have enough stored energy for these "just-in-case" situations.

We use solar PV panels to run the pump that we use near a spring to provide water for the farmhouse. It wouldn't be acceptable for us to run out of water just because there has been no sunshine, so we opted for a dual wind-sun system in addition to the charging batteries. The wind turbine acts as a back-up over the winter when there is less sunshine, and in summer, when there is more sun, the solar panels take over.

There are times (and these are surprisingly frequent) when nature provides us with so much energy the batteries are full and risk being damaged if they continue to be charged. To overcome this, we have connected a charge controller to the PV panel. It monitors the battery voltage and when the battery is full, the charge controller simply turns off the panels by disconnecting them from the battery.

WORKING OUT HOW MANY BATTERIES TO USE

The amount of energy that a battery can supply is specified in ampere hours (Ah). So, a 12-volt battery that is specified as 100Ah can theoretically deliver 1 amp for 100 hours or 100 amps for 1 hour. Multiplying the volts and amps, gives you the power (watts) the battery will produce. For this battery, then, it is possible to have:

■ 12 volts x 1 amp = 12 watts for 100 hours
OR
■ 12 volts x 100 amps = 1200 watts for 1 hour.

Back in the real world, these numbers don't quite add up as you can't expect to get more than 80 per cent capacity from your battery, i.e. 80Ah. Also, the smaller leisure batteries are not designed to deliver masses of current so you shouldn't really drain more than about 10-15 amps (that's a device of about 120 –180 watts). The pump at our spring needs 60 watts to function so we divide 60 watts by 12 volts, which gives 5 amps. As we use our pump 2 hours a day, a fully charged battery therefore lasts us about 8 days.

Important elements of a PV system

The position of your panels makes a big difference to how much energy is obtainable. South-facing is ideal and as the angle of incidence of the sun varies by season and time of day, the optimal pitch is 40° from vertical.

Flush-mounted PV panels is pitched at 40° to receive maximum average sunlight throughout the year

Grid-linked inverter turns DC into AC so we can sell it to the mains grid

Renewable obligation certificate (ROC) meter records generated energy – you can be paid for these units as well as any electricity you export

Import/export meter records the electricity you use – surplus energy goes to the grid and any shortfall comes from the grid

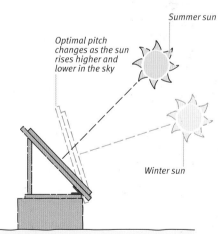

Summer sun

Optimal pitch changes as the sun rises higher and lower in the sky

Winter sun

Adjusting pitch
Optimal pitch is the angle from vertical that PV panels should be positioned to receive maximum sunlight at solar noon. This changes according to season and where you are in the world. Here in Cornwall our optimal pitch in June is 64°, but only 16° in December and we adjust our ground PVs accordingly. Roof-ground mounts and pole mounts allow you to adjust roof PVs but they are more expensive and difficult to erect.

Using solar thermal systems

Solar thermal generation is one of the simplest means of harnessing the sun's energy. It works by the direct transfer of energy; no power is generated, which means there's no mucking about with electricity. Solar thermal systems rely solely on the power of the sun to warm water and neatly provide you with plenty of pollution-free hot water for your home – as long as the sun shines.

How it works

Solar thermal units, or solar collectors, are the most widely used type of solar power. In its simplest form, a unit comprises a black heat-absorbing plate, bonded to a series of pipes that allow water to flow through them. It is housed in an insulated box with a glass cover to protect the unit from cooling winds. Sunshine passes through the glass and heats up the plate and the resulting heat is transferred to the water flowing through the pipes, which is then pumped to wherever it is to be used.

Key elements

■ **The solar collector** This is the key part of the system as it captures the solar energy. There are several different types that vary in price and efficiency, ranging from a plastic system (the cheapest and least efficient) to a copper system and finally to heat pipes inside evacuated tubes (the best and usually most expensive). Evacuated tubes are double-walled glass tubes with a vacuum between the layers to stop heat escaping. They have black-painted copper fins attached to a heat pipe inside them, which transfers heat up to a manifold, or "junction", where cold water passes over it and is instantly heated up to a higher temperature. As you decide which type of solar collector you wish to purchase, remember that in this context size really does matter, as you want to capture as much solar energy as possible.

■ **Solar hot-water tank** This is usually double-insulated, so when you heat water it is still warm and available for a shower next morning. There is a sensor at the top of the tank that allows you to confirm the temperature of the water.

■ **Solar water feed** This is placed at the bottom of the tank so when it's sunny you get masses of free hot water. But when you have to pay to heat the water, for example by using the boiler, you only heat the top portion rather than the whole tank.

■ **The controller** This is the brains of the outfit and it makes the simple decision that if the collector is hotter than the tank, it turns the pump on to circulate the hot water until the whole tank has heated up; if the collector is cool it turns the pump off.

Our thermal set-up

Our house at Newhouse Farm is listed, so we had to install our solar thermal system on an outbuilding. To overcome the losses we expected because of the water travelling a great distance from outside to the hot-water tank, we installed a slightly bigger system than was theoretically required and made sure that the pipes were heavily insulated.

System efficiency

Our system averages out to the equivalent of turning an electric immersion heater on for 3–4 hours a day in the summer and about 30 minutes per day in the winter. It was a revelation to discover that we still get enough solar energy to help heat our water – even in the middle of the winter.

Header tank

Hot water to taps and shower

Immersion heater as back-up

Controller

Solar hot-water feed

Solar collector

Pump

Cold-water feed

Secondary hot-water feed from woodburner back boiler

SITE CHECKLIST

■ **How much do you pay** for your hot- water bill?

■ Do you have a **south-facing** roof or shed?

■ If you live in a **conservation zone** or have a listed building, you must first secure planning permission from your local planning authority.

■ If you are not granted permission, another option would be to use a **ground-mounted system**.

■ Are there any grants available in your local area?

■ Have you researched different manufacturers and checked what they quote as the peak kWh performance per m²? Compare this to other companies to find an efficient system at the right price.

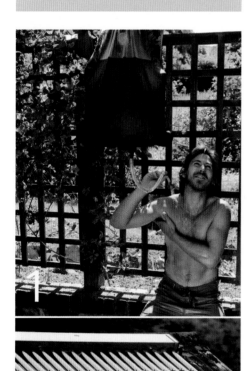

1. Camping solar showers are black plastic carriers that are filled with water and left in full sunlight – they will heat up in a couple of hours. **2. Our solar collectors** comprise evacuated tubes with heat pipes connected to the manifold at the top, through which water flows and is heated.

DIY solar shower

It is possible to make your own garden solar shower for next to nothing using a recycled radiator, a large black plastic dustbin, and a variety of leftover materials. An ideal location for the shower would be a disused outhouse or large garden shed with a south-facing roof for mounting the collector to receive maximum sunlight. When you're ready to start using your shower, fill the reservoir with enough water so that it comes above the level of the top pipe from the collector, then leave it to heat up. Empty the reservoir after each use to prevent the water from turning into an unhealthy bacterial soup; refill using a garden hose.

Collector made by rinsing out an old radiator and painting one side black with waterproof paint

Wooden box lined with insulation

Insulated outlet pipe feeds hot water to top of reservoir

Hose inside reservoir is attached to a block of wood so it floats and ensures the warm water at the top is used first

Insulated hose connects to shower head

Tank connector links shower head to hose

Glass or plastic lid for extra insulation

Copper inlet and outlet pipes are soldered to the radiator and connected to the tank

Cold water feeds into the collector from the bottom of the reservoir.

Thermal siphoning
As the water in the collector heats up, it starts to rise and, in turn, is replaced by cooler water coming into the bottom of it. This is called thermal siphoning and ensures the reservoir of water heats up. If you don't have an old radiator you could use the coolant grill from an old fridge or freezer and mount it on a sheet of metal – for our collector, we cut open an old water tank and beat it flat.

Use chemical-free washing products and the water can be recycled via a reed bed filtration system (see pages 80–81)

63

Harnessing wind energy

Wind power ultimately derives from the action of the sun warming the earth and creating weather patterns. Here in the UK we benefit from strong winds, mainly caused by depressions coming in from the Atlantic Ocean. A wind turbine uses that wind to create electricity: the wind turns the blades, which rotate a series of magnets past coils of copper wire, which generate electricity.

Wind on your plot

Jutting out into the Atlantic Ocean, Cornwall is a windy place and here at Newhouse Farm we harness this free energy with a grid-linked turbine that provides mains electricity for the house, and a stand-alone turbine that we use to charge batteries in order to power a pump for the spring. The term "stand-alone" simply means that this turbine isn't connected to the national grid.

The stand-alone turbine works with a solar PV panel (see pages 60–61) as part of a dual system. This underlines the first thing to bear in mind when considering a wind energy option: wind is not classed as "firm power" as it does not always blow. As a result, wind power has to be part of a mix of generation capabilities, or else you have to store the energy you harvest in batteries (see pages 56–57) for times of low or no wind.

There are two other important things about wind that you should know if you are considering installing a wind turbine:

■ **Wind speed matters** – lots. The power you can get from a wind turbine is proportional to the cube of the wind speed (i.e. speed x speed x speed). You can get hold of information about average wind speeds in your area by doing an internet search and then use these figures to see if it's worth your while installing a wind turbine. Even if you don't receive a lot of wind, with the right kind of turbine it's still possible to generate electricity.

■ **Local wind turbulence** is another crucial factor. The key to a good output from the turbine is to have "smooth" wind (known as "laminar") with no turbulence (see box, below). A wind turbine will never be efficient in turbulent air since it will be trying constantly to change direction. In addition, the rotor speed fluctuates, which will reduce the power output of the turbine and also increase the wear and tear.

With a bit of preparation you will be in a good position to make that most crucial decision of where to locate the turbine. Get it right and whenever the wind blows you'll be

COMING TO GRIPS WITH TURBULENCE

Turbulence is caused by obstacles on or near the ground, which change the wind from a smooth flow from one direction into vortices. These cause the wind to rapidly change speed and direction, which is not a good thing for a wind turbine (see below left). As a result, a turbine on the coast will probably get "better air" compared to one in the middle of a city, where there are many more obstacles causing turbulence. But local deviations in the strength and laminar quality of the wind can be huge, even out in the countryside where you'd think air flowed freely. The illustration below, right, shows how obstacles can effect turbulence. As a general rule, to avoid turbulence, plan for a turbine to be 6–9m (20–28ft) higher than any obstacle within 100m (330ft). If in doubt, higher is always better.

The turbulence caused by an obstacle begins twice its height before reaching the obstacle and carries on for 10–15 times the height after the obstacle, peaking at twice its height.

The grey areas above show where turbulence is created when the wind blows over hills (long areas of turbulence) and over a cliff, where the turbulence is relatively short.

1. **The stand-alone turbine** stores the energy it creates in a battery. 2. **Our two turbines** are situated on opposite sides of a small valley for optimum wind power. 3. **The grid-linked turbine** is atop a sturdy tower that has steel guys to help keep it in place on particularly windy days.

rubbing your hands with glee at all that free power. Get it wrong and you will not only get disappointing results, but you will waste a lot of time, money, and effort.

How to buy

Not so long ago, commercially bought wind turbines were very expensive and if you wanted a lot of power for your pound, then the only real way forwards was to build your own.

Growing environmental awareness, cheaper foreign imports, and increased competition have created a huge market for wind-generation products. This means it's much more economical than it once was to buy an off-the-shelf system and have it installed. On the other hand, building your own brings huge rewards and is a lot of fun. You'll find it's relatively easy to source all the components of the turbine (see pages 66–67).

A quick internet search will reveal most of the commercial turbines that are available. The market is constantly changing, so to make a good buy you need to check out all the claims made by turbine manufacturers, especially those about their rated power. Manufacturers will claim different power outputs that are based on different wind speeds, so they become difficult to compare. For example, a turbine rated 500W at 8m (26ft) per second is almost the same as one that claims 1,900W at 12.5m (40ft) per second.

The best thing to do is to ask for the power curves based on how you will use the turbine, for example to charge a 24V battery. Power curves show the power supplied by the turbine at different wind speeds. This will then allow you to compare like with like.

House-mounted systems

There are systems that mount onto the side or the roof of your house. For people in urban and suburban locations this may be your only option and, if so, it is still possible to obtain reasonable performance using one of these systems. This isn't the way we'd go, however, and you need to be aware of a few issues relating to roof-mounted installations:

■ **Turbulence** can have a negative effect. Just imagine the kind of turbulence around a huge obstacle like a house – a roof-mounted turbine is located in this zone of turbulence.

■ **Wind turbines create noise.** If a turbine is mounted directly on to your house, the sound may be very noticeable and could become a source of irritation, not only for you but also for your neighbours.

SITE CHECKLIST

■ Do you understand how the **wind blows** on your plot?
■ Have you found out the **wind speed** for your area?
■ Have you established the **direction** of the prevailing wind?
■ Have you identified **topographical features** that form obstacles and create turbulence? Have you worked out how they might be overcome?
■ Have you looked into **planning permission**? Virtually all wind turbines need this and the following factors need to be investigated before planning permission is granted: proximity to power lines, airports, roads, and railways; shadow flicker; noise; electromagnetic interference; siting and the landscape; ecology, archaeology, and listed buildings; disturbance during construction.

Components of a wind turbine

If you are to harness the wind, you will require all of the items that are discussed on these pages. If you are intending to build your own turbine, most bits can be bought on the internet at very reasonable prices. This allows you to customize the turbine to your own needs, for example if your location isn't very windy you may need bigger blades.

Blades

A very clever chap call Betz calculated that, even with the best designed blade in the world, you can only ever harness 59 per cent of the wind's energy. So, if you can harness only some of the energy, it is important that you have good blades that are as big as possible.

Designing blades is a little complicated and the choices vary: cheaper blades have a constant angle of attack and width (rather like a plank), while complex ones vary in width and look twisted. The better the blade, the more efficient your turbine. The turbine will also be less noisy, especially in high winds, and it will be easier to start the blades spinning.

Electrical generator

It may not seem like it when you look at a wind turbine, but the blades rotate relatively slowly with only a couple of hundred rpm, even in high winds. Because of this low rpm, there is really only one type of electrical generator to use: a permanent magnet alternator (PMA), which can start generating useful power at as little as 50 rpm and can have an efficiency of 90 per cent. A few points worth noting:

■ **Buy a multiphase alternator**. This produces continuous power resulting in much reduced "cogging". Too much cogging can make it hard to start turning the blades.

■ **Efficiency**. Check out the power curves of any PMA that you are considering using.

■ **Rectifiers**. If you intend to use the turbine to charge batteries, you will need to change from AC to DC (see box opposite). Some manufacturers of PMAs and wind turbines have rectifiers built in, while with others you have to buy or make your own at extra cost.

High-speed protection

It is essential that all wind turbines have an emergency shutdown device to prevent them being damaged in high winds. If a turbine over-spins, due to either heavy weather or a malfunction, there is a risk of mechanical damage. If a blade breaks off, it can travel a long way and potentially injure someone.

Furling systems

The term "furling system" describes a system that turns the rotor of the turbine away from the direction of the wind, either horizontally or vertically, to prevent damage. Furling not only protects the turbine from over-spinning, but will also reduce excess loading on the tower and its supports. Check out these designs:

■ **Variable pitch blades.** These form the best but most complex system. The blades automatically adjust their pitch, depending on the wind speed.

■ **Tail furling.** The turbine and tail are mounted to the side of the yaw bearing and the tail is hinged onto the turbine body.

■ **Tilt-back furling.** The turbine is hinged so it can tilt backwards.

■ **Blade flexing.** The blades bend back and twist during high winds.

The parts of a wind turbine aren't numerous, but there are choices to be made for the blades, inverter and generator. Tail furling (**1**), flaxing blades (**2**), cheap/noisy blades like planks (**3**), well-designed, efficient blades (**4**), electrical generators (**5**), electrical generator with integrated blades (**6**), pure sine inverter (**7**), charge controller (**8**), cheap quasi-sine inverter (**9**), switch-over switch (**10**), and home-made monitoring capability (**11**).

Shutdown systems

These are systems that can be used to manually shut down the turbine for maintenance or weather protection.

■ **Electrical shutdown.** This is the most popular method of shutdown. One advantage of using a PMA is that if the AC outputs are shorted, the PMA becomes very difficult to turn and so stops the blades from turning. A change-over switch is installed to prevent damage to the PMA.

■ **Mechanical shutdown.** This forces the turbine out of the wind or applies a brake to stop the blades turning.

Tower

There are two main types of tower for installing wind turbines:

■ **A tilt-up tower** can be assembled on the ground and then raised into the vertical position. It also has the advantage that it can be tilted for maintenance. However, this type of tower usually requires guys to keep it steady and will therefore take up a larger area.

■ **A fixed tower** is assembled in situ, usually using a crane, and the turbine is fixed on to it later. This type of tower can be free-standing and relatively trouble-free. To maintain it, however, you have to climb up the tower or move it to the ground.

Whichever system you go for, it must be extremely strong. A 2.5cm (1in) steel pipe may feel strong if you have 1m (3ft) of it, but it is very easy to bend 10m (33ft) of steel pipe. Some people recommend that you should spend at least as much on the tower as you do on the turbine, and we'd be inclined to agree with them.

Electrical set-up

There are two main types of electrical systems that usually apply to wind-generation installations.

■ **Direct grid-tie systems**. These systems are usually only an option on larger turbines. There are two main components: the turbine and a grid-tie inverter. These systems can link to the electricity grid in the same way as the solar PV system (see page 61).

■ **Battery storage**. This stores the electricity produced by the turbine in batteries until it is needed. It can, if necessary, then be converted by a suitable inverter to 240V AC to run mains equipment. The advantage of battery storage is that the electricity can be stored and then used, even if the wind stops blowing. Most installations use lead-acid batteries, which is why the voltage of most systems is in multiples of 12V. Forklift or submarine batteries also work well if you can find them. If you intend to store energy in batteries, you will have to ensure the battery bank is close to the turbine.

BATTERY STORAGE SET-UP

Turbines are usually optimized to match the voltage of the battery bank that you will be using, such as 12V or 24V. The turbine usually produces AC electricity, which must be converted before it can be used to charge batteries. Lead-acid batteries always "hold" the voltage generated by the turbine to their own voltage until they are fully charged. When the voltage increases dramatically, it could easily "boil" the batteries (which will ruin them and creates an explosion hazard). To prevent this happening, use a charge controller and a dump load. Heating elements are the best dump loads. Don't use light bulbs or motors as they have a large start-up current, which could damage the charge controller.

The elements of battery storage

■ **The rectifier** converts AC electricity to DC, which can then be used to charge batteries.

■ **The battery bank** holds the electricity generated by the turbine.

■ **The charge controller** monitors the charge state of the batteries and when they are full diverts the incoming electricity into a dump load.

■ **The dump load** takes the excess electricity and so must be able to cope with the maximum amount of power produced by the turbine.

■ **An inverter** converts DC power from the batteries to AC and will be needed if you want to power the main electricity, which runs on 240V AC.

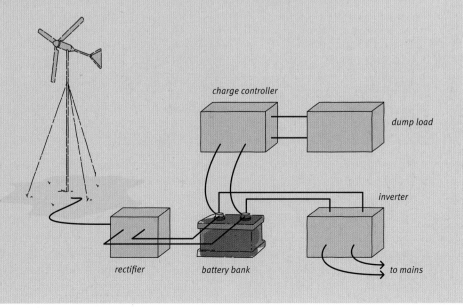

charge controller

dump load

inverter

rectifier   battery bank   to mains

Harnessing water energy

Anyone who has carried watering cans back and forth to their crops knows that they are heavy, and therein lies a blessing and a curse. As water flows downhill it has lots of energy which can be harnessed, but to transport it to a convenient location, such as a water tank, takes a fair bit of effort, and additional energy, which we have to provide.

Water power

The most efficient way of harnessing the energy in moving water is to use a water turbine, which converts water power into rotational power at its shaft. This is then converted to electrical power by a generator.

Waterwheels are covered on pages 72–73, so here we are looking at a hydroelectric system. This is a series of interconnected components, with water flowing in one end, and electricity coming out of the other (see opposite page).

Getting started

Before you can begin planning your system, or estimating how much power it will produce, you will need to make a few essential measurements:

- **The flow**, which determines how much water is available to use.
- **The head** is the vertical distance between where you plan to start capturing the water and where you intend to use it.

These are the two most important facts you need to know about your site. To measure them, see pages 70–71. You simply cannot move forwards without these measurements as they determine everything about your hydroelectric system, including the pipeline size, turbine type, rotational speed, and generator size. Even costs are impossible to estimate without flow and head measurements, as you need them to calculate the potential power output generated by your hydroelectric system.

Once you have obtained your measurements, do an online search for domestic water turbine companies to find those that can either build and install the whole thing for you, or, if you have some engineering experience, supply the components for you to make one yourself.

The turbine

This important piece of equipment is the heart of the hydroelectric system. Its efficiency determines how much electricity is generated. There are two main types:

- **Reaction turbines** run immersed in water and are used in low-head/high-flow systems. Makes include Francis, Propeller, and Kaplan.
- **Impulse turbines** operate in air and are driven by one or more high-velocity jets of water. They're typically used with high-head systems and use nozzles to produce the high-velocity jets. Examples of these turbines include Pelton and Turgo.

There are many types of turbine and making the right selection requires considerable expertise. A Pelton design, for example, works best with a high head, whereas a Crossflow design works better with a low head but high flow.

SITE CHECKLIST
- **Have you sought** permission for your water power system from the Environment Agency? And have you purchased an abstraction licence? You will need this permission if you are re-directing more that 20,000 litres (4,300 gallons) of water per day.
- **Have you measured** the flow and head (see pages 70–71)?
- **Have you discussed** your system calculations with potential installers to see if you have satisfied the minimum requirements?

1. This Pelton turbine is an example of an impulse-type turbine driven by high-velocity water jets. **2. Even small streams** may be able to create enough power to run a turbine.

A hydroelectric system

The major components of a hydroelectric system are a water diversion, a pipeline for creating pressure in the water, a turbine and generator for generating electricity, a tailrace for exiting water, and transmission wires. You need to divert water from a stream by building the diversion, where water enters the pipeline that feeds your turbine.

An expert must match *the turbine design to your flow and head. This will ensure that the turbine works efficiently and generates the maximum amount of power.*

Water diversion
At the start of the system you need to build a water diversion. This is a deep pool of water that creates a smooth flow and removes dirt and debris before it reaches the pipeline.

The pipeline
Water is transported to your turbine via a pipeline that forces the water into a limited space and creates pressure as gravity takes it downhill. Its diameter, length, and route affect the overall efficiency.

The turbine and generator
Your system's efficiency depends on the turbine's design, especially the water entry and exit points. Controls ensure the generator constantly spins at the correct speed. Both the turbine and generator must include an emergency shutdown.

The tailrace
This directs water back to the water course. If part of the tailrace is a sealed pipe below the turbine, it can increase the head.

The open stream dissipates energy as it travels downstream.

Deep pool of water creates a smooth, air-free inlet to the pipe

The water diversion is located at the highest point of a hydro system. Build a dam for the water to pool into before being directed into a pipeline.

The pipeline focuses all the water power at the bottom of the pipe where the turbine is connected.

Transmission wires

The electrical equipment must be installed in a powerhouse for safety and protection.

The turbine is located at the bottom of the slope.

The generator is driven by the turbine.

The tailrace directs water away from the turbine and back to the water course.

Avoid using *all your water, as plants, fish, birds, and other wildlife rely on the stream for survival.*

Taking measurements for head and flow

Before you set up your hydro system measure the flow and head of your water. These measurements will help you to determine the viability of the system. Flow is expressed as volume (litres or cubic feet) per second or minute. Stream levels change through the seasons, so it is sensible to measure the speed of water flow at different times of the year. Greater flow means greater power. The head is measured as a vertical distance in metres or feet. The higher the head, the greater the pressure – and the greater the available power.

MEASURING THE FLOW

Method 1: Measuring how long it takes to fill a container

■ **Build a temporary dam** with a single outlet pipe. Place a container of a known volume at the end of the pipe. Use a stopwatch to time how long it takes to fill.

■ **Divide** the container volume by the seconds. For example:
15-litre bucket
Time to fill = 3 seconds
Flow = 5 litres/second.

Temporary dam forces the water through a single outlet pipe

The time it takes to fill the container is the "flow"

Small stream method
This is an ideal way to calculate the flow of very small streams.

Method 2: Measuring with a float

■ **Measure the average depth of the stream**. Lay a plank across the stream and measure the stream depth at 30cm (12in) intervals. To work out the average depth, add all the measurements together and divide by the number of measurements you have made.

■ **Calculate the cross-sectional area** of the stream. Multiply the average depth you just worked out by the width of the stream. For example, if the average depth is 0.2m (8in) and the width is 1.5m (60in) then the cross-sectional area is 0.3 sq m (3.23 sq ft).

■ **Measure the speed of the stream** by marking off a 5m (5yd) length of the stream that includes the point where you measured the cross-section. Place a weighted float that can be seen clearly in the stream, a good distance upstream of your measurement area, and then use a stopwatch to time how long it takes to cover the length of your measured section. The stream speed will probably vary across its width, so record the times for different locations and calculate an average. To work out the speed, divide the distance travelled by the time it took. For example, if it took 10 seconds for the float to travel 5m:
Speed = 5/10, or 0.5m per second (equivalent to 18in per second).

■ **Calculate the flow**. Multiply the speed by the cross-sectional area.
Flow = 0.5m per sec x 0.3 sq m
    = 0.15 cubic m per second.
This is equivalent to 150 litres (33 gallons) per second.

■ **Account for friction**. Because a stream bed creates friction with the moving water, the bottom of the stream moves a little slower than the top. This means the actual flow is less than our calculation. By multiplying the result by 0.83, we get a more accurate rate: Flow = 0.15 x 0.83 = 0.1245 cubic m per second. This is equivalent to 124 litres (28 gallons) per second.

Mark a length of 5m or 5yd of the stream

Time a weighted float to see how long it takes to travel 5m (5yd).

Calculations for large streams
Use this method if the stream is fairly consistent in width and depth for a section 5m (5yd) in length.

Select a plank that spans the width of the stream and mark it at 30cm (12in) intervals.

MEASURING THE HEAD

Method 1: Using horizontal planks and vertical poles

■ **Decide your pipeline intake point,** then measure 1m (3ft) from it and hold a measuring pole vertically at that point. Place a horizontal plank from the intake point to the vertical pole.

■ **Measure the height** on the vertical pole from the horizontal plank to the ground and note it.

■ **Repeat to the bottom of the hill.** Ensure each plank starts from where you took the last measurement.

■ **Add up** all the measurements taken from the vertical pole. The result is the "head".

Find a friend
This job is easier with two people. One holds a horizontal plank with a spirit level on it; the other holds a vertical measuring pole or long ruler.

Pipeline intake

Spirit level placed on horizontal plank

Ensure the plank is horizontal

The measuring pole must always be vertical

Add together the heights of the verticals to establish the head

Method 2: Measuring pressure
If you measure the pressure in a hose, you can calculate the elevation change of your system. This method relies on the fact that each vertical foot of a head creates 0.433 pounds per square inch (psi) of water pressure (10 vertical feet would create 4.33psi).

■ **Run a hose** (or hoses) from your proposed intake site to your proposed turbine location.

■ **Attach an accurate pressure meter** to the bottom end of the

hose and completely fill the hose with water. Read the gauge on the meter. If the pressure were to read 4.33psi, the head would be exactly 10ft; if it reads 6.49psi the head would be 15ft.

Fill the hose with water from a watering can

Pipeline intake

A pressure meter attached to the end of the hose gives an accurate psi reading of pressure

Make sure there are no high spots in the hose that could trap air

Using a garden hose
If the distance is short enough, you can use one or more garden hoses to measure the head.

HOW MUCH POWER IS AVAILABLE?

Now you can roughly estimate the power output from your system. Note, however, these figures don't account for the inevitable losses from your system, so actual power output will be considerably less.

Theoretical Power (W) = flow (litres/sec) x head (metres) x gravity (9.81 m⁻²)

If, for example, a stream has a flow of 150 litres per second and a head of 10 metres, the maximum theoretical power is:

Theoretical power = 150 x 10 x 9.81 watts
= 14,715 watts (14.7kW)

What is brilliant about this figure is that you can see just how much electrical power your hydroelectric system could theoretically make.

14.7 kW for one hour = 14.7kWh.
In a day, this totals 14.7 x 24 = 352.8kWh.
In a year, this totals 128,772kWh.

Assuming an average house uses 3,300kWh, the stream in our example

could theoretically generate enough power for more than 40 houses.

Accounting for loss of power
The friction of the water moving through the pipeline and turbine, and the energy loss in the drive system, generator, and transmission lines, account for some loss of power from your hydroelectric system. For example, a home-sized system generating direct AC power may operate at about 60–70 per cent "water-to-wire" efficiency, measured between turbine input and generator output.

Building a waterwheel

Waterwheels are a long-established way of harnessing water power. In fact, British industry was powered by watermills for hundreds of years. The principle is simple: the wheel comprises a series of angled buckets and as the flow of water enters each bucket it pushes the wheel round before pouring out again, and this turning of the wheel can be converted into electrical power.

The waterwheel system

As with water turbines, a waterwheel system must make the most of the quantity of water flowing and the drop it falls through, or "head" (see pages 70–71). Having said that, it is still possible to operate a waterwheel system on a stream without any head, using an undershot wheel design (see box opposite).

■ **The water source** (the flow) can be a lake, river, stream, man-made mill race or, as in our case, a spring-fed stream that is diverted along an aqueduct. The diversion or sluice is usually the main civil works to be undertaken. Remember, you may need Environment Agency approval and have to pay for an abstraction license (see page 68).

■ **Aim to have the largest wheel possible** to create the maximum drop. The distance from the centre of the shaft to the inside edge of the buckets determines the torque. So, the longer the distance, the more power it creates. It is also worth considering making the wheel wider to fully utilize the flow of water rather than making the buckets deeper.

■ **To harness the power** from the rotating shaft, you can use a direct belt drive, as used to drive machinery; a gear box to increase the shaft speed so it is possible to drive a generator; or a system of cogs and chains or pulleys and belts, which can achieve the same increases in shaft speed as a gear box.

Our waterwheel system

We use our waterwheel to provide the power for all the lights at Newhouse Farm. Our wheel is only 4m (13ft) in diameter and has very little flow, so the power it produces is limited to between about 40W under normal conditions and 250W when the stream is in speight.

The waterwheel system is fed by water from an aqueduct

Though small, the wheel follows a backshot design that makes it very efficient

The permanent magnet alternator (PMA) converts power from the gear box into AC electricity

Converting water energy to electricity requires the following items: a rectifier (**1**), ammeter (**2**), charge controller (**3**), dump load (**4**), and pure sine inverter (**5**).

A 44:1 gear box increases the waterwheel's shaft speed to about 350 rpm

The rectifier converts the AC to DC for storage in batteries

The charge controller prevents excess electricity damaging the batteries

Excess energy is sent to a dump load until the batteries need to be charged up again

The pure sine inverter takes the DC from the batteries and provides 240V AC for the lights in the house

Batteries store the energy, but if the are overloaded they will be damaged

Our wheel rotates *at only 8 rpm when under load. A gear box is required to increase shaft speed sufficiently to spin the magnets that generate AC electricity (see pages 56–57).*

Maximizing efficiency

It sounds a bit trite but the one fact you need to remember is that the angle of the bucket should be 114°. You might assume that such an exact figure has a long and complex mathematical derivation, but actually it has been arrived at empirically over hundreds of years, as engineers experimented with waterwheel design. Having unveiled the great secret of waterwheels it must be said that there are still many more decisions to make and the efficiency of your system will ultimately depend on optimizing the use of the water you have at your disposal. For example, the type of wheel you choose or indeed are able to install, depending on your site, can mean the difference between 90 or 20 per cent efficiency.

What to do with the power

We store our energy in batteries (see box opposite), so that we can use more than 40W for those periods when we need lights – mainly early morning and evening. If we are generating at 40W for the full 24-hour period, then we can use 160W for a 6-hour period, which is equivalent to about 16 low-energy bulbs – more than enough for our lighting needs at Newhouse Farm!

As you can see from the details about our waterwheel system, we don't produce a great deal of electricity. But if you have sufficient power, it may be worth thinking about linking your output power to the national grid. To achieve this you would need to include a grid-linked inverter in your system.

1. If you need to include an aqueduct, it must be as level as possible so you don't lose the energy stored in the water until it is being used to turn your wheel. **2. The waterwheel** is a remarkably simple design, but it isn't always as efficient as it could be (see box, right). **3. The gear box** is crucial for getting the permanent magnet alternator (PMA) spinning and efficiently generating electricity.

WHEEL TYPES

Your major decision is what sort of wheel to build or install. This depends on the available water flow and head, the possible route for the aqueduct, and the site for your wheel.

Wheel rotation

A backshot wheel is the most efficient and can convert nearly 90 per cent of the water energy into useful power.

Wheel rotation

Overshot wheels *can achieve up to about 70 per cent efficiency when converting water energy into power.*

Wheel rotation

Breastshot wheels *are useful when there's not much head but only achieve up to 50 per cent efficiency.*

Wheel rotation

Undershot wheels *are used when there's no head and are very inefficient (only up to 20 per cent). They're like paddles that are driven by the water flowing under the wheel.*

73

Using a hydraulic ram pump

A ram pump is an ingenious device that uses the water's own pressure to move it to where you need it most – and no electricity supply is needed. With a bit of plumbing know-how, you can put one together yourself. We've installed a ram pump in our stream to pump water uphill to a bulk container behind our polytunnel, where we use it to water the plants.

What is a ram pump?

A hydraulic ram, or ram pump, is a water pump – powered by water. When water is flowing down a pipe and is suddenly stopped, the energy in all that moving water is reduced to zero with a thump. This is sometimes called the "hammer" effect. A ram pump utilizes the effect to force a portion of the water that powers the pump upwards, to a point higher than the original water source.

The mechanics

A ram pump is cheap to build, easy to maintain, and very reliable. It has only two moving parts: a spring- or weight-loaded waste valve – or "clacker" valve – and a delivery check valve.

Water flowing into the waste valve eventually forces it to close. Then the hammer effect opens the delivery check valve. This pushes some water into the delivery pipe. Because this water is being forced uphill, the flow slows down. When the flow reverses, the delivery check valve closes and the whole cycle repeats itself.

A pressure vessel cushions the shock when the waste valve closes and improves efficiency.

You also need a delivery pipe to take water to your storage tank, and a drive pipe to bring water from the water source. The pump should run indefinitely unless air gets into the drive pipe or the valves get blocked.

HOW A RAM PUMP WORKS

To power the pump, the water source has to be running water that is higher than the pump. The higher the "head", the higher the water can be pumped – up to 10 times higher than the head. Site the pump so that it has a decent head of at least 2m (6ft 6in).

The flow rate of the source water also affects how much water can be pumped and how fast. A ram pump can be used to supply a household or an entire village with minimal maintenance.

Water storage tank must be higher than water source.

Delivery pipe

Drive pipe

Hydraulic ram

Source of running water

Head of water above ram pump

The length of the drive pipe affects how often the waste valve opens and closes – the stroke period.

Height water can be pumped

RAM PUMP COMPONENTS

◼ Water flows from the drive pipe, into the inlet (**1**) and out of the open waste valve (**2**). The delivery check valve (**3**) is closed.

◼ The water picks up speed and kinetic energy, and forces the waste valve to close.

◼ The "hammer" effect raises the pressure and forces open the delivery check valve.

◼ A pressure vessel (**4**) containing air, reduces hydraulic pressure shock when the waste valve closes, prolonging the life of the pump. The pump will work without it, but less efficiently, as the vessel also creates a more constant flow rate.

◼ Water flows through the tap (**5**) into the attached delivery pipe and is forced uphill.

A ram pump *works on an endless cycle of opening and closing valves, powered solely by the pressure of water.*

PROJECT **Make and install a ram pump**

Building a ram pump entails joining different widths of copper pipe. The simplest way is to use reducers and make compression joints. To carry the water to and from the pump we used polyethylene piping. The choice of materials and pipe sizes is flexible, depending on what size valves and joints you have.

YOU WILL NEED
- Copper piping
- 2 brass T-joints
- Brass one-way valve
- Brass, spring-loaded, one-way valve
- Delivery check valve
- Brass end cap
- Adjustable spanners
- Filter and mesh cage
- Pliers
- Tap
- Polyethylene piping

ASSEMBLING THE RAM PUMP

1. Make a compression joint. Slide the end nut over the end of the pipe. Slide the olive on to the end of the pipe. Push the pipe into the connector. Hand tighten the nut onto the connector. **2. Tighten compression joints** with two adjustable spanners, twisting connector and nut in opposite directions. **3. Use the same technique** to join the pressure vessel – a length of 28mm (1in) copper pipe sealed with the end cap. **4. Join** the delivery check valve in the same way.

ATTACHING THE PUMP TO THE WATER SUPPLY

5. Attach a filter to the drive pipe to stop debris clogging the system. Ensure it is submerged – we tie ours to a post under the water. **6. Fit** an additional coarse mesh basket to stop larger bits of debris sticking to the filter. **7. Run the drive pipe** from the water source to the pump. **8. Connect the drive pipe** to the pump. Water should flow freely through the waste valve. **9. Fix the ram pump upright**. We built a frame from spare timber and lashed the pump to it.

10. Unscrew the waste valve to adjust the spring. **11. Cut the spring down** using pliers if it won't close, or add a stronger spring if it won't open. **12. Connect** the delivery hose. **13. Push in** the "clacker" element of the valve with a finger, to charge the ram and start normal operation.

Conserving water

We take a plentiful supply of clean water for granted in the developed world, but in recent years droughts and a less-than-efficient capture and distribution infrastructure have led to hosepipe bans in some areas. Combined with rising water rates, this has made us aware that drinking water should be valued and used more sparingly. Here are some ideas for conserving this precious resource.

Using less water

Treating water so it's safe to drink when it comes out of the tap takes time and energy. Water is heavy, too, so moving it around is significant. To get an idea, fill an upstairs bath from an outside tap using buckets. Now imagine the "work" or energy needed to move water to your bathroom from the nearest water treatment station, which is miles away.

So before you even think about harnessing your own water supply or using rainwater, try to reduce wastage. Simple ways include:

Take showers not baths, but do not use power showers which can use nearly as much water as a bath.

Dual-flush toilets. Devices can be fitted to older loo handles so the cistern flushes only when the handle is held down. With this, you can use as much or as little water as you wish. Or why not pop a water saver into the cistern (see box below)?

Aerated taps and shower heads add air to the water to give the effect of using more water for less.

Dishwashers and washing machines should be run on **full load** and **economy** settings. An efficient machine may cost you more initially but it will save throughout its life, especially when water and electricity rates inevitably increase.

Reusing grey water

Waste water from all sources – other than the toilets – is known as grey water (sewage is sometimes referred to as black water). Many grey-water recycling systems collect and treat waste water from showers, baths, and wash basins rather than the more contaminated water from washing machines, kitchen sinks, and dishwashers. It can be reused where you do not need drinking-water quality – for flushing toilets and watering gardens, for example.

Before deciding to install a grey-water recycling system you should compare how much you are likely to generate (which depends on the number of baths and showers taken), with your demand for reclaimed water (which depends on the number of toilet flushes or volume required for the garden). Only then can you calculate the potential savings.

Treating grey water

You can't simply collect grey water in a tank for reuse. It doesn't take a lot of imagination to picture what happens if waste water containing dead skin, hair, etc., is left to stand for a period of time. Treatment of the water is essential, and can be based on either physical or biological filters, or a combination of both. You will also need somewhere for a storage tank of an appropriate size. The systems are expensive and they need energy to power them.

DIY LOO WATER SAVER

You can buy a ready-made water saver, but it's just as easy to make your own from a plastic bottle. Put it underneath the large cistern float. When the toilet is flushed, the water that is sitting in the saver isn't used in the flush, saving that much water.

To make a water saver cut the top off a 1 litre (1¾ pint) plastic bottle. Add pebbles to the base to weigh it down. Stand it upright in the toilet cistern.

Your own water source

If there is a spring, stream, or even an old well on your plot, you can be far less reliant on mains water.

Before you look at water treatment systems, decide what you will use the water for. If you plan to use it only to flush the toilets, you won't need to do much to it – simple filtration will remove debris. If you plan to drink it, you'll need a purification system.

Filtration

There are a number of ways to filter water, each with varying degrees of effectiveness, and different costs, but all with the same general purpose of improving the hygienic and aesthetic qualities of the water.

■ **Activated carbon filters** have been around for a long time and work by absorbing and removing unwanted compounds. They have a very large surface area of highly porous material that attracts and holds chemical pollutants. They are used primarily to improve taste and odour.

■ **Water distillation** involves heating the water to boiling point and then condensing the steam. An obvious drawback to this system is that it requires a large amount of energy. Generally, the distilled water is very high quality, but tastes flat as there

Compost loo

A typical compost loo has two chambers: while one is in use the other is composting the contents. When the second chamber is nearly full, you can use the compost from the first compartment. For composting to work properly, urine must be separated from solid waste. There are absolutely no bad odours and a clever fly trap takes care of pests.

Instead of flushing *sprinkle half a cup of sawdust down the loo and – very important – close the lid.*

Composting loo in action
Our compost loo at Newhouse Farm has been in use for about four years and the first compartment is not yet full (we made it slightly bigger than necessary – oops).

Air vent

The urine separator: men and women pee forward when seated so the urine hits the curved separator connected to the guttering and collection barrel.

Jam jar fly trap
(see right)

Bucket of sawdust
and mug on a string

Urine runs
down the
guttering

Removal
hatch

Poo
pyramid

Wall divides
chamber into
two halves

Urine collects in barrel
of straw, which ends up
on the compost heap

The fly trap lures flies towards the light. Once they've gone through the plastic funnel into the jam jar, they can't get back out. The trap won't work unless the loo seat is closed.

is less oxygen dissolved in it. You can make a solar still to distill water, using the sun as an energy source.

Sand-based water filters have been used for more than 100 years to treat waste water. They can be employed on a large scale to treat a water supply for a whole community, or they can be scaled down to suit an individual household (see pages 80–81). Most require a constant flow of water to work correctly.

Reverse osmosis filters force water under pressure through a semi-permeable membrane. They allow water through but filter particles such as bacteria, toxins, and salts.

Ultraviolet (UV) filters kill the majority of bacteria and viruses in the water that passes through them. However, they won't remove chemical pollutants. For a UV filter to work

effectively, the water must be filtered first to remove any solid particles, so there is nothing for bacteria and viruses to hide behind and avoid being zapped.

In a typical system, UV radiation from a lamp passes through a special quartz-glass sleeve and into the untreated water, which flows in a thin film over the lamp. The glass sleeve keeps the lamp at an ideal working temperature of 40°C (104°F).

UV treatment does not remove organisms from the water, it merely inactivates them. The intensity of the lamp decreases over time, and it needs to be replaced regularly. UV treatment is an effective technique, but the disinfection only occurs inside the filter unit, which means that any bacteria introduced afterwards can be an issue.

Water from wells and springs

One of the reasons we moved to Newhouse Farm was that it had a spring. We realize not everyone is fortunate enough to have such an accessible water source, but you may be able to find water by drilling down to the water table, or if you have an older property, you may have an old well that has been capped.

We have our spring water tested regularly by our local council's environmental health department, just in case it becomes contaminated somewhere down the line. We use it for everything except for the cold water tap in the kitchen, which is mains water, and we also have a mains water backup system.

Harvesting rainwater

In the UK there is no real shortage of water; in fact, the rain tends to be a regular topic of conversation. We measured the surface area of the roof on our house, researched the average rainfall, and calculated that about 207,000 litres (45,534 gallons) of water fall on our roof every year – never mind the outbuildings! When we realized that even our little shed received more than 4,000 litres (880 gallons), the logic was obvious. Even if you don't want to invest in a whole system (see box opposite), at least install a couple of water butts.

Unfortunately, rain doesn't fall regularly throughout the year. If you want to use rainwater you will have to store it. A big underground tank is expensive, but fitting a system that isn't big enough to meet your needs is a false economy and means you will end up using mains water as a back-up more often.

On average we use 153 litres (34 gallons) of water per person per day in the UK (in the US it is about 489 litres or 108 gallons), which is shocking when you consider we only drink about 2 litres (3½ pints) each.

1. **Pump water** directly from a stream for a domestic water supply if you don't have a well or spring. **2. Battery-powered pump** draws water from the stream to irrigate the greenhouse. **3. Water butts** are the simplest way to collect rainwater from sheds and greenhouse roofs for use on your plot.

Rainwater harvesting system

Before designing a system, decide how much water you need to store. Check your water meter to see how much you use in a day and calculate what size tank to install.

Filtering rainwater

A vortex rainwater fine filter installed in the underground piping removes debris and diverts 90 per cent of clean water to the storage tank. It consists of a stainless-steel, fine-mesh filter in a polypropylene housing and needs cleaning regularly.

Rainwater is best used *for supplying household appliances rather than for drinking water. It would need more complex filtration and purification systems to make it safe to drink.*

Guttering collects rainwater from roof

Stored water is used to flush loos, and for the washing machine and showers

Underground tank to store rainwater

Rainwater passes through vortex filter before being stored

Outside tap

Automatic switch to mains back-up in case tank runs dry

Mains water in

Overflow and trap

Pump moves water to house

Waste water drains away to sewers or reed bed

Rainwater enters the vortex filter and debris is filtered out (**1**). Clean water (**2**) goes into the tank and dirty water (**3**) flows into the drain.

PUMPING FROM WELLS AND SPRINGS

In a shallow well or spring, you can use a pump that floats on the water surface. But if you don't know the level of the water or don't have easy access to it – for example, in a bore hole or a deep well – use a submersible pump.

Water pumped to storage tank in house

Water pumped to storage tank in house

Wind turbine and solar panel charge the battery that powers the pump

Door shuts out sunlight and prevents ecosystem forming in the water and contaminating it

Brick lining

Polyethylene piping

Polyethylene piping

In a shallow well a demand pump on a floating platform moves up and down with the water table

Sink a submersible pump below the water level in a deep well or bore hole

Built-up front ledge to keep level up and prevent flow back

Inlet pipe just below water level of well

12V demand pump

100m (109yd) to house

Two options *for pumping from a well, depending on depth of water. Pumps use DC and can be run from a wind turbine or solar panel.*

The spring water supply system *at Newhouse Farm pumps water to a holding tank in the loft, using a 12V demand pump. A pump starts when the water level drops below a certain depth in the tank and the ballcock opens.*

Using sand filters and reed beds

If you are lucky enough to own land that has a spring you can use for drinking water, you will need to filter and then purify it first with a sand filter. How about building your own sand filter? Then you will need to deal with the waste water and sewage your household produces. This is where reed beds come in – they're environmentally friendly, as well as being truly functional.

Using a sand filter

Sand filters require no energy or chemicals to filter water, and need very little maintenance. They filter out small particles, and remove more than 90 per cent of bacteria, making them an excellent primary filter. It's a good idea to use an ultraviolet filter afterwards (see page 78). Sand filters are generally used in tandem with a water storage tank, which produces a constant flow of water.

Before setting up a sand filter and drinking water from a well or spring, ask your local environmental health department to test the water to see if it will be suitable. If their analysis shows traces of metal and chemical pollutants, you may want to use a reverse osmosis filter too.

If you intend to use more than 20,000 litres (4,440 gallons) a year, contact the Environment Agency for details of abstraction fees.

Using a reed bed

A vertical-flow reed bed is a sealed, gravel-filled trench with reeds growing in it (see box opposite). The common reed (*Phragmites australis*) oxygenates the water, which helps to create the right environment for colonies of bacteria to break down unwanted organic matter and pollutants. The reeds also make the bed attractive to wildlife.

Before you build a reed bed, you need to notify the Environment Agency and your local planning department. Then install a settlement chamber to separate the solids from the liquid effluent. An existing septic tank is fine, or you can a make a new, similar, chamber. You will also need to deal with the solid sludge that separates out, just as you do with a septic tank.

The downside to reed beds is that they use up lots of land space and they do take quite a long time to produce clean water.

Final treatment stage

If you are intending to drink the water or give it to your livestock, or if it is issuing into a stream, we recommend a two-stage water treatment system: a vertical flow bed (see box opposite) for the initial treatment, and then a horizontal flow bed for the final stage of treatment.

The horizontal-flow bed is a lined shallow bed that produces an oxygen-depleted environment to enable bacteria in the reeds' root zone to break down nitrates. The water runs through the bed from one end like a stream and you can plant it with bog plants such as yellow flag (*Iris pseudacorus*) and marsh marigold (*Caltha palustris*). The purified water is clean enough to run into a fish pond or soakaway.

1. Reed-bed filters are based on wetland ecosystems that naturally purify water flowing through them. They can be used as a finishing treatment in sewage plants or on a domestic scale if you have space. **2. The common reed** (*Phragmites australis*) grows to about 2m (6ft 6in) high. In wetlands, it forms an important habitat for insects and birds. Buy your plants from specialist suppliers or grow from seed, but don't take them from the wild.

How a sand filter works

Raw, untreated water, known as the "supernatant", passes through the filter from the top to the bottom of the tank, under pressure from the water above the sand. This process takes up to two hours, and, generally, the smaller the grains of sand, the more effective the filter.

Filtering the water
Algae grow on top of the sand and form a sticky net that strains out large particles. Small bits of unwanted organic matter form a green slimy layer in the top 2cm (¾in) of sand, which is eaten by protozoans and bacteria.

Cleaning the filter
Drain and clean the filter every 3 months. Take off the top 2cm (¾in) of sand; rinse it clean and return it to the filter.

Internal sides of the tank should be rough, so the water cannot run quickly down the sides and has to pass through the sand.

Inlet pipe from spring

Chicken wire to keep out leaves and debris

Tank built of concrete slabs, or polyethylene tank, no smaller than 1sq m (1sq yd)

Light-proof and fly-proof lid

Top layer of water should be no less than 30cm (1ft)

80cm (32in) of fine, non-silt sand

Settlement storage tank

Synthetic membrane with tight weave or old nylon curtain

10cm (4in) of washed pea gravel

Water exits filter tank

Overflow with flyscreen

Outlet pipe

How a vertical-flow reed bed works

Vertical-flow beds work by gravity and need a fall of more than 2m (6ft 6in). Their effluent flows onto the surface of the bed and percolates slowly through the layers into an outlet pipe, which leads to a horizontal-flow bed. There is no standing water, so there should be no unpleasant smells.

Digesting the waste
Waste water flows through layers of sand, reed roots, gravel and stones, and is cleaned by millions of bacteria, algae, fungi and microorganisms that digest the waste, including sewage.

Getting the size right
Design your reed bed to allow 1 sq m (1 sq yd) per person in the household, and allow for about 100 litres (22 gallons) flow per person per day.

Plant four reeds per sq m (sq yd) in late April and May. They can take up to two years to fully mature.

Waste water inlet pipe

Impermeable plastic or clay layer to contain the bed. You can even use a series of old bathtubs.

5cm (2in) layer of stones, 20mm (¾in) in diameter

70cm (2ft 4in) layer of stones, 5cm (2in) in diameter

10cm (4in) layer of washed sand

15cm (6in) layer of pea gravel

Paving slab holds pipe in place

Filtered water runs into a horizontal flow bed

Using biofuels

The simplest definition of biofuels is any fuel that is obtained from a renewable biological resource. This distinguishes them from fossil fuels, which where laid down millions of years ago and are considered non-renewable. Some examples of biofuels are wood (in its many forms), elephant grass, ethanol, methanol, biodiesel, and even animal waste.

Wood

As a fuel source, wood is sometimes described as "biomass", which means vegetable mass that is used as a source of energy. Biomass is sub-divided into woody biomass and non-woody biomass, which includes materials like animal waste, high-energy crops (sugar cane, rape, and maize), and some biodegradable by-products from food processing.

The most common type for domestic use is woody biomass, which can fuel a range of appliances, from open fires to ultra-modern pellet-burning boilers and room heaters. By far the best wood is free wood, though it usually takes considerable effort to cut it to size and season it. However, even if you buy your timber for fuel, it is usually significantly cheaper than oil or gas, and, if it is sourced locally, there's the additional environmental benefit in lower transport miles, emissions, and pollution.

Apart from the sun's rays, open fires are probably the oldest form of heating known to man. Everyone knows that an open fire forms a mesmerizing focal point, but it is extremely inefficient, with only about one fifth of the heat generated from the fire being radiated into the room, while the remainder goes to waste up the chimney.

Wood burners

Unlike fires, modern wood burners can be about 80 per cent efficient, which means the vast majority of the available heat warms the room. In real terms, putting three logs on a woodburner for the evening will provide you with a similar amount of heat as putting 12 logs on an open fire. As if that isn't enough reason to invest in a woodburner.

A well-designed burner is very efficient, pre-heating the air that is drawn in prior to combustion so that the flow of gases will ensure that as complete combustion as possible takes place. The high temperature and complete burning that takes

CHOPPING WOOD

You can use either an axe or a hydraulic log splitter to split rounds, but in our minds, there is no competition. Our hydraulic log splitter has been a great buy as it makes short work of splitting logs and is much safer than wielding an axe. Before investing in a hydraulic log splitter, you need to think about a few factors, such as:

■ **Power/size** – ours has a seven-ton push, which is enough for us.

■ **Vertical or horizontal design** – our log splitter operates horizontally, which suits us perfectly as we will never split logs too big to lift onto it.

■ **Safety first** – you must wear goggles at all times.

When chopping kindling it's useful to have a large block of wood set at a convenient height, a sharp axe, and a sharpening stone to hand. A couple of productive hours of chopping will supply a few months' worth of kindling. We also save all our little off-cuts of wood for kindling in a dry area of the pole barn.

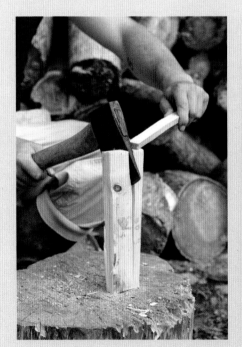

Never hold the wood you intend to chop; instead, hold it steady using another offcut while you cut into it with an axe.

A hydraulic log splitter is relatively expensive, but in the long run it will save you money, time – and your back.

ECOFANS

We use a clever device called an ecofan to circulate the warm air around our woodburner. It uses the Seebeck Effect: when two dissimilar semiconductors (p-type and n-type) at the same temperature are connected together they establish a static electric potential difference. When the bottom of the fan sits on the hot wood burner and the fins at the top are cooler, electrons flow (a current). This current powers the fan's motor, with no batteries or cables attached!

1. If you have felled trees on your plot, split them and then leave them to season for a couple of years before burning. **2. Elephant grass** looks like a crop of maize and yields 10–18 tons of biomass per hectare. **3. An ecofan** on a log burner circulates the warm air.

place in one means less residue collects in your chimney so it needs sweeping less frequently.

Commercial woodburners are usually made from cast iron or steel, but ceramic fires are also available. If you want to make one yourself, there are patterns on the internet that show how to make a woodburner or sawdust burner out of old gas cylinders.

If you are to use wood as a fuel, it needs to be well seasoned (ideally left for a minimum of two years after cutting in a dry, ventilated store) and it must be free of preservatives, paint, or galvanized nails, as these can all emit harmful gases when burned.

At Newhouse Farm all our heating is provided by four woodburners. The heat is then transferred round the house using a Heat Recovery Ventilation system (see pages 42–45), and we only have to empty our ash about once a week.

It's also possible to fuel your central heating with wood by installing a back-boiler attached to certain higher output woodburners, or by installing one of the new technology wood pellet- or chip-burning boilers. If using a log-fired woodburner with a back boiler, take into account that the burner will not heat the room it is in to the same degree as it would normally because the heat is being diverted around the pipes and radiators instead. Also be prepared to feed your burner large quantities of wood to make it function properly.

Wood-pellet boilers

There has been a recent increase in the popularity of domestic and small, industrial wood-pellet boilers. The wood pellets are generally the by-products of sawmills, though an increase in demand has led to new plants that produce the pellets commercially. Despite the fact that this processing takes energy, pellets are nearly carbon neutral and much less detrimental to the environment than a fossil fuel-powered system.

Modern domestic boiler systems can achieve efficiencies of nearly 90 per cent because they are computer controlled to achieve the best results. For wood pellets to compete with fossil fuels in terms of convenience, automatic methods of delivering pellets to the burner have been developed. This greatly increases the time between refills.

Wood chip boilers

Woodchip boilers can be as flexible as wood pellet boilers. Indeed, it is probably easier to source chips locally than pellets, but therein lies some of the issue; fuel quality may vary, depending upon your source.

Elephant grass

Growing elephant grass (*Miscanthus*) for fuel is relatively new in the UK. These crops are essentially biological solar panels and batteries as they capture sunlight and store it in a form that can be readily harvested and used as fuel. Companies will plant the grass for you with specialist equipment on non-prime agricultural land and after a year of fairly careful weed control and a bit of fertilizer, the grass should be established. In a couple of years, it grows up to 3m (10ft) tall annually. Sell your crop to power stations, or commercial Combined Heat and Power (CHP) systems are available.

Biodiesel

Biodiesel is the biofuel equivalent to conventional fossil diesel and it can be made from vegetable oils or, less frequently, animal fats. Biodiesel is not raw vegetable oil, but an ester created by reacting vegetable oil with an alcohol. The scientific name for this is "transesterification" – the reaction of a triglyceride (fat/oil) with an alcohol to form esters and glycerol. At Newhouse Farm we use waste vegetable oil (WVO), which is vegetable oil that has been used for cooking, to make our biodiesel.

Pros and cons

There are many benefits to using biodiesel instead of conventional diesel as a fuel.

■ **Biodiesel is nearly carbon neutral**. Although energy is required to make it, when the vegetable crop was growing it was absorbing CO_2, and when the fuel is combusted roughly the same amount of CO_2 is released.

■ **As biodegradable as sugar**, biodiesel is less toxic than table salt.

■ **Biodiesel reduces emissions** of tailpipe particulate matter, hydrocarbon, and carbon monoxide from most modern, four-stroke compression ignition engines.

■ **Biodiesel has a very low concentration of sulphur.** Sulphur in other fuels can lead to sulphur dioxide being produced and as a result, acid rain. The amount in biodiesel is significantly lower than in traditional diesel and is comparable to ultra low sulphur diesel (ULSD).

All this makes it sound like the new "wonder fuel", but there are a few disadvantages to using biodiesel:

■ **Biodiesel starts to coagulate** at a higher temperature than fossil diesel, which can be a problem if the fuel is used in cold climates.

■ **On some older diesel engines** it has been known to dissolve the rubber seals within the fuel system and engine – a bad thing.

■ **Biodiesel is a great source of food** for microbes – add some water and they will have all they need to multiply and become a problem, resulting in blocked filters.

The all-important reactor

If you're serious about making your own biodiesel, you will need to build yourself a reactor. This is less scary and complicated than it sounds, but it does require a certain amount of engineering know-how and isn't something we can comprehensively cover in this book. What you don't need is a whole lot of specialist equipment; we built ours from a recycled water tank housed in a galvanized metal frame. The maze of pipework beneath is explained overleaf on page 86.

Starting the process

Before you begin making biodiesel, it is essential that you first clean and dry your WVO (see box opposite). Then you can move on to the science. Biodiesel is produced from the reaction of triglycerides (vegetable

1. Our reactor is made from an old copper water tank topped with a metal dustbin lid. **2. Biodiesel and glycerol** are mixed together when first reacted. They are then left to stand so they separate. **3. The heavy glycerol** is very dark compared with the brighter biodiesel. The difference in colour makes it easy to see when all the glycerol has been drained off.

oil) with methanol. Unfortunately, if you just mix the two together, nothing will happen, so you need a catalyst. In this case, an alkali is needed and those most commonly used are sodium or potassium hydroxide.

To aid the delivery of the solid catalyst into the biodiesel reaction, it is first dissolved in the methanol. The amount of methanol needed is about 20 per cent of the volume of oil used. For example, if you were using 50 litres of oil, then you would need 10 litres of methanol.

There is a standard amount of catalyst needed for the biodiesel reaction – many people agree that it is 3g per litre of oil, although some use 5g without any problems. If WVO is being used, then a titration (chemical analysis) must be carried out to determine the amount of extra catalyst required to neutralize the acidity of the oil. The acidity is caused by cooking in it, which produces free fatty acids (FFAs).

If there are FFAs present, they will react with the catalyst before the biodiesel reaction is complete, which results in a very poor yield of biodiesel and it will be contaminated with unreacted oil. Therefore, you need to add extra catalyst, so that after reacting with the FFAs there is still enough left to make biodiesel.

Carry out a titration

A titration must be carried out on WVO to test for the amount of FFAs present. A titration does not take a lot of time, but it can look a little complicated on paper. The basic idea is to react a small sample of the WVO (which will be acidic as it contains FFAs) with a measured amount of sodium hydroxide (which is a base). When the acid is neutralized, you can assume that all the FFAs have been used up.

Titrations are carried out on a very small scale using accurately

SOURCING, CLEANING, AND DRYING WVOS

Local restaurants, school and work canteens, and catering companies are your best bet for sourcing waste vegetable oils, or WVOs. People are usually happy to give you the oil, as it saves them time and money disposing of it, but some do demand a small charge as more of us cotton on to biodiesel.

■ **Any bits of food** must be filtered out and water removed by heating the oil. It is very important that all of the ingredients used in the production of biodiesel are as water-free as possible or you will end up with soap. if you are using new vegetable oil, it is already dry.

■ **Pour the WVO through some muslin** into a storage barrel to filter out any large pieces of food in the oil.

■ **Allow the oil to settle** so that smaller pieces of food sink to the bottom of the barrel.

■ **Draw off the oil** from a tap set about a third of the way up the barrel to remove the cleaner oil above the food contaminants.

■ **Dry the oil in your reactor**. It is of paramount importance that the oil contains no water. Heat the oil to about 60°C (140°F), then pump it around the system so there's an opportunity for the water molecules to escape. This drying process takes up to 4 hours.

measured amounts of chemicals. Steps 1 to 6 on page 87 explain how to prepare and carry out a titration. We know that all the FFAs have been used up when the pH rises to about 8.5, which is also the point at which phenolphthalein indicator solution changes from colourless to purple. This is also the point when you stop adding drops of sodium hydroxide.

It is essential that you note how many drops you have used. Each drop from the pipette contains 0.0455 ml or, to put it another way, there are 22 drops in 1ml. Repeat steps 5 and 6 on page 87 three times and take an average of the result. If one result is totally different to the others, you have probably made a mistake so ignore it and do another one. And that's it. You can then scale up these numbers to work out how

many extra grams of catalyst are required per litre of WVO.

For example, say the titrating solution required 2.5ml to use up the FFAs, then an extra 2.5g of catalyst should be used for each litre of WVO. In the example on page 87, we used 1ml of WVO (which is 1/1,000 of a litre) and a solution that contained 1/1,000g of sodium hydroxide per litre. Therefore if 2.5ml of solution is needed for 1ml of oil, then 2,500ml would be needed for 1 litre of oil and 2,500ml of solution would contain 2.5g of sodium hydroxide. Phew!

Once you know the correct amount of sodium hydroxide to add to the methanol for an efficient biodiesel reaction, mix carefully, shaking all the time, and pour into a large plastic container. Then attach to the reactor with a hose, checking for leaks.

Use a reactor to effect a separation

Heat the oil to about 50°C (122°F) and then add the methanol/catalyst solution. Place the lid on the tank so that any methanol that evaporates from the reactor will condense on it and drip back into the tank. After the whole lot has mixed for about an hour, turn off the reactor and leave its contents to settle (see box below).

Once the reaction is complete, you are left with a mixture of biodiesel and glycerol. Luckily, the glycerol is heavier than biodiesel and will therefore separate out naturally and sink to the bottom. When the glycerol has settled, drain it off.

Wash the biodiesel

The biodiesel at this stage is by no means ready to use. It will still contain some methanol, sodium hydroxide, soap, and glycerol. These impurities could easily damage parts of a diesel engine and must be removed. Luckily they are all soluble in water, so they can be "washed" out, which we do with a process called "bubble washing" using a fish tank aerator.

Add water to the reaction vessel (we use a hose attached to a funnel so the water goes straight to the bottom) in a ratio of about 1 part water to every 2 parts biodiesel.

Lower the fish tank aerator into the bottom of the tank and switch it on to the lowest setting that creates bubbles. Each bubble carries a small amount of water through the biodiesel and when it bursts at the surface, the water drop sinks back through the biodiesel and dissolves the impurities. Allow the biodiesel to wash for 2–4 hours. Turn off the air pump and leave to settle for a further hour. Then drain off the water (use the hose to watch for the colour change again). Each wash takes two hours and then the water is drained off. It should take four or five washes until the water comes out clear.

Once the biodiesel has been washed it will be slightly cloudy because it has been saturated in water. Dry it as you did the original WVO (see box on page 85) and avoid breathing in the fumes.

The final product

The biodiesel should now be ready to use. It should be a clear, amber-coloured, pH-neutral nectar. Although it is possible to get about a 98 per cent yield, realistically you can expect 80 per cent plus.

USING THE REACTOR

Our reactor comprises a water tank, immersion heater, and a set of pipes and valves. Be very careful to prevent methanol fumes escaping at the top of the tank. It's best to try to seal the lid and vent the tank to the outside. When making biodiesel, you use a reactor as follows:

■ **Slowly open** valve 4 and the methanol/catalyst is sucked in and mixed with the oil.
■ **When** the methanol/catalyst tank is empty, close valve 4.
■ **Let reaction mix** for 1 hour. Turn off pump and close valve 1.
■ **Some of the mixture will remain** in the pump and pipe. Use valve 2 to drain this off and tip it into the top of the tank (you may want to put a bit into a glass jar so you can watch it).
■ **Close all valves** and leave the whole lot to separate for about 6 hours.
■ **Drain the glycerol** once it has separated out by opening valves 1 and 2. Attach a piece of clear hose below valve 2 and watch for the colour change between the glycerol and biodiesel, which shows that the glycerol has drained off.

NB: Oil must always cover the immersion heater element when it is switched on.

If an emulsion forms when washing
■ **Stop the washing** and drain the water, leaving the emulsion/biodiesel in the tank.
■ **Close valve 2** and open valves 1, 3, and 5.
■ **Switch on** the immersion heater and pump and leave to heat up to 50°C (122°F).
■ **Turn off** the heater and pump and close the valves (drain off the pipes and put the mixture back into the tank).
■ **As the mixture cools**, the emulsion should break and the water will separate out. Adding a little vinegar to the first wash may help prevent emulsions from forming.

Old copper water tank

Clear hose to show oil level in tank

Feed from tank for methanol catalyst

Oil can be pumped through this valve to another tank

Central heating pump

22mm (⅞in) pipe

Immersion heater element

PROJECT Make biodiesel

Observe all safety procedures when handling these chemicals. Always wear suitable gloves and goggles and read the labels. Wash all equipment and rinse with deionized water before use. Read through the instructions before you start and make sure that you understand them and have everything ready.

YOU WILL NEED
- Sodium hydroxide (anhydrous)
- Propan-2-ol (isopropyl alcohol)
- Phenolphthalein indicator solution
- Deionized or distilled water
- 2ml graduated syringe
- Graduated pipettes
- Beakers, conical flask
- Gloves
- Scales (accurate to 0.1g)

1. Mix the sodium hydroxide solution by measuring out 1 litre of distilled water and dissolving 10g of sodium hydroxide into it. Measure out 100ml of the solution and add 900ml of distilled water. Stir and pour this solution into an airtight bottle and label it. **2. Measure** 10ml of propan-2-ol and add it to a conical flask. **3. Using a syringe,** measure 1ml of the waste vegetable oil. **4. Put it into the conical flask.** Swirl the contents vigorously until the oil dissolves, and then add a couple of drops of the phenolphthalein solution and mix. You must be accurate with your measuring and keep records.

5. To carry out the titration, use a separate pipette to suck up 3ml of the sodium hydroxide solution and add it to the conical flask drop by drop while swirling continuously. Each drop will cause the liquid to turn pink temporarily, and then it returns to pale yellow. **6. When it turns pink** and stays pink for 20–30 seconds, stop adding drops. Repeat steps 2 to 6 three times and do the calculations described under "Carry out a titration" on page 85, so you know how much extra sodium hydroxide is needed. **7. Measure the sodium hydroxide catalyst** and mix it up carefully with the methanol in a large container.

8. Attach the catalyst container to the reactor with a clear hose. Heat the WVO in the reactor to 50°C (122°F) and add the catalyst/methanol mixture. Turn the immersion heater off, but keep the pump running. Follow the process for opening and closing valves described on page 86. **9. As the catalyst mixes** with the oil and the reaction takes place, the oil turns from clear to cloudy. **10. Wait for the glycerol to separate out**. **11. Wash the biodiesel (see page 86)** and repeat the washing until the water comes out clear. Then dry the biodiesel again as described in the box on page 85.

Using an anaerobic digester

An anaerobic digester can take any type of organic matter, from food waste to manure and sewage, and convert it into a soil fertilizer and biogas, which can be used as an alternative energy source. It's ideal for farms and municipal waste-processing plants, and can be used on a smallholding if you produce enough waste to run the digester.

What is anaerobic digestion?

Anaerobic digestion is the process whereby bacteria that occur naturally break down organic waste material in an oxygen-free environment. These anaerobic bacteria are part of nature's waste management and are found in soils and deep waters, as well as in landfill sites. Anaerobic digestion converts organic waste into a residue, which can then be used as a fertilizer, and a biogas that can be used as a renewable energy source.

Producing biogas

In the UK we throw away about a third of the food we buy. If we add to that the waste from commercial catering and food processing, as well as farm manure and crop waste, it creates an awful lot of material that could be turned into biogas. This organic waste often ends up in landfill sites where it generates harmful methane as it decomposes – methane is 24 times more damaging than carbon dioxide as a greenhouse gas.

You can recycle your waste in a system known as a digester. This creates a controllable supply of biogas, which is a mixture of 40 per cent carbon dioxide and 60 per cent methane, plus other trace elements, and can be harnessed as a renewable energy source. Although anaerobic digestion also releases carbon dioxide, the carbon was absorbed by plants previously and so forms part of a complete carbon cycle. The released gas does not contribute to global warming in the same way as carbon released from fossil fuels, which has been trapped under the ground for millions of years.

Types of digester

There are commercial anaerobic digesters, designed for farms, which have the capacity to produce 100kW to 1MW of electricity. For a smaller plot, we've created a DIY digester (see box opposite). You can also use an anaerobic lagoon (see box below) to produce biogas in a large balloon.

1. The contents of a compost bin heat up, and naturally occurring anaerobic bacteria break down the organic material. **2. The residue** or digestate from anaerobic digestion goes back onto the land to improve soil fertility.

ANAEROBIC LAGOON

Like the digester, this anaerobic lagoon creates biogas from your waste organic material; you can buy the materials to make one from specialist suppliers. You add organic matter to a large closed balloon with no air in it – biogas plus air is an explosive combination. When anaerobic digestion takes place, the biogas balloon inflates. Heat enhances and speeds up the reaction.

Black material absorbs solar energy, warming the lagoon and speeding up the process

Digester cover

Waste inlet

Biogas outlet

Fertilizer outlet

Bubbles of biogas

Size matters
The volume of the lagoon must be right for the amount of waste you are adding. Ask a specialist to advise you.

DIY digester

We used an old muck spreader as the anaerobic digester in a system that we designed for a farmer friend. He uses it to manage the waste produced on his farm: the biogas is used to power an oil press to make biodiesel, while the fertilizer goes back onto the fields.

You can use biogas to power a generator to produce electricity, or go for a combination of heat and power and run a generator and feed heat back to speed up the digesting process. Collecting solar energy from black radiators is another way of generating the heat needed. Alternatively, simply burn the biogas for heat or use it instead of petrol to power machinery. In India and China, it is very common to build domestic digesters to power gas rings for cooking.

The digestate *is an excellent fertilizer and can be applied with a muck spreader.*

Waste goes in here

The tank is painted black so it absorbs heat, which helps the process to get started

Pipe carries gas to gasometer

Floating gas storage tank rises as gas is produced

Gas is piped to generator or burner via flash arrestor

Fertilizer outlet

Paddle pipe to stir mixture

The organic waste is broken down into sugars and amino acids before finally being turned into biogas

Storage tank filled with water to exclude air for safety

Flash arrestor (see box below)

Pump to circulate water round the system

Hot water circulates via thermal siphoning – or use a little pump

We heat the digester using black-painted radiators as solar collectors

FLASH ARRESTOR

When biogas is being burned, a flash arrestor prevents the flames and air travelling back along the pipeline and into the gasometer. Any explosion is confined to the top of the arrestor.

Burstable membrane protects bubbler

Fill cap

Biogas inlet at base

Biogas flows out to burner

Biogas bubbles up through the water

Cut a hole *in the top of the cap and place a burstable membrane to limit damage.*

Stirring up a reaction
The process can slow down if waste is allowed to separate into layers. It can take up to a month to produce biogas. Stirring the mixture speeds things up. The gas is explosive when in contact with air, so sinking the paddle pipe below the level of the liquid in the digester ensures that no air is introduced.

Reusing and recycling

We are committed to recycling at Newhouse Farm and have got sorting waste down to a fine art. But before we send anything off to be recycled – from old cabling and cardboard boxes to plastic bottles – we try to go one step further and find an alternative use for it around the house or in the garden. After all, one person's waste is another person's treasure.

The waste problem

Waste has evolved as a result of rapid economic development, but its disposal is not an entirely new problem. Court records show that in Stratford-upon-Avon in the mid-16th century, Shakespeare's dad was fined for "depositing filth in a public street". Later, mass industrialization led to an increase in waste, and in the 1800s dustmen were introduced to collect ash from coal fires.

To reduce our waste, we limit the amount we bring into our home in the first place by cutting down on packaging and disposable items, and only buying what we really need. We also aim to lengthen the life of items and reuse good materials to prevent them ended up in landfill.

When we look at a piece of rubbish, we see its whole lifecycle. First, there is the cost and embodied energy it has taken to manufacture the object. Then there's its useful lifespan. If it has been designed for only one use, this is followed by the serious question of, what next? We then look for ways to use it so it doesn't go in the bin.

Reusing different materials

Reusing is a creative, money-saving, and environmentally-friendly activity. We reuse all sorts of different materials around Newhouse Farm – it's not only a lot of fun but also an incredibly satisfying process.

Household and office rubbish

■ **Paper** can be recycled, but we first use scraps for writing notes, or stick a piece of paper over a used envelope as a label. You can even buy a gadget that turns paper into a "brick" for burning.

■ **Ink cartridges** in printers are easily refilled.

■ **Rechargeable batteries** can be reused again and again, and save toxic chemicals going into landfill.

■ **Glass jars** are excellent for storing your own jams, preserves, dried food, seeds, and chutneys. Clean them thoroughly and keep the right lid next to the right jar.

Building materials

■ **Reusing old timber** is hard work. De-nailing, sanding, and planing it can take time and effort, but the satisfaction of turning what could be termed rubbish into furniture, or using it as a building material, makes the effort worthwhile. Plus, old timber is much cheaper than new wood and you can use the off-cuts as kindling in a wood burner. Beware of creosote coatings on reclaimed timber and avoid painted wood, as it takes much more work to prepare it. Wooden pallets can be dismantled and turned into anything from a shed to a compost bin (see page 106).

1. Reclaimed beams from an old building made a strong frame for our raised bed (see page 126). **2. Rocks** grubbed up by our pigs were used to build a herb spiral (see page 159). **3. An oil drum** is easily turned into a cold smoker (see pages 250–251).

Reuse materials around the home

Some plastic bags can't be recycled, so rather than throwing them away, we stuff cushions with them. We also enjoy making our own scented candles from those irritating leftover candle ends. You'll need a packet of wicks from a candle-making supplier.

YOU WILL NEED
FOR THE CUSHIONS:
- Plastic bags
- Scissors
- Cushion cover

FOR THE CANDLES:
- Old candle ends
- Bain marie
- Silicone or paper muffin moulds
- Candle wicks

STUFFING A CUSHION

1. Cut plastic into long thin strips. You can mix different types of plastic bags and packaging, but make sure you clean them before you start.   **2. Stuff the strips** into a cushion cover. Pack it full as they will flatten down with use.   **3. The finished cushion** with eco-friendly stuffing. Shredded plastic makes great stuffing for pet beds too.

HOME-MADE CANDLES

1. Break up used candles. Keep colours separate to avoid murky coloured new candles.   **2. Heat the wax** in a bain marie. Fish out any old wicks as the wax melts. Take off heat and stir in a few drops of essential oil. Put a wick in a mould – we used muffin cases – and pour in a little wax. Leave it to set, to hold the wick fast; put it in the fridge to speed things up. Then add more wax in different coloured layers. Leave to set between layers.   **3. Remove the moulds** when the wax cools.

■ **Copper and plumbing parts** are valuable commodities. We have used them for all sorts of projects, from building a ram pump (see pages 74–75) to constructing a solar shower (see pages 62–63). If you don't reuse your copper, make sure you get a good price for it at a scrapyard.

■ **Old cables and electrical components** are slightly harder to reuse if you are not an experienced electrician, but replacing and wiring a plug is relatively simple. It's also worth stripping out the lengths of copper inside cables and using it to suspend slug-proof hanging baskets (see pages 20–21).

■ **Ferrous or scrap iron** is another great material for reusing in all sorts of projects. We keep a small metal store so that if we need to fix a wheelbarrow or build a spit roast then there is always metal available for us to weld together.

In the garden

■ **Glass** that's still in a window frame is great for building cloches or making cold frames in the garden (see pages 116–117). Once glass breaks it's harder to reuse, but we have made a heat sink in the greenhouse from broken glass, maximizing its thermal properties (see pages 118–19). Handle glass with care.

■ **Old guttering** makes a perfect tray for sowing pea seeds (see page 142).

Plastic bottles can be transformed into mini cloches (see box below), or, if you've got lots of them, make an ingenious recycled downpipe to feed a water butt. Sort the bottles into similar sizes and cut off the bottoms. Link them together with some wire, so that one fits inside another, and hang them upside down. Attach them to your shed gutter and place a butt underneath.

Egg cartons can be composted, but first we use ours for growing seedlings (see page 134).

Rubber tyres can be reused as towers for growing potatoes. Fill the base tyre with compost and add chitted potatoes. When shoots appear, stack another tyre on top and fill with more compost. Add two or three more tyres for the perfect pot.

Recycling explained

We will only consider recycling an item after we've first reused it around the house and garden, because the energy taken to recycle materials is still significant.

We were fortunate enough to follow our recycling bags to the local processing centre, which proved a real eye-opener. Once the lorry arrived on site, our bags were part of an extremely well-choreographed sorting operation. They were emptied on to a conveyor belt and plastic bags were separated by hand before the first of the clever machines did its bit.

A rotating belt with a very powerful electromagnet sucked steel cans about 30cm (1ft) off the conveyor and sent them into a huge cage. Then the main belt passed an area where an electromagnetic vortex flung aluminium cans into yet another cage. Pallets of crushed aluminium cans are so valuable they are kept under lock and key. And recycling aluminium can save up to 95 per cent of the energy needed to make it from raw materials.

The plastic bottles were separated into a huge pile and were then fed on to yet a conveyor belt where they were sorted by hand to extract any that were not recyclable. In another area of the plant, paper and card were sorted by hand.

Conventional bags for landfill are also processed at the same site and, as the bags split open, we saw bottles, tins, clothes, and many other items that could all have been recycled. But there's no way to sort

---

PROJECT **Reuse materials in the garden**

Household cardboard tubes make great biodegradable pots to start off carrot and other root veg seeds, as you can plant them in the soil, tube and all, without disturbing the roots. Plastic bottles make ideal mini cloches for individual plants.

YOU WILL NEED
- Cardboard tubes
- Potting compost
- Tray
- Seeds
- Plastic drinks bottle
- Scissors

BIODEGRADABLE POTS

1. **Fill tubes** with sieved potting compost after standing them in a tray. Sow one seed per tube. Water gently and leave to grow.   2. **Plant out** seedlings when they are growing strongly; bury the tube directly into the soil.

MAKE A BOTTLE CLOCHE

1. **Cut the base off** a 2-litre (3½-pint) drinks bottle.   2. **Place the bottle** over a plant such as a tomato to make an instant mini cloche. Use the cap as a ventilator and take it off on warm days when condensation collects in the bottle.

through it all once it's reached this stage. Recycling has to be done as far as possible in the home.

Get organized at home

Try our top tips (see box, right) to help you sort out your recycling at home – either ready for collection by your local council, or to take to the nearest recycling centre when you are next passing by.

Some enlightened councils are also collecting food waste separately for processing (see anaerobic digesters, pages 88–89), but the easiest thing to do at home is to compost your raw vegetable and fruit scraps to make a wonderful soil-conditioner (see pages 104–107 for a guide to what you can and cannot compost). We collect composting material in a little bin in the kitchen, and have found we don't need a lid as it doesn't smell – the sheer volume of vegetables we eat means that it is emptied regularly and we rinse the bin in the stream on the way back to the house. We also use a bokashi tub (see page 104) to compost all of our cooked food waste.

Generally, it's best to send textiles and clothes to charity shops or sell them at car boot sales for reuse, but they can also be recycled if there's no useful wear left in them. Some recycling centres ask you to separate textiles into manmade and natural fibres before recycling.

Shoes that still have plenty of life in them can be repaired and used by people in developing countries, as can pairs of spectacles.

RECYCLING TIPS

Recycling can be messy if you don't have a well-ordered system. We have a unit in the kitchen that is labelled, lined with the council's specific recycling bags, and easy to empty. It saves lots of hassle and is a reminder to recycle every time we walk past it.

Ready for recycling

■ **Wash tins and cans**, and flatten them before recycling.

■ **Plastics** need to be sorted into different types – councils recycle some plastics more than others. Wash and flatten bottles and containers before recycling.

■ **Carrier bags** can be take to recycling points, often outside supermarkets. Bags made from recycled polythene use one-third of the energy needed for virgin plastic.

■ **Glass** can be recycled hundreds of times, so there is no need for any waste. Recycle metal lids as for tins.

■ **Paper and cardboard** are easy to recycle and reclaimed waste paper now makes up around 63 per cent of the fibre used to produce paper and board in the UK.

■ **Foil-lined drinks cartons** and Tetrapaks are hard to recycle, but in some areas you can take them to your local recycling centre.

Recycling *materials begins at home with the sorting process.*

1. Reuse old guttering to start pea seeds off under cover (see page 142). **2. CDs and bottle tops** threaded on string and hung between stakes so that they move in the breeze make effective bird scarers. **3. Turn an old window frame** and some timber into a cold frame. **4. Cardboard boxes** laid flat make a great biodegradable mulch (see no-dig gardening on page 100).

PRODUCTIVITY Growing your own food is probably one of the most satisfying things you can do. We love the idea of not only being productive but also of growing in harmony with nature. When you get the balance right, you'll discover just how awesome nature can be and how much it is on your side. This chapter provides you with all the information you need to make the most of your plot, large or small. We put a particular focus on how to save time in the garden and extend your growing season – so you can sit out in the summer sun and still be harvesting fresh crops in the depths of winter.

Approaches to growing

Growing your own food is a big step for first-time gardeners and the range of techniques can be daunting. However, the fact that there are so many points to one simple truth: there is no right way to do it. Experiment with whatever appeals – some methods take so little effort, you won't even need to lift a spade – and you'll find an approach to suit you and your plot.

Keep an open mind

You don't have to live on a five-acre smallholding to follow organic principles or design a permaculture plot. These are simply the "tools" that can be used to cultivate your space, large or small.

Techniques have changed drastically over time, from traditional methods to intensive pesticide-based systems, and back again to natural approaches. As with many aspects of sustainability, the traditional methods are often more valuable.

We have found it worthwhile to keep an open mind to growing. We try anything once: in our opinion, once can be an accident, twice a mistake, and three times is enemy action. If a method doesn't work for you, try an alternative. Remember, sustainability is about getting the most out of your space without damaging its future productivity.

Growing organically

Organic cultivation is based on the belief that the environment and the way we grow our food are interdependent. Its principles take into account soil and climate, while avoiding the use of toxic chemicals.

How it works

■ **Enhancing soil health** by composting is one of the foundation stones of organic practice, mainly because there is lots of life in the soil compared to artificial fertilizers. These lack the humus content – the decayed plant material and soil organisms – of compost, which brings vitality and holds moisture.

■ **Crop rotation** (see page 108) reduces build-up of soil-based diseases and pests.

■ **Weeds** are controlled mechanically by hoeing or hand weeding, or by mulching (see page 100).

■ **Using green manure** – growing crops that are dug back into the soil to improve fertility – is another key organic method (see page 106).

■ **Pest control** is based on minimizing the opportunities for pests to flourish, using techniques such as companion planting (see page 101) and encouraging natural predators (see pages 120–123).

Permaculture

Permaculture means different things to different people. We understand it as working with nature rather than against it. Permaculture uses natural ecosystems as a model for growing food, linking plants, animals, and microbes. If a plot is designed around what is already growing, permaculture can fit any situation.

How it works

■ **A no-dig policy** and low-energy approach are often followed. However, it's not just lazy gardening! In permaculture, disturbing the soil is

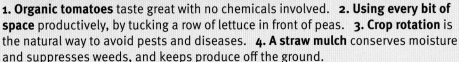

1. **Organic tomatoes** taste great with no chemicals involved.   2. **Using every bit of space** productively, by tucking a row of lettuce in front of peas.   3. **Crop rotation** is the natural way to avoid pests and diseases.   4. **A straw mulch** conserves moisture and suppresses weeds, and keeps produce off the ground.

Permaculture forest garden

A forest garden is made up of mainly perennial plants, growing as they would in the wild. A well-managed garden will yield fruits, nuts, and herbs, and annual crops such as salads can be sown in between the perennials. Growing a mix of diverse plants side by side reduces disease and pest attack: it's companion planting on a large scale.

Making a forest garden

A forest garden is ideal for well-established plots as it can incorporate mature trees. But don't let that limit your imagination. You can create a forest garden in pots on a patio by planting a dwarf fruit tree, a grapevine, herbs, and salads. Forest garden plants benefit each other: vines use trees for support; wild garlic grows in the shade of fruit bushes, leaving no space for weeds.

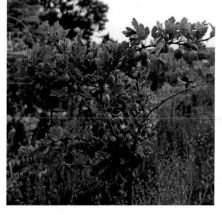

A forest garden *is planted in layers of edible perennials: here gooseberry bushes are planted alongside fruit and nut trees with lavender as low-growing groundcover.*

Fruit bushes like redcurrants, blueberries, and gooseberries can cope with light shade from the trees – mushroom logs will also thrive.

A low-maintenance garden
Perennial plants need far less attention than annual crops. Once they are planted, there is very little digging to do in a forest garden, apart from preparing small salad beds.

Fruit and nut trees such as apple, chestnut and mulberry

Fruit trees trained as espaliers and cordons

Strawberry plants

Perennial herbs such as lavender, chives, and wood sorrel

Grapevine climbing up dwarf fruit tree

Soft fruit canes such as raspberries

Annual crops in open, sunnier spots

Pond attracts frogs for pest control

Sweetcorn and nasturtiums *are annuals. The corn supports the nasturtiums, which shade the soil and keep it moist.*

Perennial edible groundcover *plants such as wild garlic and alpine strawberries help suppress weeds.*

thought to destroy its natural fertility and lead eventually to erosion.

Growing perennial crops is an important feature of permaculture. When they are well established they use up less energy than sowing a new crop each year, and weeds are less of a problem as there is less bare soil for them to colonize.

Zoning is another fundamental. Whatever needs most attention – vegetable beds, salads, and herbs – is grown close to the house. Orchards and livestock zones are further away; further still you come to field crops.

Mulching is one of our favourite permaculture principles – see below.

No-dig gardening

The normal reasons for digging are to incorporate manure and compost, remove or bury weeds, and create a good tilth for sowing. However, in no-dig gardening all manure, compost, and other organic material is applied to the surface two or three months before sowing, and is gradually incorporated by worms and other organisms. No-dig gardening feeds the soil not the plant.

How it works

Worms and their allies do the digging for you. Earthworms work on a permanent and ongoing basis that is arguably far more efficient than using a spade or a fork!

Weeds are dealt with by taking preventive action. Shallow hoeing or mulching in winter removes weeds before they have time to seed. A decent layer of light-excluding mulch left in place for at least a growing season can be used to clear the ground of tougher weeds. You can plant through the mulch – see below.

Conserving your energy is one of the key reasons for adopting a no-dig approach. Some people love digging but others are put off the whole idea of gardening by this strenuous aspect. For those who are elderly,

---

PROJECT **Easy no-dig mulching and planting**

This is the easy way to plant a vegetable bed, with no digging or weeding. It relies on mulching – blocking the light so weeds can't grow. Cardboard is an ideal mulch as it's readily available and biodegrades over time.

YOU WILL NEED
- Cardboard
- Large stones
- Watering can
- Topsoil
- Spade
- Sharp knife

1. Lay the cardboard mulch direct onto uncultivated ground, overlapping the pieces so that there are no gaps for weeds to grow through.   **2. Weigh down the edges** with stones to stop the cardboard blowing around.   **3. Water** thoroughly.

4. Cover with a layer of topsoil around 7.5cm (3in) deep.   **5. Leave for two weeks** and then make a planting hole by digging into the soil and cutting away a circle of cardboard.
6. Plant up (a squash is shown) and firm the soil around.   **7. Water well** and let grow!

less able, or less inclined to get muddy, no-dig is an accessible entry into the world of growing your own.

No watering

We first encountered this technique when we visited the The Lost Gardens of Heligan, the award-winning garden restoration project in the far south-west of England. It saves water in the garden and saves a lot of effort too. We've had great success with this method on our courgettes.

How it works

■ **Once a young plant** has been transplanted and thoroughly watered in, it is left to grow without being watered again. At first the plant will look a little unhealthy and may struggle, but this is only while the roots go down deeper in search of the natural water table.

■ **A strong taproot** develops as a result, and the plant thrives in dry periods due to its resilient root formation, without extra watering.

Square-foot gardening

Square-foot gardening is a new approach that evolved from the need to optimize space and reduce maintenance. It's ideal in an urban environment with limited space but works just as well for an intensively planted plot or on an experimental smallholding or city allotment.

How it works

■ **The basic concept** is to grow crops in a series of squares instead of rows. Each is about 30cm (12in) square and has a different vegetable, herb or flowering plant in it.

■ **Obvious benefits** include companion planting (see box): pest-deterrent plants like marigolds, onions, garlic, and chives are so close to the surrounding crops that their effectiveness is magnified.

■ **Succession planting** (see page 134) is much easier with this method: once a square has produced its harvest, it is easily replanted with a brand-new mini crop.

Biodynamics

First propounded by the philosopher and scientist Rudolf Steiner at the beginning of the 20th century, biodynamics treats a plot of land as an interdependent and self-nourishing system. It has a lot in common with organic principles, but biodynamics is still regarded as being at the wacky end of gardening.

How it works

■ **Biodynamics goes a step further** than the usual ecological gardening practices such as companion planting, green manures, and composting, by using a series of herbal remedies to treat the soil, plants, and even the compost heap.

■ **An astronomical calendar** is used to plan sowing and harvesting times.

■ **The dynamic aspect** takes note of biological processes. A typical biodynamic technique is to take sap rising in the morning as a sign that leafy vegetables should be harvested first thing when they are fresh.

COMPANION PLANTING

Companion planting is based on crops that grow together in a beneficial partnership, reducing the time needed for pest control and maintenance. Here are a few tried and tested combinations – experiment with your own and plant your beds with a bit more companionship.

■ **Sweetcorn, beans and squash** This Native American tradition is one of the oldest and most famous forms of companion planting. The sweetcorn serves as a trellis for the beans to climb up; the beans fix nitrogen for the sweetcorn and the squash grows around the base, keeping in the moisture and suppressing weeds. Try substituting sunflowers for sweetcorn.

■ **Onions and lettuce** Rows of onions or garlic next to lettuce and other salads create a "smell" barrier that helps stop slugs and snails getting too close.

■ **Poached-egg plant and peas** Poached-egg plants are a perennial you can move each spring to your legume bed. The flowers attract lots of hoverflies, which keep down the aphids that would otherwise spoil your peas.

■ **Basil and tomatoes** Aphids hate basil, so plant it next to your tomatoes. It's a great combination on the plate too.

■ **Nasturtiums and cabbages** Nasturtiums are a favourite food plant of cabbage-white caterpillars. Grow them as a trap crop to lure the butterflies and caterpillars away from brassicas. Add aphid-free flowers and leaves to salads.

■ **Radishes and cucumber** Reduce the risk of cucumber beetle by planting a ring of radishes around cucumber plants.

■ **Carrots and onions** One of nature's matches made in heaven: the onions drive away carrot fly and the carrots keep away the unwanted onion fly.

Keep aphids under control
Sow poached-egg plant (Limnanthes douglasii) at the same time as your peas.

Growing with hydroponics

Imagine a method of growing plants that doesn't need soil, uses a fraction of the water, and gives yields up to four times greater than traditional soil-based growing. It almost sounds too good to be true – and in the past hydroponics has suffered from being associated with white-coated scientists. Today it's a technique that anyone can try, and we have been researching how to use it at home.

What is hydroponics?

Hydroponics is a method of growing plants without the need for soil, by directly feeding the roots with a mineral nutrient solution. Setting up a system at home does involve an initial outlay of time and resources but, in the long run, it saves labour and conserves water.

We first became interested in hydroponics because of the challenge facing many people living in densely populated urban centres, with little space to grow their own food. Hydroponics makes efficient use of space and labour, and has a low impact on the environment.

At Newhouse Farm we recommend the Nutrient-Film Technique (NFT), where a very shallow stream or "film" of nutrients, 1–2mm (less than ⅛in) deep, provides plants with all the nourishment they require for healthy growth. Because the nutrient flow is so shallow the roots are still able to access oxygen, without which they would rot.

The advantages

▨ Hydroponics can be employed on stony or otherwise **difficult sites**.
▨ There's no risk of developing **soil-borne diseases**.
▨ There are **no weeds** to compete for space, nutrients, and water.
▨ **Nutrients are delivered directly** to the plants' roots, so up to four times more plants can be grown than on the same area of land.
▨ **Tailoring the nutrient mix** to suit each particular crop increases yields.
▨ Because hydroponics **uses water efficiently**, consumption can be reduced by up to 90 per cent.

▨ **Combining hydroponics** with a greenhouse or polytunnel stretches the growing season, enabling you to eat out-of-season produce.

What to grow

Plants grown hydroponically require a constant stream of diluted nutrients washing around their roots. Crops that we have had success with are herbs, summer squashes, salads, tomatoes, chillies, and aubergines. It's important to support tall-growing vegetables with wire or string as they grow, as you would normally.

The only vegetables we would not grow hydroponically using NFT are root vegetables: there simply isn't space in the growing channels for large roots. The bottom line with hydroponics is to experiment and learn as you go along.

CARING FOR CROPS

With hydroponics, successful growing depends on monitoring the nutrients and pH level of the solution.

Starting plants off

The seed-germination medium we use is coconut fibre, a by-product from the husking industry, which comes ready shaped into cubes or plugs. Germination is up to five times faster than in using traditional methods as the fibre retains water more effectively than soil. Place seeds in the middle of the plugs and feed them on a start-up nutrient (you can order this online) for a couple of weeks.

Transferring plants

Once plants reach a decent size and the tips of their roots are poking through the bottom of the cube, move the cube and plant into the growing channels.

Feeding with nutrients

Organic nutrients can be bought online from hydroponics suppliers: worm casts, krill, alfalfa, and kelp are all suitable. If you want to make your own, use the liquid fertilizer from the bottom of a wormery (see page 127) or comfrey concentrate (see page 107).

A 45-litre (10-gallon) tank will be large enough for a small-scale domestic growing system. It will need a top-up every couple of weeks to keep the water level high and to replenish the nutrients absorbed by the plants as they grow.

Monitoring pH levels

Check the pH of the nutrient solution in the tank regularly using a waterproof pH monitor. Adjust the pH by adding "pH down" powder (handle it with care), or by altering the amount of nutrients you add.

Tomato plants thrive *when grown hydroponically. With a constant supply of water and nutrients you need never worry about the fruits splitting and it saves lots of time. Set up your system under cover and you can extend the growing season and eat tomatoes for most of the year.*

Setting up a system

A hydroponics system involves growing plants in channels fed by a stream of nutrient-rich water pumped round in a continuous cycle. Ready-made kits are available but to really understand the process we recommend putting together a system yourself. You can grow plants hydroponically outside, but growing under cover gives maximum yields.

The irrigation system

To pump the nutrient solution to the growing plants, we use a simple plant irrigation system available from garden centres. This uses electricity, so there can be a small running cost. We run a 12V pump from a battery powered by a solar panel and/or wind turbine.

Growing channels

You can buy special growing channels, but we've found flat-bottomed guttering works just as well. Make lids from white plastic sheeting to keep the inside dark; this reduces algal growth and simulates the normal environment for roots. A thin layer of capillary matting down the length of the channel gives an even flow rate and healthier roots.

Growing channels need to slope gently down towards a collection channel; we adjusted their height with slivers of wood until the solution was trickling slowly down. If the gradient is too shallow, the solution collects in puddles around the roots and increases the risk of disease.

The length of channel is up to you. Ideally they will have closed ends with small drainage holes, but open-ended channels do exactly the same job, just with more splashing!

The shape of a geodesic dome *avoids warm air pockets forming, making it ideal for growing plants under cover.*

Grow in winter *with a large energy-efficient light bulb to simulate summer light, a fish tank heater to warm the nutrient solution, and bubble plastic to insulate the channels.*

A typical set-up
A simple trestle table is ideal for the growing channels, leaving plenty of space for the nutrient tank underneath.

The nutrient solution trickles down the growing channels, which are raised slightly at one end.

Growing channels made from flat-bottomed guttering

Nutrient solution is pumped along irrigation pipes from tank to channels.

More guttering collects the solution as it runs out of the channels.

A lid on the tank keeps the solution warm and reduces evaporation

Battery charged by solar PV panel or turbine

12V pump with an adjustable flow rate of 12 litres (21 pints) an hour is ideal

Tank containing nutrient solution

Layer of insulation

An irrigation pipe takes the solution back to the tank ready for reuse.

Plants in coconut-fibre plugs sit on a layer of capillary matting.

Achieving a productive plot

Growing your own food is relatively easy; plants require little more than nutrients and water to survive. But to improve productivity and get impressive harvests, a little more effort is needed. Regular watering, feeding, and thorough maintenance make your plants stronger and more resilient to weeds and garden pests. Providing your crops with optimum soil conditions is the key.

Looking after the soil

It's good gardening practice to think of the soil structure as the foundation of a productive plot. Whether you have a raised bed in an urban area or a large smallholding, you'll get better results if you add plenty of rich organic materials to the soil. At Newhouse Farm we make huge amounts of our own compost year on year to replenish our raised beds. We enrich our soil with green manure crops and animal manure, and make our own liquid fertilizers to boost certain crops in the growing season. Nurturing the soil is a bit like mixing together the right ingredients in a cake: it directly determines how well your fruit and vegetables "rise". We find it's a very hands-on aspect of growing and really gets you back to the roots of a productive plot.

Make your own compost

Composting is the process whereby the natural decomposition of organic matter is accelerated to create a rich growing material. Bacteria, fungi, and microorganisms thrive in the right conditions and will break down waste quickly to provide a great source of quality compost to use around your plot. Successfully making your own compost depends on getting the mixture just right.

Any compost heap will naturally break down eventually and turn into something useful, but to avoid a smelly wet mix or a pile of dry matter, you must get the balance right between materials high in carbon and those that are high in nitrogen. At Newhouse Farm we always try to mix one part "greens" with at least one part "browns". We also add activators to speed it all up (see box); most work by providing a nitrogen boost to kick-start the process.

Browns (high in carbon)
- Straw
- Dead leaves
- Cardboard
- Shredded paper
- Loo rolls
- Egg cartons and egg shells
- Twigs and plant stems
- Sawdust

Greens (high in nitrogen)
- Grass cuttings
- Uncooked fruit and vegetable scraps and peelings
- Tea bags and coffee grounds
- Manure
- Urine
- Weeds and fresh plants

COMPOST COOKED FOOD

Above all, you should never waste food and always try to be inventive with leftovers. If you do have cooked food, meat, fish, and dairy products to dispose of, however, it's possible to compost them using the Bokashi system. This turns cooked food waste into compost in an odourless, compact unit, using a type of bran that contains microorganisms. The process is anaerobic, so the container must be airtight. The microorganisms ferment the waste, then you can add it to your conventional compost bin.

Add cooked food scraps and a handful of bran. Bokashi also makes strong liquid fertilizer: dilute with water to feed plants or use neat to unblock drains!

TRY THIS
- **Add an activator** Compost just happens, but if you want it in a hurry, add an activator to speed up the process. Try any of these.
- **Urine** Men's works better than women's (it's the hormones).
- **Grass cuttings** Add sparingly in thin layers.
- **Comfrey leaves** Even the old ones leftover from making concentrate (see page 107).
- **Seaweed** Collect it fresh, from below the tide line.
- **Manure** Add a little at a time.
- **Nettles** Don't forget to wear gloves when picking.
- **Topsoil** Contains lots of microorganisms which will help to get the heap going.
- **Compost from an old heap** Also full of microorganisms.

Cool composting

The cool composter is probably the most common style of compost bin. It doesn't retain much heat but instead encourages a large worm population to break down materials, along with a huge collection of microorganisms. Just lift the lid and add small amounts of waste regularly. Don't add weeds with seed heads: these must be hot-composted to destroy the seeds or you will end up sowing weeds on your vegetable beds when you dig in the compost.

Cool composters are easy to use. We recommend emptying them out every couple of months and turning the compost before putting it back in. Use a fork to mix it up. If it looks too wet add more "browns"; if it's too dry and fibrous, add more "greens". We have several cool composting bins that we use on rotation for a ready supply throughout the year.

Hot composting

Composting at higher temperatures kills weed seeds and reduces the spread of plant diseases, but you won't find many worms in the mix – it's too hot for them. Heat-loving anaerobic microorganisms do all the work in a hot compost heap.

When we first arrived at Newhouse Farm we cleared a lot of uncultivated land for vegetable beds. This in turn presented the challenge of what to do with all the unwanted weeds. We didn't want to waste the plant

1. Green plant material is rich in nitrogen, so add it to your compost heap. **2. Mix it** 50:50 with dry "brown" material such as straw. **3. Plastic cone-shaped bins** are ideal for cool composting. **4. Cool compost in progress.** The bottom layer is ready to use but the top goes back in the cone for a bit longer. **5. Retain the heat** in a hot compost bin with a layer of old carpet. **6. Spread** home-made compost on a vegetable bed, then fork it in.

material, so we built a few big hot-composting systems out of pallets.

Wooden pallets are available all around the world – free of charge if you scavenge them. Fix them together using some big nails or string, to create two adjoining wooden boxes that can be used in rotation, each about one cubic m (1.3 cubic yd) in volume. The wood helps to retain the heat created by the composting process. For extra insulation, line the insides of the boxes you have built with big bits of cardboard and stuff bubble wrap inside the hollow bit of each individual pallet.

It may also be worth using a shredder to cut up some of the materials if you are processing large quantities. To maintain the temperature in a hot compost heap, you need to turn the compost regularly to aerate it. Use a fork to shift the outside to the inside and vice versa; it's hard work but well worth it. Covering the heap with black plastic or some bits of old carpet helps to retain the heat too.

Using a wormery

One of the main advantages of composting with a wormery is that when it's designed in vertically stacked tiers, it takes up so little space. In an urban environment we'd ecommend one as your first choice. Build your own (see page 127) or buy one readymade. The main attraction is the liquid fertilizer or worm tea that collects in the base. It's high in nitrogen and phosphates – a rocket fuel for growing plants.

Making leaf mould

Leaf mould is an excellent way of making your own compost, to use as a soil conditioner, to improve both drainage and water retention, or for potting up seedlings. Simply collect fallen leaves and place them in black plastic bags with some small holes in them. Leave them for about a year and then enjoy – a simple compost recipe but worthwhile. If you are making leaf mould on a larger scale, we recommend building a big cube-shaped cage using four wooden

posts and some chicken wire. Shred the leaves before adding or collect them using a lawn mower: it chops the leaves up and mixes them with grass, which is high in nitrogen, creating a magic compost mix full of microorganisms and water.

Using green manures

Green manures are crops grown specifically to help build a good soil structure and maintain fertility. They are not harvested; instead they are dug straight back into the soil. Once considered an agricultural technique in farming, growing green manures is increasingly popular with small-scale organic gardeners.

At Newhouse Farm we have been using them for a few years as part of our crop rotation and are pleased with the results. Not only do they look attractive, they also help to protect bare soil from erosion, as well as providing a good covering blanket to keep the beds free of weeds. Green manuring is simple. Choose a suitable crop from those listed on

---

PROJECT # Dig a compost trench

Compost trenches are a really good alternative to a conventional compost heap, particularly during winter when normal compost bins have cooled down and are slower to deal with waste. They are completely smellproof, quick and easy, and a great source of food for young plants; the decomposed material provides a rich supply of nutrients right where it is needed at the roots of the growing plants.

1. Choose a space in a vegetable plot that will have runner beans or peas growing in it next season. In autumn, dig a trench one spade deep and a spade's width across.
2. Fill it gradually by adding vegetable scraps and kitchen waste, covering them with the original soil from the trench as you go.   **3. Once the trench is full,** leave it for a couple of months, then sow seeds or plant directly into it. Pumpkins and courgettes do particularly well on top of compost trenches.

PROJECT **Make comfrey fertilizer**

Comfrey is an excellent plant to grow in the garden. Not only does it attract a whole host of bees and pollinating insects but, by following a few simple steps, you can turn the leaves into a liquid fertilizer rich in nitrogen, potash, and phosphorus – essential for healthy plants. Comfrey is a deep-rooted herbaceous perennial that absorbs nutrients from way down in the soil. It grows best in full sun and can be cut down four or five times in a season, but remember to stop by early autumn to allow enough regrowth before winter. In our opinion the only negative issue with composting comfrey is the smell – but that just adds more character.

TRY THIS

■ **Cut the bottom** off a large plastic bottle and pack it with comfrey leaves. Stand the bottle, without its top, upside down in another container. In two weeks you'll have comfrey concentrate on a smaller scale.
■ **Substitute nettles** for comfrey in either method if you haven't got any comfrey on your plot.

1 Pick handfuls of comfrey leaves. It grows prolifically so don't worry about stripping the plant. **2 Build a stand** for your comfrey distillery – we used old breeze blocks. Place a container such as a watering can underneath to collect the concentrate. **3 Drill** a hole in the base of a butt or large plastic container with a lid, capable of holding approximately 45 litres (10 gallons).

4 Pack the comfrey leaves tightly into the container. **5 Weigh the leaves** down with some bricks to speed up the process. As more leaves grow back on the comfrey plant, pick them and add to the container. **6 After about 10 days** the leaves will start to decay into a black liquid. You should collect about 2–3 litres (4–6 pts). **Store the comfrey concentrate** in a bottle in a cool dark place, but don't seal the bottle too tightly as it may ferment in warm weather. Once the concentrate has stopped dripping into your collector, add the leftover comfrey leaves to the compost heap as an activator. Dilute the concentrate 1:15 with water and feed your plants for amazing results.

the crop rotation plan opposite and allow it to grow for a short time. Then dig it back into the soil with a sharp spade to replenish the nutrients.

You must dig green manure back in while it's young and sappy. If you leave it too long, then it defeats the point and looks more as if you have planted a bed full of weeds! Several green manures – including alfalfa, clover, trefoil, and fenugreek – belong to the legume family and can actually take up nitrogen from the air, adding extra goodness to the soil. We allow a month or so after digging them in before we plant up the beds.

A few favourite green manures
Alfalfa Sow from spring to mid-summer and grow for a few months.
Crimson clover Sow from early spring to late summer. The flowers attract insects, especially bees.

Fenugreek Sow from early spring to late summer. One of the fastest-growing green manures; useful if you have a tight crop rotation.
Trefoil Sow from early spring to late summer. Does well in shade; use it to under-sow sweetcorn or sprouts.
Mustard Sow from spring to summer to grow for about eight weeks. Goes to seed quickly in hot weather, so dig it in nice and early.
Grazing rye Sow late summer to late autumn. Ideal over winter, when it suppresses weeds.

Crop rotation
Before we head out into the garden at the beginning of each year, we plan an organized system of crop rotation. This sounds complicated but it makes sense. Simply put, some families of plants are more prone to particular diseases and have specific pests that prey on them. In addition, different plant families also need different nutrients from the soil. By moving the crops from plot to plot each year you can give them a better chance to get strongly established before problems start. At the same time the soil gets the chance to replenish itself.

Working out a rotation plan
Trying to work out a definitive rotation plan proved nearly impossible when we first started, as different experts give different advice. So we tried to understand exactly which elements of each system we liked and what logic we agreed with. After many headaches we came up with a plan that suited us and appeared to be in line with most expert advice. We divided our crops into groups, set out in the chart opposite. Green manures are included in our crop rotation too.

1. Crop rotation stops soil getting depleted and avoids a build up of pests too. **2. Sow clover** as a weed-suppressing green manure. **3. Labelling is crucial:** you've got to be organized for crop rotation to succeed.

CROP ROTATION PLAN

We divide our crops into six groups but follow a four-year, four-bed rotation by fitting salads in wherever we can and letting alliums and umbellifers share a bed. We don't include potatoes in our crop rotation because they are prone to blight where we live and need to be grown separately.

	YEAR 1	YEAR 2	YEAR 3	YEAR 4
BED 1	A&U	L	B	M
BED 2	L	B	M	A&U
BED 3	B	M	A&U	L
BED 4	M	A&U	L	B

GROUP	CROPS INCLUDE		SOIL REQUIREMENTS
Alliums (A)	■ Garlic ■ Leeks	■ Onions ■ Shallots	High organic matter; may need lime added to the soil to reduce acidity.
Umbellifers (U)	■ Beetroot family (quinoa, spinach, Swiss chard, spinach beet) ■ Carrots ■ Celeriac ■ Celery	■ Fennel ■ Parsley ■ Parsnips ■ Potatoes – unless blight is a problem where you live	Root crops need stone-free soil; a fine tilth. Soil should not be freshly manured. Some root crops also help to break up soil structure, especially potatoes.
Legumes (L)	■ Alfalfa (green manure) ■ Broad beans ■ Clover (green manure) ■ Fenugreek (green manure) ■ French beans	■ Lupins (green manure) ■ Peas ■ Runner beans ■ Tares (green manure) ■ Trefoil (green manure)	Well-drained and moisture-retentive, but not nitrogen-rich. Legumes fix nitrogen in their roots for future crops. When harvesting leave the roots.
Brassicas (B)	■ Broccoli ■ Brussels sprouts ■ Cabbage ■ Calabrese ■ Cauliflower ■ Kale	■ Kohl rabi ■ Mustard (green manure) ■ Oriental brassicas ■ Radish ■ Swede ■ Turnip	Leafy crops need nitrogen-rich soil; may need lime added to reduce diseases like club root.
Miscellaneous (M)	■ Buckwheat (green manure) ■ Courgettes ■ Cucumbers ■ Grazing rye (green manure) ■ Peppers ■ Phacelia (green manure) ■ Pumpkins	■ Squashes ■ Sweetcorn ■ Tomatoes	Some plants have so few soil-dwelling pests or diseases that they can be fitted in anywhere in the rotation
Salads (S)	■ Chicory/endive ■ Lambs' lettuce ■ Lettuce ■ Miners' lettuce ■ New Zealand spinach	■ Purslane ■ Salsify ■ Scorzonera	Not fussy. We put them in as and when, rotate within beds, and grow lots under cover – that's why they're not in the rotation plan. Succession plant.

Set up a greenhouse irrigation system

When you grow plants outside you don't have to worry too much about watering, as you expect nature to do it for you. But once you start growing plants in polytunnels, greenhouses, cold frames or cloches, they depend on you for water. Installing an automatic irrigation system will make life an awful lot easier at the height of the growing season.

Getting water where it's needed

To set up an irrigation system you first need a water source. Rainwater butts are an ideal simple solution: we have one inside our greenhouse that's filled from guttering attached to the greenhouse roof. Bear in mind that rainwater butts have a limited capacity; in a dry spell you may find yourself topping up the butt with water from the mains or elsewhere.

Water is heavy and it takes a lot of energy to move it. If you can collect and store water on land that's higher than your greenhouse, then you can use gravity to help with the watering. If you can't use gravity to reduce your workload, then technology can come to your rescue.

A simple little demand pump is all it takes to move water to exactly where you want it. A demand pump can use mains electricity or be battery operated, and will only pump – and therefore use energy – if a tap is turned on, in this case by an electronic timer. The pump is controlled by a pressure switch: when the tap is turned off again, the water pressure builds up and switches the pump off.

Delivering the right amount

The key to irrigation is to deliver the right amount of water. You'll know when you get it wrong. Splitting tomatoes are a tell-tale sign: if a tomato plant receives too little water, then is deluged with it, the fruits can't handle the sudden surfeit and the skins will split. Don't forget plants only need water during the day when they are photosynthesizing. Water in the morning and harvest in the evening when flavours are at their most concentrated. Don't take our word for it – try it with your tomatoes!

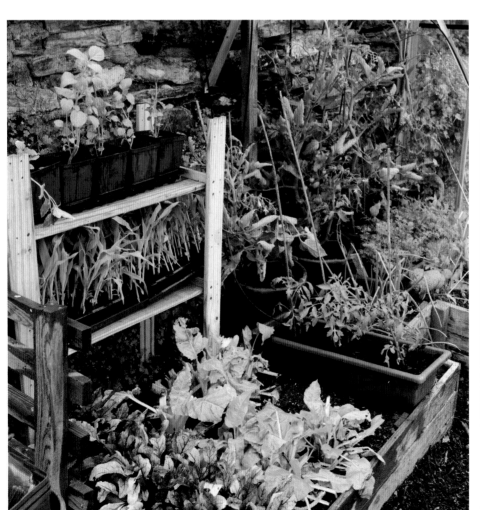

Irrigation in action A combination of sprays and drippers in our greenhouse saves us valuable time each day and the plants get watered very gently, without disturbing the compost.

TRY THIS

If you have only a few plants, these small-scale systems will keep them watered for a couple of days.

■ Take a **plastic container** with a lid. Make a hole in the lid, drape the ends of longish strips of fabric through the hole and insert a piece of pipe. Spread out the fabric strips and bury the container in compost with the pipe sticking out so you can use it to fill with water. The fabric "wicks" transfer moisture from container to compost.

■ Cut the bottom off a 2 litre (3½ pints) **plastic bottle,** turn it upside down and push the neck into the soil next to a plant. Fill it with water, which will seep into the soil.

■ **Lay a piece of fabric** on a tray and stand plant pots on top. Drape the fabric into a container of water so that the plants can draw up moisture by capillary action.

PROJECT Install an automatic watering system

A few hours arranging leaky pipes, drippers, and sprayers and connecting them to a water supply will save you many more hours of watering. Your system will pay for itself in terms of increased yields.

YOU WILL NEED
- Leaky pipe system, dripper system, spray system or any combination of these
- Water source
- 12V demand pump
- Rechargeable, deep cycle or leisure battery
- Hose pipe
- Battery-powered pump timer
- Small block of wood

INSTALLING A LEAKY PIPE

1. Install the system before planting up. Lay the perforated leaky pipe on the compost in a way that will distribute moisture to the maximum growing area. Use small sticks to hold it in position and serve as markers.   **2. Bring both ends together** and join them to the water supply hose using a T junction. Connect the supply hose to your automated system (see below).   **3. Add compost** to cover the pipe.   **4. Plant up the bed,** avoiding the sticks marking the leaky pipe.

INSTALLING DRIPPERS AND SPRAYERS

1. Arrange sprayers so the nozzles deliver water to each pot.   **2. Continue** building up the system; drippers are ideal for hanging baskets.   **3. Add dual-purpose** attachments to act as misters or drippers.   **4. Add a small black end stop** when you get to the end of a run of piping.

CONNECTING UP TO THE WATER SUPPLY

1. Make a float from a block of wood for the hose drawing water from the butt, so it takes water from the top, rather than the bottom where sediment collects.   **2. Mount the pump and timer** to a wooden box unit using the supplied fixings. Our unit has a sloping roof to keep the battery dry and you could mount a solar panel on the roof to charge the battery. Connect the pump to the battery; the timer has its own internal battery. Connect the timer to the pump with a length of hose, and connect a supply hose to the timer.   **3. Connect the pump** to the water butt with another length of hose, keeping the distance between them as short as possible.   **4. Bring all the supply hoses** to a single junction close to the timer beside the pump. You can run several systems at once but the water pressure will drop. Connect the junction hose to the timer. Switch on and experiment!

Growing under cover

Growing under cover is not a gardening technique for secret agents. It's the process of extending the growing season by using a greenhouse, polytunnel, or smaller-scale options such as cloches and cold frames, to create warmer conditions for your plants. This allows you to produce fresh vegetables for longer, grow some foods out of season, and grow exotic crops from warmer climates.

Why do it?

To become self-sufficient you need to maximize the growing potential of your plot, starting crops early to ensure successive harvests, and avoiding lean periods later on.

A greenhouse or polytunnel may be expensive, but the benefits soon pay off – from growing salads in winter to giving tender plants a head start in spring. Some foods travel across the world to reach us, leaving a trail of environmental issues in their wake. A greenhouse is a way to grow them at home, rather than giving them up or feeling guilty every time we eat a strawberry out of season.

Small-scale options

From mini cloches for individual plants to home-made cold frames, you can still give plants on smaller plots extra protection without putting up a polytunnel or greenhouse. Even city dwellers growing herbs and salads on windowsills can experience the benefits of growing under glass.

Cloches

Cloches are essentially protective covers for plants. We have tried tent-style cloches covered with polythene, low plastic tunnels with inverted U-shaped wires, glass frames, and hard corrugated plastic sheets bent into a curve. One of our favourite methods is simply to place a clean jam jar over a newly transplanted seedling – a modern take on a Victorian glass bell cloche. We also cut the bottom off big plastic bottles and place the top half over the plant, unscrewing the cap for ventilation in warmer weather.

Cold frames

Traditionally used for hardening off seedlings before planting out, we've found cold frames are ideal for raising seedlings from scratch and for extending the season of salads and herbs. A cold frame's key design

1. A traditional glass cloche can protect a single plant. **2. The shape of a geodesic dome** prevents frost pockets forming. **3. DIY cloche** can be made from a cut-down plastic bottle. **4. Harden off** plants in a cold frame before planting out. **5. Open vents** and door in a greenhouse to keep the air circulating.

feature is that it can be accessed easily for watering and harvesting. Using an old window for the top saves lots of effort and is a great way to recycle (see pages 116–117).

Windowsills
Growing plants on a windowsill may not sound like the most aspirational approach to growing food under cover but it can be successful. Young plants thrive in warm, slug-free conditions and, because you see them regularly, they get more attention and grow well, provided you rotate them so that all sides receive equal light.

Large-scale structures
With the warmth and protection of a polytunnel or greenhouse, it's more than viable to become self-sufficient in a range of vegetables. What you lose in ground space on your plot, you more than make up for with the extra weeks of growing time gained.

Greenhouses
A greenhouse has to be one of the nicest places to work in winter. The warmth and smells make it a bit like going on holiday.

As with all methods of growing under cover, choosing where to site it is crucial. Our greenhouse is orientated east-west on a south-facing wall, which gives lots of light and the wall acts as a heat sink.

Greenhouses are expensive to buy new but are often available second-hand if you are prepared to dismantle one. They can be surprisingly productive for their size if you get the layout right. Optimize vertical space by installing tiers of shelves for pots and trays, and by hanging baskets inside. Try growing tomatoes, herbs, aubergines, chillies, and salads, and starting off all sorts of seedlings.

In winter the temperature should not fall below 4°C (40°F) at night and it can get surprisingly warm in sunny

6 STEPS TO SUCCESS
Follow these guidelines to get the best from plants grown under cover.

■ **Ventilate often**, even in winter, to prevent problems like red spider mite developing. A heat sink (see pages 118–119) helps to keep air circulating, or open the door and roof vents to draw air through.

■ **Don't overplant**: too many plants too close together are more susceptible to pests and diseases.

■ **Nourish the soil** in permanent beds with a good supply of liquid fertilizer or new compost. If you use soil intensively it can become depleted of nutrients.

■ **Monitor the temperature**: frost is still an issue under cover. Even a water butt or small pond will help to warm the air, but a fan-assisted heat sink is ideal (see pages 118–119).

■ **Clear away detritus** from dead plants and fallen fruits, etc. to reduce the chances of pests and diseases building up.

■ **Water automatically** by installing an irrigation system and plants need never go thirsty (see pages 110–111).

GROWING UNDER COVER

PRODUCTIVITY

UNDERCOVER JOBS
Exotics such as chillies have to be grown under cover in temperate climates; you'll get an earlier harvest from many crops if you start off seedlings in a greenhouse or polytunnel; and a protected environment can fool other vegetables into cropping out of season.

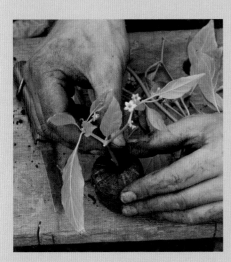

Take cuttings *from chillies. Remove a few leaves to increase the chances of success, and pot up in a rehydrated coir plug or cutting compost (see page 135).*

Start off sweetcorn *seedlings under cover for an earlier harvest. Harden them off (see page 134) before planting outside when there's no longer any risk of frost.*

Harvest rainbow chard *all year round by growing it in beds under cover in a polytunnel or by putting cloches over plants outside.*

weather. Installing a heat sink (see pages 118–119) will keep the air warm in winter, and will also circulate air in summer to keep the temperature down and reduce the risk of disease. To stop a greenhouse overheating, hang a damp towel in the open doorway and keep the roof and side vents wide open.

Polytunnels

Commercial polytunnels are a familiar part of our landscape but they're not just for farmers and market gardeners. We built our first one at the bottom of a small suburban garden.

Polytunnels are often made from polythene or PVC stretched over metal frames and are simple to put together. Dig down around the frame and lay some turf over the edges of the plastic; this keeps it stretched tight and avoids any embarrassing kite fiascos in high winds.

At Newhouse Farm we have built raised beds down either side and installed benches for potting up seedlings. We added a pond to help retain heat and encourage frogs to keep down pests. In summer the pathway down the middle is full of pots holding the taller plants like tomatoes and cucumbers, which grow incredibly well tied up to the centre of the frame and are easy to harvest by walking along the rows.

Geodesic domes

Geodesic domes are not new; they have been around since the beginning of the 20th century. Championed by inventor Buckminster Fuller, they are designed to have a minimum external surface area but with far fewer internal building supports, giving maximum growing space.

Geodesic domes also make the most of solar energy. Sunlight shining into a conventional structure like a greenhouse creates warm air pockets that can damage plants. The dome shape promotes good air circulation and prevents pockets developing.

We ordered our geodesic dome in kit form. Putting together a building that gains its strength only when the last piece is put in place is a bit of a nightmare, but a lot of fun. We think it looks like a spaceship. For more on geodesic growing, see pages 102–103.

Conservatories

Most conservatory owners know that they are excellent places to grow plants. You can start off an array of seedlings in a conservatory and make it a permanent home for exotics. Citrus and olive trees, grape vines, and physalis plants do particularly well.

TYPE	PROS	CONS
Cloche	■ Cheap to construct – free if you make it out of scrap. ■ Ideal for gradually hardening off seedlings (see page 134). ■ Protects vulnerable young plants from pests.	■ Can get easily knocked over or blown away. ■ Only useful when plants are small. ■ Time-consuming technique.
Cold frame	■ Easy access for weeding, watering, harvesting. ■ Simple and cheap to make.	■ Not enough room for tall plants such as tomatoes.
Windowsill	■ Almost everyone has one. ■ Big plants like tomatoes will be extremely productive.	■ Tall plants may reduce daylight entering the room. ■ Stand pots in a tray to protect paintwork when watering. ■ You must rotate the pots.
Greenhouse	■ Productive growing space with the right layout. ■ Relatively easy to assemble.	■ Can be expensive.
Polytunnel	■ Cheaper than a greenhouse. ■ Large space available for growing.	■ Not as durable. ■ Not a good option on a windy site.
Geodesic dome	■ No warm air pockets. ■ More space for tall plants. ■ Admits maximum amount of light. ■ Aerodynamic shape – great on windy sites. ■ Fits into the landscape because of its completely curved nature.	■ Challenging to assemble from a kit or to build from scratch. ■ Expensive.
Conservatory	■ Great for exotics. ■ Part of the house so plants get maximum care.	■ Very expensive. ■ Temperature control is essential.

Using a polytunnel

Polytunnels are great places to grow everything from spinach to salads, but their usefulness doesn't end there. Use the space to dry garlic, onions, and herbs before storing, and to bring tender plants such as citrus trees under cover in winter – and make a workstation where you can repot plants or take cuttings. Our polytunnel is a carefully planned mix of permanent plantings such as vines and olives, crops such as tomatoes and cucumbers that will spend their entire life under cover, and others that benefit from a warm start but are destined for the vegetable plot. We even have a propagator in the polytunnel, which acts as a double skin to retain the sun's heat and is ideal for starting off tomato and melon seedlings.

Hang up garlic *to dry in the airy warmth of a polytunnel before storing it.*

Maximize productivity

Use your undercover space to start plants off early, keep salads and herbs producing over winter, and grow more exotic crops such as melons and aubergines that won't survive outside in a temperate climate.

Growing tomatoes *in a polytunnel gives big yields and they are easy to harvest. Support plants using strings attached to the frame.*

Beetroot seedlings *for planting out and to cut as salad leaves.*

Vine growing direct in the soil

Tall tomato and cucumber plants tied to polytunnel frame

Starting off peas in guttering

Salads sown in succession for continuous cropping

Olive trees do best under cover in a temperate climate

Small pond acts as a heat sink and encourages frogs

Lemon tree brought under cover in winter

Grown under cover, strawberries don't get splashed with mud or pecked by birds

Spinach seedlings ready to transplant

Rows of herbs

Potting bench

Space below bench is handy for storing potting compost

Large propagator with shelves and its own cover

Pest control *is simple if you keep chickens. Let them loose at the end of season to root out and eat any overwintering pests.*

PROJECT **Build a cold frame**

In its simplest form a cold frame is a box with a glass lid that helps seedlings to grow by enhancing the environment they are in and protecting them from extremes of weather. Rather than buying new materials to build one, we always recommend looking around to see what bits and bobs you have available. Reusing old windows or panes of glass is a much greener option – and it's cheaper.

YOU WILL NEED

- Drill
- Spirit level
- Hammer
- Punch
- Tape measure
- Hand saw
- Screwdriver
- Wood: planks, uprights, and battens
- Old window plus extra glass or plastic
- Sliding hinges
- Nails
- Rawl plugs
- Screws
- Stones or glass bottles

Use a cold frame to start off frost-tender plants early and to harden them off before planting outside

Position the lid at an angle so that rain runs off it and to give maximum growing space for larger plants

Large stones, heat-storage bricks, or glass bottles heat up during the day and give out warmth at night

Gravel helps to retain moisture so the plants will need watering less frequently. It also keeps seedlings' roots at a good growing temperature

Site the frame against a south-facing wall for added warmth

MAKING THE BASE

1. Make a simple box by screwing horizontal planks to a framework. The size of your box will depend on what you use for a lid. We based ours on an old window. Make the uprights from standard 50 x 25mm (2 x 1in) lengths of wood. We used some leftover planks for the sides – 150 x 25mm (6 x 1in) are ideal – and we saved on wood by positioning the cold frame against a raised bed and wall. **2. Check the sides** of the box are level. **3. Add a brace** across the back of the box to keep it square.

MAKING THE LID

4. Use an old window for the lid. Screw two sliding hinges to opposite ends of the top edge of the window frame. Slide on the other half of each hinge. **5. Screw the other hinge halves** to a length of wooden batten the same width as the lid. **6. Flip the hinges shut** and hold the lid in its final position, resting it against the wall and the front edge of the cold frame base. Mark the position of the batten on the wall, then lift the lid down. **7. Slide the bolts** out of each hinge to separate lid and batten. **8. Drill** the batten to the wall using rawl plugs and screws, following the guide marks you made earlier.

CONSTRUCTING THE SIDES

9. **Measure** and cut timber for the triangular side-wall frames, with the lid in place. Remove lid.   10. **Mark the angle** of the joint for the side-wall frame. Do this at both ends. Cut the angles.   11. **Drill** the side frame in place using long screws at an angle. Measure the triangular space and cut a pane of glass to this size.   12. **Nail narrow battens** to the inside edges to stop the glass falling inwards.   13. **Fit glass** against inner battens and nail additional narrow battens on to the outside to hold it in place. Take care not to smash the glass. Use a nail punch to keep your hammer that extra safe distance away! If you don't feel confident about cutting glass to fit, use tough see-through plastic sheeting or bubble wrap and staple it to the frame.

USING THE COLD FRAME

14. **Fill the cold frame** to within 10cm (4in) of the top with large stones, heat-storage bricks or glass bottles filled with water, allowing space for warm air to circulate and be absorbed.   15. **Place an old paving slab** on top of the stones, again leaving room around the sides for air circulation. Adjust it until it's level.   16. **Fill a plant tray** with gravel and level the surface. Place it in the cold frame.   17. **Slide the lid** back on to the hinges. Stand trays and pots of seedlings on the gravel – taller plants at the back, small ones at the front. Keep a length of wood handy to prop the lid open, to acclimatize plants gradually and harden them off (see pages 112–115).

ALTERNATIVE USES
Make maximum use of your cold frame with these ideas.

Make a hotbed
Line the base with plastic then half fill it with fresh horse manure. Mix in some straw and leave to ferment. Wait until the strong smell of ammonia disappears, then add about 30cm (1ft) of topsoil. Plant or sow when the soil temperature is about 27°C (81°F). Great for initial germination of plants.

Drying seeds
Use your cold frame to speed up the drying process when preparing seeds to store. Keep the lid slightly open to allow moisture to escape.

Cold frame turned solar dryer
Spread seeds thinly to dry. Use trays to keep different varieties separate.

Making a greenhouse heat sink

Even growing under cover, plants still need extra protection from frost. Greenhouses and polytunnels heat up quickly but, sadly, cool down just as fast. The challenge is to find a way of keeping the temperature above the danger zone where plants can be damaged – we're not saying warm, just warm enough. That's where the heat sink comes in.

What is a heat sink?

A heat sink is something that can capture the sun's heat and store it during the day, then give it off when required – like a night-storage heater.

Rather than trying to generate heat to keep our greenhouse frost-free, we like the idea of capturing it. Even in the depths of winter the sun warms greenhouses and polytunnels, but the lack of insulation means the heat disappears quickly as the sun sets.

So we decided to stop some of that free heat escaping and store it. Our system uses a small fan that runs continuously. During the day it blows warm air through a box buried in the ground and filled with lumps of glass – the heat sink. At night it blows cooler air through the warm glass, which warms the air. This warm air stops the temperature in the greenhouse falling below freezing. For added frost protection we also built our lean-to greenhouse against a south-facing stone wall, whichitself acts as a heat sink.

Construction

Our heat sink is a hole roughly 1cu m (1.3cu yd), dug in the floor of the greenhouse. We reckoned this would be big enough for our 2.4 x 4m (8 x 13ft) greenhouse. We insulated the hole with discarded polystyrene to stop heat being lost to the earth, before filling it with imploded glass to absorb the heat. Imploded glass has amazing thermal properties but we realize it's not always that easy to get hold of this specialist type of glass: rocks, stones, glass bottles or jars – filled with water – will work just as well. Making the pipework is a great opportunity to recycle odd bits of leftover plumbing. You'll need a variety of connectors and lengths of standard plastic piping. Drill holes to perforate the pipes before assembling. Start with a T-junction connector where the inlet pipe enters the ground and connect a series of pipes to form a big loop that returns to the T-junction. There's no need to apply sealant between joints.

The benefits of a heat sink

▨ **Very little power** is needed to run the system, which relies on an inexpensive computer fan designed to run for years on very low power. You can generate the power yourself if you use a solar PV panel to charge up the battery.

▨ **No nasty fumes** from conventional paraffin greenhouse heaters.

▨ **Unexpected frosts** won't catch you out. The heat sink runs regardless so no need to constantly check the weather forecast.

▨ **Prevent diseases** such as botrytis by keeping the system running all year round to circulate air.

The results

It's very hard to say exactly how efficient our system is, but combined with the south-facing rear wall, it has managed to keep our greenhouse frost-free. Salads continue to grow deep into the winter – no mean feat considering we regularly have frosts with temperature sometimes dipping as low as -6°C (21°F). A winter of extra productivity and the system paid for itself: not a bad investment.

How the heat sink system works

We all know hot air rises and that's what this system relies on. During the day a fan sucks hot air from the apex of the greenhouse roof, down through some piping and into a network of perforated pipes to warm up the heat sink. At night the fan draws down cool air, which is then warmed by the heat sink and in turn warms the greenhouse – simple!

A frost-free greenhouse
Store the sun's energy in a heat sink and use it to warm up your greenhouse at night.

During the day the fan draws warm air from the top of the greenhouse, down through the pipe.

At night the fan draws cooler air down through the pipe.

A south-facing wall *and water butt act as secondary heat sinks. The white pipe takes air to the main underground heat sink.*

Plastic piping

Warmed air blows out of the vent at night.

Fan in plywood box

Deep-cycle leisure battery

Water butt acts as secondary heat sink

Heat sink vent

Site the heat sink below central walkway or under shelves to keep growing space free

Solar PV panel

Wooden heat sink lid

Hole in the floor insulated with a layer of polystyrene

During the day warm air circulates through the sink, heating the glass.

Lumps of glass or stone

Network of perforated pipes connected to the main downpipe

At night, cooler air circulates through the sink and is warmed by heat stored in the glass.

INSTALLING THE FAN

1. Wire up the fan.   **2. Make a small plywood box** to house the fan. Make a lid to seal the box. Cut out holes in the sides to fit the air pipes, and drill holes for the wiring.   **3. Connect the fan** to a deep-cycle leisure battery using crocodile clips. Screw lid onto the fan box. Keep battery and fan box in a plastic crate to protect from damp. Cut holes in the crate to match the holes in the fan box for the air pipes.   **4. Push the pipes** through the holes in the crate and into the fan box.
5. Connect the battery to a small solar panel outside the greenhouse and the system is up and running.

Gardening in harmony with nature

We encourage wildlife on our plot because improving biodiversity is an effective method of pest control and boosting productivity. This dedicated wildlife garden illustrates different ideas and the benefits they bring, so that you can choose suitable elements to add to your own plot. And don't forget, urban gardens can be wildlife havens too.

KEY TO GARDEN PLAN

1 Nettle patch
2 Bird nesting box
3 Bat box
4 Small pond
5 Rock-pile habitat for slow worms
6 Bee B&B
7 Flowers for useful insects
8 Ladybird hotel
9 Nectar station for bees and butterflies
10 Bumble bee house
11 Bird table
12 Hedgehog house
13 Log-pile habitat
14 Mini wildflower meadow

Flowers for butterflies (7)
Attract butterflies with flowers such as Michaelmas daisies and they'll move on to pollinate your crops.

A wildflower meadow (14)
Plant a traditional meadow to benefit all wildlife – tall grasses provide safe cover for little creatures and birds like to eat the seeds, while wildflowers attract butterflies and bees.

Make a log pile (13)
Stack up logs, vines, and other twiggy trimmings, securing the pile in place with strong branches hammered in vertically, to create a habitat for frogs, newts, and toads, which shelter in the gaps.

Birds as pest control
Some birds snatch insects on the wing, other species eat at ground level – sparrows love to munch aphids and caterpillars.

Feed the birds (11)
Hang up fat balls packed with nuts and seeds.

Dig a pond (4)
Frogs, newts, and toads need water to breed – and the good news is they all eat slugs and other garden pests.

Bee hotel (6)
Bamboo canes in a plant pot will encourage solitary bees to take up residence.

A dew-covered spider's web
Spiders are an important part of a garden's ecosystem, playing their part in keeping down insect pests and being in turn a valuable food source for small garden birds like wrens.

Encouraging wildlife

Simply by gardening organically, without chemicals, you've already made your plot wildlife-friendly, even if you do nothing else. By adding a few extras such as nectar-rich flowers and a small pond or bird table to attract the right wildlife, we've noticed a positive effect on the productivity of our cultivated areas for little effort and outlay.

Making habitats

Different creatures like different environments. A shady log pile will shelter frogs and toads, while a rock pile in a sunnier spot will encourage slow worms. You need them on your plot because they all eat slugs.

A nettle patch attracts ladybirds. Adults and larvae eat huge amounts of aphids (up to a 100 a day!) and polish off pests such as potato beetles, mealy bugs and whitefly.

Set up a hedgehog house – a wooden box with a narrow entrance tunnel – to encourage hedgehogs to stay. They eat slugs and other pests such as cut worms and wire worms.

Create wildlife corridors

Use these to link habitats and help insects and small animals to move around the garden. All you need to do is leave areas along boundaries, under hedges, and against fences to grow unchecked. You could even ask your neighbours to do the same and the result would be a natural wildlife highway across your neighbourhood.

Planting for wildlife

Native plants are the best choice for encouraging biodiversity as they support a wider range of wildlife. Bees like flowers that are rich in nectar such as borage, lavender, lemon balm, mint, chives, and other herbs. Useful insects such as hover flies and parasitic wasps, which prey on aphids, prefer flat flowerheads packed with lots of tiny flowers, so plant dill, fennel, yarrow, daisies, and poached-egg plant.

Don't deadhead flowers – seedheads make good snacks for small seed-eaters. Cornflowers, teasel, and sunflowers are ideal.

Feeding

Put seeds and nuts out when natural food is in short supply, then birds will be used to visting your garden by the time insect pest populations build up. Feed early bees and butterflies when flowers are scarce by investing in a nectar station. It looks a bit like a bird feeder but it holds a sponge soaked with sugar water and is bright yellow to attract insects.

Nest boxes

We see birds as both friends and foes. It's great to have their company in the garden, but our fruit bushes need netting to prevent them from harvesting before us. On the other hand, birds like to eat insect pests, and so we encourage them to visit. Nest boxes help: set them up out of reach of cats, and facing between south-east and north to avoid them overheating in strong sunlight.

Insect houses

As well as a bee B&B (see opposite), leave clay pots stuffed with moss and dry grass at ground level for bumble bees, which hibernate underground.

Cater for overwintering ladybirds by opening a ladybird hotel. You can make your own by drilling a log full of holes (see the bee B&B for tips) and setting it vertically on a pole. Or cut short lengths of hollow bamboo and twigs, tie them into bundles and hang them around your plot.

These small changes can make a big difference to a useful insect's survival rate.

1. **Ox-eye daisies** have flat open flowers that attract useful insects. **2. Teasels** are great dual-purpose wildlife plants: bees like the flowers and birds eat the seeds. **3. Poppies** are another favourite of bees and other beneficial insects.

PROJECT Construct homes for wildlife

There are occasions when you can improve on nature. A home-made bee B&B makes an ideal shelter and nesting site for solitary pollinating bee species such as mason bees. And we'd say that digging a pond is one of the most wildlife-friendly steps you can take in your garden: it's a water source for small birds and mammals, and a vital breeding habitat for frogs.

BUILD A BEE B&B

1. Use a flat piece of wood for the base. Cut a log to size to fit the base.   **2. Drill** a range of holes in one end of the log using drill bits of various sizes. Drill at a slight upward angle so that rain can't drip in. **3. Add a bracket** to the base and screw the base to the log.   **4. Make a roof** with some spare wood.   **5. Attach the B&B** to a south-facing wall or fence, near bee-attracting plants, and wait for the bees to move in.

MAKE A WILDLIFE POND

Dig your pond at least 60cm (2ft) at its deepest. It must have a shallow area too. Rake the soil to remove sharp stones, then spread out the underlay and liner. Use one or two rocks to hold them in place while you fill with water. Edge with stones or rocks.

Fill your pond with rainwater if possible; if you have to use tap water, let the pond stand for a week to drive off any chlorine before adding plants.

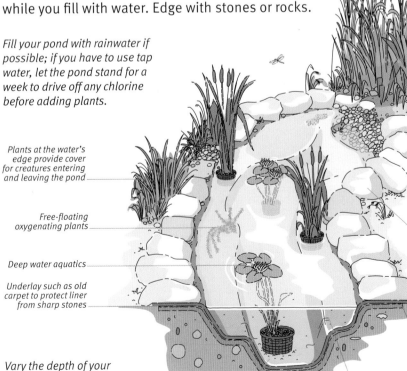

Shallow "beach" area for creatures to climb out easily

Plants at the water's edge provide cover for creatures entering and leaving the pond

Free-floating oxygenating plants

Deep water aquatics

Underlay such as old carpet to protect liner from sharp stones

Edging stones hold pondliner in place

Flexible pondliner fits any shape

Vary the depth of your pond to suit different plants and pondlife.

Deep water for pondlife to survive freezing

"Shelf" for shallow-water plants

Add oxygenating plants *A bucketful from another pond will also contain creatures from pond snails to water beetles and will boost biodiversity.*

Dragonflies *spend part of their lifecycle under water. They eat midges and other insect pests.*

Growing in urban spaces

Space may be restricted in towns and cities, but it's still possible to grow some of your own food in a small garden or even on a balcony or large windowsill. By using simple and intensive gardening methods you'll soon be picking salads and herbs, or even fruit and vegetables – and they can all be grown conveniently just outside your back door.

CROPS FOR URBANITES

If you have limited space, use these guidelines to decide what to grow.
■ Is it something you love to eat?
■ Is it expensive to buy?
■ Is it easy to grow?
■ Is it little work for a high yield?
If a crop ticks all of these boxes, go ahead and grow them.

Our suggestions

■ **Salads** are expensive to buy but easy to grow at home. Have a go at rocket and lamb's lettuce, or cut-and-come-again varieties, the leaves of which can be picked all summer.
■ **Easy growers** include garlic, onions, and carrots.
■ **Quick croppers** like radishes work well in between rows of slower-growing crops.
■ **Perennials** can be low maintenance and highly productive. Try perpetual spinach and soft fruit, as well as a selection of hardy herbs.
■ **High-yielding crops** should be your staples. These include runner beans, carrots, courgettes, leeks, swede, chard, and tomatoes.

Salad plants Keep picking rocket (top) all summer long; nasturtium flowers add a peppery tang to salads.

Think outside the box

Balconies, flat roofs, and even sloping roofs can all help to optimize your area for growing food, while using vertical walls makes sense in an urban environment where space is severely limited.

But you don't have to sacrifice everything for food production. Balancing productivity with a place to relax after work is easy to achieve if you rethink what is considered ornamental. Chard with colourful stems, architectural artichokes, and peas and beans grown for flowers as well as crops will all make your space more beautiful. And include flowers that work harder; some act as natural pest controls (see page 101) while others can be eaten (see page 157).

Growing in containers

Almost any fruit or vegetable will grow in a container, and this form of gardening offers a manageable introduction to growing your own. Container growing is cheap, easy, suitable for any size of plot, and movable. We spent years moving from house to house with our collection of kitchen-garden plants in pots, ranging from herbs to fig trees.
■ **Use any type of container** for growing plants, from terracotta pots and plastic bottles cut in half to old paint tins and buckets.
■ **Drill drainage holes** in the bottom of your containers. Cover the holes with a layer of broken pots or small stones to prevent them clogging up.
■ **Plants in pots are not self-reliant:** water them regularly, feed them, and replace the compost each spring.

Growing in raised beds

Raised beds are ideal for areas where there's no soil or it's poor quality. Building a raised bed (see page 126) makes planting and harvesting so convenient; you can even make beds at waist height to avoid back strain.
■ **A wide range of materials** can be used to build a raised bed.
■ **Raised beds on hard surfaces** are like containers, and you'll have to water and feed plants regularly.

Growing in hanging baskets

Hanging baskets aren't just for flowers you can grow fruit and vegetables in them too. Strawberries, tumbling tomatoes, salads, and herbs will thrive in them. Use a bracket to fix baskets to a wall, or hang edible hampers from trellis or fencing.
■ **Pests like slugs and snails** find scaling hanging baskets a mission impossible, especially if you hang them up with copper wire, which they will be loath to cross.
■ **Baskets dry out quickly**, which means they need regular watering, so consider an automatic irrigation system (see pages 110–111).

Growing vertically

Vertical growing imitates the natural world, which has three productive layers: trees, shrubs, and herbaceous plants (see forest gardens, page 99).
■ **Try interplanting**. Grow tall, thin vegetables between short bushy ones to maximize your space.
■ **Add climbing plants** – anything from runner beans to grape vines – to transform walls, fences, pergolas, and trellis into productive areas.

PROJECT # Plant up a hanging basket

We used a basket we made from willow withies, but you've probably got one lying around that will do just as well. You also need a tough plastic liner, such as a section of an old compost bag. We planted our basket with alpine strawberries. They're easy to grow from seed and produce fruit the same year. Or try salad leaf mixes, herbs such as thyme and basil, and tumbling cherry tomato plants.

YOU WILL NEED
- Basket
- Plastic for liner
- Compost, straw
- Copper wire
- Strawberry plants

1. Line the basket with plastic and pierce a few holes in it for drainage. Fill with compost. Use copper wire to make a handle to hang the basket. **2. Make holes** in the compost and insert the plants. Firm compost around plants. Water well. **3. Mulch with straw** to reduce evaporation and keep soil moist. **4. Hang** the basket up in a sunny spot. Water daily.

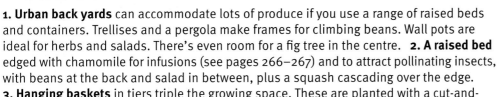

1. Urban back yards can accommodate lots of produce if you use a range of raised beds and containers. Trellises and a pergola make frames for climbing beans. Wall pots are ideal for herbs and salads. There's even room for a fig tree in the centre. **2. A raised bed** edged with chamomile for infusions (see pages 266–267) and to attract pollinating insects, with beans at the back and salad in between, plus a squash cascading over the edge. **3. Hanging baskets** in tiers triple the growing space. These are planted with a cut-and-come-again spicy salad leaf mix, which you can pick for many weeks over the summer.

Build a raised bed

Building a raised bed is a great way to turn a small space, even one where there is no soil, into a productive plot. Of all the different gardening methods we've experimented with, our raised beds take the least effort to maintain. They are easy to weed and water, there's less bending involved – ideal for older gardeners – and the soil doesn't get compacted as it is never walked on.

YOU WILL NEED
- Hammer
- Ruler
- Pencil
- Saw
- Electric drill
- Nails, screws
- Wood – salvaged floorboards are ideal and cheap
- Pond liner or tarpaulin
- Hardcore
- Compost

Decide where to build your bed. *We made ours against a south-facing wall to absorb more heat during the day and retain it overnight. It's shown planted with squash, chamomile, lettuce, and runner beans.*

BUILDING THE FRAME

1. Cut wood to length. Vary the lengths of the pieces, so that in the first layer the front overlaps the sides, in the second layer the sides overlap the front, and so on. Staggering the end joints in this way strengthens the frame. The average size for a raised bed that is easy to reach from all sides is 60cm x 90cm (2ft x 3ft). **2. Screw** each layer together. We used long Posidrive screws. **3. Build up the frame** in layers. **4. Strengthen** the finished frame by adding corner posts.

LINING AND FILLING THE BED

5. Line the bed. We used a piece of old pond liner and attached it to the wall using a wooden batten. **6. Fold the liner** to fit, then nail the edges to the frame. The liner stops moisture soaking into the wood and retains moisture in the compost. **7. Fill** the bottom 10cm (4in) with broken pottery and stones for drainage. Add good-quality compost, water it well and start planting.

TRY THIS
- **Lift some slabs** on your patio and use them to build a raised planter. Stand them on end and bury them up to half their depth for stability.
- **Dismantle an old rockery** and reuse the stone – it stores heat and keeps your plants' roots warm.
- **Experiment:** build walls from old car tyres (see page 48) or glass bottles cemented together. Or stack a few tyres on top of each other for an instant raised bed or potato tower.
- **Add "key holes"** to a deep raised bed. This creates an E-shaped bed, with recesses that allow you to reach plants at the back easily.

PROJECT **Make a wormery**

Conventional compost bins take up a lot of space and the process can be slow. A wormery turns kitchen waste into superb compost quickly, thanks to the action of brandling worms. These aren't earthworms but worms that live in leaf litter on top of the soil. A wormery re-creates their ideal habitat, which is warm, dark, and damp. The easiest thing to do is to buy a kit, which consists of a series of stackable units, and comes with a tub of worms. As you fill each unit with waste you simply add another on top. The worms also produce a liquid nutrient that filters down through the wormery – we call it worm tea. Dilute it about 1:10 with water before feeding it to your plants.

A wormery in action *takes up minimal space and even has room for a plant. Copper tape keeps slugs away.*

DO FEED YOUR WORMS
- Fruit and vegetable peelings
- Tea bags and coffee grounds
- Paper and cardboard (shredded)
- Old socks (not synthetic fabrics)
- Flowers
- Pet and human hair
- Fallen leaves
- Small amounts of grass cuttings
- Dust from the vacuum cleaner
- Raw egg shells

DON'T GIVE THEM
- Meat, fish, and dairy products
- Dog and cat faeces
- Too much citrus or too many onions
- Cooked food

ASSEMBLING THE WORMERY

1. Stand the base unit with the tap on a level piece of ground close to your kitchen. Push one of the corrugated rings firmly into place. These stop the worms escaping.   **2. Stack the unit** with the fine mesh bottom on top of the base unit and add the tub of worms to it.   **3. Feed the worms** with some fresh kitchen scraps. Chop up any big pieces first. Feed them small amounts until they settle in.   **4. Cover** them with shredded paper. Lift the paper up to add food. You can tell when the worms are coping with the waste you give them: they will be active and you'll see they are composting what you put in.

5. Add another corrugated ring and composter unit. Add a final ring to the top unit and put the planter on top to act as a lid.   **6. Fill** the planter with potting compost.   **7. Plant** the planter with vegetables or herbs. We added a courgette. The top planter doesn't benefit from the worms below – it's just a way of making every bit of space in your plot productive and a neat finishing touch to your wormery.

CARE TIPS

- **Start using** the unit above when the bottom composter is full of scraps. Take a couple of handfuls of worms and waste from the bottom layer to start up the next one. When the worms are in full production they will compost scraps within a couple of weeks.
- **Drain off** the worm tea weekly.
- **Inspect** your worms regularly. If the compost looks dry over the summer, add a little water. If it looks too damp, then add more paper, cardboard, or a bit of straw.
- **Don't add more scraps** if there are no worms on the surface of your food waste. Too much food will starve your worms of air, leading to a soggy slimy mess and eventually even worm fatalities.

Taking on an allotment

If you have a small garden, an allotment provides valuable extra space in which to grow your own food. Most are also very social places, where you can swap seeds, exchange produce, and pick up tips from other keen plot-holders. An allotment allows you to practise planting on a larger scale, too, and you can grow enough to preserve and store your produce for year-round use.

WHAT TO GROW

Try our recommended annual crops for first-time allotment holders.
- **Garlic** is very easy to grow and can be stored for months.
- **Leeks** are high-yielding crops for a winter harvest.
- **Beetroot** is another high-yielding crop. You can use the young leaves in salads, as well as the roots.
- **Squashes** store well for winter but they require a lot of space to grow.
- **Rainbow chard** is one of our favourites. It has incredibly colourful stems, and it grows quickly.
- **Radishes** grow rapidly – sow them between slower-growing crops.
- **Broad beans** can be sown in early spring and autumn for a steady seasonal supply, but watch out for pest damage and disease.
- **Climbing and runner beans** make the most of vertical space. Grow them at the northern end of your plot so they don't shade other crops.
- **Courgettes and summer squashes** need little work for a high yield. Try a no-watering policy (see page 101).
- **Potatoes** are a no-brainer on an allotment. If you want to optimize your space try growing them in stacks of tyres, barrels, or old compost bags, as well as in the ground.

Courgettes taste best *when small, before they turn into marrows.*

Assess your time

The problem with allotments is their sheer popularity. Waiting lists can be long, and by taking on an allotment you will inevitably be delaying someone else's chance to grow their own food, so if your garden at home isn't used for crops, cultivate that first. Also think about how much time you will be able to give; if you don't keep your allotment looking ship-shape, you might be asked to give it up. The obligation to keep your plot tidy and productive is a great incentive to get the most out of it, but the pressure can be daunting. We would recommend applying for your first allotment with a friend or neighbour if you are in any doubt about how you will cope.

Read the rules

Allotments are governed by bye-laws that vary across the country. On some it may be possible to keep hens, bees, pigeons, rabbits, even pigs, but you can expect restrictions on planting trees, putting up fencing or a shed, subletting, digging a pond, or using the plot for business purposes.

First steps

You rarely get to choose your plot, and will probably be forced to work with what you're given. This presents a great opportunity to do a mini site survey (see pages 170–171). Look at the slope of the land and type of soil. Note which areas get the most sunshine and which are shady.

Before you start planting, condition the soil with plenty of well-rotted manure and fertilizer (see pages 104–109), and perhaps some sharp sand, mushroom compost, or wood ash if it is heavy clay.

When deciding what to grow, think about what will be most suitable for each of your productive sites. For example, grow herbs and salads that you use most days at home – perhaps on a balcony or windowsill – and plant crops that require less attention on your allotment. You can also start seeds off at home, then transplant them to the allotment.

Grow perennials

One of the great things about perennials is that they need little maintenance – ideal if you don't have much time. They are also relatively hardy. You could go for soft fruit such as strawberries, raspberries, and

TIME-SAVING TIPS

- **Mulch areas** to reduce weed growth (see page 100) until you are ready to work them.
- **Try solarization**, which also helps to suppress weed growth. This novel technique involves laying clear plastic sheets over large freshly dug areas and keeping them in place with stones or wood. Once the ground has heated up to about 26°C (80°F), plant seedlings that you've grown on your windowsills at home, directly into the ground. Cut two slits in the plastic in a cross shape, peel it back and plant. Keep plants well watered. Any weeds that start to sprout under the plastic won't be able to withstand the heat and will wither and die. This is also a great way to reuse plastic.
- **A no-watering policy** for summer squashes and courgettes reduces the workload (see page 101).

gooseberries, and a variety of vegetables, including perennial rocket, perpetual spinach, globe and Jerusalem artichokes, and, of course, rhubarb. Although it's not edible, comfrey is also worth growing as a useful fertilizer (see page 107).

If your site has restrictions on planting trees, try dwarf varieties or training trees as cordons or step-overs – you may be able to fit them in without breaking the rules.

Access to water

Keeping plants well watered can be a challenge. Sites usually have taps, but they may not be close to your plot. To preserve water, plant your crops further apart than the recommended spacing, giving the roots more room to search for moisture. Also mulch between rows to reduce evaporation and help to retain soil moisture. If you have a shed on your allotment, attach a water butt to capture rainwater from the roof.

Sheds and structures

If you are allowed to put up a shed, it will save you carrying tools to and fro – especially useful if you live some distance away. Add a decent lock to store equipment safely. If you have a garden at home too, you'll need to double up on basics, such as a spade and fork. For the ultimate well-organized shed, see pages 130–131.

Other permanent structures to consider are a cold frame to protect small plants (see pages 112–113 and 116–117), and a double compost bin made out of old pallets to recycle all your allotment's organic waste.

1. **All the features** of an ideal allotment, including shed, compost heap, and organised beds. **2. Water butts** collect a significant amount of rainwater from a shed roof. **3. Plant runner beans** at the north end of your plot so they won't cast shade. **4. Fruit cages** and fleece tunnels protect plants from pests.

Setting up a well-equipped shed

The shed is the hub of Newhouse Farm, the store for the tools and equipment we need to keep it all going. We love our tools and tend to favour manual over mechanized. Of course some modern machines are best suited to getting a job done, yet in general, especially on a smallholding, we believe the more traditional tools really do help you become more connected to the land and thus more productive overall. Hand tools are also nearly always cheaper and easier to maintain.

KEY TO SHED

1. Spades
2. Garden fork
3. Rake
4. Post driver
5. Scythe
6. Long-handled shovel
7. Axe
8. Broom
9. Pitchfork
10. Sledge hammer
11. Hoe
12. Mattock
13. Pickaxe
14. Tool rack
15. Fishing rod (pp.215–216)
16. Shelving
17. Squashes storing over winter (pp.164–165)
18. Egg incubator, infra-red lamp (p.194)
19. Bee-keeping equipment (pp.212–213)
20. Demijohns for brewing (pp.254–261)
21. Hand trowel
22. Hand fork
23. Watering can
24. Petrol can
25. Plant pots
26. Dibber
27. Bin for animal feed
28. Wheelbarrow
29. Bucket
30. Spare wellies
31. Riddle
32. Lawnmower
33. Bee suits (pp.212–213)
34. Screw press (pp.256–261)
35. Apple chopping box (pp.260–261)
36. Straw for animal bedding
37. Sack trolley
38. Chitting potatoes (p.146)
39. Industrial wood chipper (pp.82–83)
40. Rotovator

Hanging tools up *saves space in a small shed.*

Spades (1) *receive plenty of use and it's worth investing in really solid ones that won't bend.*

A dibber (26) *is useful for repotting small plants and for planting onion sets. Look out for different sizes.*

A riddle (31) *is ideal for sieving soil or home-made compost to get rid of stones and bits of twig.*

Store squashes (17) *on the shelves if your shed is frost-free. Turn them regularly so they don't rot.*

Shelves and hooks *keep a big shed tidy and well organized. Use a floor-standing rack to stop tall tools falling over. Put trays and boxes on the shelves to store small items neatly.*

A screw press (34) *for squeezing fruit to make wine, cider, and juices.*

The scythe (5) *has been neglected lately, but we believe it is one of the smallholder's greatest tools.*

WHAT TO GROW The variety of plants that you can grow for food is absolutely amazing, from quick-growing salads to slow-maturing walnut trees. By growing under cover you can also try out some more exotic crops, for the sheer fun and challenge of it but also to reduce your food miles and still be able to enjoy a few tropical treats. Our philosophy is: try growing anything once and if it grows well and you enjoy eating it, grow it again! There is something very special about planting fruit and nut trees that you know will provide produce for generations to come. And don't ignore nature's larder of wild foods to forage...

Sowing and planting

Successful sowing and planting is all about getting the timing right – from starting seeds off under cover so that the seedlings are ready to plant out when there's no risk of frost, to waiting for the soil to warm up before sowing outside. You also need to keep sowing every month to guarantee a harvesting throughout the growing season. See pages 136–9 for a calendar to help plan your year.

Preparing the soil

Choose a warm area for a seed bed and add plenty of well-rotted organic matter, such as home-made compost, to improve it. Spread over the soil in autumn and fork in or leave the worms to do it for you. Compost not only adds nutrients, it also improves structure, making clay soils easier to work and sandy soils more moisture retentive.

Dig heavy clay soils in autumn and leave the frost to break up large clods. Any left in spring can be easily broken up with the back of a rake. Another option if your soil is clay or full of rubble, is to build raised beds on top of it (see page 126).

Before sowing seeds, rake the soil to achieve a crumbly, stone-free structure, known as a "fine tilth".

From seed to bed

Buy seeds from a catalogue or garden centre; we also save our own seeds from vegetables we have grown (see page 164). Having space to start some seeds off under cover is invaluable. Polytunnels, cloches and cold frames protect seedlings from frost and pests (see page 112), and in temperate regions, they allow you to start your growing season earlier and make the most of short summers.

We sow seeds in a range of trays, pots and modules, using our own home-made compost, sieved to remove lumps and twigs. Pots are ideal for big seeds such as courgettes and beans; module trays or egg boxes allow you to sow small seeds in individual units, which minimizes root disturbance when transplanting.

Thinning out

Seedlings grown in trays need thinning out so that they have more room to grow. Water them first, then hold a seedling between your thumb and forefinger and pull gently. Leave seedlings at 2.5–4cm (1–1½in) spacings. Transplant thinnings into seed trays to grow on – or eat them.

Hardening off

Plants grown under cover need to be acclimatized before transplanting outside. Set trays outside and bring them in at night, or open the lid of a cold frame during the day and close it at night, until there is no risk of frost.

Succession sowing

Sowing at intervals throughout the year maximizes the growing season and avoids gluts. For example, start peas off under cover in February to harvest in May; then sow a few rows each month from March to July, and you'll be picking till October.

1. Thinning and transplanting basil seedlings, to give them space to grow.
2. Raking to create a fine tilth ensures good contact between seed and soil.
3. Use a drill marker – string tied to two stakes – to sow seed in a straight line.
4. Add compost before planting out seedlings to give them a nutrient boost.

PROJECT **Basic techniques**

When you can see a pot or seed tray is full of roots, it's time to transplant seedlings. Sow seed outside when the soil has warmed up and is not too wet: follow packet instructions, but as a general rule, sow thinly and not too deep. Plant fruit trees and bushes in winter when they are dormant.

TRANSPLANTING SEEDLINGS

1. Gently ease the seedling (an alpine strawberry) out of the module. Hold it at the base of the stem and push up from below. **2. Use a dibber** to make a hole – either in a pot of compost or outside in the soil – and set the plant at the same depth it was growing at in the tray. **3. Firm the soil** round the roots and water well.

SOWING OUTDOORS

Use a spade to make a ridge in the seed bed. **1. Sow seeds** thinly into a shallow drill made by drawing your hand or the side of a rake through the top of the ridge. These are radish seeds. **2. Cover** with finely sieved soil tilth. **3. Tamp down** the sides of the ridge with a spade. Water and leave to grow. Thin out the seedlings after a week or two, if overcrowded.

PLANTING UP CUTTINGS

1. Measure out equal volumes of home-made compost and sharp sand. Sieve the compost to remove lumps. **2. Mix the compost and sand** well. Sand improves drainage and reduces the risk of rotting. **3. Use the mixture** to fill pots and push one cutting – these are gooseberries – into each pot. Water well and leave them to grow in a sheltered spot. Do not allow the pots to dry out.

PLANTING TREES

Dig a hole twice as wide and as deep as the rootball. Drive a stake into the hole before planting. **1. Plant the tree** at the same depth it was growing at – you'll see a soil line on the stem. Mix the excavated soil with compost and use it to fill in around the roots. Firm in gently with your foot. **2. Tie** an old bicycle inner tube round the trunk and nail it to the stake. **3. Water well**. Add a mulch, avoiding the stem.

PLAN THE GROWING YEAR: VEGETABLES

Our aim is to be able to harvest something to eat from our vegetable beds virtually all year round. For the most part we succeed, especially with a greenhouse and polytunnel as back-up. A key to achieving our aim is succession sowing (see page 134). By sowing a couple of rows of salad leaves every few weeks throughout the summer the plants mature at different times, giving us a staggered harvest. In autumn we carry on sowing and harvesting in the greenhouse for winter salads.

Use these charts to help you plan when to sow and when to harvest crops. We've indicated the best spacings between rows and between plants in a row. We've also

CROPS	SPACINGS		J	F	M	A	M	J	J	A	S	O	N	D
	ROWS	PLANTS												
Asparagus	45cm (18in)	45cm (18in)				P	H							
Aubergines	60cm (24in)	60cm (24in)	S	S	S	T	T		H	H	H			
Beetroot	23–30cm (9–12in)	10cm (4in)				S	S	S	SH	SH	H	H	H	
Broad beans	25cm (10in)	25cm (10in)		S	S	S	S	H	H	H	H		S	
Broccoli, sprouting	60–75cm (24–30in)	60–75cm (24–30in)		S	S	S	S	T	T	H	H	H	H	H
Brussels sprouts	25–45cm (14–18in)	25–45cm (14–18in)	H		S		T					H	H	H
Cabbages	30–50cm (12–20in)	30–50cm (12–20in)	H			S	S					H	H	H
Carrots	15cm (6in)	5–8cm (2–3in)		S	S	S	SH	SH	SH	H	H	H	H	H
Cauliflowers	50–75cm (20–30in)	50–75cm (20–30in)				S	S		T	H	H	H		
Celeriac	45cm (18in)	30cm (12in)			S	S	T			H	H			
Chillies		pot grown			S	S					H	H		
Courgettes/marrows	60–120cm (24–48in)	60–120cm (24–48in)					S	S	T	H	H	H		
Cucumbers	45–75cm (18–30in)	45–75cm (18–30in)			S	S	S	T		H	H			
French beans	45cm (18in)	10cm (4in)					S	SH	SH	H	H	H		
Garlic	15cm (6in)	15cm (6in)	S						H	H	H		S	S
Ginger		pot grown			P	P					H	H		
Globe artichokes	90cm (36in)	90cm (36in)				P			H	H	H			
Horseradish	30cm (12in)	30cm (12in)				P			H	H	H			
Jerusalem artichokes	90cm (36in)	45cm (18in)	H	P	P								H	H
Kale	30–60cm (12–24in)	30–60cm (12–24in)	H	H	SH	SH	SH	S	T					H
Kohl rabi	30cm (12in)	15cm (6in)				S	S	SH	SH	SH	H	H	H	

indicated where you can gain extra time by starting seeds off undercover before transplanting outside – or where a tender crop has to spend its entire lifecycle in a greenhouse. See pages 140–147 for more specific growing instructions on and our recommendations for the most rewarding vegetables to grow.

KEY TO CHART

S	sow		S	sow under glass
P	plant		P	plant under glass
T	transplant		T	transplant under glass
H	harvest		H	harvest under glass

CROPS	SPACINGS ROWS	PLANTS	J	F	M	A	M	J	J	A	S	O	N	D
Leaf beet	45cm (18in)	30cm (12in)	SH	SH	SH	SSH	SSH	H	H	H	H	H	H	H
Leeks	30cm (12in)	15cm (6in)	H	H	SH	SH	H	T	T		H	H	H	H
Onions	30cm (12in)	5–8cm (2–3in)			S	S	S	S	H	H	H			
Parsnips	20–30cm (8–12in)	10–15cm (4–6in)	H	SH	S				H	H	H	H	H	H
Peas	45–60cm (18–24in)	8–10cm (3–4in)		S	S	ST	ST	SH	SH	H	H			
Peppers	30–50cm (12–20in)	30–50cm (12–20in)		S	S	S			H	H	H	H		
Potatoes	45–75cm (18–30in)	30–38cm (12–15in)			P	P	P	H	H	H	H			
Pumpkin/squash	60–120cm (24–48in)	60–120cm (24–48in)				S	ST	S	H	H	H	H		
Radishes	15cm (6in)	2.5cm (1in)	S	S	S	S	SH	SH	SH	SH	H	H	H	
Rhubarb	90cm (36in)	90cm (36in)		H	PH	H	H	H	H			P	P	P
Runner beans	45cm (18in)	23cm (9in)				S	ST	S	H	H	H	H		
Salad leaves	25–45cm (10–18in)	25–45cm (10–18in)	H	SH	SH	SH	SH	SH	SH	SH	SH	SH	H	H
Scorzonera/salsify	30cm (12in)	15cm (6in)	H	H	S	S			H	H	H	H		
Shallots	23cm (9in)	10cm (4in)				S	S		H	H	H			
Sorrel	38cm (15in)	38cm (15in)		P	P				H	H	H	P	P	
Spinach	30cm (12in)	8–15cm (3–6in)	H	H	H	SH	SH	H	H	SH	SH	H	H	H
Swede	38cm (15in)	23cm (9in)	H	H				S	S			H	H	H
Sweetcorn	30–60cm (12–24in)	30–60cm (12–24in)				S	ST		H	H				
Tomatoes	25–45cm (10–18in)	25–45cm (10–18in)	S	S	S	S	T		H	HH	HH	HH	H	
Turnips	15–23cm (6–9in)	15–23cm (6–9in)	H	H	SH	S	S	S	S				H	H
Wild garlic	10cm (4in)	10cm (4in)			H	H	H					P	P	

PLAN THE GROWING YEAR: FRUIT AND NUTS

We've given spacings for between rows and between plants in a row for mature fruit and nut trees in case you're planning an orchard. But we realize that even one sweet chestnut is too many for average gardens. Patio varieties of fruit trees and pots of strawberries and blueberries make fresh fruit available to all.

KEY TO CHART

P	plant		P	plant under glass
H	harvest		H	harvest under glass
X	prune		X	prune under glass

CROPS	ROWS	PLANTS	J	F	M	A	M	J	J	A	S	O	N	D
Apples, pears	2.5–5m (8–18ft)	2.5–5m (8–18ft)	XP	XP	P					XH	XH	H	P	XP
Apricots, peaches	3.6–6m (12–20ft)	3.6–6m (12–20ft)	P	P	P	X		H	H	H	H	H	P	P
Blackberries	1.8–2.2m (6–7ft)	1.8–2.2m (6–7ft)	P	P	P				H	H	H	X		P
Black/red currants	1.8m (6ft)	1.8m (6ft)	P	P	P			H	H	H	H		XP	P
Blueberries	1.5m (5ft)	1.5m (5ft)	P	P	XP				H	H	H		P	P
Cape gooseberries	25–45cm (14–18in)	25–45cm (14–18in)				S	S				H	H		
Cherries	6–7m (20–25ft)	6–7m (20–25ft)	P	P	XP			H	H	H	H		P	P
Figs	3.6m (12ft)	3.6m (12ft)	P	P	P	X			H					P
Gooseberries	1.2–1.5m (4–5ft)	1.2–1.5m (4–5ft)	P	P	P			XH	XH	H			XP	P
Grapes	1.8m (6ft)	1.2m (4ft)	P	P	P							H	XP	P
Hazel/cobnuts	4.5m (15ft)	4.5m (15ft)	P	P					X		H	H	XP	P
Kiwi	3m (10ft)	3m (10ft)	P	P	P								H	P
Lemon		pot grown	XP	P	P					H	H		P	P
Medlar, quince	5–8m (12–25ft)	5–8m (12–25ft)	P	P	P						H	H	XP	P
Mulberry	4m (13ft)	4m (13ft)	P	P	P					H	H		P	P
Olives	1.8m (6ft)	1m (3ft 3in)	P	P	P								HP	XP
Pecan, honey locust	1.8–10m (6–33ft)	1.8–10m (6–33ft)	P	P	P						H	H	XP	P
Plums, damsons	2.4–4.5m (8–15ft)	2.4–4.5m (8–15ft)	P	P	P		X	X		H	H		P	P
Raspberries	2m (6ft 6in)	30–37cm (12–15in)	P	XP	P			H	XH	H	H	H	H	P
Strawberries	90cm (3ft)	45cm (18in)	P	P	P			H	H	H			P	P
Sweet chestnut		5m (16ft)	P	P	P						H	H	P	P

PLAN THE GROWING YEAR: HERBS

Herbs do well in pots, window boxes, and indoors on a windowsill, so everyone can grow them. Some can be picked all year round; others are annuals. We've indicated the best spacings between rows and between plants in a row. If you've got space to grow rows of annual herbs, you'll be able to dry some for winter.

KEY TO CHART

S	sow	**S**	sow under glass
P	plant		
T	transplant		
H	harvest	**H**	harvest under glass
X	prune		

CROPS	SPACINGS ROWS	PLANTS	J	F	M	A	M	J	J	A	S	O	N	D
Bay		1.2m (4ft)	H	PH	PH	H	H	H	XH	XH	H	PH	PH	H
Basil	30cm (12in)	20cm (8in)		S	S	S	TH	SH	SH	H	H	H		
Chives	30cm (12in)	30cm (12in)			S	S		H	H	H	H	H		
Coriander	30cm (12in)	15cm (6in)	H	H	S	S	S	SH	H	H	SH	SH	SH	SH
Dill	30cm (12in)	23cm (9in)				S	S	SH	SH	H	H			
Marjoram	20cm (8in)	60cm (24in)				S	S		H	H	H	H		T
Mint	30cm (12in)	30cm (12in)	H	H	PH	PH	H	H	H	H	H	H	H	T
Parsley	23-30cm (9-12in)	23-30cm (9-12in)					S	SH	SH	SH	H	H		
Rosemary	15cm (6in)	90cm (36in)	H	H	H	S	H	H	XH	XPH	H	H	H	H
Sage	15cm (6in)	60cm (24in)			S	S	S	S	XH	XH	H	H		
Tarragon	60cm (24in)	60cm (24in)					P	H	H	H	H			T
Thyme	60cm (24in)	15cm (6in)	H	H	H	H	P	PH	XH	XH	H	H	H	H

Plant up basil thinnings and grow them on for even more plants. Growing Mediterranean herbs such as basil under cover guarantees success.

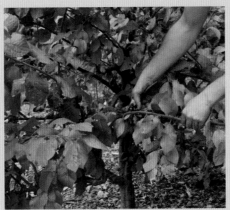

Pruning and training apples and other fruit trees boosts the crop, helping fruit ripen by opening up the tree and letting in more light (see pages 154–155).

Squashes and courgettes are staples in our kitchen. We enjoy courgettes in summer and store squashes for winter soups (see pages 164–165).

VEGETABLES TO GROW

Nothing beats the satisfaction of picking and cooking your own home-grown produce, from the first runner beans to late winter leeks. The biggest problem is deciding what to grow in the first place. We see it as a matter of balancing the "must haves" with the "should haves" and adding a few of the vegetables we think are a bit decadent, such as globe artichokes. You also need to take into account the suitability of your soil: there's more information on this on pages 104–109.

The must haves

These are the basics that give you crops to eat all year (for tables of the growing year, see pages 136–139). With a little planning and succession planting you'll be able to pop out to the garden to harvest something useful at any time of year. Sow seed outdoors, unless otherwise stated.

Beetroot (1)

Beta vulgaris

■ **How to grow** Beetroot has a long season: succession sow monthly throughout spring and summer, starting in April. Sow thinly, a couple of seeds every 10cm (4in), about 2.5cm (1in) deep and in rows about 30cm (1ft) apart. Thin them out when the seedlings are about 2.5cm (1in) tall.

■ **Problem solving** Beetroot needs regular watering or it will be tough and woody to eat.

■ **Harvest, cook, store** When harvesting, twist off the leaves 5cm (2in) above the roots to stop them bleeding. Store in clamps or in a box of sand in a cool place (see pages 164–165). Young leaves can be used in salads and when thinning rows the small beetroots are tasty too.

SUPPORTING BROAD BEANS

Taller varieties of broad bean need support to stop them flopping over and the beans becoming an easy target for slugs. Trellis laid horizontally does the trick. Knock in stakes about 30cm (1ft) tall at each corner of the bed to hold it in place.

Broad beans (2)

Vicia faba

■ **How to grow** It is mild in Cornwall in the far south-west of England so we sow our broad beans in November for an early harvest. Elsewhere sowing is usually February to May. Sow about 10cm (8in) apart and 5cm (2in) deep. We tend to plant in blocks so we can use trellis to support the growing beans (see box), though staggered pairs of rows with a 60cm (2ft) gap between them works well.

■ **Problem solving** The biggest pest is blackfly: pinch out all the growing tips where they gather. If you do this before they really take hold, you should have lots of succulent, untouched bean tops to eat.

■ **Harvest, cook, store** You should be able to pick beans from late spring all the way through to early autumn. They can also be dried for winter use, when they'll need soaking for 8 hours and boiling for 40 minutes. In spring, steam bean tops or cook them in butter.

Broccoli (3)

Brassica oleracea
Cymosa Group

■ **How to grow** Purple-sprouting is the hardiest and most prolific variety – that's why we grow it. It's a great vegetable for late autumn and winter. Sow the seed in individual plugs or very thin drills in April under cover. When robust enough, transplant seedlings to their final growing position outdoors: leave about 45cm (18in) between them as the mature plants are huge.

■ **Problem solving** Birds love broccoli too, so hang up a bird scarer or protect plants by stringing cotton between twigs to stop birds landing. Stake plants as they grow or try the trellis support system (see box): they can get top-heavy.

■ **Harvest, cook, store** Cut stems before flower buds open. Cut the central spear first. Keep cutting and plants will carry on producing for most of the winter, provided you don't strip all the stems at once. Purple sprouting is great stir-fried. Broccoli can be frozen, but the result is such a poor imitation of the fresh vegetable that we don't bother.

Brussels sprouts (4)

Brassica oleracea
Gemmifera Group

■ **How to grow** It wouldn't be Christmas without Brussels sprouts. For the festive season sow your Brussels around Easter in individual plugs or thinly in drills under cover; transplant seedlings at the end of May, leaving at least 60cm (2ft) space between them, and then wait for winter.

5 6 7 8

■ **Problem solving** Brussels are a low-maintenance veg, but watch out for birds, which will eat seedlings as well as helping themselves to the final crop. Protect seedlings by stringing cotton between twigs; hang bird scarers near mature plants.

■ **Harvest, cook, store** Start picking sprouts from the base of the stem – use a sharp knife. Don't forget, sprout tops are also good eating. Sprouts can be frozen (blanch them first) but we prefer to eat them in season.

GROW CARROTS IN LOO ROLLS

Grow carrots in cardboard tubes from the middle of loo rolls. These make great biodegradable pots: fill them with compost and plant seeds in the top. The narrow tube encourages long straight root growth and makes transplanting really easy.

Carrots (5)
Daucus carota

■ **How to grow** Sow carrots thinly in rows 15cm (6in) apart and set the seeds about 1cm (½in) deep. Sow in succession from late winter through to early summer. There are lots of varieties, from carrots shaped like golf balls to roots that come in shades of yellow, white and purple. They all have one thing in common – they taste great.

■ **Problem solving** Companion plant with onions to deter carrot fly, which will help to protect the onions against onion fly too.

■ **Harvest, cook, store** You should be able to harvest from June to December if you have succession planted. Lift maincrop carrots in October before the frosts and store in a clamp (see page 165) or root cellar (page 181). Pulled straight from the ground, wiped on a sleeve, and then crunched, carrots are a good way to get kids to eat vegetables. We like roast carrots and grating them into carrot cake.

Celeriac (6)
Apium graveolens var. *rapaceum*

■ **How to grow** There is no doubt that every kitchen garden needs celery or celeriac – the flavour is invaluable in so many dishes. We chose celeriac as it's easier to grow. Raise seedlings under cover in early spring. Plant them out at the end of May, about 30cm (12in) apart and 45cm (18in) between rows.

■ **Problem solving** Generally maintenance free, though slugs can be a problem.

■ **Harvest, cook, store** Harvest the roots from autumn and all through winter – leave them in the ground rather than lifting and storing. Eat them raw or cooked: they are a pain to prepare because it is difficult to scrub all the dirt off, but practice makes perfect. The leafy tops can be used in warming winter broths.

Courgettes, squashes, and pumpkins (7)
Cucurbita family

■ **How to grow** We grow a lot of squashes and courgettes. Sow seeds under cover in April, in individual pots. Plant them out at the end of May. We always follow a no-watering policy (see page 101), which saves us a lot of hard work. Squashes and pumpkins take up a lot of space, but are good trailing down over raised beds, or grow them up netting and trellis.

■ **Problem solving** Slip a square of old carpet or slate under larger fruits to keep them clean and stop them rotting.

■ **Harvest, cook, store** It's essential to keep picking courgettes and summer squashes while they are young: miss a couple of days and all of a sudden you have marrows in your vegetable rack. Frying garlic, courgettes, summer squashes, and a handful of tomatoes in olive oil makes a very quick and easy, colourful meal. Store squashes and pumpkins on open shelves in a frost-free outbuilding. They will keep for months and are a useful standby for winter soups.

Kale (8)
Brassica oleracea Acephala Group

■ **How to grow** Kale is an old-fashioned vegetable and appears to have fallen from favour somewhat – we think it deserves better. It is very hardy and tasty, plus it's dead easy to grow and will flourish nearly everywhere. Sow seed in May and transplant the seedlings in July to their final position.

■ **Problem solving** More or less trouble-free.

■ **Harvest, cook, store** Pick kale from November all the way through to the following May. It's a great standby – we nip out and whip off some nice-looking leaves when we need greens in a hurry. There are a number of different varieties – we like the curly kale. Like most brassicas it can be frozen, but we think it is only truly tasty and appetizing when freshly picked.

1

2

3

4

Leeks (1)
Allium porrum

■ **How to grow** Growing prize leeks is a mystical art, but we're just interested in growing them to cook with. We sow them in drills about 15cm (6in) apart and 1cm (½ in) deep. When they're big enough to transplant – when they are about 20cm (8in) tall – we get a handful of the plants, twist off all but 5cm (2in) of the green, and separate them. Using a dibber, we make holes in the ground, about 5cm (2in) deep, and then place one leek in each hole. A good watering will fill the hole sufficiently – there's no need to firm the soil in place. They grow well, even in cold, wet areas.

■ **Problem solving** More or less trouble-free.

■ **Harvest, cook, store** Leeks may look like they're growing in the plot most of the year, but that's because they can be left in the ground and lifted as needed, from September all the way through to May. It's comforting to know they are out there to be harvested all winter. Always ease the plant out of the ground with a fork or you will end up tearing off the outside layers or even pulling the leek apart. Please don't forget exactly how good the green part of the leek is. For some reason supermarkets have a tendency to chop off all the greenery to make handling and display more convenient – what they are really doing is throwing away the goodness. By all means chop off the tips, but cook the rest!

Onions and shallots (2)
Allium family

■ **How to grow** Onions are usually pretty cheap to buy but there is something special about having a plait of your own home-grown hanging up ready to use. We grow onions from sets – miniature onion bulbs – rather than from seed, because the plants have better disease resistance. We plant them out in late winter, spacing them 10cm (4in) apart, in rows about 25cm (10in) apart.

■ **Problem solving** Onions grown from sets have a tendency to "bolt" or flower too early. If this happens, cut off the flower stalk and use the onion straight away.

■ **Harvest, cook, store** The delicate flavour of shallots makes them popular with chefs but we mainly use them very early in the season as a substitute for spring onions – mature shallots are small and fiddly to prepare. Spring-onion-size shallots are usually ready long before the first true spring onions. Main-crop onions are ready to harvest around July.

Parsnips (3)
Pastinacea sativa

■ **How to grow** We know parsnips are not as popular as they were but we felt they had to be on our "must have" list. Our efforts at growing them have been quite hit and miss. The little seeds can blow away easily, so take care when planting: we spread them very thinly, a couple of seeds every 15cm (6in), in rows 30cm (12in) apart, at a depth of 1cm (½in). We sow them around Easter. They are slow to germinate. Thin out when the parsnips are the size of a golf ball.

■ **Problem solving** Dig over the soil and pick out stones to avoid growing misshapen roots. Improving the soil with well-rotted compost helps to produce long, straight parsnips.

■ **Harvest, cook, store** We dig our parsnips from October

GROWING PEAS IN GUTTERING AND SUPPORTING WITH WILLOW STICKS

When starting off peas under cover we grow them in waste lengths of plastic guttering, with holes drilled in it for drainage. We sow the seed in zig-zag formation. When the seedlings are big enough and the risk of frost is past, it is really easy to slide them off the guttering into a prepared trench outside.

Support peas with sticks to stop them trailing on the ground and becoming slug food. There is absolutely no point in buying bundles of pea sticks: any twigs and small branches will do the job of keeping the pea plants off the ground and growing upwards. We use willow offcuts left over from pollarding our trees: we like to find a use for every scrap.

5 6 7 8

to the following Easter. The parsnips are happy sitting in the ground waiting for you to come and get them, but the tops wither away so you have to remember where you planted them. We really enjoy eating them, either roasted or curried in soup. They are a family favourite, and let's not forget they were one of our staple foods before the potato turned up. The thinnings are lovely cooked in butter.

Peas (4)
Pisum sativum

■ **How to grow** Sow peas under cover in late winter and plant out when the risk of frost has passed. Continue sowing every couple of weeks until early summer, sowing outside once the weather warms up.

■ **Problem solving** Using pea sticks to support plants helps to reduce slug damage (see left). Taller varieties may need further support, such as netting stretched between posts.

■ **Harvest, cook, store** Start picking in June and continue until September. The first peas of the year are great to eat straight from the plants; when tiny we munch the whole pods as raw mangetout. The growing tips are tasty sautéed in butter and the empty pods can be turned into a lovely country wine (see page 258).

Radishes (5)
Raphanus sativus

■ **How to grow** It is so quick and easy to grow radishes that many gardeners think it beneath them. By summer you may have had a surfeit, but we always keep a row or two on the go. Sow seed in drills about 15cm (6in) apart and 1cm (½in) deep, from February to August. Radishes are also great sown as a quick crop in between rows of slower-growing veg.

■ **Problem solving** Flea beetles may attack the leaves but the

FORCING RHUBARB

We "force" rhubarb by covering plants with a heap of well-rotted manure in spring and putting an old half barrel on top. We take the barrel off when the pale shoots emerge from the top of the rich manure. Tradition says that once a plant has been forced, it needs to rest for two years before you do it again, but we force our rhubarb plants every year and they are fine!

radishes themselves aren't usually affected.

■ **Harvest, eat, store** Pull radishes while they are still small: the larger they are, the tougher they can be, and the hotter. Enjoy them fresh in salads – you can't store them for any length of time.

Rhubarb (6)
Rheum x *hybridum*

■ **How to grow** Yes, we know you eat it like a fruit, but rhubarb is a stalwart perennial of the veg plot. It's easiest grown from crowns – rooted pieces of plant. Set them 90cm (3ft) apart. Create more plants by dividing every five years.

■ **Problem solving** Generally trouble-free.

■ **Harvest, cook, store** Leave new plants to establish for a year, then harvest any time from February until July. Pull the stalks, don't cut them. As well as crumbles and fools, rhubarb can be used in chutney and jam. It freezes well. Don't forget the leaves are toxic.

Runner beans (7)
Phaseolus coccineus

■ **How to grow** Sowing runner beans in pots in the greenhouse and transplanting them out as early as the frost allows is one of our yearly rituals. You can also sow straight into the ground later on. We grow

ours on wigwams; leave 23cm (9in) between plants, stick in bamboo canes and tie them together at the top.

■ **Problem solving** Lots of people are put off runner beans because they think they are tough and stringy. There is absolutely no reason to suffer tough beans. You can buy "stringless" varieties, but by far the easiest answer is to pick them young and often.

■ **Harvest, cook, store** Keep picking so the plants keep producing: surpluses can be blanched – plunged in boiling water briefly – and frozen.

Salad leaves (8)
Lactuca and others

■ **How to grow** Growing salad, especially lettuce (*Lactuca*) and rocket (*Eruca*), is one of the easiest things to do well. Sow thinly in drills 30cm (12in) apart and 1cm (½in) deep. This ensures that the seeds are well spread out and not as much thinning is needed. Choose "cut and come again" varieties and sow in succession – you'll be cutting salad all summer long.

■ **Problem solving** Use beer traps and plastic collars made from cut-down bottles against slugs, and encourage natural predators (see pages 166–167).

■ **Harvest, eat, store** Cut the leaves in the morning when they are freshest.

Spinach (1)
Spinacia oleracea

■ **How to grow** We reckon Popeye had the right idea; spinach is good for you – and it's very easy to grow. To pick spinach all year round, keep succession planting in rows about 30cm (12in) apart and at a depth of 2.5cm (1in). Don't be tempted to plant too much at once, as the leaves are best eaten young. There are varieties of perpetual spinach but in our opinion they don't taste

anywhere near as good as annual spinach.

■ **Problem solving** Can "bolt" or run to seed if it doesn't get enough water.

■ **Harvest, cook, store** We cut off handfuls with a pair of scissors: it will grow again quite quickly, allowing for a second harvest. Sadly, after all the effort of picking and washing, spinach cooks down to very little. The young leaves are great raw in salad. Blanch the leaves before freezing them.

Tomatoes (2)
Lycopersicon esculentum

■ **How to grow** Tomatoes are an easy crop to grow on window sills, balconies, under cover and outside. At Newhouse Farm we grow the majority of our tomatoes in the greenhouse, starting them off in small pots and trays in March, and transplanting them to bigger pots as they mature. Keeping them in pots does require quite a lot of compost and watering, but they do extremely well. Tomatoes need feeding regularly. We use our worm tea (see page 127) and comfrey fertilizer (see page 107); they help the tomato plants to remain healthy for significantly longer each season. Support plants with canes or tie them in to strings running down from the greenhouse roof.

PINCHING OUT TOMATOES

Pinching out the diagonal side shoots that grow at an angle between the side shoots and the main stem of a tomato plant encourages the plant to form fewer, bigger fruits. If you don't do it, you get lots of smaller fruits. You can pot up the pinched-out side shoots and grow them on into new plants, if you have time.

■ **Problem solving** We have problems with blight, which is a disease that damages tomatoes and potatoes: we've tried to counter the problem by growing the plants upside down, which is meant to prevent blight from establishing. Use a hanging container and plant young tomato plants through a hole in the base; the plants' roots grow upwards. In our experience it's reasonably effective – and a good talking point.

■ **Harvest, cook, store** Pick tomatoes when they are completely ripe: cut them just above the flower stalk. Try growing different varieties for cooking, salads, etc. If you have a glut, freeze tomatoes – skin them first, then cook them for 10 minutes or so and sieve to make your own home-made passata. They also bottle well (see page 240). At the end of the season green tomatoes make great chutney, or ripen in a bowl with a banana.

The should haves

If time and space are tight then you may have to sacrifice some of the "should haves", but if you can squeeze them in, they are all worth growing.

Asparagus (3)
Asparagus officinalis

■ **How to grow** It is worth having an asparagus bed for

the sheer seasonal indulgence, even though it takes time for the plants to establish. Plant one-year-old "crowns" in April (see box opposite).

■ **Problem solving** Go out after dark with a torch and pick off any slugs – feed them to your hens or ducks.

■ **Harvest, cook, store** Cut your first spears two years after planting and then annually in late spring. Start cutting when the spears are 10cm (4in) long. Use a knife to cut them off just below the surface of the soil. Stop cutting in June and allow the plant to grow. We love the spears simply steamed and served with butter. You could freeze some if you have spare.

Cabbage (4)
Brassica oleracea
Capitata Group

■ **How to grow** Some people may class cabbage as a "must have" crop, but there are other brassicas that we would rather grow. Of course, there is nothing nicer than a neat row of cabbages if you have the space. Sow spring cabbages in summer and Savoys in spring for winter eating.

■ **Problem solving** Birds will peck at the seedlings, so set up a bird scarer (see page 167). Caterpillars can be a problem later on; pick them off by hand and feed them to your hens.

5 **6** **7** **8**

■ **Harvest** Cut spring cabbages from April onwards and Savoys in winter. As before, we don't think brassicas freeze that well from a taste point of view.

Cucumbers (5)
Cucumis sativus
■ **How to grow** Cucumbers are relatively easy to grow and every year we marvel at how many we get from each plant. In our first year at Newhouse Farm we picked well over a hundred from one plant!

Okay, it's confession time – our cucumbers look nothing like the ones you buy in the shop. They tend to be a lot shorter and fatter and, dare we say, tastier. Sow seed under cover in April or outside in June.
■ **Problem solving** Spray greenhouse cucumbers with water to increase humidity and discourage red spider mite.
■ **Harvest, cook, store** Carry on cutting cucumbers until the first frosts. Try pickling them if you have a glut, or make tzatziki.

PLANTING ASPARAGUS CROWNS

Dig a trench and make a shallow mound at the bottom of it. Set the crowns on the shallow mound, placing them at least 45cm (18in) apart. Spread out the roots and cover them with soil. Keep mounding up the soil as the plants grow, so that you end up with them growing on a ridge. This will get higher over the years as you add

mulches and well-rotted manure. Asparagus plants are perennial, so site the bed carefully – you can't start moving them around. For the same reason, you must pull out every bit of couch grass, ground elder, dock, and any other pernicious weeds before you plant your asparagus because they will be impossible to dig out later.

French beans (6)
Phaseolus vulgaris
■ **How to grow** French beans are less prolific than either broad or runner beans. From a 3m (10ft) row you can expect 9kg (20lb) broad beans, 27kg (60lb) runner beans and a mere 4.5kg (10lb) French beans – however, they are very fine eating. Sow seeds outside in May and carry on succession sowing until late June.
■ **Problem solving** Young seedlings are vulnerable to slugs so set plenty of beer traps. Support your beans with trellis or willow wigwams and avoid them being easy targets for ground pests.
■ **Harvest, cook, store** Pick beans from July to October. Like runner beans, you can leave the pods on the plant to fatten up and then dry the beans for winter use – or blanch and freeze the tender young beans.

Globe artichokes (7)
Cynara cardunculus
Scolymus Group
■ **How to grow** Globe artichokes are magnificent, thistle-like perennial plants that take up a lot of space for very little produce. That said, we love them and they taste great. For best results plant rooted offsets (like suckers taken from the base of a mature plant): it's easier than growing from seed.

■ **Problem solving** Set beer traps for slugs while plants are small. Once they are full size they can cope with a few tattered leaves.
■ **Harvest, cook, store** Wait a year before harvesting the heads, then cut them every summer. Pick them before they flower, when they become a popular hideout for insects. You can pickle the bases or "hearts" but preparing them is a bit fiddly and time-consuming.

Jerusalem artichokes (8)
Helianthus tuberosus
■ **How to grow** Jerusalem artichokes are prolific, but we know very few people who consume the whole harvest. Our pigs usually benefit from part of ours. Although they are tasty, we have nicknamed them "fartichokes" because of their propensity to cause wind. Think carefully about where you site them: these 2.2m (7ft) high daisies are invasive and once you've planted them they are nearly impossible to get rid of. But on an exposed plot they make a great, productive wind break with pretty flowers.
■ **Problem solving** More or less trouble-free.
■ **Harvest, cook, store** Dig up tubers from November onwards. Roast them along with other veg or make them into soup.

145

1 2 3 4

Kohl rabi (1)

Brassica oleracea
Gongylodes Group

■ **How to grow** Kohl rabi is not very popular in Britain but has a following in Europe. Sow seed from April to July.

■ **Problem solving** Use a bird scarer to keep birds away from the young plants.

■ **Harvest, cook store** Leave in the ground and dig up as needed from midsummer on. Simply trim off the leaves, scrub and slice. They make a cracking gratin or mash them with butter.

Potatoes (2)

Solanum tuberosum

■ **How to grow** Space is the only reason we have not listed spuds as a "must have". You can buy local potatoes cheaply in season. But they never taste as good as those dug from the garden and put on the plate within the hour! Plant seed potatoes from late March to April depending on whether they are earlies or maincrop.

■ **Problem solving** Protect against frost by drawing soil over leaves with a hoe.

■ **Harvest, cook, store** Dig earlies from June, maincrop from September. Harvest promptly before slugs move in. Home-grown potatoes are sweet and tasty with a little butter. Store maincrop varieties in a clamp (see page 165).

146

Swedes and turnips (3)

Brassica napobrassica and *B. rapa*

■ **How to grow** We plant more than we will ever need of these great winter staples and use the less perfect ones to feed our pigs. Sow seed in May.

■ **Problem solving** Keep birds away from the young plants.

■ **Harvest, cook, store** Dig up roots from October onwards. Store in a clamp (see page 165). Some of us love mashed swede; others claim it is punishment, not nutrition.

CHITTING POTATOES

Seed potatoes should be encouraged to begin sprouting (or "chitted") before you plant them outside. Several months before planting, lay the potatoes out in a dry, cool, frost-free place. It should be light, but out of direct sunlight – a shed with a window is ideal.

Sweetcorn (4)

Zea mays

■ **How to grow** Sweetcorn need plenty of sun to ripen the cobs successfully. Sow under cover in April and plant out after danger of frost has passed.

■ **Problem solving** Stake plants on windy sites.

■ **Harvest, cook, store** Pick the cobs in late August/September. Eat as soon as possible after picking before the sugar content turns to starch.

Why not try

We wouldn't give these top priority, but that doesn't mean you shouldn't experiment with the following veg.

Aubergine (5)

Solanum melongena

■ **How to grow** Here in the far south west of the UK we can get away with growing aubergines outside but we usually have some in the greenhouse too. Start seed off in pots in March under cover. Stake and feed plants as for tomatoes.

■ **Problem solving** Red spider mite can be a problem. Reduce the risk by spraying with water to keep the humidity up.

■ **Harvest, cook, store** Pick aubergines once they are at least 10cm (4in) long and the skin is shiny. Watch out for the prickles on the little green caps and on the stalks.

Cauliflower(6)

Brassica oleracea
Botrytis Group

■ **How to grow** Cauliflowers are challenging to grow, needing well-manured soil that hasn't been recently dug and, above all, regular watering. Grow different varieties and you can cut cauliflowers from spring to autumn. Sow seed in spring and thin seedlings as they grow. Transplant so that mature plants will be 60cm (2ft) apart.

■ **Problem solving** Keep birds away from the young plants with home-made scarers.

■ **Harvest, cook, store** To eat them at their best, cut them while the heads are still tightly packed – loose florets mean they are past their prime. Fold in the leaves and cover with a piece of slate for a week first. We've got a great recipe for piccallili and we like the florets raw with dips. If you want to freeze caulis, separate the florets and blanch them first.

Chilli (7)

Capsicum annuum

■ **How to grow** Chillies are really easy to grow. At Newhouse Farm we have tried everything from small Scotch bonnets that blow your socks off to more refined banana peppers. All are fast-growing annuals that do best in warm summers and like a bit of

5   6   7   8

humidity. In temperate climates they are definitely best grown under cover and sown in spring.
■ **Problem solving** Look out for red spider mite – misting with water can help prevent attacks and chillies like the humidity.
■ **Harvest, cook, store** We use chillies in fresh salsas and curries and with roasted seeds and nuts. To dry them, string them up and hang in a dry, airy spot. You can freeze chopped chillies – remove seeds first.

SPROUTING SEEDS

Sprouted seeds are nutritious and tasty in salads. Our favourites include radish, broccoli, sunflower (shell them first), and chickpea. First, soak them in water for 24 hours. Then lay them in a sieve in a well-lit position. Every day rinse the seeds with clean water and tip them back in the sieve. They will sprout 4 or 5 days later. Rinse, shake, and store in a fridge – eat within two days.

Ginger
Zingiber officinale
■ **How to grow** If you like fresh ginger, try growing your own from a root from the grocer or supermarket. Look for a portion of root that has a bud on it. Start it off in a small pot in spring and repot as it grows. Grow ginger under cover in temperate climates. It's a tall plant with grass-like leaves.
■ **Problem solving** As ever, in the greenhouse, red spider mite is a problem. Spray with water.
■ **Harvest, cook, store** Tip out the pot in autumn and harvest your roots. Replant a bit and use the rest. We use it to make ginger beer (see pages 254–255). You can freeze ginger.

Horseradish
Armoracia rusticana
■ **How to grow** Horseradish grows in moist, rich soil and can tolerate a shady position.
■ **Problem solving** It is highly invasive: plant it in a secluded part of the garden where you can easily restrain it.
■ **Harvest, cook, store** Instead of buying jars of horseradish sauce we now make our own. You can dig up and harvest horseradish about nine months after planting: save the smaller roots for replanting. It tastes extremely good with smoked mackerel. Freeze the roots or store in a clamp (see page 165).

Leaf beet (8)
Beta vulgaris var. *flavescens*
■ **How to grow** Leaf beet, or chard, is easy to grow – we often find it self seeds and pops up in the veg bed unannounced. Sow seed in April and thin the seedlings to 30cm (1ft) apart. Rainbow chard has ruby red, orange, yellow and pink stems.
■ **Problem solving** Trouble-free, apart from the odd bit of slug damage to leaves.
■ **Harvest, cook, store** Pick leaves all summer long. We like leaf beet as you get two veg for the price of one: steam the stalks and cook the leaves separately like spinach. Freeze them in the same way too.

Peppers
Capsicum annuum
■ **How to grow** Grow peppers just as you would tomatoes but keep them in the greenhouse.
■ **Problem solving** If stems flop over stake them up.
■ **Harvest, cook, store** Pick peppers in late summer.

Salsify
Tragopogon porrifolium
■ **How to grow** These root vegetables look like small, thin, darker-coloured parsnips but taste vaguely mushroom-like. Sow in April.
■ **Problem solving** Plant seeds in a deep compost-filled hole for straight roots.

■ **Harvest, cook, store** Dig up in October and cook immediately, Peel them once they're cooked.

Scorzonera
Scorzonera hispanica
■ **How to grow** A root vegetable similar to salsify, but with black skin. Sow in April.
■ **Problem solving** See salsify.
■ **Harvest, cook, store** Dig up in October. Blanch and eat in salads. Store salsify and scorzonera in a clamp or root cellar (see pages 165 and 181).

Sorrel
Rumex acetosa
■ **How to grow** Sorrel likes a shaded damp spot.
■ **Problem solving** If a plant starts to look a bit tired, divide it and replant the pieces.
■ **Harvest, cook, store** Pick regularly and add to soups and salads. It has a lovely lemony flavour and is good for making your own pesto.

Wild garlic
Allium ursinum
■ **How to grow** Order plants from a nursery. Plant in a shady damp spot to mimic its habitat.
■ **Problem solving** Generally trouble-free.
■ **Harvest, cook, store** Pick leaves in spring for best flavour and add to soups, salads, and risottos. The flowers are edible too: add them to salads.

1

2

3

4

FRUIT AND NUTS TO GROW

Growing a wider range of fruit and nuts is one of the advantages of a smallholding. In an average-sized garden it's easy to add climbers such as grape vines and kiwis, while blueberries and dwarf fruit trees thrive in pots on a patio.

Soft fruit

The great thing about soft fruit is that you don't have to wait long for results. Unless otherwise stated, plant as bare-root plants from October to March. They need little maintenance other than weeding and mulching, and yields can be phenomenal.

Blackberries (1)

Rubus fruticosus

■ **How to grow** Here at Newhouse Farm we would never plant blackberries – but that's because we are lucky enough to have lots in the hedgerows. Once a year they cease to be thorny invaders and become prickly baskets of tasty fruit. If you need to buy plants look out for thornless varieties – ideal for smaller spaces – and juicy hybrids like loganberries and tayberries. Grow on wires and posts or train against a wall.

■ **Problem solving** On a smallholding and in many gardens brambles can be a nightmare. If you inherit some wild brambles on your plot, try to tame them by shaping them into easily accessible blocks.

■ **Prune** If growing blackberries on wires, cut out all dead wood in autumn and tie in new canes.

■ **Harvest, cook, store** Pick fruit from July to August. As well as crumbles, we always make jams and jellies, and open freeze surplus berries on trays before bagging them up.

Blackcurrants and redcurrants (2)

Ribes nigrum, R. rubrum

■ **How to grow** Blackcurrants are easy to grow and thrive on cool, heavy soil, even on clay. Mulch them generously each spring using well-rotted manure. Bushes are heavy cropping and the fruit has a high vitamin C content. Redcurrants are yummy and particularly useful to grow against awkward north-facing walls and in shady areas – ideal for an urban garden.

■ **Problem solving** Put up netting to stop birds stripping your crop. Watch out for redcurrant blister aphid on the leaves in summer. Cut stems back as far as the first fruits if symptoms appear.

■ **Prune** For blackcurrants, prune between November and March. Remove one-third of the stems: they can become overcrowded in the middle of the bush. For redcurrants, see gooseberries for instructions.

■ **Harvest, cook, store** Pick in July and August. Separating the small berries from their trusses is tedious. Some people prefer to cut off entire fruiting branches and strip the berries in the kitchen. We pick ours by hand so that the stored energy in the branches can return to the plant. We make our blackcurrants into pies, jams, and jellies. Redcurrants are great in summer pudding and in jellies to serve with roast lamb. Both berries freeze well.

Blueberries (3)

Vaccinium corymbosum

■ **How to grow** Blueberries are a mountain fruit that does really well in a temperate climate. They grow best in groups so that they can cross-fertilize each other; you'll need two varieties that flower at the same time for pollination. Unless your soil is acidic, you'll need to grow them in raised beds or big tubs filled with ericaceous compost, which has a low pH. Plant bushes in April or May.

■ **Problem solving** Always water bushes with rainwater to keep the soil pH low.

■ **Prune** Not necessary.

TAKING GOOSEBERRY CUTTINGS

Increase your stock of fruit bushes by taking cuttings. Gooseberry cuttings are simple to take in early autumn. Choose a stem that grew this year and make an angled cut across it (see left). Your cutting should be about 15cm (6in) long. Push it into a small pot of compost and keep it in a sheltered spot or cold frame. It will start producing fruit in two years. Or grow new bushes from suckers – new shoots that grow off the parent bush. Cut off a sucker (see left), making sure you take some roots with it, and pot on.

5　**6**　**7**　**8**

■ **Harvest, cook, store** Pick berries from July to September when they have turned from light blue to a pewtery deep blue-black and are soft to touch. We like fresh blueberries in fruit salads or pack them into muffins. We freeze any surplus for making smoothies.

Cape gooseberries and tomatillos (4)
Physalis peruviana,
P. ixocarpa
■ **How to grow** These are annuals with a difference – each cape gooseberry is enclosed inside a papery lantern. The tomatillo (pictured) is a close cousin. Plants must be grown in a greenhouse or inside. Sow seed February to March. Look after them like tomatoes: use canes or string to support the growing plants.
■ **Problem solving** Spray regularly with water to reduce red spider mite.
■ **Prune** Not necessary.
■ **Harvest, cook, store** Pick from August to October when the berries are bright orange. Tomatillos are excellent in a Mexican salsa. Cape gooseberries taste sweet but smell rather odd.

Cranberries (5)
Vaccinium oxycoccos
■ **How to grow** We grow cranberries to go with our

home-reared Christmas turkey. Plant bushes in March. They grow well in a sunny, sheltered position and need regular watering. If growing them in a pot, stand it in a wide saucer topped up with water, and use ericaceous compost as cranberries need acidic soil.
■ **Problem solving** Use rainwater rather than tap water, to keep soil pH low.
■ **Prune** Not necessary.
■ **Harvest, cook, store** Pick berries in September and October. Cranberries are easy to freeze, ready for Christmas.

Gooseberries (6)
Ribes uva-crispa
■ **How to grow** Gooseberries need rich moist soil and regular watering. Plant bushes in autumn: mulch with leaf mould.
■ **Problem solving** Pick off sawfly caterpillars by hand and buy plants resistant to American gooseberry mildew.
■ **Prune** Cut back old wood in winter; prune strong lead shoots by half to an upward-pointing bud. Cut out cross shoots and shorten laterals. Summer prune in July so that fruits have maximum exposure to sunshine to ripen. Aim for an open cup shape so you can reach in to pick the berries.
■ **Harvest, cook, store** Pick from May to July. The smaller the berries, the more sour they

are. We also grow dessert varieties, which are red and much sweeter and don't need cooking. Like other berries, gooseberries freeze well.

Grapes (7)
Vitis vinifera
■ **How to grow** We have planted a small vineyard on a south-facing slope and have had a few vines growing under cover for years. We water indoor vines regularly and give them liquid tomato feed once a week in spring. Outside we feed our vines by mulching in spring

---

TRAINING GRAPES

Train the main stem *upwards with a cane. Train some lateral stems horizontally on wires. In winter prune the laterals to two or three buds from the main stem. In summer stop them from getting too long by "nipping" out the growing tip three or four leaves beyond each developing bunch of grapes.*

---

and autumn. They grow on thin topsoil on a clay-based subsoil.
■ **Problem solving** We grow mulberry trees at the end of the rows of vines. They have an anti-fungal property that helps protect the vines from disease.
■ **Prune** Shape the frame in the first few years. Then prune annually in December (see box).
■ **Harvest, cook, store** Pick grapes from August to October. Grapes are one of the fruits we grow for their fermenting potential – they taste great too.

Kiwi fruit (8)
Actinidia deliciosa
■ **How to grow** Kiwi fruits are exotic but do well in a temperate climate. Choose a self-fertile variety so you only need one plant. For best results grow against a south-facing wall or in a polytunnel.
■ **Problem solving** Generally trouble-free.
■ **Prune** You don't have to prune them, but if you don't, kiwis take up lots of space; pruning also encourages more fruit. Do it between November and February. Train sideshoots on wires and, after a couple of years, nip out growing shoots about 15cm (6in) beyond the last fruiting buds.
■ **Harvest, eat, store** Pick fruits from October to December. They can be eaten straight from the vine as they don't keep too long.

1 2 3 4

Melons (1)
Cucumis melo

■ **How to grow** We pride ourselves on our melons. We sow seed in pots in April and add a cane for each plant to grow up and some netting to support the fruit, but you can grow them on the ground. Melons are very sensitive to cold so do best under cover.

■ **Problem solving** Plant melons on mounds to avoid neck rot – damage between the base of the stem and the top of the root brought on by wet conditions at soil level.

■ **Prune** Pinch out growing tips two leaves after a developing melon. This stops the plant wasting energy on growing and puts it back into the fruit.

■ **Harvest, cook, store** Melons ripen from August to October. They don't store well.

Raspberries (2)
Rubus idaeus

■ **How to grow** Raspberries are always expensive in the shops, but luckily they grow well in wet and cold areas and have a long picking season. Raspberry canes like well-drained soil in a sunny position. Support them with a couple of stakes at each end of the row with some wire running between them.

■ **Problem solving** Cover with netting to prevent bird theft.

■ **Prune** In winter, prune the majority of canes all the way back to just 3cm (1¼in) above the ground. Leave a few unpruned. As time goes on leave more and more canes unpruned. Try pruning the canes at different levels so that you have a nice spread of fruit.

■ **Harvest, cook, store** Raspberries ripen from July onwards and can carry on until October depending on variety. They are great fun to pick, though they don't all make it safely to the kitchen – gardener's perks! They are delicious as they are, made into jam or preserved in liqueurs for a winter treat (see page 241).

Strawberries (3)
Fragaria x *ananassa*

■ **How to grow** Strawberries are one of our must haves. Plant them from March to April on ridges for drainage. Plants have a relatively short life of cropping (three to four years) so try to propagate some of your own from runners – mini plants on the end of a long stem.

■ **Problem solving** Avoid slug attack by growing plants in hanging baskets – but they will need heavy watering. When growing conventionally we mulch plants with straw in summer to keep the fruit from rotting by lifting it off the ground. Net plants to stop birds getting the fruits before you do.

■ **Prune** Not necessary.

■ **Harvest, cook, store** Pick fruits in July. If you have a glut, make some jam or open freeze the berries on trays before bagging them up.

Fruit trees

Fruit trees are an excellent long-term way to cut down on your food miles – especially if you store some apples for winter eating. Plant varieties that suit your local environment: look around and see what is growing well in nearby gardens. Many dwarf varieties of fruit tree will even grow well in a container on a patio. All are best planted when the trees are dormant, between October and March (see page 138). Fruit trees are an investment for the rest of your life, so take your time and do it properly. Training fruit trees not only saves space, it increases yields too. We explain some common styles on page 154.

PICKING APPLES FROM TALL TREES

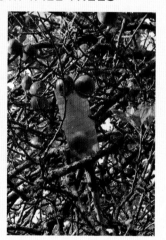

Pick apples before they fall to reduce problems in the orchard – rotting windfalls attract wasps and can spread disease. This home-made contraption is ideal for picking apples individually from traditional tall trees. Cut the bottom off a plastic fizzy drinks bottle. Push a broom handle through the neck of the bottle and hold it in place with gaffer tape. Manoeuvre the bottle so that an apple sits inside, then shake gently to detach it from the branch. This takes longer than shaking the apples down, but you'll have fewer bruised fruits, which don't keep as well.

5

6

7

8

Apples and pears (4)
Malus domestica
and *Pyrus communis*

■ **How to grow** Both trees like annual heavy mulching with rich compost. Pears like to grow in a more sheltered spot than apples and are more fragile. Pears normally need another tree within 100m (110 yd) to serve as a pollinator, or you can buy a family pear tree that has three different varieties that will self-pollinate grafted onto one trunk. Apples and pears are available in dwarf varieties.

■ **Problem solving** Codling moth larvae burrow into apples. Use pheromone traps to catch adult moths before they mate.

■ **Prune** Pears don't need specialized pruning. Trim long shoots in summer and again lightly in winter. For apples, see information on page 155.

■ **Harvest, cook, store** Pick from July to October. Depending on variety, some apples are best eaten early, others will keep well into next year. Store apples and pears in trays in a cool, dry place. As well as tarts and pies, apples make a good base for herb jellies.

Apricots, peaches, and nectarines (5)
Prunus armeniaca, *P. persica* and *P. persica* var. *nectarina*

■ **How to grow** Apricots, peaches, and nectarines like a sunny, sheltered position. We are fan-training our nectarines on a south-facing wall.

■ **Problem solving** Flowers open early when pollinating insects are rare, so hand pollination helps. If short of space, grow patio apricots in pots – they produce full-sized fruit even though they are barely 1m (3ft) tall.

■ **Prune** Remove dead wood as necessary.

■ **Harvest, cook, store** Pick from July to September. Apricot jam is delicious. Eat the best peaches and nectarines; preserve the rest in brandy or dry them (see pages 242–245).

Cherries and plums (6)
Prunus avium
and *P. domestica*

■ **How to grow** Cherries and plums are easy to grow. They work best fan-trained against a south-facing wall or in a sunny, sheltered position.

■ **Problem solving** Protect fruit from birds with netting. Plums are a wasp's favourite food, so pick ripe fruit daily.

■ **Prune** Pruning increases the chance of silver-leaf disease, so do it as little as possible.

■ **Harvest, cook, store** Pick cherries in July, plums from August to September. We make plum jam and chutney, and try to save some cherries for bottling in brandy.

Figs
Ficus carica

■ **How to grow** Figs are a solid Newhouse Farm favourite and do remarkably well in a temperate climate. They grow well in containers and do even better if you move them under cover in winter and water and feed regularly. They grow best when their roots are restricted: it improves fruiting.

■ **Problem solving** Generally trouble-free.

■ **Prune** Between December and January. Make sure you remove all unripened fruit and fruitlets or they will reduce next year's crop.

■ **Harvest, cook, store** Harvest figs from August to September, when they feel soft and when the "eye" on the bottom of the fruit has opened up a bit. They should be moist, sweet, and fragrant. The right time to pick them is just before they would fall off the tree naturally. Eat immediately.

Lemons (7)
Citrus limon

■ **How to grow** Lemons are the easiest citrus trees to grow in a temperate climate. It's best to grow them in large pots and bring them inside over winter. When growing lemons in pots, you need to "top dress" them every year or so by removing the top 2.5 cm (1in) of compost and replacing it with fresh. This is best done in spring.

■ **Problem solving** Mist with water to reduce red spider mite.

■ **Prune** Shear them right back in winter to a compact shape. Try rooting the prunings.

■ **Harvest, cook, store** Pick lemons from July to October. Watch out for their spiky bits when harvesting.

Why not try?
We wouldn't give olives top priority, but that doesn't mean you shouldn't have a go. Our experiment is still in its early stages, but here's what we've found out so far.

Olives (8)
Olea europaea

■ **How to grow** We have yet to get a decent crop from our olive trees, but patience is a virtue and so we will wait. In the UK they do best under cover. Olives grow particularly well in sandy soil interspersed with clay layers. You may need to water small trees in hot summers.

■ **Problem solving** Grow olives on a slope to avoid their roots sitting in too much water.

■ **Prune** Heavy pruning needed. Consult a specialist book.

■ **Harvest, cook, store** Pick olives in late summer. You can't eat them straight from the tree: try pickling them in brine first (see page 236).

1   2   3   4

Old fruity favourites

These less well-known fruit trees are returning to popularity – and about time too.

Medlar (1)
Mespilus germanica

■ **How to grow** Medlars are medium-sized trees with highly unusual fruits that look like little wooden rose hips. They are tough hardy trees and like a sunny open spot. You can even grow them in a large container, such as a half barrel.

■ **Problem solving** Generally trouble-free.

■ **Prune** Avoid pruning as fruits are produced at branch tips.

■ **Harvest, cook, store** Pick in October when the fruits have almost rotted, or "bletted", to a rich golden yellow. Eat the flesh with a teaspoon – enjoy it with cheese and a nice glass of port – but don't eat the seeds. Medlars don't keep: make jelly with any surplus.

Mulberry (2)
Morus nigra

■ **How to grow** Mulberries don't travel well, so really the only way to taste them is to grow your own. We grow the black variety rather than white mulberry, whose leaves silkworms eat. We've planted them alongside our grape vines. They come into flower quite late so avoiding any frost damage.

■ **Problem solving** Generally trouble-free, though birds help themselves: you'll know about it when you find mulberry-stained bird poo on the paths or, worse, the washing.

■ **Prune** Thin branches in winter if necessary to maintain the tree's shape.

■ **Harvest, cook, store** Pick from August to September. Watch out for juice stains: wear old clothes when harvesting. The fragrant fruit tastes of raspberries dipped in red wine. The berries soon deteriorate once picked, so freeze any surplus immediately or make them into jam, jelly or wine.

Quince (3)
Cydonia oblonga

■ **How to grow** Quince trees grow to about 5m (16ft) high and produce fruit like enormous golden pears. They like damp soil and prefer a sheltered spot. They don't flower until late spring so are usually safe from frost damage.

■ **Problem solving** Thin the fruits as they develop to get bigger, better quinces.

■ **Prune** None required.

■ **Harvest, cook, store** Quinces ripen in October. They are too hard to eat raw so have to be cooked. They won't last much longer than a few weeks, so use them quickly: try adding a few slices to an apple pie. We enjoy quince poached in rosewater syrup with elderflower cream.

Nut trees

Nuts are a great source of protein and relatively easy to grow. Plant trees any time from October to March. Harvesting normally takes place between September and November. Most nuts can be stored for about six months in a dark, dry environment. Here are some of our favourites that we grow at Newhouse Farm.

Almond (4)
Prunus dulcis

■ **How to grow** Best grown as fans on south-facing walls. Almonds are just like peach trees – you can hardly tell them apart – and need similar conditions. They have beautiful blossom that appears before the leaves in spring.

■ **Problem solving** Throw a sheet of plastic over trees in winter to keep buds dry and prevent peach leaf curl disease.

■ **Prune** Try to avoid pruning: it increases the risk of diseases such as peach leaf curl. As a last resort, prune in spring when new growth starts.

■ **Harvest, cook, store** Pick almonds in autumn and rub off the leathery skin (wear gloves to do this); then dry and store.

PROTECTING YOUR FRUIT CROP

A fruit cage is extremely effective as a defence against birds. We leave the door to our fruit cage open in early summer so that birds can eat any pests, but close it when the currants and raspberries are ripening. We keep it closed in winter too, when birds like to snack on the buds of the currant bushes.

Netting fruit bushes or rows of strawberries is another option. Make a tunnel by pushing bent hoops of plastic piping into the ground and stretching netting over the top. Peg netting into the soil to stop birds sneaking underneath. Don't lay it directly on top of fruit – birds will peck straight through it!

5   **6**   **7**   **8**

Hazelnuts and cobnuts (5)
Corylus avellana

■ **How to grow** Hazel nuts are very tasty and the trees can be used for hedging and coppiced for firewood, plant supports, and making your own hurdles. Cob nuts are a cultivated variety of hazel nut.

■ **Problem solving** Birds and squirrels love the nuts and often strip the crop before you get a chance to pick. You can't get ahead of the game and pick unripe nuts – they need to ripen on the tree. Visit trees daily and start picking as soon as the husks start to turn brown.

■ **Prune** Keep trees to a manageable height by pruning in winter – or follow a coppicing routine (see page 182).

■ **Harvest, cook, store** Pick nuts when ripe in autumn. Eat them straight away or, if you are going to store them, take off the husks first.

Sweet chestnut (6)
Castanea sativa

■ **How to grow** A low-maintenance tree that erupts with loads of yummy nuts in spiny shells. They are huge trees, so not for a small plot.

■ **Problem solving** Generally trouble-free.

■ **Prune** No pruning necessary.

■ **Harvest, cook, store** Knock down the nuts in autumn and take them out of their shells – wear gloves! You will find up to three nuts per shell. Leave them to dry, then store. If you roast chestnuts on an open fire or in the oven, pierce the shells first with a skewer or they'll explode – messily.

Walnut (7)
Juglans regia

■ **How to grow** Walnut trees are definitely a long-term investment. They are very slow-growing and can reach 33m (110ft) high, so consider the location carefully before planting. Grafted varieties can crop within three to four years but with traditional types it's more like 10 to 15 years.

■ **Problem solving** Grow in a sheltered spot to avoid frost damage to flowers.

■ **Prune** Shouldn't be necessary, but if you need to take out a branch or two, do it in autumn to avoid the sap bleeding.

■ **Harvest, cook, store** If you want to pickle walnuts, harvest them before the shell forms. Otherwise pick them later, rub off the sticky skin and dry them – they store well.

Why not try?
Here are a couple of unusual trees that we plan to try. They are a long-term investment but look to be worth experimenting with, especially using permaculture principles in a forest garden (see page 99).

Pecan (8)
Carya illinoinensis

■ **How to grow** We tend to associate pecans with the southern USA, but in fact they are hardy. The main drawback is how long they take to mature and produce nuts – anything from 10 to 20 years. A mature tree can be 30m (110ft) tall and 20m (65ft) wide.

■ **Problem solving** Keep well watered while establishing to avoid powdery mildew.

■ **Prune** Rarely needed, but if you do have to take out a branch or two, do it in autumn to avoid bleeding.

■ **Harvest, cook, store** Pick in October when husks open.

The nuts keep best if frozen. Dry them at room temperature for a couple of weeks first.

Honey locust
Gleditsia triacanthos

■ **How to grow** These multi-purpose trees are native to North America. The seedpods are edible, the flowers attract bees and trees can be coppiced and leaves used as fodder.

■ **Problem solving** Protect young trees from severe frost until established.

■ **Prune** Shouldn't be necessary. Watch out for thorns on mature trees.

■ **Harvest, cook, store** Collect pods as they fall. The pulp inside is edible – use it to make beer! – but the pods are more commonly used to feed sheep, cattle or pigs.

ORCHARD BIRDS

Letting geese, ducks, and hens have free run of an orchard or allowing them to forage under fruit and nut trees benefits birds and trees. The birds supplement their diet with all manner of insects and stop pest populations building up. Geese are traditional orchard birds and will also keep grass under control by grazing. Use tree protectors, or don't let them in until trees are mature.

Pruning, training, and grafting

Pruning will make your fruit trees more productive, increasing yields and fruit quality, as well as making harvesting a whole lot simpler. Training is a more specialized form of pruning and is used to restrict a tree's growth to create formal, space-saving shapes; grafting is a method of making more fruit trees, which mature quickly and bear fruit sooner, for very little outlay.

Pruning fruit trees

The point of pruning is to increase yields and create an open tree shape that's more convenient for harvesting. It's also needed when a tree is suffering from any of the three Ds: Dead, Dying or Diseased branches. Pruning has many more complex quirks depending on different trees and it's worth consulting a book that's entirely dedicated to the subject.

Pruning generally falls into one of two categories: either summer or winter pruning. Winter pruning is a great time to tidy up the tree and remove any dead or diseased bits.

Summer pruning

This stimulates growth of fruit buds ready for the next year, opens the tree up to sunlight so that the fruit will ripen better, and is a good time to prune trees that you are training into espaliers, fans, and cordons, because the shoots are more flexible then. Do it once the leaves are dark green and the bark has started to turn brown and woody at the base of the shoots – towards the end of August. In cold areas it may be autumn before shoots are mature enough to prune. See the directory on pages 148–153 for specific advice on different trees.

Tools to use

For pruning thin shoots up to around 2cm (¾in) in diameter you need pruning shears. To deal with bigger branches, invest in a pruning saw and a pair of long-handled loppers. You'll need them for coppicing woodland too (see pages 182–183).

Training

Training fruit trees is an ideal way to grow fruit on a small plot. It can take advantage of warm south-facing walls and fences that help fruit ripen quicker, and makes harvesting easier. All trained shapes need support of some sort. Run horizontal wires across a wall or fence; use posts and wires for free-standing trees (see below). Once established they are easy to maintain.

Popular styles of training
By training fruit trees into neat space-saving shapes you can fit them into small spaces and improve productivity.

Grafting fruit trees

We tend to leave grafting to the experts but it's worth learning. Grafting combines the properties of two different varieties: strong roots and trunk (the rootstock) with top-quality fruit (the scion). All trees you buy have been grafted.

Budding is useful for grafting a favourite apple, for example, on to a less productive tree. Whip-and-tongue grafting creates a new tree.

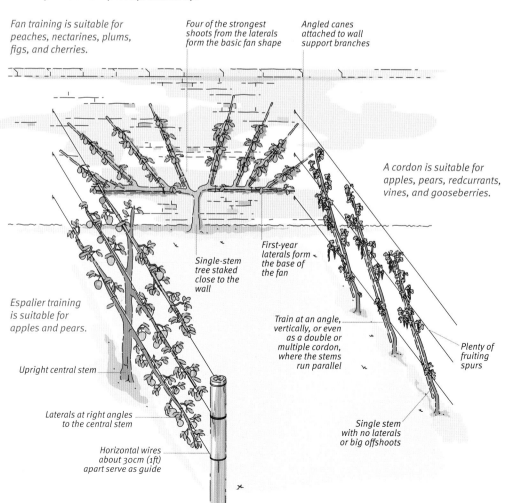

Fan training is suitable for peaches, nectarines, plums, figs, and cherries.

Four of the strongest shoots from the laterals form the basic fan shape

Angled canes attached to wall support branches

A cordon is suitable for apples, pears, redcurrants, vines, and gooseberries.

First-year laterals form the base of the fan

Single-stem tree staked close to the wall

Espalier training is suitable for apples and pears.

Train at an angle, vertically, or even as a double or multiple cordon, where the stems run parallel

Plenty of fruiting spurs

Upright central stem

Laterals at right angles to the central stem

Single stem with no laterals or big offshoots

Horizontal wires about 30cm (1ft) apart serve as guide

PROJECT **Prune an espalier apple tree**

Summer pruning is crucial to maintain the shape of a formally trained espalier tree. The basic techniques shown here apply to other styles of training, as well as to pruning straightforward bush-type fruit trees. Use sharp shears and always cut above an outward-growing bud.

1. Cut cleanly with the shears at a shallow angle facing away from the leaf. Leave a small gap between the cut and the last leaf bud. **2. Cut back leafy shoots** that have grown up directly from the main horizontal branches to three leaves above the base clump of leaves. **3. Tie in sideshoots** growing out of the vertical stem by training them along a wire and incorporating them into the shape. If the tree is becoming overcrowded, remove them completely.

4. Trim back any shoots that are growing out at an angle from the espalier instead of along its length. **5. Take off the top** of the tree. **6. The finished tree** has a precise tiered shape that makes harvesting easy and saves space in the garden.

PROJECT **Grafting techniques**

BUDDING

To be successful, budding needs to be done in midsummer. Choose a healthy cutting about 30cm (12in) long for the scion and graft it to a strong healthy branch of your rootstock tree.

1. Cut a piece of bark with a leaf bud from the scion **2. Cut a T-shaped slit** in the bark of a branch of the rootstock tree. **3. Peel back** the flaps of bark and insert the bud. Fold the flaps of bark back down around the bud. **4. Bind the stem** with grafting tape. Your chosen variety will grow from the newly grafted bud. As the bud grows, cut back the old stem of the rootstock above the grafting point so that all the energy goes into the new variety.

WHIP-AND-TONGUE GRAFTING

For this technique, best carried out in February, you will need a year-old rootstock. Start by taking a healthy cutting about 23cm (9in) from the scion tree in December. Heel it into the ground to keep it dormant. Rootstock and scion should be roughly the same diameter – ideally about 2.5cm (1in).

Cut off the rootstock at 15–30cm (6–12in) above ground level. **1. Make a sloping cut** across the rootstock 5cm (2in) long and slice into it thinly to form an upward-pointing tongue. Make a similar cut in the scion, just behind a bud, to form a downward-pointing tongue. **2. Interlock the tongues** on scion and rootstock. **3. Bind together** with grafting tape.

HERBS TO GROW

Herbs usually do extremely well in pots and containers and are a great starting point for growing your own produce. Grow herbs that you like eating and remember you are more likely to use them if they are close to the kitchen. Here are some of our favourites.

Bay (1)
Laurus nobilis

■ **How to grow** Bay is an evergreen that requires very little maintenance. It grows extremely well in pots or containers and is a great herb for an urban space.

■ **Harvest, cook, store** You can dry bay leaves to store them but as we have a bay tree, we pick and use the fresh leaves at any time of year. They are crucial for a good casserole.

Basil (2)
Ocimum basilicum

■ **How to grow** Basil can be grown as a perennial in warmer countries but in cooler climates it's usually grown as an annual. The fact that we have been growing basil from seed every summer for many years says something about how tasty we think it is. Basil grows very well in a sunny position, provided it is watered regularly. It is good practice to pinch out the growing tips to help preserve the plant's bushy shape and to remove the flowering shoots to ensure a decent supply of young leaves.

■ **Harvest, cook, store** There's nothing better in summer than a snack of our own tomatoes and basil on fresh bruschetta. The big mature leaves are the tastiest. Basil doesn't really dry and store well so the leaves are best used fresh.

Chives (3)
Allium schoenoprasum

■ **How to grow** Chives are hardy perennials and a member of the onion family. They grow in small clumps. Sow seed outside in spring when the soil warms up, in a warm, sunny position, or propagate by dividing existing clumps and replanting in good compost. Chives will grow in almost any soil but they like humidity so we tend to plant them next to our ponds. If seed is sown under cover, leaves can be harvested in just a couple of weeks.

■ **Harvest, cook, store** The hollow, grass-like leaves are great snipped over potato salads and omelettes. We also use the pinky-purple flowers as a tasty garnish in summer salads. Yes, chives can be frozen or dried but nothing beats the taste of the freshly picked herb.

Coriander
Coriandrum sativum

■ **How to grow** We love coriander. Sow seed from late spring into a fairly rich soil in a sunny position. We succession sow coriander to guarantee a ready supply. We are also lucky enough to be able to grow coriander and other annual herbs under cover in winter, thanks to our greenhouse heat sink (see pages 118–119).

■ **Harvest, cook, store** The leaves and seeds can be used in a huge range of dishes, including lots of spicy Asian cuisine. Follow the instructions for dill, below, for harvesting the seeds.

Dill
Anethum graveolens

■ **How to grow** Dill is a hardy annual with highly aromatic dark brown seeds and lively tasting leaves. Sow dill seeds in situ and be sure to keep the area very well weeded as the seedlings don't grow well with competition. To ensure a good seasonal supply, succession sow seed from late spring to early summer.

■ **Harvest, cook, store** The leaves are delicious with fish and our favourite recipe has to be the Scandinavian salmon dish gravad lax. They are also excellent with cucumber or fresh in salads. To harvest the seeds simply cut the base of the plant when the flower heads turn brown and tie the stems into loose bunches. Cover the heads with brown paper bags and hang upside down somewhere airy for a few days. Open the bag and you'll find plenty of dry ripe seeds ready to store in a glass jar. If you want to dry the leaves for use in winter, make sure you cut them when the plants are about 30cm (12in) tall and before they start flowering.

Marjoram
Origanum majorana

■ **How to grow** There are many different varieties of marjoram and to make things even more confusing some of them are called oregano. As a general rule, marjoram varieties are hardy perennials while oregano varieties (*Origanum vulgare*) are usually tender plants. Gourmets claim the latter have the finest flavour. Both do well in pots or in a sunny spot in the garden.

■ **Harvest, cook, store** Both marjoram and oregano are vital herbs for pasta sauces and for sprinkling over pizzas. The leaves dry successfully (see pages 242–243) but you should be able to keep a pot or two going on the kitchen windowsill or on a shelf in the greenhouse over the winter.

Mint (4)

Mentha species

■ How to grow There are lots of different varieties of mint and most of them are tasty. Mint spreads very quickly and is best planted away from other herbs, either against a wall or in a bucket or box in the herb bed to control its roots – take the bottom of the bucket out to allow drainage. It can tolerate a degree of shade and needs lots of water.

■ Harvest, cook, store We use our mint to make everything from mint sauce to go with lamb to tzatziki, to help us get through our summer cucumber glut. We also enjoy it freshly picked in a cup of mint tea. Mint can usually be harvested all year round, but it's worth potting up a few roots for winter and bringing them indoors to a kitchen windowsill, just in case.

Parsley (5)

Petroselinum crispum

■ How to grow Parsley is one of the most well-known herbs and has made its mark in culinary circles with its unique taste and versatility. It is also a very good source of vitamin C and iron. We sow parsley each year into rich soil that has a fine tilth; it likes to be kept well watered.

■ Harvest, cook, store Dry the leaves at high temperature by blasting them in a microwave for a few minutes. Add fresh parsley as a garnish: it loses its flavour in slow cooking.

Rosemary (6)

Rosmarinus officinalis

■ How to grow Rosemary is a delightful evergreen shrub: some species can grow to about 1.5m (5ft), so choose carefully. You might consider using it for a hedge. It likes light and dry soil. Sow seeds in spring or alternatively take some cuttings from a neighbour's plant (ask first!). Take them in late summer from non-flowering shoots and push into a pot of compost. Keep in a frost-free environment until the following spring when they can be planted out. Prune established plants in spring after the first flowering.

■ Harvest, cook, store Late summer is probably the best time to pick leaves for drying but as rosemary can be harvested all year round, we don't tend to bother. We often use rosemary when cooking meat or roasted vegetables and almost always as a fragrant addition to the barbecue.

Sage (7)

Salvia officinalis

■ How to grow Sage is an aromatic perennial. It grows to about 60cm (2ft) in the right sunny position with well-drained soil. For best results, grow from cuttings taken in late spring. Cut bushes back at the end of the summer to prevent them from becoming too woody.

■ Harvest, cook, store Sage is great for flavouring stuffing and makes a very tasty pesto mixed with garlic and pine nuts. Cut leaves and hang up to dry at the end of summer – be warned, they take a long time to dry.

Tarragon

Artemisia dracunculus

■ How to grow Tarragon is a very untidy but vibrant perennial herb that usually comes in two varieties: French and Russian. We recommend growing the French variety rather than the coarser Russian. Take cuttings and keep them indoors as French tarragon is susceptible to cold weather and may die over winter. Drainage is important: plant it on sloping ground in a sunny position, or near the top of a herb spiral (see pages 158–159).

■ Harvest, cook, store Leaves can be dried but they are best frozen. Add to chicken dishes or infuse a sprig in vinegar to use in salad dressings.

Thyme (8)

Thymus species

■ How to grow Thyme is another great perennial that thrives in a well-drained, dry position. It's best grown from cuttings taken in early summer, rather than from seed. For best results cut shoots about 15cm (6in) long from the tips of the plant, avoiding the woody base stems. Prune it after flowering to stop it getting too straggly.

■ Harvest, cook, store Thyme can be dried successfully but as it is evergreen we usually carry on picking it even in winter. It's great in all tomato recipes.

EDIBLE FLOWERS

We like to liven up our salads with a scattering of edible flowers. While most people are familiar with borage flowers floating in their summer Pimms, they are often surprised to find nasturtiums, calendula or pot marigolds, wild garlic flowers, and heartsease in amongst the lettuce. Chives add a nice touch of pink. As with all ingredients for a salad, shake flowers free of insects before adding.

157

Create a herb spiral

Growing herbs in a 3D spiral uses the plants themselves to create the ideal conditions for each other, in a kind of compatibility arrangement. The other advantage if you have only a small plot is that the spiral structure makes maximum use of vertical space as well as horizontal – almost like a gardening skyscraper. But don't let that put you off: it's fantastically simple to build.

How it works

A herb spiral works on the premise that some plants require more sunlight and drainage, others like shade and damp soil. The clever thing about the spiral is that it allows for a variety of different conditions in such a small space, giving each herb its own little microclimate.

Permaculture in action

A spiral also means you can plant more densely, which is a major principle of permaculture (see page 98–101): high-yield growing in as little land as possible. The height of the spiral creates drainage for herbs like rosemary, thyme, and sage, and also provides cover and allows moisture to collect on the lower north side for herbs like chives and wild garlic that prefer damper, shadier conditions. As the herbs grow and become established, the spiral casts shade – even in full sun.

Getting started

Consider the location of your herb spiral carefully. For the spiral to work and the sun-loving plants to thrive, it needs to be placed in a sunny location, ideally south-facing to receive sun throughout the day. The spiral will cast its own shade but it can't create its own sun!

You can work out the sunniest areas in your plot simply by observing where the sun falls throughout the day, but a compass is useful when you're planning the planting scheme.

"Zoning" is another key design principle of permaculture: plants that need most attention or are in frequent use should be grown closest to the home, so try to position the spiral near to the house.

Gathering the materials

An assortment of medium-sized stones are ideal for building up the spiral walls, thanks to their stability and heat-absorbing qualities – another clever aspect of the design that maximizes the growing year by encouraging early growth. But, before going out and buying any materials, remember the mantra "Reduce, Reuse, Recycle". We used stones because that was what we had lying around (see box opposite), but there is no end to the different materials you could try – from wood to bricks to old wine bottles.

TRY THIS

■ **Experiment** with different herbs, planting them in the appropriate position in the spiral.

■ **Wine bottles** work well as a building material. Make sure you fill them with earth before you start to improve their strength and enable the walls to absorb and retain some of the sun's heat.

■ You could include a **small pond** at the bottom of the spiral on the northern side to grow watercress and encourage frogs into the garden, which help with natural pest control. Dig a shallow hole, line it with impermeable material and edge with additional stones (see page 123).

■ Add **alpine strawberries** to your herb spiral: they thrive in the shady gaps between plants and provide a great snack for whoever is picking the herbs.

SUGGESTED PLANTING PLAN

Use the plan to position herbs according to their preferred growing conditions.

Shade-loving plants face north

Driest conditions at the top of the spiral

You could make a small pond here

Damp and shady

Dry and sunny

Sun-loving plants face south

Stones hold the soil in place and act as a heat sink

NORTH-FACING HERBS
1 Wild garlic
2 Mint
3 Chives
9 Parsley
10 Sorrel
11 Tarragon

SOUTH-FACING HERBS
4 Marjoram
5 Thyme
6 Chamomile
7 Coriander
8 Basil
12 Sage
13 Rosemary

PROJECT **Build and plant a herb spiral**

Laying a mulch below the spiral saves digging the ground beforehand and helps to prevent weeds from growing up through your herbs. If your spiral is in the middle of the lawn, make a mowing edge with some slate like we have – you'll appreciate it in summer.

YOU WILL NEED
- String and pencil
- Tape measure
- Scissors/Stanley knife
- Trowel
- Watering can
- Pile of medium-sized stones
- Eco-mulch or cardboard
- Old slates or tiles (optional)
- Compost or topsoil
- Herbs for planting

1. Measure out the circle on the ground to a diameter of about 1.5m (5ft); the age-old technique using a pencil and string will give you a reasonably accurate circle. Roughly mark out the edge with stones.   **2. Cut strips** of mulching material or cardboard slightly larger than the circle, so that they extend beyond the stones. Position the mulch under the stones.
3. Place old roof slates or tiles, if using, under the stones to make a mowing edge.

4. Lay an extra piece of slate in the centre to weigh down the mulch, then start building the spiral inwards from the north-facing edge   **5. Add compost** or topsoil as you go to give the spiral stability. Make sure that the lowest stones in the spiral are sitting directly on the mulch, not on a layer of compost.   **6. Spiral the stones** upwards, adding height with compost and packing it between the stones as well. The herb spiral needs to be at least 50cm (1ft 8in) tall.

7. Make the spiral wall taller on the south-facing side by adding more stones. Position the herbs according to the planting plan.
8. Plant the herbs and water well.   **9. Harvest herbs** once they are established. Here, sage, chives, wild garlic, marjoram, and tarragon are thriving, with alpine strawberries filling the gaps.

PROJECT **Grow your own mushrooms**

One of the biggest worries about foraging for mushrooms in the wild is identifying the edible ones. Growing your own eliminates the risk – you can confidently sample lots of different types without needing to be an expert mycologist. They'll be cheaper than shop-bought ones and whichever of these two methods you try, you'll be reusing a waste product.

A fun and easy way to grow mushrooms uses an old paperback book. We tried pearl oyster mushrooms. In the wild they grow on dead or dying hardwood trees but we grew them on our windowsill at home.

The other method uses logs and dates back to China a thousand years ago. Back then, they simply placed freshly felled logs next to ones that had mushrooms growing on them and waited for them to spread. These days we can buy spawn plugs – small lengths of grooved dowel that contain the mushroom's root system, or mycelium, to insert in a log. Look out for shiitake, pearl oyster, or chicken of the woods spawn plugs.

YOU WILL NEED – BOOK METHOD
- Mushroom spawn (order online)
- Paperback book with 200–400 pages
- Plastic bag and elastic bands
- Mister spray bottle

YOU WILL NEED – LOG METHOD
- Axe
- Narrow spade
- Post-hole digger
- Gorilla bar
- A hand drill and 8mm drill bit
- Logs that have been felled within the last six months, about 1.2m (4ft) long and 15–18cm (6–7in) in diameter
- About 50 mushroom spawn plugs per log (order online)

BOOK METHOD

1. Soak the book in warm water for 20 minutes. Squeeze the bubbles out of the book while it is underwater to get rid of most of the air. Take the book out of the water and squeeze it again, so that it is wet but not saturated. **2. Carefully open the book** and break up the mushroom spawn. **3. Gently spread** some on the pages. **4. Press** the pages together. Repeat this process every 50 pages or so throughout the book, until you have used all the spawn.

5. Put a few elastic bands around the book and place it spine down in a see-through bag. Seal the bag and label it with the date. Keep in a warm place away from direct strong sunlight and draughts – about 20°C (68°F) is ideal and in winter keep it near a radiator or heat source. After 24 hours the spawn will begin to activate. In about two weeks the paper will be covered in a white fuzz – the mycelium, or mushrooms' roots. When the edges of the book look white, place the bag in the fridge for two days. **6. Remove from the fridge** and open the bag, folding it down to just above the top of the book. Put it in a light position (indirect sunlight) and water regularly with a plant mister. **7. Harvest** oyster mushrooms when they are about 10cm (4in) across.

GROWING TIPS
- **Maintaining high moisture** levels is very important as mushrooms are mostly water. Growing them in a book means they need a bit of attention, but no more so than any indoor houseplant and you can expect a harvest much faster than with the log method.
- You may get as many as **three crops** from your book. There's no need to put it back in the fridge – the mushrooms should just continue to grow as you harvest them.
- **Dry mushrooms** in a solar dryer (see pages 242–243) then store them in airtight jars.

LOG METHOD

1. Choose a disease-free hardwood log and trim off any side branches and twigs. Remove any lichen or moss. Try not to damage the bark: it will help to retain moisture when the mushrooms start growing. Moisture is top priority for mushroom cultivation. **2. Dig a hole.** Your site should be damp, shady, and sheltered from strong winds. Use a gorilla bar to get started. **3. Finish off** with a post-hole digger: the hole should be about half as deep as the log's total length. **4. Stand the log** in the hole and secure it firmly by back-filling with rubble and soil. The log will draw up water from the earth.

5. Drill holes at right angles into the log. Make them half as deep again as the length of the spawn plugs. Stagger the holes at 10–15cm (4–6in) intervals in a diamond pattern, going all around the log. **6. Push the spawn plugs** into the holes immediately after drilling – make sure your hands are clean. Then tap them in place with a hammer. **7. Water** the log thoroughly. Place a pot or piece of cling film with an elastic band over the top of the log. This will help to limit moisture loss by evaporation. Continue to water in hot weather. If the log gets too dry, the bark will flake off; if it sprouts green mould you have overdone the watering. **8. Repeat with more logs** if you have space. In 12 to 18 months your crop will be ready. Pick mushrooms when they form clumps of about 15cm (6in) across. Use a sharp, short knife and cut close to the bark.

Any hardwood log can be used for growing mushrooms but we've had great success with beech, oak, and birch.

TRY THIS

■ **Tree stumps** are ideal for growing mushrooms, as their roots still draw up plenty of moisture from the soil, but you must inoculate the stumps within several months of the tree being cut down. Drill only the outer ring of sapwood on the face of the stump, then insert spawn plugs.

■ **The north side** of a building can be ideal for the log method. The wall will keep the logs a bit warmer but don't position them too close to the building or they won't get any rain.

■ **Tray culture** gets great results with button mushrooms. The trays should be about 20cm (8in) deep and filled with well-rotted horse manure. Sow dry mushroom spawn on the surface and cover with damp newspaper. Store the trays in a garage or shed. Remove the newspaper after about two weeks when the mycelium has grown. Cover the surface with 5cm (2in) of normal topsoil and water well. You should be picking mushrooms in two weeks.

1

2

3

4

FORAGING FOR WILD PLANTS

Foraging was once vital for the survival of hunter-gatherers. Now it's a popular pastime – even in cities people gather free food from parks or footpaths. Before picking and eating any wild plants, however, be certain that you've correctly identified them. We recognize veg in the supermarket but have lost the skills needed to scan a hedgerow for edible treats. Get yourself a plant identifier and, if in doubt about a plant, don't eat it!

FORAGER'S CODE

■ **Eat only** what you have identified as being edible.
■ **Leave plenty** for others, including wildlife – pillaging is bad foraging etiquette.
■ **Gather fruits widely** from scattered plants, not just from one individual. Leave some for plants to set seed.
■ **Be selective** – pick only the young tender leaves, the best-looking fruits.
■ **Avoid roadsides** because of car fumes and don't pick low-growing plants next to footpaths, where dogs might have sprayed urine.
■ **Take a bag** whenever you go on a walk – just in case.
■ **Give as well as take**. Volunteer to help lay a hedge or put up bird boxes.

Spring salads and roots

Spring is the perfect time to pick the first green tops of nettles and unusual early salads and to dig up various roots. Look for them in hedgerows and field edges.

Nettles (1)
Urtica dioica
Excellent cooked or made into tea. Use the freshest tender top leaves, cook in a little water and serve as a side dish with butter. Cooking destroys the sting, so your tongue won't tingle!

Beech leaves
Fagus sylvatica
Young beech leaves are a vivid bright green, oval in shape with lots of distinctive pairs of veins. Pick the early softest leaves and try them raw in a cheese and tomato sandwich or lightly steamed as a vegetable.

Rosebay willowherb (2)
Epilobium angustifolium
Steam the young shoots, or boil in a very little water, as you would asparagus.

Hawthorn
Crataegus monogyna
A small tree with deeply lobed leaves and very abundant, strong-smelling blossoms that open in May. The tender young leaves make an interesting

addition to salads. As the name suggests, watch out for thorns!

Burdock
Arctium lappa
A tall, thistle-like plant with round, purple flowers – but it's the root you want, which is absolutely delicious. Peel and cut into chunks to add to stews, or cut into thin sticks, fry in oil and serve like chips.

Dandelion
Taraxacum officinale
You've probably got some growing in your garden and

THE DIGGING STICK

One of the forager's oldest tools is a digging stick made from strong wood – hazel is ideal. Give it a sharp, bevelled, chisel end and harden it by heating in the embers of a fire. Excavate a deep hole alongside a plant. Dig all the way to the bottom of the root and on all sides and lever out the root. Fill in the hole afterwards!

you'll find them on waste land. The roots are very tasty in stews or in stir fries, and you can roast and grind them to make a coffee substitute. Mix young leaves in with salads. They're tricky to uproot and a digging stick is a great help (see box).

Wild garlic (3)
Allium ursinum
Our favourite wild plants! They grow in woodland margins and you can often smell them before you see them. Eat the leaves wilted in butter as a side dish, or mixed with potatoes for a tasty fried wild garlic champ.

Wood sorrel
Oxalis acetosella
This pretty plant grows on the woodland floor in spring and looks like oversized clover, with delicate pinky-white flowers. The heart-shaped leaves have a strong lemony flavour, great sprinkled in soups or salads – just don't eat too much as they contain oxalic acid that can upset digestion.

Summer fruits

On summer walks we fill our baskets with fruits, roots, and something succulent.

Marsh samphire
Salicornia europaea
A green succulent plant, it will often carpet areas around salt

5

6

7

8

marshes or mud flats. Delicious pickled, then served with ham on toast. Like many wild greens, the taste is hard to describe.

Horseradish

Armoracia rusticana

The leaves look like dock leaves: large, long, and coarse. Find them in fields and wasteland. Grate the very strong-tasting root and mix with cream and some lemon to make a basic horseradish sauce.

Blackberry

Rubus fruticosus

A fruit with a rich foragers' tradition; many of us have fond childhood memories of picking baskets full. Avoid gathering next to busy roads as the pollution will spoil the fruit.

Elderberry (4)

Sambucus nigra

These hedgerow berries make very good wine. Earlier in the season we also pick some of the fragrant flowers to make our very own elderflower champagne (see page 259).

Wild strawberry (5)

Fragaria vesca

These little strawberries are very tasty – more delicate in flavour than the cultivated kind but well worth collecting. Find them on the edges of woodland and shady lanes.

Crab apple (6)

Malus sylvestris

This underrated fruit makes tasty jelly. It's easy to forage: just hold out a basket and shake the branches. Look for trees in mixed hedges.

Autumn harvest

Traditionally autumn was a time for gathering and storing nuts for winter, with people behaving very much like squirrels. It's also a good time for fungi but they are notoriously difficult to identify. We haven't covered them here; instead we recommend going on a fungi foray led by an expert.

Sweet chestnut

Castanea sativa

The nuts are contained in sheaths covered in hundreds of thin, green spikes. We think that these make the best stuffing for Christmas turkeys. If you pierce them with a knife first they are excellent roasted in front of an open fire.

Walnut

Juglans regia

Mature trees have huge crops. If you know where one is growing wild then keep it a secret and enjoy the benefits once a year. The compound leaves comprise several pairs of leaflets. See page 153 for tips on storing and preserving.

Hazel (7)

Corylus avellana

It takes a fast-draw forager to beat the squirrels to these yummy nuts. Hazelnuts are tasty cooked in all sorts of ways. We like to store them as winter treats but make sure they are completely dry, otherwise they will rot and your crop will be wasted.

Winter fruit and seashore food

Wrap up warm and, if hedgerow pickings are thin, head to the seashore instead.

Sloes

Prunus spinosa

Sloes are the fruit of the blackthorn tree and look like clusters of tiny purple plums. Picking sloes is an annual ritual for us. Although they are too bitter to eat, we use them to flavour gin (see box).

Rosehips

Rosa canina

Rosehips are a great source of vitamin C and can be eaten raw if you scrape out the hairy seeds. They're also good for making syrup.

Edible kelp

Alaria esculenta

Kelp has long brown fronds and is found in rock-pools or deeper water. Cut into short lengths

and soak them in warm water for 5–10 minutes before adding to stir-fries.

Dulse

Rhodymenia palmata

A tasty seaweed from the intertidal part of the shore. Identify it by its rich red colour.

Sea lettuce (8)

Ulva lactuca

Its stunning emerald green colour makes sea lettuce easy to identify. We use it in stir fries.

SLOE PRICKER

We cut a cork from a wine bottle in half lengthways and stuck lots of pins through it to make a sloe-pricking tool. Use it to pierce the skin of sloes when making sloe gin; it helps the flavour and juice to infuse. To make sloe gin you need 250g (8oz) sloes and the same weight in sugar. Fill a wide-necked bottle half way with pricked sloes and sugar and top up with gin. Shake for the first couple of days to dissolve the sugar. It'll be ready to drink after two months.

Storing the harvest

Growing your own produce is one of the most exciting aspects of living a more self-sufficient lifestyle, especially with an effective storage regime to back it up. A well-thought out system means your excess harvest won't end up as fodder for livestock or cause the compost bin to overflow. More importantly, it helps you to maintain a supply of fresh food all year round.

Harvesting for storage

As a general rule, harvest produce for storage when it is at its peak. It should look healthy, ripe, and ready to eat, but there are a few exceptions. With vegetables such as squashes, wait until the stem has dried out and shrivelled a bit, and the skin doesn't dent when you press it with your fingernail. Equally, wait a bit longer before picking apples and pears, which are best harvested for storing near the end of the growing season. For best results store only late-ripening varieties and leave them on the tree for as long as possible. You'll know they are ready when they can be gently lifted off the branches.

Try not to damage crops as you pick them or dig them up. Don't waste time trying to store damaged or diseased produce – either send it to the compost bin, or give it to pigs or chickens as fodder.

Cleaning and trimming

Brush off most of the excess soil from root crops but don't scrub or wash them – you can do that just before you cook them. Similarly, don't trim off any unshapely knobbly bits: the exposed cut could start to rot in storage. But do remove the leafy tops from roots before you store those, as they will take some of the moisture from the root and can turn slimy later, ruining anything they are touching.

In the store room

For thousands of years people lived without fridges and plastic-wrapped food. They used natural larders, pantries, root cellars, and store rooms to keep food edible. At Newhouse Farm we keep our produce fresh for months in our store room. A store room needs to be at a cool and constant temperature, and should be frost-free. It doesn't have to be dark like a root cellar (see pages 180–181), but it shouldn't have direct sunlight, which will make the room too warm and can discolour produce. The humidity should be ambient: too wet and produce will develop mould and fungal problems; too dry and your vegetables will shrivel.

Ventilation is important: fly-proof mesh across windows and vents lets air in while keeping pests out.

SEED-SAVING TIPS

■ **Leave seeds to ripen on the plant,** but cut them before they scatter naturally. Cut the stalks and place the seed heads upside down in a paper bag, to collect seeds as they dry.

■ **Briefly soak seeds** from fruits like tomatoes in water to wash off the "jelly" before drying on a hard surface – on kitchen paper you'll never get the paper off the seeds!

■ **Shell peas and beans** from the pod before drying and storing.

■ **Dry seeds in a cold frame** to speed up the process (see page 117).

■ **Store them** in labelled paper envelopes, in an airtight container in a cool, dry room.

■ **Save bags of desiccant** that come with electronic equipment and use to keep the moisture out of your store.

Runner bean pods *dry out and split to reveal ripe beans ready to store.*

1. Cut squashes for storage when the stem attaching them to the plant has dried out. **2. Beetroots** will store for longer without their leaves. **3. Dry onions** before storing them – this can take several weeks.

Hanging produce

This is a great way of making stored food inaccessible to vermin while allowing good air flow. We hang vegetables like garlic, onions, and sweetcorn from strings, while suspending squashes in netting avoids having to turn them regularly when they are sitting on shelves.

Using trays

Onions and apples store particularly well on trays with slats or chicken wire bases to allow air to circulate. Apples are best wrapped individually in paper to stop one rotten apple spoiling the rest. Deeper trays can be used to store beetroot, Jerusalem artichokes, carrots, and parsnips in sand or sawdust. Put a layer of sand in the bottom of the tray and arrange the roots so that they don't touch. Layer sand and roots, finishing with a final covering of sand. Fill trays in situ to save the effort of moving them. You can also store roots in a barrel (see page 180). For other methods of preserving food, see pages 224–225.

1. **Use deep trays** to store layers of root vegetables in sand. 2. **Hang** onions, garlic, herbs, and chillies from the roof. 3. **Keep** home-made drinks, preserves, cured hams, and eggs, as well as fruit and veg, in a well-organized store room. 4. **Dimpled cardboard trays** are another way to keep apples separate in storage.

PROJECT **Make a potato clamp**

Clamping is a traditional way of storing potatoes if you haven't got a store room or root cellar. Site a clamp in a sheltered spot as it isn't guaranteed frost protection. Store only best-quality potatoes and watch out for slugs. You can use the technique to store any root vegetables and fodder beets for livestock too.

YOU WILL NEED
- Fork
- Colander
- Straw
- Spade

1. **Dig up** your potatoes and leave to dry – a colander is ideal – for a couple of hours, before laying them on a base of straw or bracken. 2. **Arrange them in a pyramid** and cover with more straw. Then leave them to breathe for an hour or two. 3. **Cover the pyramid** with a layer of earth 15cm (6in) thick. Allow some straw to poke through the soil, to let air get to the crop. Pat the sides flat with a spade: make them steep so that rain can run off.

Problem solving

Our way of dealing with pests, diseases, and weeds is to use an integrated approach that takes into account the soil and the crops themselves. This means getting to know your pests and their natural predators. It's a method that places great store in the old expression "prevention is better than cure". It's not perfect, but it's cheap – and there's no risk to people or the environment.

DEALING WITH WEEDS

Keeping on top of weeds before they become a problem is the best approach. Mulching is extremely efficient at suppressing weeds (see page 100). Where it isn't possible to mulch, hoe off weeds regularly when they are small, especially on dry, sunny days when they will shrivel and die. Bigger weeds may need removing with a small fork or trowel. Always deal with weeds before they set seed. Remember: "one year's seeds means seven years' weeds." Digging is a satisfying way of clearing overgrown areas but sadly the benefits can be short-lived. It exposes dormant seeds that will germinate and create as many weed problems as you've solved. Try covering the ground with a cardboard mulch instead, let the weeds die down, then plant through.

Two ways to tackle weeds. *Mulching (top) suppresses weeds by blocking out light. Hand weeding is the best way to get rid of long-rooted dandelions.*

Start with the plants

To get the best results from our crops we start by buying seed of pest-resistant varieties – usually traditional, local, proven varieties. Then we grow strong healthy plants that will be more resistant to attack. We boost our plants by feeding the soil. Worm tea (see page 127) is useful as it contains all sorts of beneficial fungi and bacteria, not just nutrients.

We also focus on the environment: crop rotation (see pages 108–109) reduces the risk of disease building up in the soil; good spacing between plants allows air to circulate, which helps reduce disease; winter digging exposes pests to bird predators; and companion planting in spring and summer (see page 101) attracts beneficial insects to deal with pests. Interplanting – growing two crops together – is confuses crop-specific pests like carrot fly. These preventive methods are highly effective, but you should keep a watchful eye too.

Animal pests

Moles are difficult to deal with. They eat huge amounts of worms, damage plant roots, and build mole hills in undesirable spots. Get a specialist trap and check it daily.

Birds can be deterred with a traditional scarecrow, which work best moved around over the season. Plastic bottles make good bird scarers, or string up old CDs to create moving reflections. We use netting to stop birds getting at our soft fruit or young brassicas. Fine netting will also stop cabbage white butterflies and turnip moths laying eggs on leaves.

Rabbits can devastate a garden. The best option is to fence them out with 2.5cm (1in) wire netting. Bury it at least 15cm (6in) below the surface and make it at least 60cm (2ft) high.

Small pests

Aphids can devastate a salad or bean crop. We recommend interplanting with marigolds (*Calendula officinalis*), which works by attracting hoverflies that eat the aphids. Other predators include ladybirds, which you can encourage by building a ladybird hotel and placing it near crops (see page 121). When aphids appear on broad beans or peas, we pinch out the tips where they cluster, and throw to the pigs.

Leatherjackets are big, fat, white, ugly larvae of the crane fly. They eat all sorts of plant roots. Whenever we dig one up, we feed it to the ducks.

Caterpillars are easy to spot and pick off by hand – or use barriers such as Enviromesh or fleece, which allow light to reach plants but keep out butterflies and other insect pests, and even birds and rabbits.

Cabbage root fly can be foiled by laying a 15cm (6in) square of rubber carpet underlay around the base of plants. This stops the fly laying eggs close to the roots.

Slugs and snails are deterred by a barrier of copper tape fitted around individual plants or pots. It works wonders, but is expensive. Try this if you don't like squashing or cutting them in half with a pair of scissors (best done at night with a head torch). We have tried other deterrents such as egg shells, coffee granules and soot, but find beer traps work best for us. The smell attracts slugs and snails, who fall in and drown. Empty them regularly to avoid an unpleasant concoction developing.

Diseases

Cleanliness helps to avoid problems in the first place. Scrub pots and trays before using, pick up fallen fruit and leaves, and burn diseased plants.

Blight affects tomatoes and potatoes, causing brown and black marks on leaves and fruit. Remove and burn infected leaves quickly. It is a wet-weather disease, so provide plants with good drainage. We've dealt with the problem by growing our outside tomatoes upside-down!

Club root is a soil-borne disease affecting brassicas. If a problem, grow plants in a cardboard box filled with fresh compost and sunk into the soil.

Grey mould, or botrytis, affects all plants grown under cover. It starts with brown spotting on the foliage, followed by furry mould. Improve air circulation, avoid overwatering, and burn infected shoots.

Rust appears as yellow, red, and brown pustules on leaves. It can kill an entire onion crop. Burn affected leaves, don't wet the foliage when watering, and avoid high humidity.

Silver leaf can develop on fruit trees, especially plums. A silvery hue appears on leaves. Cut back branches 15cm (6in) beyond the affected area.

1. String up CDs and bottle tops to deter birds. **2. Make a bird scarer** from a plastic bottle. Cut side "wings" so it spins in the breeze. **3. Pour beer** into jars set level with the soil to trap slugs and snails. **4. Eject aphids** with a high-pressure blast of water. **5. Pick off caterpillars** as you spot them and feed to your chickens. **6. Netting** keeps birds and butterflies from brassicas. **7. Jagged edges** on cut-down plastic bottles, plus copper tape, discourage slugs and snails from reaching lettuces.

WORKING LARGE AREAS If you are lucky enough to have a large plot to work on you'll also have lots more decisions to make. This chapter is intended to guide you through the decision-making process and to give you some food for thought. Without wanting to sound too negative, you will have to be careful to ensure that you don't bite off more than you can chew – and, to fully milk the eating analogy, it is important to remember you can only eat an elephant a bite at a time! It is a real privilege to be the custodian of land so enjoy your time and don't forget the countless generations who have worked it before you.

Observing, planning, and designing

It's hard to resist jumping in with both feet and getting stuck in, but time spent planning your plot can save you from expensive mistakes further down the line. Gathering as much local information as you can and making a detailed site map will help you to make your dreams come true without too many false starts – and you may uncover some fascinating history at the same time.

Start by observing

Ideally, you should take notes throughout the seasons before making permanent decisions. In our first year, for example, we waited to see where frost pockets developed before planting our fruit trees, and monitored wind speeds in different sites before erecting a turbine.

For a comprehensive picture of your land, speak to previous owners and neighbours or research old photographs and maps. Part of our motivation to plant an orchard was discovering a 400-year-old map that showed the whole of our valley covered in fruit trees. Both local knowledge and the nature of the land itself should influence any decisions you make. The result will be a well-designed landscape that grounds your dreams and ambitions in reality.

Planning your plot

Now you've got to the exciting stage. First decide which existing elements of your plot you are going to keep, and which have to go. Then think about what you are going to produce on your plot, and why. What kinds of fruit and vegetables do you like eating? Do you want to keep poultry?

Our advice is: don't over-stretch yourself. Your energy and enthusiasm will fade if you take on too many projects and don't have time to step back, gain some perspective, and think to yourself: "This is the life".

Designing your plot

The design that you eventually come up with will never be a finished thing. Nature constantly moves the goal posts – anything from the weather to the local slug population has the power to alter your plans. But this unpredictability is what makes life fun. We often stray from the initial idea, but this is another advantage of the organic lifestyle – allowing yourself the luxury of diverging.

1. Assembling a geodesic dome is a flat-pack challenge. **2. Digging a channel** for the pipe that brings water from the spring to the buildings at Newhouse Farm. **3. The water wheel** starts to take shape next to the barn.

DESIGN TIPS

- Site your **vegetable garden** in a sunny, sheltered place near the house.
- Keep **toolshed and compost bins** close to the vegetable patch.
- Align rows of fruit and vegetables from **north to south**, to catch the sun.
- On a slope, **plant across the contours** to prevent erosion.
- Plant **fruit bushes** densely to make harvesting and netting easy.
- Use **fruit trees** as a way of hiding ugly features.
- Earmark **south-facing walls** for delicate fruits like peaches and vines.
- Site **wind turbines** away from sources of turbulence, or plan to build them high enough.
- Keep **poultry** near to the house so it's easy to let them out and put them away at night.
- **Geese** are noisy: site their pen near the entrance of your property and they'll act as watchdogs!
- A south-facing roof is ideal for **solar PV panels** or **thermal collectors**.

Conducting a site survey

Making a map is without a doubt the best way to get to know your land. A well-observed map fits everything together spatially and helps you to visualize your plans. But resist the temptation to add your ideas onto the map at this stage – it makes the process much more confusing. Simply record what is already there, and always mark north and south.

Filling in the details

Record your site's dimensions as accurately as you can – to scale if you have the patience. Try using a print out of your plot from Google Earth on the internet and lay tracing paper on top. Then you can add extra information such as the sunny and shady areas, and different soil types. Consider drawing a separate map of your buildings at a larger scale to show details such as services, mains, and utilities.

Look beyond your boundaries. Are there tall neighbouring trees or large buildings that cast shadows? Areas such as these may be harder to utilize, so highlight them on the map.

Newhouse Farm in the early days was in need of attention, from clearing the land of brambles and gorse to fixing the roof and sorting out the plumbing.

Mapping out the options

Annotate your map with extra information, from soil types to prevailing winds and sun traps.

Observe a stream throughout the year and measure the flow in different seasons (see pages 68–71).

Make a note of wildlife habitats such as ponds, wildflower meadows, and bird nesting sites.

Large trees cast shade

Main access track to smallholding

South-facing wall ideal for fruit trees

Stream to power waterwheel

Windy enough for a turbine

South-facing slope valuable for crops, or site for an earth shelter

Marshy ground ideal for willow

Frost pocket: avoid planting trees here

Ideal roof for PV and/or solar panels

Exposed slope for wind turbine tall enough to surmount existing trees

Woodland for coppicing

Very steep north-facing slope can be planted with woodland

N

S

Shady lane for mushroom logs

Secluded spot for beehives

FINDING WATER

Find water on your plot by using a willow divining rod. Dowsing, or doodlebugging as it is known in the US, may sound wacky, but don't knock it until you've tried it. Finding springs using this ancient method is an amazing experience and it could even help you cut your water bills.

Creating boundaries

Losing a crop of carefully tended vegetables to farm animals on the rampage is one of the most frustrating things that can happen on a smallholding, so we always make sure our livestock is securely contained. A mixture of permanent hedging and fencing, together with easily assembled temporary enclosures, helps us keep animals where we want them.

Permanent enclosures

Hedges, walls, and fences are traditional permanent boundaries, used the world over to contain animals – or to keep them out. All need regular maintenance to keep them fit for purpose.

How to plant a hedge

Hedges are bushes that have been trained to form an impenetrable mass that livestock cannot push through. Once planted, they are cheap to maintain. A traditional quickthorn hedge is planted with thorn bushes (normally whitethorn, *Crataegus laevigata*). Use seedlings about 15cm (6in) tall and set them in two staggered rows with about 45cm (18in) between each plant and 23cm (9in) between rows. Protect from livestock using conventional fencing for at least the first four years. This extra fencing is the most expensive aspect. Once the bushes are mature, you can lay the hedge.

Hedge-laying (see opposite) encourages the plants to produce dense growth that contains livestock efficiently and creates an important habitat for wildlife. It is ideal for nesting birds and for dormice.

Traditionally, a professional hedgelayer can lay a "chain" or 20m (22yd) a day. Seven years after laying a hedge, the regrowth can be as high as 4.5m (15ft).

Dry-stone walling

Dry-stone walls are built by laying together large closely fitting stones without using mortar. The old walls on our boundary are animal proof but need regular repairs. We also built a wall from scratch. The trick is to dig a level foundation trench and use flat angular stones that fit together snugly. You can buy stones from a salvage yard or building suppliers, but it is not cheap. It makes sense to build dry-stone walls only if you've got plenty of stones on your land.

Wire fencing

Wire is expensive but relatively durable and makes an effective boundary. A good wire fence needs to be tensioned, so buy a wire strainer to achieve this. This simple tool can also strain slack or broken wire, including barbed wire, and can exert up to 2 metric tonnes (2 tons) of pull,

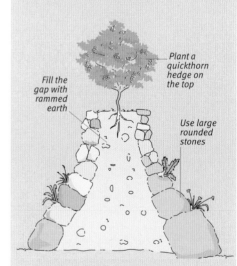

THE STONE HEDGE

Where we live in Cornwall in the far south-west of England, this form of hedging is extremely popular. It is basically a cross between a stone wall and a living hedge.

Building a stone hedge

Use large rounded stones to construct a pronounced batter – that is, two walls that lean towards each other. Make the walls around 1.2m (4ft) tall. Fill the gap between them with rammed earth and plant a quickthorn hedge on the top. Plants will also grow in gaps between the rocks. Stone hedges are valuable habitats for small mammals and reptiles, as well as for plants.

Fill the gap with rammed earth

Plant a quickthorn hedge on the top

Use large rounded stones

A typical stone hedge *should be as wide as it is tall, and the width at the top of the wall should be half the width of the base.*

1. Fencing for sheep and goats needs to be at least 1m (3ft 3in) high.
2. Dry-stone walls should be twice as wide at the base as the top for stability. Different regions have distinctive styles.

Lay a hedge

A hedge needs to be at least 2.5m (8ft) tall for laying and the technique is usually carried out when most of the leaves have fallen. The stems to be laid are called "pleachers" and should be the straightest, best-looking stems in the hedge. Remove dead or bent, twisted stems as you work your way along. This is the Blackdown style of hedge-laying, specific to a region of the West Country.

HEDGE-LAYING TOOLS YOU WILL NEED
- Stafford bill hook (1)
- Tenterden bill hook (2)
- Short-handled slasher (3)
- Kent pattern hand axe (4)
- Hedging maul (5)
- Hedging rake (6)
- Leather gloves (7)

1. This hazel hedge was laid about eight years ago and is starting to look gappy. **2. Clear brambles and nettles** from the base using a bill hook and slasher. **3. Select a pleacher** and, using a sharp bill hook, make a vertical cut through the stem so that it is pliable enough to be laid down. Although the technique looks drastic, the pleacher continues to grow.

4. Trim the stob – the cut-away stump – and any whiskers of wood, to reduce rotting. **5. Lay the pleacher down** horizontally. **6. Roughly weave** the pleacher into those that have already been cut and laid, to hold it in place. **7. Cut a crook** from the hedgerow – look for a post with a natural hook at the end, to hold the pleachers in place. Sharpen the base with the bill hook.

8. Hook the crook over the pleachers facing inwards. **9. Use the maul** to hammer the sharpened base into the ground. **10. The finished hedge.** The pleachers throw up vertical growth along their length and the cut stump will also send up six to eight stems.

so the pressure on fence posts can be considerable and they will need anchoring (see box below).

Match the fencing height to your livestock. Goats need fencing that is at least 1m (3ft 3in) high so that they can't jump over. You can increase the height of standard stock fencing (square netting) by adding two extra lines of wire. Put up fencing about 1.15m (3ft 9in) high for cattle, and 80cm (2ft 7in) for pigs and sheep. To keep deer out, you need a fence that is at least 1.9m (6ft 3in) high.

Post and rail fencing

If you have oak or chestnut trees to coppice, you could make your own post and rail fencing from stakes. Split them in half to make the uprights and into quarters to make the cross rails. Post and rail fences are good enough for most livestock and for marking out footpaths, but obviously won't keep rabbits out of a vegetable plot.

Temporary enclosures

When grazing sheep, cattle, or pigs on fodder crops, you need a way of confining them to one area at a time. The method is quick and easy to set up and dismantle. Such temporary enclosures are also important when you need to corral sheep for shearing or lambing, or to inspect their feet.

Electric fencing

With electric fencing it's easy to create a secure temporary boundary in no time at all. We always use electric fencing for our pigs and poultry. It helps protect poultry from potential predators if the voltage

WIRE FENCING

Wire fencing is only as strong as the posts that hold it. Use a post rammer to set them firmly in the ground. If necessary, add box anchors to stop posts being pulled straight out again under tension when you use a wire strainer to take up slack in the wire.

Bury a boulder or large stone as a box anchor. Corner posts need two, to take the strain in each direction.

Square-meshed stock fencing with a single line of barbed wire on the top will stop pigs and cows straying.

Temporary wire fencing such as diamond netting will contain sheep. Roll it up when not in use.

TWO TYPES OF HURDLE

Lightweight gate-style hurdles can be used for instant pens; woven wattle hurdles make short-term fences. Make gate-style hurdles out of any wood that splits easily, such as ash or chestnut; thin stakes make lighter hurdles. Sharpen the end stakes, then use mortices to join horizontals. Nail cross braces to the horizontals for strength.

Use a frame *to make a wattle hurdle. Space holes 23cm (9in) apart and weave between stakes with willow or split hazel.*

To assemble an enclosure *place solid posts in the ground at intervals and attach hurdles between them with twine.*

Wattle hurdles *make good temporary fences, but they don't last more than a few years. They also look good in the garden, but take quite a long time to make. See pages 280–281 to find out more about basic weaving techniques.*

is high enough and the fencing is in good condition.

Electric fencing is also effective with cattle, but it doesn't always work with sheep as their thick fleeces don't conduct electricity easily. You can up the voltage to high levels of 4,000–5,000 volts with three strands of wire or consider using electric netting when your sheep are lambing to protect them from foxes. But under normal circumstances the best way to secure sheep temporarily is with diamond wire netting or hurdles.

The simplest electric fence uses one strand of hot wire. Position it at nose level for pigs and cattle. For pigs that's about 30cm (12in) off the ground.

If you set up a small solar panel to trickle charge your battery, you won't have to take it back to the workshop every time it needs recharging. The whole set up can be rolled up and put away in minutes.

Hurdles

Lightweight and easy to move around, hurdles are ideal if you have a ready supply of coppiced wood (see pages 182–183), and are ready to build your own (see box opposite). Alternatively, you could make more permanent, woven wattle hurdles, which make good, cheap, short-term fences (see box opposite).

Temporary wire fencing

Wire netting that can be rolled up is particularly useful as a temporary fence. Diamond netting is easiest to work with as square-meshed netting may get bent out of shape.

PROJECT **Set up electric fencing**

Electric fencing is cheap and effective, and can be set up or taken down in moments. It can be adapted for a range of livestock by varying the height of the hot wire – the ideal position for any animal is nose height. Pigs are remarkably intelligent animals, for example, and it only takes one belt on the nose for them to learn it's best not to cross the line.

YOU WILL NEED
- Plastic stakes
- Electric wire
- Control unit and battery
- Watering can, plastic crate

1. Clear the grass around the perimeter to reduce "bridging" – losing electricity into the ground where grass touches the wire. Set out plastic stakes. Space them close enough so the wire doesn't sag. **2. Feed the wire** around the stakes. **3. Set the wire** at an appropriate height. In this set-up all the strands are "live". **4. Check again** for grass touching the wire.

5. Firmly push the spike of the control unit into the ground. This acts as an earth, so wet the ground for good conductivity. **6. Connect the control unit** to the fence and the positive and negative terminals to a fully charged battery. We then cover our battery with a plastic crate. **7. Test the fence** by touching a piece of grass to the wire. If it's working, you'll know (get someone else to do this if you have a weak heart or a pacemaker). Remember to tell visitors that the fence is live.

1 2 3 4

FODDER CROPS TO GROW

Rearing livestock on a small scale is a great way of becoming more self-sufficient. However, animals often need more food than they can obtain from grazing and this extra feed can be expensive. In the past this was why most livestock was slaughtered before winter when fresh food could not be spared. Agriculture then developed so that planting crops to feed livestock through the harder months became the norm. It's now perfectly viable for a smallholder to subsidize winter feeding with crops specifically grown as fodder. For some you will need to use a seed drill for best results; others can be sown broadcast by scattering handfuls of seed.

Fodder cereals

Cereals are not just a crop for farms with hundreds of acres; growing them on a smallholding can easily be achieved with a bit of hard work. Most cereals grow quickly and should smother any weeds.

Barley (1)

Hordeum distichum

■ **How to grow** Barley will grow in surprisingly poor conditions. It does like a finer seed bed than other cereals and should be sown in spring, from March onwards when the soil is warming up and drying out. Sow at 247kg (544lb) per hectare (100kg/220lb per acre) using the same method as oats.

■ **Harvest** Cut barley late when the ears are bent over, the grains have gone pale, hard, and yellow, and the straw is dry.

MAKING HAY

Leave grass to grow in a field or orchard. Cut with a scythe in early summer when the grass is tall, either just before or just after flowering, but before it goes to seed. To make a haycock, erect a 1.8m (6ft) tripod of wooden poles tied together at the top and around the structure. Place a bent piece of tin on the ground facing a windward side; this will keep the air flow circulating through the haycock. Cover the structure with hay and leave to dry. When dry, store in a hayshed and feed to livestock such as cattle, goats, and sheep in autumn and winter.

Store loose in a stook (see box below right) until it's completely dry. Then thresh it, which can easily be done by either bashing handfuls against the back of a chair or by beating it with a home-made flail. Feed the grain to pigs or cattle. You should always soak grain for at least 24 hours before feeding. Don't waste the straw: your livestock will appreciate it for food and bedding.

Maize (2)

Zea mays

■ **How to grow** Maize is another excellent fodder crop. Sow in spring into light soil, about two weeks after the risk of frost has passed. Sow at about 37.5kg (83lb) per hectare (15kg/33lb per acre) at a depth of 7.5cm (3in) in rows 38–75cm (15–30in) apart. Put up a scarecrow to stop rooks sweeping down and eating all the freshly sown seed.

■ **Harvest** Ripe maize cobs are great for cattle or you can feed them the whole plant in summer like grass. Maize can even make good silage: cut it when green, crush, and store it in plastic sacks so it ferments. Of all the fodder crops maize is definitely one of our personal favourites – especially as we love eating it too! To harvest the cobs simply walk along the rows, rip out the

ears and then drop them into a sack. They'll keep you and your livestock very happy indeed.

Oats (3)

Avena sativa

■ **How to grow** Oats grow well in damp cold places. In wet areas they are best sown in spring. In drier and warmer conditions they are better suited to winter sowing – but make sure you have a scarecrow ready at this time of year as birds like to snack on them. The seeds should be sown into a coarse seed bed

HOW TO MAKE A STOOK

To construct a stook, secure two sheaves together, standing them upright so that the grainy heads stick to each other. Add more pairs so that they won't blow over in the wind. Leave the stooks for about three weeks to dry thoroughly, then bring under cover.

with small clods about the size of a child's fist. Ground that has been turned over by pigs using their snouts is ideal. Sowing is most easily done in a biblical fashion by holding a bag full of seeds and broadcasting them over the ground. Sow oats at 100–125kg (220–276lb) per hectare (40–50kg/88–110lb per acre). Then harrow the ground, which involves pulling – either by manpower, horse or tractor – a spiky "bush" or attachment called a harrow to cover the seeds and mix them into the ground. When some of the oats reach 15cm (6in) tall, harrow again to kill weeds and open up the surface.

■ **Harvest** Cut the oats when there are still green bits in the straw. Tie into sheaves – grab-sized bundles tied around the middle. Make a stook with the sheaves (see box opposite). Sheaves can be fed directly to cattle alongside their grass diet, at a rate of one sheaf per beast per day. Oat straw is generally accepted as the best cereal straw for feeding.

Rye (4)
Secale cereale
■ **How to grow** Rye grows well in cold, dry conditions and light sandy soil. It is planted in a very similar way to oats. Sow in autumn for best results as it grows fast.

Rye is known as a catch crop due to its quick-growing habit. The other excellent thing about rye as a fodder crop is that birds don't like it much so the success rate is high.
■ **Harvest** If you plant rye straight after a crop of potatoes, it will be ready to be grazed off by sheep or cows in spring when other greens are in short supply. This space can then be planted with another spring crop. It also makes good straw bedding or animal feed.

Fodder root crops
Roots are useful as winter fodder for animals, as well as being delicious in the kitchen. Root vegetables store up energy in the summer and retain all the nourishment as they lie dormant over the winter. They are packed with goodness and can seriously supplement your animals' diet.

Fodder beets and mangolds (5)
Beta vulgaris
■ **How to grow** Sow seeds at 4–5kg (9–11lb) per acre (10–12kg/22–26lb per hectare) into a fine seed bed at the beginning of April. Make rows 55cm (22in) apart and thin them to around 23cm (9in) between plants.
■ **Harvest** Mangolds can yield huge crops but are not as rich

in protein as fodder beet. Pull both in autumn before the first frost and place in piles covered with their leaves until you have time to clamp them (see page 165). Wait until after New Year's Day before feeding them to pigs and cattle: this reduces the risk of any toxins being present. Neither crop is nice enough to eat – like bland-tasting tough old beetroot – but some people do grow mangolds specifically to make wine.

Turnips and swedes (6)
Brassica rapa and *B. napus*
■ **How to grow** Turnips and swedes do extremely well in wet and cold conditions. Sow into a fine seed bed in May in drills at a rate of about 0.5kg (1lb) per acre (1kg/2lb per hectare) and then thin out to one every 23cm (9in). Try to hoe between plants a couple of times as they are growing to reduce competition from weeds.
■ **Harvest** Lift both turnips and swedes some time after Christmas and store in clamps (see page 165). Alternatively, try grazing sheep directly on the growing crops in fenced strips, which you extend each day. After the sheep have finished, let your pigs out into the field to root up all the leftovers. Don't forget to lift and store some roots for use in the kitchen too.

Fodder brassicas
These tend to be nutritious, hardy crops for autumn and winter feed for lambs or cows; fodder brassicas are also good for suppressing weeds and so they clear the ground ready for future plantings.

Cabbage (7)
Brassica oleracea
Capitata Group
■ **How to grow** Sow cabbage seeds in early April in drills 50cm (20in) apart, in well-manured soil.
■ **Harvest** You get double-value feeding when you grow fodder cabbage. You can cut and cart the cabbages to cows when they're ready to harvest, usually around October. Then you can let your pigs out on to the ground where they will turn up all the edible roots with their snouts.

Kale (8)
Brassica oleracea
Acephala Group
■ **How to grow** Sow seed as for cabbage above. Kale tends to have a higher yield and is rich in protein.
■ **Harvest** As with cabbage, you get double-value from kale as you can feed livestock on both leaves and roots. Start grazing animals on kale from early autumn onwards, then let pigs into the field.

1 **2** **3** **4**

Mustard and rape (1)
Brassica juncea and *B. napus*

■ **How to grow** Sow mustard from March onwards by drilling at 10–12kg/22–26lb per hectare (4–5kg/9–11lb per acre). Sow rape in summer by drilling at 2.4kg/5lb per acre (6kg/13lb per hectare); it can be ready for your animals to graze in 12 weeks and will carry on producing until Christmas. If you grow rape and keep bees, be aware that your bees will harvest rape nectar voraciously but the honey they produce is not at all palatable.

■ **Harvest** Like turnips and swedes, both mustard and rape are ideal for strip grazing.

Other fodder crops

Sunflowers and Jerusalem artichokes look stunning – the artichokes are also a member of the sunflower family. More importantly, they will fatten up your pigs in winter.

Jerusalem artichokes (2)
Helianthus tuberosus

■ **How to grow** Plant Jerusalem artichokes any time after Christmas. Set the tubers every 30cm (12in), in rows 90cm (3ft) apart. They are prolific and you will find that the following year, despite thorough harvesting, tubers will sprout up again in the same place.

■ **Harvest** Instead of wasting time digging up your Jerusalem artichokes, simply put your pigs in an enclosure with them, giving them access to a few plants at a time, like strip grazing. They will root them up and happily eat them for weeks, while you save plenty of money on your normal feed costs.

Sunflowers (3)
Helianthus annuus

■ **How to grow** We grow sunflowers as a dual-purpose crop, harvesting the heads for the chickens – and ourselves – and letting the pigs in to forage on the stems and leaves. Sow 2.5–4cm (1–1½in) deep at roughly 4kg/9lb per hectare (1.5–2kg/3–4lb per acre).

■ **Harvest** The seeds are ready to harvest when the back of the flower head turns brown. We scrape out the seeds and dry them. Leave some heads for wild birds.

UNUSUAL CROPS TO GROW

Climate change is a reality. We have seen a noticeable change in conditions here in Cornwall and evidence shows the same is happening all over the world. Wherever possible, we embrace changes to our advantage and try to focus on the glass half-full perspective. If the weather

conditions are warmer in the summer, we see it as an opportunity to grow unusual crops and reduce the amount of food we import. It also happens to be quite a lot of fun!

Bamboo (4)
Phyllostachys species

■ **How to grow** Bamboo is an incredible crop. It grows quickly, is very strong and is excellent in damp areas. Some species are even edible. We decided to plant it at the bottom of our plot where the land is fairly wet but well drained. Here it acts as a windbreak for the vines further up the hill and thrives in the moist conditions. Bamboo can be grown all over temperate regions. It needs little care and attention, thriving naturally and spreading profusely through its root system. We planted *Phyllostachys nigra* which has black canes and *P. glauca*, which forms good clumps and spreads well. Choose species carefully; some bamboos are rampant and will spread rather too efficiently.

■ **Harvest** Cut canes regularly to remove older or decaying culms or stems and let in enough light for the rest of the plant to flourish. Harvest canes annually near the end of summer. We love the idea of being self-sufficient in as many materials as possible, so never

again needing to buy a single bamboo cane for the garden was reason enough to plant bamboo. Any larger growth that we get in years to come we plan to weave together and build some form of garden shelter or seating area.

Flax or linseed (5)
Linum usitatissimum

■ **How to grow** Flax is one of the UK's oldest crops –used to make linen and also linseed oil, a rich source of omega-3. Flax seed grows best in well-drained soil, rich in organic matter. Sow in drills in late spring and cover lightly with soil.

■ **Harvest** The seed capsules are ready to harvest in late summer when most have turned brown. Mow the crop, rake it up into sections, and let it dry. The dried seeds can be pressed to make oil or milled for flour. The husks make a rich oil cake for cattle and the rough straw a base layer for animal bedding.

Hemp
Cannabis sativa

■ **How to grow** Hemp grows well on most soil, but avoid poorly drained or sandy ground. Prepare a weed-free seed bed and sow from late April to early May when the risk of frost has passed. Make drills at a depth of 2.5cm (1in) and leave 13–25cm (5–10in)

5
6
7
8

between rows. Hemp plants tend to be very competitive and once they are mature they will smother any other plants with their tall, dense canopy. The environmental benefits of hemp compared to crops such as cotton are unquestionable. It is grows fast, needs little water and no pesticides or chemicals. It is also important to understand that hemp is not the same as wacky baccy! The agricultural variety has almost negligible levels of cannabinoids.

■ **Harvest** Hemp is a versatile crop and can be made into all sorts of natural products, such as insulation, fabric, paper, and animal bedding.

Hops (6)
Humulus lupulus

■ **How to grow** After a hard day working the land, there are few things more enjoyable than going to the local pub and enjoying a well-deserved pint of beer. By chance we prefer our local brewery's ale rather than imported lager, so the ensuing "beer-miles" are not too bad. However, if you are serious about becoming more self-sufficient then growing your own hops is worth trying. Hops are relatively easy to grow in well-drained soil with plenty of manure. First, remove any perennial weeds and grass

growing in the area and then lay bits of hop roots, from 30–60cm (1–2ft) in length under a good layer of manure or compost. Space these bits of root 1m (3ft) apart. Male and female flowers are produced on separate plants. It's the female "cones" you need for brewing and for best flavour they should be unpollinated, so dig up any male plants that grow.

■ **Harvest** Cut the flowers when they are blooming and the

TRAINING HOPS

To make picking easier *and keep your plot neat, train hops on a traditional-style frame with 3m (10ft) tall strings; the hops race up them when they burst into life in spring. If you have space, try a "maypole" with strings running from the top of a central pole – or train hops on a pergola instead of a grapevine and create a shady place to sit.*

inside is full of a yellow powder that will be the key ingredient in your very own beer (see page 254). Dry them thoroughly by hanging from wires over a stove or wood burner. Store the hops in a hessian sack until you are ready to use them.

Rice (7)
Oryza sativa

■ **How to grow** Although better known as an Asian crop, rice is in fact grown in large quantities in America and Southern Europe. What makes rice tricky to grow further north is that it requires summer temperatures of over 20°C (68°F) for most of its growing season, which can be up to four or even five months. Rice also needs plenty of water. We recommend growing it under cover (with a minimum temperature of 10°C/50°F) and using a ram pump to supply the irrigation system (see pages 74–75). Prepare a seed bed that has warmed up in spring and rake the seed in well after sowing. Flood the bed with water once. As the rice plants grow, keep the bed well watered, making sure that the water is below the top of the shoots. When the plants are about 20cm (8in) tall, thin them to about 10cm (4in) between plants and continue to keep your small-scale paddy field wet. Transplant the

thinned seedlings to a second bed. Seeds can be difficult to source: we recommend growing mountain rice.

■ **Harvest** Cut the plants at the end of summer, when the rice spikelets are hard and yellow-coloured or turn from green to brown. Drain the patch and allow the rice to dry for 2–4 weeks in the greenhouse.

Tea (8)
Camellia sinensis

■ **How to grow** Tea is native to China and India but has more recently been grown in other parts of the world. It is an evergreen plant from the camellia family. Plants are best propagated from cuttings and grown under cover for the first couple of years. Outside on a south-facing slope, a standard tea bush will grow to about 1m (3ft) tall, and needs selective pruning to make it easy to pick the young leaves. Position tea plants about 1.5m (5ft) apart in rows, with 1m (3ft) between each row. We are growing our own tea thanks to the climate in the south-west of England. It so happens it is very similar to the climate in Darjeeling. Best go get the kettle on...

■ **Harvest** Bushes take six years to mature before they can be picked. Pick the tender young tips every 7–10 days in the growing season.

Storing crops on a larger scale

When you're growing crops for animals and humans you need more storage space. A root cellar is designed to keep vegetables fresh for months on end. We think there is something very satisfying about eating a stored carrot in spring or having turnips to feed to our pigs on cold winter days. And if you've made hay in summer, you'll need somewhere weatherproof to keep it.

The hay shed

Once hay is harvested and dried (see page 176), you'll need a covered hay shed to keep it dry. Wet mouldy hay breaks down quickly and is not only unhealthy for animals to eat, it's a fire hazard – hay heats up as it rots. If it gets too wet, mix it into your compost bins or use as a mulch.

Site the shed close to livestock housing so you don't have far to lug the hay. Make the sides from vertical wooden slats about 7.5cm (3in) apart, to allow the hay to breathe but stop it getting wet. Design the door so there is enough headroom to walk in while holding a pitchfork of hay – this will avoid backache later! The shed should be solid and wind-resistant but don't waste large sums of money on what is essentially a rain-cover for dried grass.

Grain store

Grain that has been threshed to separate it from straw needs to be kept safe from vermin. Metal bins with lids are a good option or try a traditional grain store bucket raised off the ground. Keep straw under cover in the same way as hay.

Some cereals, such as oats, can be fed to livestock without threshing. Store these cereals in sheaves (see page 176) under cover.

Storing root vegetables

Root cellars are designed to store large quantities of produce all through the year without refrigeration. Their design is based on the fact that most root crops keep best in cold, humid, dark conditions, with plenty of room for air to circulate. Traditional root cellars were built wholly or partly below ground. The ideal site is carved into a north-facing slope. They don't need windows – roots must be kept in the dark, just as they were when they were growing. Site your root cellar close to the house. The last thing you want in winter is to get cold and wet fetching produce. Keep a wind-up torch hanging inside the exterior door to the cellar so you can see what you're doing.

Temperature

Put a thermometer in the cellar and check it regularly. The ideal temperature range is between 0–4.5°C (32–40°F). Install an intake vent near the bottom of the cellar wall to draw in cool night air and, at the high point of the cellar, another vent to let out warm air. Use the vents to control the temperature: open at night if the cellar gets too warm.

Humidity levels

High humidity is best: about 90–95 per cent will stop root vegetables from shrivelling. Use a hygrometer to measure it accurately. The easiest way to increase humidity is by pouring water on the floor. Earth floors maintain higher humidity levels than concrete.

Ventilation

Keeping air circulating in the cellar also helps remove ethylene gas produced by vegetables as they ripen. Left to build up, it can cause other veg to ripen quickly, and make them smell bad or start to sprout. Use the cold and warm air vents to control circulation and temperature.

MINI ROOT CELLAR

If you have an old wooden barrel don't even think about cutting it in half and turning it into two planters. Sink it into the ground against a wall close to the kitchen and turn it into a mini household root cellar.

Converting the barrel to a store

Dig a slight dip in the ground next to the wall and start layering up rocks so that the barrel can be positioned at a 45° angle with the lid facing outwards. Fill the barrel with harvested root crops, packing straw around them for insulation. Back fill with earth behind the barrel, add a layer of straw and another layer of earth, except above the barrel opening. Add a wooden board for a door.

Layer of earth 60cm (2ft) thick

Layer of straw

Wooden board with handle

Barrel at 45° angle

Building a root cellar

If you haven't got a natural slope to house a root cellar, you can achieve a similar effect by building it partly below ground and heaping soil over the top to create an earth berm (see pages 48–49). You will need advice from a structural engineer to create a framework strong enough to hold the weight of earth. Make your cellar at least 1.5m x 2.5m (5ft x 8ft).

Fitting out the cellar
Add plenty of shelves for storage. Make them from a durable hardwood such as oak that won't need treating with wood preservatives, which can taint stored produce. Spread a thick layer of gravel on the floor to stop your feet getting wet when you pour water on the ground. Or use large shallow pans of water to adjust the humidity instead.

Traditional root cellars *in Canada built into the slope of a north-facing hill, with turf roofs and solid doors for insulation.*

Making use of natural factors
The design of a root cellar relies on earth's insulating properties combined with the tendency of warm air to rise.

Adjustable vent to let out warm air

Air circulates when the vents are opened and cools the air in the cellar.

Plastic damp-proof membrane above 15cm (6in) concrete ceiling

North-facing earth berm keeps cellar cool

Hardwood shelves for storing produce

Gap between shelving and wall allows air to circulate

Breeze block or brick walls

Circulating air stops ethylene gas building up

Stone foundations

Gravel over earth floor

Cold-air vent with adjustable intake

Wire mesh on both vents keeps out insects and rodents

Double door system stops warm air entering when you do

HOW LONG WILL FOOD KEEP FRESH?

The length of time that roots stay edible varies greatly, depending on how well you regulate the temperature, ventilation, and humidity. It is a case of trial and error until you learn the unique qualities of your individual root cellar. There is no reason why most stored produce should not last a whole year in the right conditions.

Produce to store

- Beetroot
- Carrots
- Celeriac
- Fodder beet
- Jerusalem artichokes
- Kohlrabi
- Mangolds

- Parsnips
- Potatoes
- Salsify
- Scorzonera
- Swedes
- Turnips

Managing a wood

Productive woodlands have been carefully managed in the UK for centuries, and we believe that some form of control is really beneficial, as it helps to keep trees strong and healthy, and can extend their life. It also makes good economic sense, allowing you to become self-sufficient in fuel, as well as providing a shelter belt for crops and playing an important part in nature conservation.

Woodlands for fuel

Small woodlands are most often managed to provide a source of firewood for the home. You can season it by storing it under cover with good air circulation for at least a year – the longer you store it, the better it burns. If you have firewood to spare, you can sell it or make charcoal (see pages 184–185).

Construction and crafts

Roundwood is wood that's in the same state as it was when felled. It isn't worth much money, but is useful for building simple structures, like sheds and barns. Coppiced wood is ideal for fencing, basketry (see pages 280–281), and green woodworking techniques (see pages 282–283).

You may need permission from the Forestry Commission to fell trees. Some are protected by preservation orders or may be growing in a conservation area – check with your local authority. Trees with trunks less than 8cm (3in) in diameter when measured 1.3m (4ft 3in) above the ground are fine to fell yourself. For all others, call in a professional.

Livestock and woodland
- **Pigs** kept in woodland enjoy eating acorns and beech mast.
- **Cattle and sheep** allowed the occasional foray into the woods can help to regenerate the vegetation.
- **Chickens** are woodland birds.
- Holding an occasional **pheasant shoot** brings in extra income.

Managing a coppice

Coppice comes from the French word "couper", meaning to cut, and it's a sustainable way to harvest large quantities of timber from your trees. Plant the trees close together and, when the trunks are about 23cm (9in) in diameter, cut them in winter to just above the ground. Tall, straight poles will grow from the stumps, and you can then repeat the procedure every few years and harvest the wood. Ash, hazel, and willow are ideal.

If you have an existing coppice that has been left for several years, divide it into "coupes", or areas to be coppiced. The diameter of a coupe should be about 1.5 times the height of the trees. For fencing and firewood, cut the trees every 10–15 years. Harvest one coupe at a time within this cycle; don't cut all the coupes in one go, as this will disrupt the natural ecology. A short cycle of 3–4 years is known as a "short rotation coppice". Use willow for this, and turn the slimmer poles into woodchip biomass for heating (see pages 82–83).

1. Coppiced hazel trees planted close together grow tall and straight towards the light. **2. Chickens** enjoy foraging in the willow and dogwood coppice at Newhouse Farm. **3. Using a log splitter** reduces logs from mature trees to a manageable size for a stove.

Creating a new wood

Planting a mixture of conifers and broad-leaved trees helps to ensure biodiversity and provides the best environment for wildlife. Your plot will benefit too, as woodland creates an effective windbreak for crops.

Getting started

Siting a new wood is easy. Choose land that is not good for much else, such as north-facing slopes, poorly drained land, and infertile soil.

Spacing is important. If trees are too far apart, they will grow with short trunks and too many branches, and if planted too close together, they will be tall and spindly. The best technique is to plant closely and then thin out the trees as they grow (see page 135). Buy bare-root trees from a nursery and plant in winter, or grow your own saplings from seed (see below).

In a mixed woodland of conifers and deciduous trees, the conifers create shelter for wildlife in winter, and early nesting sites for birds in spring. They also retain warmth in autumn so that deciduous trees hold on to their leaves for longer, which improves their growth rates.

Growing your own saplings from locally collected nuts and seeds ensures your new trees are truly local species.

Putting up boxes for dormice and birds is just one way of making your woodland more wildlife friendly.

Plastic tree guards protect saplings from rabbits and hares. Remove them as the trees mature.

TOP TREES

Our suggested trees for planting a small-scale woodland for timber and firewood:

■ **Sweet chestnut** Awesome for timber, fast growing, strong.
■ **Oak** Slow growing and slow burning too.
■ **Ash** Tough and resilient with deep roots. Fast growing. Excellent firewood as it splits easily and even burns when it's green.
■ **Larch** An unusual deciduous conifer. Very fast growing. Makes good fencing.
■ **Cherry** A good hardwood for sweet-smelling firewood.
■ **Elm** Great for making chopping boards or butcher's blocks, sadly almost extinct now in Britain.
■ **Silver birch** One of our favourites for burning but it must be well seasoned.

PESTS AND PROBLEMS

Newly planted saplings are most at risk from animal pests, such as deer and squirrels, which can damage mature trees too.

■ **Deer** damage is easy to spot, as they eat all the leaves and nibble the twigs up to a definite, visible line. Put up fencing 1.8m (6ft) high, or shoot them.
■ **Grey squirrels** munch on the bark of many broad-leaved trees and will often eat the leading shoots of young saplings. Reduce their population by poison, traps, or shooting.
■ **Rabbits and hares** strip the bark of young saplings, which kills the young trees. Protect trees with guards or fencing.
■ *Rhododendron ponticum* is an invasive shrub that casts such heavy shade that nothing else can grow below it. Keep it under control if you value biodiversity; ideally dig it all out if you have the energy.

Making charcoal

Thousands of tonnes of charcoal are burned on barbecues in the UK each year but most comes from tropical rainforests and endangered mangrove swamps on the other side of the world. Yet charcoal has been made in this country for centuries, and it's easy to build a kiln and make some on a small scale, so why not give it a go and enjoy truly satisfying summer barbecues?

What is charcoal?

Charcoal is made by heating wood with insufficient oxygen to burn, but to a temperature high enough to drive out water and volatile gases. Charcoal burns slowly to a very high temperature. In Europe it was used for thousands of years for smelting metals until coal took its place, and traditional blacksmiths still prefer to use charcoal in their forges. It is also popular with artists for sketching, but today its main use is for barbecues.

Its slow-burning properties make charcoal perfect for outdoor cooking, but never use it on an open fire indoors, as it produces toxic carbon monoxide when it burns.

Buy local

Wood from British trees is less dense than timber used for imported charcoal, making it far easier to light and quicker to heat up for cooking.

Local forestry volunteer groups often make charcoal as an annual fundraiser, using the money for woodland management. If everyone in the UK decided to buy locally produced charcoal we'd all get better quality as a result. When we can't buy locally, we buy bags with the Forest Stewardship Council (FSC) logo. This non-profit organization promotes conservation of the world's forests and guarantees products come from well-managed sources.

BARBECUE TIPS

■ **To speed up the cooking process** try this method of lighting. Take an off-cut of a metal pipe and stand it on top of the barbecue tray to make a "chimney". Stuff the bottom with paper, add some kindling and light it. Once the kindling catches, add charcoal via the top of the pipe. When the charcoal starts to burn, put on some oven gloves and carefully lift the pipe upwards so that the glowing charcoals spread across the tray.

■ **Don't start cooking** until the bed of hot embers has been glowing for 10–15 minutes.

■ **When the charcoal is ash grey** it's reached the right temperature.

A TRADITIONAL CHARCOAL CLAMP

The clamp was built with logs arranged in a criss-cross pattern around a central hole. More wood was stacked around the logs to form a mound about 3.7m (12ft) across and topped with layers of leaves and turf, with a few vents at the bottom. Once lit the collier tended the fire constantly for two weeks, making sure it smouldered but didn't break into flames, until blue smoke signalled the charcoal was ready.

Make a modern trench version

A charcoal pit is a good idea if you have the space and want to make a large batch. Dig a decent-sized trench and fill it with wood. Set fire to the wood and when it is fully ablaze cover the trench with a couple of sheets of corrugated iron. Then quickly shovel earth on top, burying the sheets of metal and cutting off the oxygen supply. Leave the heat to work its magic. After several days, open up the trench and remove your newly made charcoal.

A traditional charcoal clamp should smoulder but never burst into flames.

Collier lights the clamp by throwing fire embers into the chimney vent

A clamp is around 1.8m (6ft) tall

Short lengths of wood

Layer of leaves, twigs and turf

Vent

Ladder to reach the hole at the top to light the fire

DIY charcoal kiln

We made a small kiln out of an old oil drum, which produces more than enough charcoal for our summer barbecues. To keep home-made charcoal in good condition, store it in sealed bags so that it doesn't get wet. Use it for cooking, blacksmithing, or drawing.

Using the kiln

First, light a wood fire in the drum to burn off any remaining residue (see page 251). Then, using an angle grinder, cut off the base of the drum around the metal rim, leaving three protruding cams. This disk will later form the lid. Turn the drum over and drill five holes in what will now be the base. Place the base on some bricks and seal it with soil and turf, leaving an air vent 15cm (6in) in diameter. Fill the kiln by standing a wooden post in the middle and stuffing offcuts of construction timber and hardwood around it. To light the kiln, carefully pull out the central post to leave a chimney, and drop lighted paper and kindling into the hole. Once the wood is burning, place the lid on the cams, and seal around it with sand. When the smoke from the kiln turns from white to blue, close off the air supply by rotating the lid to cover the cams. Leave overnight – your charcoal will be ready the next day. Take care not to inhale any dust when removing it.

Home-made charcoal *is cheap to make from wood that would otherwise go to waste, and it's also easy to light.*

Making charcoal
For best results use hardwood offcuts and monitor the air flow carefully.

The disk cut from the original base of the oil drum forms the lid

Metal cams support the lid and close off the chimney holes when needed

Smoke will change from a thick white plume to a blue haze, normally after about three hours

Rotate the lid to close the chimney holes and leave the drum to stand overnight

Upside-down oil drum

Seasoned wood cut into wedges, from 2–5cm (¾–2in) thick

To make your own artists' charcoal simply stuff a tin can tightly with 10cm (4in) lengths of willow and place the can in your kiln along with the other wood

Five well-spaced inlet holes in base of kiln

Soil and turf to seal base

Bricks to raise kiln off of ground

Inlet hole for air 15–23cm (6–9in) in diameter

CHARCOAL TIPS

■ **Wear a mask** when removing the charcoal so that you don't inhale any dust.
■ **More ash than charcoal** shows that the wood has burned rather than heated up. Next time reduce the size of the air inlet hole at the base and pack the surrounding turf more tightly.
■ **Wood that is charred**, rather than fully formed charcoal, didn't get hot enough. You may have put the lid on top of the fire too early, or the air hole needs enlarging.

ANIMAL HUSBANDRY By keeping animals you take a huge step towards leading a self-sufficient life. Even just a couple of hens can give you a real sense of independence. If you choose to produce your own meat, however, there are stark facts to be faced. Meat does not come pre-sliced and wrapped in cellophane, and we know lots of people who have problems killing their livestock. To give your animals the best possible life, and then to dispatch them with the least amount of stress, seems to us the sensible way to produce meat. You can be certain commercially-farmed animals are not shown the same respect.

Keeping chickens

People have been keeping hens for thousands of years. The Ancient Egyptians, Greeks, Chinese, and Romans all enjoyed the benefits of rearing chickens for eggs and meat. Nowadays they are still ideal domestic animals, whether you live in an urban or rural area. However you like your eggs in the morning, if they come from your own free-range chickens nothing compares to their great taste.

Choosing the breed

We generally try to mix our small flocks to include pure breeds and some hybrids. Hybrids are used commercially and you can expect lots of eggs. Traditional breeds look more interesting and are useful to have as broody hens if you want to rear your own chicks. Light Sussex and Rhode Island Red are ideal for both eggs and eating but are ignored by commercial farmers because of their small eggs. We tend to opt for bantams, which are smallish breeds: they are relatively low cost to feed and you don't need much space. For a small plot, especially an urban one, we would recommend getting only a few hens and not bothering with a cockerel (see box opposite). As long as you keep fewer than 50 birds in total, including other poultry, there's no need to register your flock with DEFRA (see www.defra.gov.uk).

What age to buy?

Day-old chicks are very cheap to buy but are unsexed, so you won't find out which are cockerels until later. This is good if you want some birds for meat but bad news if you simply want plenty of eggs. There's also the expense of heating their enclosure when they're young and giving them extra feed until they're ready to lay.

Pullets

These are birds that can be anything from about eight to 20 weeks old. You can easily buy them in batches of all females – no worries about cockerels. They take a little more

OUR FREE-RANGE PHILOSOPHY

The key for us has always been to provide our chickens with as much free roaming space as possible. On our suburban plot we let them out into the garden in the morning and locked them away at night. Now on our smallholding they have a substantial area to roam. Chickens are traditionally woodland birds and appreciate being in our willow coppice. They're also at home in open fields, where they supplement their diet with insect pests and weed seeds. However, there are disadvantages to the free-range lifestyle. Hens will start laying eggs in hidden places instead of their nest boxes. If it becomes a problem, keep them in their run till midday, until they start laying inside again.

Good to eat?
To check how old an egg is, put it in a bowl of water. A fresh egg lies on its side at the bottom (left); rotten eggs float (right).

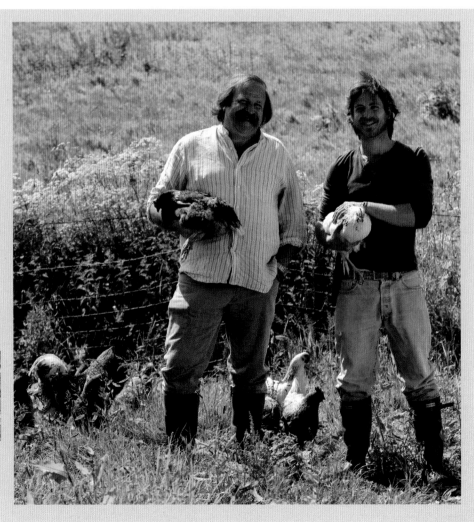

feeding before they start producing eggs but are a good age to buy.

Point-of-lay pullets

At 20 weeks old hens start laying eggs. Their first season tends to be their most productive. You have to spend a bit more to get point-of-lay pullets, but we have occasionally found it worth while, especially when our existing hens are getting a bit old and we want a few more daily eggs.

Year-old ex-battery hens

Commercial battery farms kill their hens after their first year of laying. After they've reached their productive peak they no longer have value. There are huge animal-welfare issues that are associated with battery hens. Often they spend their whole life in an area no bigger than an A4 piece of paper; they lose their feathers, never learn how to scratch, and generally look a sorry state. We buy battery hens and give them a second chance. They are normally hybrids and are excellent layers. It's a humbling experience to see a maltreated animal rediscovering its instincts and enjoying its first dust bath or struggling to eat its first worm. The colour of their combs changes from a sickly pale pink to a healthy red in just a few weeks. Not only is it a feel-good thing to do, but battery hens are productive and cheap.

1. Marans are one of our favourites. They tend to be very hardy and lay large, deep-brown eggs. **2. Light Sussex** are a lovely old English breed and are great layers as well as good table birds.
3. Buff Orpingtons are placid birds that lay smallish eggs. They are excellent hens for fostering chicks. If you don't plan to breed from your flock, don't choose these hens as they have a tendency to go broody. **4. Rescued hybrid battery hens** adapt quickly, soon thriving in their new free-range environment, and are reliably good layers.

COCKEREL PROS AND CONS

A cockerel is a great way of keeping a free-range flock together; he will shepherd them and protect them from predators. Our latest, William, lost his tail feathers defending his ladies from a fox and walked around with an unsightly stump for a few months afterwards. Another reason to keep a cockerel is that it gives you the opportunity to rear more chicks, at little expense, if you let a hen go broody. The disadvantage in urban areas is their tendency to act as an alarm clock, so apologies to all our neighbours who have been woken up over the years.

Housing and basic care

Whether you keep chickens in an urban garden or on a smallholding, they have the same needs: a cosy nest box to lay in, a patch of ground on which to scratch and forage, and – most important – somewhere to sleep at night, safe from predators. We built our big chicken coop inside a shed with an outside run attached. This makes cleaning them out easy, even on a rainy day. We have also got a movable ark (see pages 192–193) down in the field. A movable system is ideal for gardens: it gives hens access to grass and you can change its position when the land is looking a bit hen-pecked. All chickens need somewhere to perch during the day and to roost at night, constant fresh water and, of course, tasty food.

Chickens like to perch *as they are woodland birds – ideally on a round branch to avoid damaging their feet.*

KEY TO CHICKEN RUN

1. **Outside run**
2. **Dust bath under shelter**
3. **Mesh roof on outside run**
4. **Indoor run within shed**
5. **Pulley system to operate door**
6. **Door to outside run**
7. **Staggered perches**
8. **Nest box with access hatch**
9. **Hen access to nest box**
10. **Vermin-proof feed store**
11. **Access for humans**
12. **Sawdust on floor**
13. **Rat-proof feeder**
14. **Bowls of grit and oystershell**
15. **Automated water supply**

Dust baths are a vital way to get rid of parasites like lice; make one by filling a shallow wooden box with fine silver sand and keep it somewhere covered from the rain

Give grit and oystershell in small pots to aid digestion and avoid calcium deficiency

Chickens must have clean water and an automatic watering system saves a huge amount of time – if you fill up their water manually, do it regularly

MAKING A PERCH FOR A MOVABLE RUN

Even though the sleeping quarters are raised off the ground in a movable ark (see pages 192–193), hens still need simple free-standing perches to roost on at night. **1. Saw** a piece of freshly cut wood to length. It should be around 7.5cm (3in) in diameter. Leave the bark on. Cut two supports from thicker trunks.
2. Fix the perch to each support using long screws, ensuring no sharp edges protrude. **3. Install** the perch.

A simple movable run *with secure, sheltered accommodation for night-time. Move to fresh grass every few days.*

Avoid corrugated iron roofs: they get too hot in the summer and too cold in winter

Perches should be wooden, rounded, and at least 75cm (30in) off the ground and about 7.5cm (3in) wide; stagger them so that the droppings can fall straight to the floor, not on to other birds

Hens enter nest box from inside run

Chickens like a warm cosy nest box to lay eggs in, with plenty of fresh straw; these nest boxes have hinged doors for easy collection

Keep the feeder indoors, away from falling droppings, and hang it above ground to make it rat-proof; cover the floor with sawdust and clean out regularly

Traditionally, chickens were fed on kitchen scraps and spare grain. We still give them some kitchen waste, but are very careful to avoid any contamination – they only have veg scraps, no meat. We supplement their free-range diet with a combination of mixed corn and layers' pellets, which we store in a secure metal bin to stop rats and mice helping themselves.

Let your chickens out to roam *during the day, even in frost. The only time you'll need to keep them shut in is when there is deep snow on the ground. Remember, egg production will drop in winter – it's controlled by the hours of daylight.*

POTENTIAL PROBLEMS

Keeping chickens is generally straightforward, but you may need to use some of the following techniques and solutions.

Trimming a cockerel's spurs

This will stop your hens from getting hurt during mating. Wrap the cockerel in a towel and hold him firmly. Use wire cutters to trim the spurs a little at a time. File them smooth when you're done.

Making the cut
Avoid the vein: stop at the first sight of blood below the surface.

Red mites

Parasites that emerge from the woodwork at night. To deal with them, keep the coop clean and get a remedy from a vet.

Scaly feet

Caused by burrowing mite. Isolate affected birds and consult a vet.

Broody hens

If one of your hens has gone broody and you don't want any more chicks, place her in a small slatted coop for a couple of days. The cold air circulating underneath will deter her from sitting.

The cooler
This coop has a slatted floor to stop the broody hen sitting comfortably.

Build a chicken ark

A movable chicken ark is ideal for small gardens, as it keeps your chickens where you want them while giving them access to grass. When a patch wears out you can simply lift the ark and move it on to pastures new. Raising the nest box above the run makes maximum use of the space available for the chickens to move about. This ark houses two or three hens comfortably.

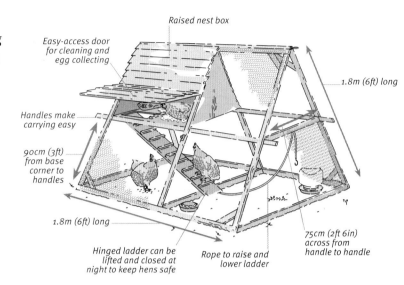

Raised nest box

Easy-access door for cleaning and egg collecting

1.8m (6ft) long

Handles make carrying easy

90cm (3ft) from base corner to handles

1.8m (6ft) long

Hinged ladder can be lifted and closed at night to keep hens safe

Rope to raise and lower ladder

75cm (2ft 6in) across from handle to handle

YOU WILL NEED

- Handsaw
- Circular saw, jigsaw
- Power drill/driver
- Wire cutters
- Tape measure, pencil
- Hammer
- Pressure-treated planks, battens
- Plywood, feather boards
- Chicken wire
- Staples, pins, screws, nails
- Hinges, latch, clasp, rope

MAKING THE FRAME

1. Cut planks to size and screw them together. We used 1.8m (6ft) square frames that were a convenient fit for chicken wire of 90cm (3ft) width. Screw angled brace supports into the corners of each frame, except for the corner where the door will be located.   **2. Fit the final corner brace** on the inside edge of the frame, so that the door to the ark will fit flush in the corner. Rest one frame on the other while working for stability. **3. Fix a vertical strut** into the centre of each frame. Attach longer horizontal struts to the inside of the frame, protruding at least a hand's span each side of the ark. These will be used to carry it, so fix them at waist height and sand the ends to make them comfortable to handle.

4. Work out the ideal width to maximize space for the chickens while making the ark easy to carry and prop the frames against each other.   **5. Take measurements.** Ours was 1.5m (5ft) wide at the base and 75cm (2ft 6in) wide at handle height. Cut lengths for horizontal central and base struts.   **6. Mark angles** and cut ends to fit.   **7. Fix base struts** to inside edge of the long verticals, and central struts to the inside edge of the horizontals. Fix an additional horizontal strut higher up, to attach the nest-box door frame (see step 12).

MAKING THE NEST BOX

FEATHER BOARDING

To fit boards, secure screws without over-tightening, lift the edge and slide the next layer under. Once in position, tighten top screws and repeat process.

8. Measure the floor for the nest box, and cut out from plywood using a circular saw or handsaw. Cut out a hen-sized access hatch using a jigsaw. Screw the floor to the supporting struts. **9. Measure, cut, and attach** plywood end pieces for the nest box. **10. Make a ladder** from a 0.3 x 1.2m (1 x 4ft) plyboard plank. Pin on rungs made from battens, using a block of wood as a spacer. Hinge the ladder to a section of plank and screw the plank to the underside of the floor, level with the access hatch. **11. Clad one side** of the nest box with feather boards (see box); fit them to about halfway down on the other side.

12. Construct a door big enough for you to collect the eggs; aim to make the height such that the bottom of a feather board will fit over the top part of the hinges. **13. Fit it flush** with the main frame and let it overhang the nest box floor to avoid draughts. Add hinges. **14. Complete the feather boarding,** attaching those covering the door to its frame. You can also add a simple clasp for a padlock. **15. Attach a capping timber** to the top of the ark to stop rain dripping through the roof joint.

ATTACHING CHICKEN WIRE

17. Make another door to fit one of the bottom rectangles. Strengthen the door with two corner braces at opposite ends. Attach hinges to one of the vertical sides. Cut chicken wire to size and staple it in place.
18. Screw the door hinges in place and attach a latch to keep out predators. **19. Continue** attaching chicken wire over the whole frame, taking care not to leave any loose edges. Snip off any sharp ends.
20. Install a drinker and feeder, and introduce your chickens!

How to increase your flock

Which comes first: the chicken or the egg? Well, we have always started with chickens and increased our flocks from their eggs – that's why we keep a cockerel (see page 189). But for a beginner we recommend buying fertilized eggs (do this online) and incubating them yourself. It's harder work than leaving it to nature, but it's the least risky way to build a flock.

Hatching your own

An electronically controlled incubator takes care of the temperature and humidity, but you'll still need to turn the eggs three times a day so that the embryo does not get stuck on the shell (see box). Incubation is about 21 days. After seven days, "candle" the eggs to check they are fertile (see box). Stop turning them on day 19.

After hatching, leave the chicks in the incubator for the first 24 hours and don't worry about feeding. Then move them to a heated brooder, where they will live for the next six weeks. The brooder must be rat-proof, with wood shavings on the floor and an infra-red lamp above. Ideally, the temperature should be 35°C (95°F); then reduce it by 3°C (5.4°F) a week.

The natural way

It is easy to tell when one of your hens is broody. She won't leave the nest box and fluffs up to twice her size when you peer in. She will make loud noises and if you move her she'll go straight back to her eggs.

If you want her to hatch chicks, you must move her to her own house. Firstly, so that the chicks are safe and secondly, so that she doesn't discourage all the other hens from coming in to the nest box to lay.

Her house should be warm and cosy, with food and water nearby. We find it easiest to move broody hens at night. After that, there is very little to do – other than provide chick crumb and water for your new chicks.

DIY HATCHING

■ **An electronic incubator** allows minimal handling, which can cool the eggs or introduce bacteria.

■ **Warm it up** before the eggs arrive. In a still-air machine the ideal temperature is 39.4°C (102.9°F), measured 5cm (2in) above the eggs. Set the humidity to 75–80 per cent.

■ **Label eggs** with the date they were added to the incubator.

■ **Turning the eggs** Using your pencilled date label as a helpful marker, rotate each egg through 180 degrees every time you turn it.

■ **Candling the eggs** Cut two holes in opposite sides of a cardboard box. Hold an egg in front of one hole and shine a torch through the other and examine the yolk. Discard infertile eggs and those with the blood ring of a failed embryo.

What to look for
From left: failed embryo, infertile egg with clear yolk, fertile embryo.

■ **In the brooder** Show your chicks where the water is by dipping their beaks in it, and drop food in front of them like the mother hen would.

■ **Using an infra-red lamp** If it's too hot, chicks move away from the lamp; too cold and they huddle below.

Broody Buff Orpingtons are great foster hens. Give them a clutch of fertilized eggs to sit on and they will hatch the chicks and raise them as their own.

PROJECT **Prepare chickens to eat**

Killing one of your chickens and preparing it for a meal is relatively simple. The first time you do it, it's a good idea to get an experienced person to help so that the chicken is rendered unconscious immediately and doesn't suffer.

KILLING AND PLUCKING

DO
■ Make sure that the bird has not been fed for 24 hours so that its digestive system is empty
■ Get someone to help
■ Stay relaxed
■ Pluck the chicken straight away when it's still warm
■ Wash your hands between plucking and drawing

DON'T
■ Panic
■ Use too much force
■ Kill a bird in front of other chickens
■ Tear at the feathers or you'll rip the skin

1. Take both legs firmly in your left hand and hold the head cupped in the palm of your right hand, with your index finger and middle finger either side of its neck. **2. Stretch** the neck down so that the head bends backwards. Stretch until the neck is broken: don't go too far as the head will come off. **3. Tie the feet** and hang the chicken. Start plucking immediately. It is far easier to do while the bird is warm. Pluck the wing feathers, followed by the leg feathers, then the body.

DRAWING

4. Cut from the bottom of the neck up to the head. **5. Sever** the neckbone and remove it, along with the head. **6. Put your finger** inside the gap and loosen the innards by moving your fingers inside the cavity. **7. Turn** the chicken and slit between the vent and tail, being careful not to pierce the rectum or you'll contaminate the flesh. Cut all round the vent.

8. Pull the vent carefully away from the body; it should come away quite easily now that you've cut it free. **9. Draw out** the intestines, gizzard, lungs, liver, and heart with the vent as you keep pulling it steadily. **10. Remove the crop** from the neck end of the chicken, being careful not to pierce it. Tuck the flaps of skin back inside at either end of the bird. Gently singe the skin with a flame to burn off any remaining fluffy feathers. **11. Truss the bird** up ready for roasting. Cut off the feet and tie the wing tips to the legs, then wrap the string round the hocks and the end of the tail.

Keeping turkeys

The first Christmas at Newhouse Farm we ordered an organic turkey from our local butcher. It was a lovely bird, but with a huge price tag. Next year we did the sums and reckoned we could rear them for about a third of the price. So we fattened a dozen, giving them lots of room and organic feed, and it was a resounding success. Watching them grow is fascinating and they make great presents.

Choosing what to buy

We buy birds that are 5–6 weeks old rather than day-olds, because it cuts down on the hassle of providing lamps and looking after them when they are at their most fragile. We normally buy 12 Norfolk Black turkeys, which are too young to sex at a glance. We would expect to know which are stags and which are hens by about 12–13 weeks. As long as you keep fewer than 50 birds in total, including other poultry, there's no need to register your flock with DEFRA (see www.defra.gov.uk).

The best breeds to choose from are:

Bourbon Reds are an American breed that originated in Kentucky and Pennsylvania and can grow to a monstrous 15kg (33lb). Their feathers are a reddish-chestnut colour and their tail feathers are white.

Bronze are named after the unusual colour of their feathers, which are a green copper-brown in the sun. Bronze turkeys often require artificial insemination to reproduce due to the large size of their breast meat. We have found them a calm bird to keep that can grow very large.

Buff turkeys have reddish buff-coloured feathers and the hens can be good egg producers. The added advantage of a buff turkey is that the pin feathers are nearly white, so it looks great when plucked.

Narragansett are extremely tasty birds that are more hardy than most other breeds due to their mixed genetic selection. Narragansett turkeys are traditionally known for having a calm disposition and making good mothers.

Norfolk Black are our favourites and possess striking black plumage.

CLIPPING WINGS

If you want to restrict the movement of your turkeys, clip one of their wings. Clip both wings and they will put lots of effort into flying and eventually take off, whereas one wing means they are lopsided and spin back to earth. When clipping, simply cut off their primary feathers with a sharp pair of scissors at the point where they line up with the next layer.

Get someone else *to hold the turkey as you clip the wing feathers.*

1. Turkeys don't have great eyesight, so they may need coaxing into their shed at night. **2. Give them organic feed** and clean them out regularly. **3. Turkeys** will thrive with plenty of space to enjoy.

They are slower to mature than many commercial breeds, but it's more than compensated by their really tasty flavour. Having said Norfolk Blacks are slow to mature, the stags can still reach a good 11kg (25lb)!

Housing and basic care

Turkeys must be kept separate from chickens to guard against the fatal blackhead disease. We keep our turkeys outside in a small paddock surrounded by electric fencing to keep out any hungry foxes (see page 175 for how to set one up). They have a decent-sized shed to shelter in and a big perch in the middle of their enclosure, which they sit upon and practise vulture impressions.

We feed our birds with turkey grower's pellets, which have less protein in them than commercial turkey feed. The reason we are able to use this type of feed is because we usually get birds as early as possible in the season, so that they have plenty of time to grow in size naturally and obtain a great deal of their protein by snacking on the insects and bugs in their enclosure.

When looking after turkeys, it is also vital to provide a good source of grit for them to eat. This acts as an aid to digestion, enabling them to mash up their food in their crop and digest the goodness, ensuring they grow nice and big during the year.

Top turkey tips

■ **Keep your turkeys clean!** Meaning the bedding and food containers – and give them plenty of fresh water. By keeping their house clean there is then far less chance of one of your birds getting ill.

■ **Shut them up at night**. Sounds like common sense, but free range doesn't mean providing the local fox with an early Christmas present.

■ **Leave the ground to rest** for 12 months before a new batch of turkeys return to the same spot. This helps avoid the dreaded blackhead, which is a parasite that lives in earthworms and gut worms. Signs of a problem are sulphur-yellow droppings and, more often than not, a dead turkey.

■ **Consider** homeopathic worming alternatives.

■ **If you plan to keep breeding stock** so you can enjoy turkey all through the year, buy some special leather saddles as protection for the hens. These sit on their backs and stop the stags from damaging them too much while mating. The saddles need to stay on in spring and come off in early autumn.

KILLING LARGE BIRDS

Slaughtering turkeys needs to be fast and efficient. We calmly take the birds one at a time to a barn. Then we place them upside down in a suspended traffic cone. One of us holds the legs while the other two place a broom handle on either side of the turkey's neck. They firmly squeeze the handles together and twist and push them down while the person holding the legs pulls up. This separates the vertebrae in the neck and then we immediately slice the jugular with a sharp knife. Once dead, the birds are hung up by their feet and we pluck them straight away (see page 195).

Doing the deed alone

To kill a turkey solo, place a broom handle over its neck, twist and press down with your feet, whilst pulling it up by the legs.

The "suspended traffic cone" method *requires three people to make it as efficient and kind as possible.*

Working alone *requires greater coordination and strength to ensure the job is done quickly and humanely.*

Keeping ducks and geese

Geese are absolutely amazing to rear yourself. We find that they are hardy, tough, and surprisingly self-reliant – almost the perfect self-sufficient animal – but they can be noisy and a handful if you're not used to big birds. Ducks are also extremely useful animals to keep on your plot, but you'll find they can be fairly messy!

Why keep ducks and geese?

Provided you have a source of fresh water, ducks are great to keep for four reasons: their delicious eggs, which make the best cakes in the world; they are tasty table birds; they are selective eaters that are less likely to scratch garden beds than chickens; and they can be useful at keeping down the population of pests like slugs. Geese are first class grazers and are great guard birds, with their noisy honking serving as an intruder alert. They usually start laying enormous eggs in February and March. Soft-boiled for breakfast, you'll find you need a whole regiment of soldiers to dip in them. Put in cold water, bring to the boil for six minutes – perfect! Bear in mind, though, that geese are large birds and need to be treated as such. Respect them when you pick them up or you will receive a strong wallop from their wings.

Choosing what ducks to buy

Whether you are choosing ducks or geese, you can buy them as either young birds or as eggs and raise your own. Among the best breeds of duck to choose from are:

■ **Aylesbury** table ducks are famous as large birds for eating. They weigh up to 4.5kg (10lb).

■ **Indian Runners** don't have much meat on them but they are good egg layers – on average, you can hope for about 180 eggs a year. They have a distinctive upright stance and stroll around like penguins.

■ **Khaki Campbells** can lay over 300 eggs a year!

■ **Muscovy** ducks are heavy and placid, and make excellent mothers. They are very good fliers, so you will probably want to clip their wings (see page 196). Be careful when you pick them up as their feet have sharp claws. Muscovies are thought to descend from a goose, but we class them as our favourite ducks.

■ **Welsh Harlequins** are good all-round birds. They are decent layers and are big enough to be an impressive table bird.

Choosing what geese to buy

There are many breeds to consider:

■ **Brecon Buffs** not only look lovely they also taste great!

■ **Chinese geese** are excellent egg

GREEN GEESE

Traditionally, rearing geese was inextricably linked with the growth and decline of green grass. Goslings begin grazing when the grass is fresh in spring and then, when the grass slows down around September, we slaughter them. It is a harsh natural cycle, but efficient. In the past, they were called Michaelmas geese in Britain as their butchery tied in with the 29 November, and in America geese are often bred to coincide with Thanksgiving feasts.

Keeping "green geese" *makes good financial sense and mows the lawns.*

layers and can be ready to slaughter as early as 8 weeks.

■ **Common English** is generally the standard goose, often an Embden crossed with a Toulouse.

■ **Embden** is an excellent, very large table breed.

■ **Roman** is particularly good if you want a goose that can be killed when it is young, but still have plenty of breast meat to enjoy.

Housing

Housing ducks and geese is not very complicated.

■ **Ducks will live happily** in a conventional hen house, easily

DUCKS TO WATER

Ducks need to be able to periodically submerge their heads to clean their eyes and nostrils. We believe that it's only really fair to keep ducks – and geese, for that matter – if you have running water on your plot or at least a pond regularly topped up with fresh water. Flowing water and a pond are ideal, but if you don't have either of these, you must ensure that you can provide them with a deep container of water that you can regularly change.

One of our Muscovy ducks *enjoys a paddle in the stream with her young.*

adapted and placed near a pond or stream – water is essential to a duck's wellbeing. You may want to provide a ramp into the house as ducks are clumsy and can easily damage themselves, but they don't need a perch. Additionally, the housing should be rat- and fox-proof, draught-free but well ventilated, and always have fresh dry bedding. Ducks enjoy a wander, but we keep ours in a fenced-off area with a pond most of the time, to avoid stepping in duck poo each time we leave the house.

■ **Provide geese** with larger houses than ducks. The traditional design is an open, three-sided construction, often made with straw bales. We always protect them from foxes at night by locking them away in a small shed. Geese are vulnerable to rats and foxes when they are young or when they're sitting on eggs. We use an electric fence with poultry wire to stop them roaming (see page 175).

■ **Geese require** a bit more space for grazing than ducks or chickens, and we have found that our small orchard is perfect for them. Although they are officially classed as water fowl, they don't absolutely need a pond. All they require is access to water to keep their nostrils and eyes clean by immersing their heads. A large container will do until you make something a bit more permanent such as a small pond, but it must be deep and the water changed regularly.

Feeding

■ **Ducks aren't grazing birds** like geese, but they will supplement their diet with grass if you give them the access. We feed our ducks corn daily to increase the number of eggs they lay and to fatten them up nicely. They are also partly carnivorous and will happily eat slugs, snails, worms, frogs, and insects. Therefore, in spring before we start the next round of crop planting, we allow our ducks

access to the vegetable beds to find and eat any hiding pests. Don't get carried away and give them free range of your beds all year round, though, as they will damage young brassicas and eat peas and lettuce without a care in the world.

■ **Geese eat grass** like living lawnmowers and can even be used for weeding between strawberry plants or vines, as they don't normally eat broad-leaved plants.

■ **When you get your goslings**, feed them chick crumbs for the first couple of months, reducing quantities after four weeks as they start to graze more

on grass shoots. Then, when the geese are fully grown, occasionally substitute their grass diet with corn feed if you want to fatten them up.

Slaughtering ducks and geese

For both ducks and geese we would recommend that you follow the methods described for large birds on page 197. Geese are larger and should be killed by a team effort, but some smaller ducks can be killed single-handed. You can kill your ducks at about 10 weeks old but we leave ours for much longer (see page 195). Kill geese at 5–6 months old.

1. Imprint yourself on goslings by being around when they hatch and for the first few days. They'll flock to you much more readily when they're bigger. **2. Shutters, mesh,** and a lockable door, will help protect the goose house from predators. **3. These Indian Runner ducklings** are particular favourites – we enjoy their perky natures.

Keeping pigs

Pigs are at the heart of our smallholding. They plough and manure the land as well as providing us with tremendous meat. Pigs are highly intelligent animals and are capable of coming when they're called and showing individual character. But here at Newhouse Farm we are omnivores and enjoy eating a bacon butty, so our pigs don't have names and we don't become too attached to them.

Choosing what to buy

Rare-breed pigs such as Berkshire, Cornish Black, and Tamworth, tend to be much hardier than specialized commercial hybrids and are better suited to outdoor smallholding conditions. Ideally, you want your pig to put on weight fast and not have any health problems.

You can often look at the history of certain pedigree animals in the records of a pig breeder to get an indication of the size they'll grow to and whether they will be better suited for making bacon or for processing the meat as sausages.

Berkshires are one of Britain's oldest breeds. They are early maturing pigs and have a high proportion of lean meat.

British Saddleback is a hardy breed with an excellent foundation in many cross-breeding programmes.

Cornish Blacks have a thick fat layer, which keeps them happily warm over winter.

Gloucester Old Spots were bred originally to live in apple orchards. They are hardy and make great bacon.

Landrace is a popular breed in Denmark and Sweden, due to their long backs for bacon production.

Large Whites provide top-quality back bacon and are extremely popular commercially.

1. We collect our new weaners in a large cage on the back of our pickup and borrow a stock trailer from a friend when we take them to the abattoir.
2. Choose weaners with long, lean backs. **3. Pigs from a reputable dealer** are more likely to remain healthy. Check out their history in the breeder's records.

Tamworths are a lovely, medium-sized, red coloured pig that is extremely hardy, even in northerly areas such as Scotland and Canada.

How to buy pigs

You will need to register your property as an agricultural holding, before buying pigs. There will be paperwork to fill out when you buy. You'll need to keep records, tag each animal, and abide by regulations when you need to transport livestock. Visit www.defra.gov.uk for more information and check with your local authority.

We would not recommend buying your first batch of pigs from a local livestock market unless you are very experienced or have a knowledgeable friend to help you. Often farmers will off-load some of their inferior stock at market and you won't know what you're looking for. Instead, develop a relationship with a reputable farmer, who should then sell you good stock because, if the pigs don't do well, you won't go back to them again and they end up losing good business.

Gilt weaners

The easiest and most economical way to buy pigs is to get some 8-week-old weaners that have already been weaned for a couple of weeks and run around actively. The rear ends should be clean and keep an eye out for any signs of lameness.

It is best not to buy breeding stock straightaway because, as a beginner, it is nearly impossible to select genuinely good stock. Breeding pigs also involves much more equipment, attention, and expertise. We like to leave that side of things to local experts and concentrate our efforts on the fattening-up side of things, so we always buy gilts. These are young female pigs that have not mated nor had any piglets. We opt for gilts rather than boars as the pork does not end up tasting "pissy" – a colloquialism for meat tainted by male hormones as the young boar matures.

Transporting your pigs

Getting your newly bought pigs home involves a bit of planning. In many countries there are strict rules governing the movement of animals and penalties if you don't adhere to them, so check them out via DEFRA or your local authority.

A key piece of equipment when moving pigs is a length of plyboard with two holes cut in the top to hold it at each end. This enables you to successfully shepherd your pigs in and out of trailers or to new pastures.

Housing and basic care

Most of the equipment that you will need to keep pigs is easily available from agricultural suppliers, but some equipment, such as feeders and electric fencing, can be expensive to buy new, so look out for it at farm auctions. If you are buying second-hand equipment, make sure you disinfect it first and scour it with a wire brush. When choosing the pig sty, ensure it is well insulated against the cold. The more energy your pigs put into growing bigger instead of keeping warm, the better.

HAPPY PIGS

One of the main motivations for rearing our own pigs is that the animal welfare of factory-farmed pork can be horrendous. Commercial farming often denies pigs space to move around and their feed can be pumped with a cocktail of chemicals resulting in cheap, tasteless pork. Such intensive farming has often escaped scrutiny, which is surprising considering we are so keen to get on our high horses about other taboo meat production. If you can't rear your own pigs, you can still choose to eat free-range organic pork.

We are strong believers *that happy pigs are tasty pigs!*

PROJECT **Set up a pig pen**

The focal point of a pig pen will be the house or sty. We always place the door facing away from the prevailing wind and build it on a raised pallet to stop rising damp. The shell is then covered by some corrugated iron. Don't go spending much money on their housing, but do use large nails or screws and make it strong enough to withstand a fully grown pig enjoying a good back scratch!

YOU WILL NEED
- Electric fence
- Pig sty
- Straw
- Water bowl
- Stone weight
- Trough
- Organic feed

1. **Before moving your pigs** into their pen, surround the area with an electric fence (see page 175). **2. Keep the pig sty** topped up with plenty of fresh straw, putting a whole bale in at a time. **3. Ensure there is plenty of water** in the pen to satisfy a pig's thirst. If possible, sink the container into the ground, as well as putting a weight in it, to prevent the pigs knocking it over. **4. To prevent the feed** from being trampled into the ground in their pig-like enthusiasm to get at it, place it into a trough twice a day.

1. **Keep your pigs** in overgrown areas so they can root around for treats and clear the ground. 2. **Throw fresh greens** into the pen. 3. **In hot weather**, make a muddy patch to serve as a wallow.

Pigs and water

Pigs drink copious volumes of water and their container will need topping up regularly. We position it near the edge of the fence so that we can easily fill it. In hot weather you should also create an area of wet mud that the pigs can use as a "wallow". Wallowing helps the pigs to cool down and the layer of dried mud on their skin offers some protection against sunburn.

Feeding pigs

The feed that we use is an organic pellet that contains plenty of protein and carbohydrates and is in addition to a foraging diet of grass, wild weeds, and roots.

When the weaners are young we allow them to eat as much as they want from an automatic feeder placed next to their house. When they get to 10 weeks we start to feed them twice a day. Regardless of age we feed them 1kg (2¼lb) of food each morning and evening. For us that means giving our two pigs a large full scoop of food twice daily and they do fine. We continue with this method of feeding until slaughter (see opposite).

You can throw the food over the ground for them to forage for, but as it is the most expensive part of the pig-rearing process, and they often end up urinating on it or trampling it into the ground, we pour it into their trough to avoid waste. Conversely, we do make a point of throwing fresh greens and fodder crops all over their enclosure for them to search for.

We like to give our pigs access to fresh pasture with plenty of roots for them to dig up and eat. It is also a good idea to plant fodder crops on the land before they move in to save money on their feed bills.

Serving your pigs household waste is illegal as there are now many regulations restricting the feeding of pigs with any waste that has been in your kitchen. This is to avoid the spread of disease. However, if you top and tail your vegetables in the garden and position your beds near to where the pigs live, then you will find they can still eat plenty of fresh peelings and spoiled vegetables.

When you feed them, call loudly each time with a distinctive noise. This will train them to come to you and makes it much easier to shepherd them if they escape. Our pig-calling noise sounds like "ShoooEee!", but it's completely up to you...

Slaughtering and butchering pigs

Once your pigs weigh 65–80kg (140–180lb) you can slaughter them at any time. We normally keep our girls for 9–10 months before slaughtering them, which is much longer than commercial farms, but gives us more of their digging and manuring power to help cultivate bits of land.

There are so many regulations covering the killing and eating of pigs on your own land, we recommend sending them to a local abattoir instead. Visit the abattoir to check you are happy with the price and services they offer. This also takes the stress out of the visit on the day of the slaughter, as you'll know what's in store. To move your pigs, tempt them into the trailer using pig boards, your signature pig call, and some food. Once in the abattoir, take them along for their appointment and say your goodbyes. The next day you can collect a scraped carcass split into two halves to butcher at home, or ask a butcher to prepare the cuts for you.

Make your own sausages with the aid of an electronic mincer and ready-prepared sausage skins.

Some of our favourite cuts
One pig provides so many different types of meat for you to enjoy. A deep freeze is especially useful post-butchering.

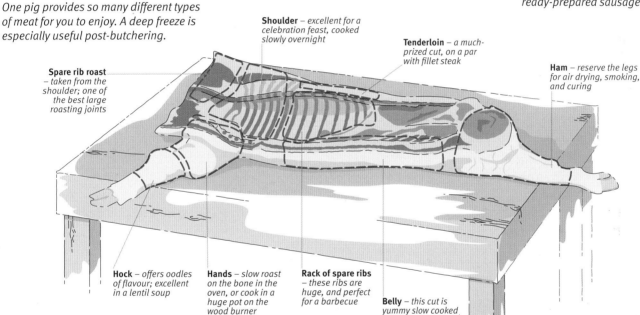

Spare rib roast – taken from the shoulder; one of the best large roasting joints

Shoulder – excellent for a celebration feast, cooked slowly overnight

Tenderloin – a much-prized cut, on a par with fillet steak

Ham – reserve the legs for air drying, smoking, and curing

Hock – offers oodles of flavour; excellent in a lentil soup

Hands – slow roast on the bone in the oven, or cook in a huge pot on the wood burner

Rack of spare ribs – these ribs are huge, and perfect for a barbecue

Belly – this cut is yummy slow cooked with oriental spices

JOINTING BASICS

Butchering meat requires a large wooden butcher's block, a meat saw, and some sharp knives. In addition, an electronic mincer saves a huge amount of effort when making sausages –if you have a hand-powered one "good luck", and we bet you'll get an electric mincer next time!

Shoulder To separate the shoulder, cut between the fifth and sixth ribs.

Tenderloin Remove this in one long strip from inside the backbone.

Ham Cut the flesh cleanly with a saw, then remove the H-bone with a knife.

Keeping sheep and goats

Rearing sheep reduces our reliance on imported meat and wool that travel thousands of kilometres to reach us. It takes commitment and skill to look after a small flock and it's not something to undertake lightly. Goats tend to be hardier than sheep and are great at reclaiming a neglected smallholding, as they eat anything, from brambles to weeds. Both sheep and goats produce excellent milk.

Register your property

If you intend to keep sheep and goats you must register your property as an agricultural holding. You'll have to fill out forms when you buy animals and keep records, tag each sheep and goat, and abide by regulations when transporting livestock. Visit DEFRA's website, www.defra.gov.uk and check with your local authority.

Choosing sheep

Geography is important. On an exposed site with poor grazing, a primitive hardy sheep such as Soay or Ouessant is best. Some modern breeds are highly specialized, others are more general-purpose. If you want sheep mainly for meat, for example, go for a quality carcass breed such as the Texel.

Ouessant are a primitive breed, which means they haven't been overbred and are very hardy.

Dorset Horns can lamb more than once a year. They produce good quality wool and a high milk yield.

Border Leicester is an elegant English sheep. A prolific breeder, they produce good mutton and wool.

Southdown is a manageable size and matures early.

Soays are similar to wild sheep, with good milk yields and lean meat.

Texel is an excellent meat sheep. Both sexes have horns.

How to buy sheep

Buying good-quality sheep can be daunting for the first timer. Visit local livestock auctions, and ask a farmer for advice before you start. Always look at the seller's performance records, and check that sheep have good teeth – they should be broad, short, and fit squarely in the mouth.

Start small, with three ewes for example, or two orphaned lambs, until you feel confident that keeping sheep will fit in with your lifestyle.

Choosing goats

Goats are gregarious animals, so you should keep at least two.

Saanen can get quite big, but have high milk yields on good grazing.

Anglo-Nubian have lower milk yields but of top-notch quality.

Toggenburg are fairly small, but do well on larger, free-range areas.

Golden Guernsey are small, with lower milk yields than large breeds.

Angora are renowned for their soft mohair fleeces and high milk yields.

How to buy goats

As a rule, goats with strong legs, a wedge-shaped rear end, and strong backs are likely to be good animals. You can get more information by joining a goat-keeper's organization.

Buy weaned kids or goatlings between 1–2 years old. Despite being a bit more expensive to buy, they are cheaper to feed than young kids that need milk.

1. Ouessant sheep from France are small and easy to carry – ideal for a smallholder. Primitive breeds such as these don't flock together in the way other sheep do. **2. Feed hay** to sheep in winter if grazing is limited. Use a covered rack to keep the hay dry and clean.

1. Well-brought-up goats shouldn't butt their handlers. **2. British Alpine goats** produce milk with high butterfat.

FEEDING GOATS

Goats need huge amounts of fibre, which they get from browsing on brambles, thistles, and twigs. Provide them with hay all year round – on average, a milking goat will need about a bale a week. Also give your goats a salt lick and a constant supply of fresh water.

Supplement grazing *with special goat mix from your local agricultural suppliers. It provides extra energy. Suspended feed troughs stop goats fouling in their food and then refusing to eat it.*

Hay, straw, and, occasionally, kale, *are best fed in a rack. The bars should be 5cm (2in) apart and at least 75cm (2 ft 6in) above the ground. Make it easy to reach from outside the goats' enclosure.*

Housing and basic care

▓ **The land needed for sheep** varies greatly depending on the size of the breed and the quality of pasture – the grassland and mixed vegetation that grazing animals feed on. As a rough guide you could keep about 10 ewes on a 0.4 hectare (1 acre), but you must have more land available so you can move them on. Moving sheep onto new pasture on a six-to-eight week rotation reduces the build up of parasites on the land and also conserves the grass.

Sheep shouldn't need any housing beyond the natural shelter offered by outcrops of rocks and trees, although some rare breeds are susceptible to wet and cold weather. It may also pay to have a shed to move the ewes into when they are lambing.

▓ **Goats don't like rain or cold.** Most need a draught-proof shelter to sleep in at night. If you are building one from scratch, put in a concrete floor to make cleaning easy – the manure is great to add to compost. Also, try to provide your goats with an outdoor daytime shelter as a bolt hole in case of bad weather.

Securing your animals

▓ **Good fencing for goats** is essential (see pages 172–175). Bear in mind a wise old saying: "Goats spend 23 hours of the day planning their escape and the last hour executing it." Anyone who keeps goats will soon become aware of the constant battle to stop them from escaping and eating the contents of the fruit and vegetable garden.

▓ **Tethering goats** is another option, but it is time-consuming; as with sheep, you need to move them regularly to prevent the land from becoming contaminated with a build-up of parasites.

▓ **For temporary sheep fencing** try hurdles. Use them to put together small enclosures when you need to examine their feet, give them medication, or round them up for shearing or at lambing time.

▓ **For permanent boundaries** you can build stone walls, plant hedgerows, or use wire-netting fences topped off with a strand of barbed wire (see pages 172–175).

Feeding and drinking

▓ **Sheep** should not require much supplementary feed if they have good grazing. If you have restricted access to grass, then feed them pellets – in troughs to avoid waste – or give them a rack filled with good-quality hay. They will also need a clean, fresh supply of water, in a bowl fixed at least 0.5m (20in) above the ground to prevent them fouling it.

▓ **Goats** are best fed by grazing them on scrubland or pasture. They will thrive on heather- or gorse-covered hillsides and in deciduous woodland, but will not do so well in coniferous woods. They also require hay and supplementary mixes.

Breeding sheep and goats

▮ **Mate or tup sheep** in the autumn. For less than a dozen sheep, it's too expensive to keep a ram; we suggest borrowing one. Rub some reddle (any dark-coloured earth) on his chest so that you can see when he has served all of your ewes. Keep your ewes on poor pasture for a few weeks before tupping – this is called flushing the flock – then move them onto good pasture with the ram.

▮ **Sheep's gestation period** is 147 days and lambing normally starts in late February or March. It can mean late nights and stressful days, much like being a doctor perpetually on call. A good shepherd allows sheep to get on with it alone, while remaining vigilant. The first signs of a ewe giving birth will be that they choose a place away from the rest of the flock and repeatedly lie down. A water bag appears first followed by the feet and nose. When the lamb is born, the ewe licks away the mucus and membrane from its head to stimulate it. If a ewe has been in labour for more than an hour and is obviously in discomfort, call a neighbouring farmer or vet.

When all the ewes have lambed, move them to the best pastures you have. New mothers and offspring will thrive on good nourishment.

▮ **Take goats to be mated** – it is usually cheaper than keeping a billy goat yourself. The advice for kids is the same as for lambing, although the gestation is a few days longer.

Castrating goats

If you plan to eat billy kids castrate them before they're three months old, as this stops their meat from tasting too strong. The most humane method is to use an Elastrator, available from agricultural suppliers.

POTENTIAL PROBLEMS

▮ **Blow flies** lay eggs in the damp wool around the sheep's bottom. Cut away the affected fleece, and prevent a recurrence by spraying the back of the sheep with a pesticide spray from the vet.

▮ **Foot rot** can be a problem for both sheep and goats on damp ground. Keep hooves trimmed. If animals get foot rot, walk them through a foot bath of formalin.

▮ **Sheep's lungs** can fill with fluid and they may drown if they get stuck on their backs. Always tip them over if they're lodged upside down.

▮ **Intestinal worms in sheep** need treating. Invest in a gun for dosing a whole flock; if you only have one or two animals, use a syringe.

▮ **Abscesses in goats** are best lanced and kept clean with antiseptic solutions. Ask a vet to help with this procedure.

▮ **Dose goats against fluke** if they have access to wet or marshy land.

Jointing a sheep

Fat lambs are ready for slaughter at four months old; sheep between one and two years are for mutton. We recommend finding a good local slaughterhouse to do the job. They may be able to hang the carcass for you for a few days, to improve flavour, but more often than not you'll need to find a cold space to hang the meat at home. We think good British lamb or mutton is under appreciated. These are our favourite joints.

A good fatty leg of mutton *that's full of marbling is best for roasting.*

The best cuts on the carcass
We ask for the carcass to be cut in half, but prefer to do the butchering at home, to end up with the joints we like to cook.

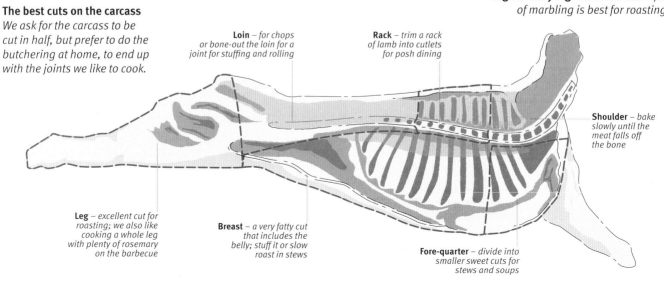

Loin – *for chops or bone-out the loin for a joint for stuffing and rolling*

Rack – *trim a rack of lamb into cutlets for posh dining*

Shoulder – *bake slowly until the meat falls off the bone*

Leg – *excellent cut for roasting; we also like cooking a whole leg with plenty of rosemary on the barbecue*

Breast – *a very fatty cut that includes the belly; stuff it or slow roast in stews*

Fore-quarter – *divide into smaller sweet cuts for stews and soups*

PROJECT # Shear a sheep and dye wool

Shearing takes lots of practice. Try learning the ropes on a neighbouring farm first. We don't spin fleeces as it's easier to get it done by a professional – you'll find information on local spinning services online or at your nearest agricultural suppliers. However, we do like dyeing our own wool with natural plant dyes. You can get an amazing range of colours from the unlikeliest sources, from onion skins to privet leaves. Treat the wool first with a mordant – a chemical that "bites" into the wool to fix the colour.

YOU WILL NEED
- Hand shears
- Large saucepan
- Alum
- Cream of tartar
- Onion skins

HOW TO SHEAR A SHEEP

1

2

3

1. First clip all the wool off the stomach, down to the udders, taking care not to chop off her teats. **2. Next shear her down one side,** starting at the throat and around the side of her neck and head. Keep going as far down as you can reach; then roll the sheep over and shear down the other side. The fleece should now come right off her body except at the hindquarters. **3. Lay the sheep flat on the ground** and shear the fleece away from the back and hindquarters. Tidy her up with a trim of her hind legs and tail so that the other sheep don't laugh at her.

DYEING WOOL WITH NATURAL EXTRACTS

1

2

3

1. Weigh out the same amount of onion skins as the weight of wool. Let them sit in a big pan of water overnight, then boil for an hour. Strain off the dye.
2. Wet the wool thoroughly, then boil it in a mordant solution of 110g (4oz) of alum in 18 litres (4 gallons) of hot water and 25g (1oz) cream of tartar. (Always keep a separate set of pans for dyeing; never use cooking pans). **3. Add the mordanted wool** to the hot dye and soak for an hour, stirring occasionally. Drain and dry the wool. Onion skins give a rich orange colour. Reuse the dye water for a paler, beige wool.

NATURAL DYES

Clockwise from left, wool dyed with natural plant colours:

- Apricot skein: **madder**
- Beige skein: **blackcurrant**
- Beige ball: second use of **onion skin** dye.
- Primrose yellow: **weld,** or try **gorse shoots** or **privet leaves**
- Orange: **onion skin**
- Grey/blue: **blackcurrant**
- Purple: **logwood** (a tropical tree), or try **willow roots** or **bilberries.**

Keeping cattle

Imagine how great it would feel to supply all of your own protein and dairy products. In our opinion, keeping cattle is the epitome of self-sufficiency, but before you take on any animals, remember that it is a serious commitment. Although one of the more complicated and time-consuming challenges, it can be extremely rewarding.

Choosing what to buy

Keeping cattle involves much more effort and a larger financial outlay than buying a few chickens. You will need extra sheds and an acre of pasture for each cow. Visit local farmers and experienced neighbours to learn the ropes and think carefully about how many cattle you want to keep on your land. Do you want to produce beef to sell or just enough for your home, friends, and family? How much milk and dairy products do you use on average in a month? Do you want to add the job of milking cows twice daily to your routine?

EXAMINING A HEIFER

As well as examining the younger heifer, ask to have a look at her mum; this will give you a good indication of what she's going to end up like.
- **Make sure that she is calm** and reasonably tame.
- **Feel the udder** carefully to see if you can detect any lumps; these can be caused by mastitis, which blocks the flow of milk.
- **If the cow is in milk,** then ask if you can have a go at milking her. Check the workings of each teat and see how calm she remains. She is likely to be a bit frisky as you will be a stranger to her, so cut her some slack before passing judgement.
- **Go on to check** the cow's teeth to determine her age. A mature cow at five years old has eight incisors on the lower jaw. As the cow grows older, her age can be gauged by the wear, but this takes an experienced eye.
- **Ask if she is tuberculosis tested** (TT) and also free from brucellosis.
- **Don't buy her** if the farmer tells you up front that she has a problem, such as a blind quarter, where one quarter of her udder has no milk in it.

One cow will be keep you in all the milk that you could possibly need. If you have a beef animal, you will also have more than enough meat.

You will have to decide between dairy cows, beef cows, or more traditional dual-purpose cows. We don't keep cattle because of lack of space, but we have good friends and neighbours who share an enthusiasm for older, dual-purpose breeds and natural rearing techniques.

Our favourite breeds of cattle for smallholdings include:

- **Ayrshires** can be white and red and are perfect if you are looking for a tough breed that produces plenty of high quality milk. They fatten early and can remain productive for up to 12 years.
- **Dexter** is our favourite breed. Their beef is delicious. Their small size makes them easier to butcher and preserve, and satisfies the needs of a single family.
- **Herefords** are excellent for beef.
- **Jerseys** are docile and hardy, and produce excellent high-quality milk that's ideal for making butter and cheese. Jersey cows also live for a long time and can really become part of the family.
- **Short Horns** are excellent dual-purpose cows, suitable for a small herd. They are hardy and long-lived, rear calves very easily, and make good foster mothers.

How to buy cattle

Buying a cow is easier said than done, but before you even venture out to an auction, you must first register your property as an agricultural holding. There will be paperwork to fill out when you buy your cattle. You'll need to keep records, tag each animal, and abide by regulations when you transport your livestock. You will also need up-to-date paperwork when you take cattle to the abattoir. Visit defra.gov.uk for more information and check with your local authority.

The first time you visit an auction, go with an experienced friend or farmer. You can find good deals at auctions, and the best cows to choose between are a "first-calver" and an older cow.

- **A first-calver** is a heifer that has had just one calf and is therefore producing lots of milk. The farmer will probably have bred her specifically to sell, so you know that she will be a good cow and you can start milking her straightaway. The disadvantage of buying a first-calver is that you are both beginners, and she may be a bit flighty at first, and as nervous as you are when being milked. Also, her teats will be smaller and harder to squeeze than those of a mature cow.
- **An older cow** is more likely to have a placid nature as well as elongated, well-milked teats, making her easier to milk. The drawback is that she won't be with you for so long.

Housing and basic care

Cattle usually only need to come in under cover to be milked or to eat dry hay. Look over the fence and see what your neighbours do at different times of the year; they will know the individual climate and conditions better than any weather forecaster, and be able to advise you about extra shelter that your cattle may need.

More fussy breeds that produce high milk yields will want to go inside to eat extra food when the weather is bad or if the grass is not in prime condition. If you intensively rear cattle indoors over winter, you can have great results, but it is much more expensive to supply them with straw and extra food.

If you have spare outbuildings on your plot, you may choose to use one as a designated milking shed, and another house for your cattle to sleep and eat in over winter.

The amount of food you will need for your cattle depends on the breed, their size, and their ability to adapt to the environment. Equally, they will need different-sized rations at different times. Normally, cattle receive a "maintenance" ration and then a little bit more, known as a "production" ration, when they are being milked. Add food according to how much milk they are giving. We prefer hardy breeds, such as Dexters, that thrive on grass and a simple supplement of hay.

If your cows are looking fatter or thinner, adjust their feed of hay and pellets accordingly. Watch how much milk they produce, how hungry they are, and if they appear healthy. If in doubt, ask local farmers, vets, or agricultural suppliers for advice.

Mating

Smaller cows can be mated after 15 months, but most bigger cows should wait until 20 months. They can only can be mated when they are in heat, or "bulling". At this time, a cow will have a slightly swollen vulva, moo more noisily than normal, and mount other cattle or allow another cow to mount her. Bulling occurs at 21-day intervals, and only lasts for about 18 hours, so keep your eyes open if you want to catch your cows at the right

1. Dexters are small, hardy, and dual-purpose, and they love to browse. They produce a high-quality meat that is much in demand. **2. High-fibre cattle pellets** top up the basic dietary requirements of cattle producing high milk yields. **3. Keep a salt lick** in your cattle's field; it's a easy source of sodium and other minerals. **4. Dexter cattle** are ideal to rear traditionally as a suckler-herd that lives as a family group. Regular handling ensures that the cattle are calm and easy to look after.

time. Once you have chosen a cow that you want a bull to mate with, take her to a neighbour's farm or bring the bull to her. Alternatively, you can call your local artificial insemination authority.

Calving

Outdoor hardy cattle will normally calve on their own, with no real trouble. You're fairly likely to go out one day and see your cow licking a newly born calf. If, however, the calf has not sucked from its mother's teat within an hour of birth, hold it to its mother and make it suck. It may be necessary to tie up the mother while you do this. If you are bringing your cows in regularly, make sure it is a draught-free environment so that the calves don't get too cold. Never turn out calves without their mothers into cold, winter fields.

Milking

Milk your cows twice a day, preferably at 12-hour intervals. You will quickly find your own routine, bringing them in for an hour's milking in the morning and evening. Normally one cow will have to produce one calf a year if she is to produce milk. This means that you will not only have to milk them daily, but also have calves to keep an eye on.

Encouraging milk flow

To get milk from your cows, you will have to take calves away from their mothers early on. The mother will bellow loudly for a couple of days after this. Substitute yourself for the young one, so that your cow allows you to milk her as a calf would. Feed the calf separately with milk in a bucket. This may seem cruel, but cows are not human; they have shorter memories and it's just one of the realities of milking your herd.

Alternatively, you may prefer to remove one calf from its mother and try to pass it off as a twin on to another. If you can persuade the foster mother to accept a young calf alongside her own, you will free up the original cow for milking. You have to be a bit lucky to get away with this, but try tying up the foster mother to a post and coaxing her with some good food as a distraction.

Yet another option is to reach a balance where the calf takes its share of milk and then you take the rest.

PROJECT ## How to milk a cow

Before you start milking, wash the cow's udder, massaging it to stimulate the flow of milk as you clean. Then wash the rear end of the cow to prevent any nasties dripping into your nice clean milk pail. Also wash the teats and your hands before you begin, and make sure that you give the cow something tasty to eat to distract her.

YOU WILL NEED
- Washing equipment
- Small stool and pail

1. Position a small stool on the right-hand side of the cow and grip the pail between your knees. **2. Grasp the two front teats,** one in each hand, and squeeze them at the top with each thumb and forefinger to trap the milk in the teats.
3. Move your hands down, bringing in your middle fingers.
4. Bring in your little fingers so your whole hand is around the teat. **5. Squeeze the milk** from the bottom of the teats. Then release the teats and repeat the process in a rhythmic rolling action. Use common sense to squeeze at the right pressure.

1. A calf reaches puberty at about 9 months and is ready to breed from by 15 months. **2. Teaching a calf to suck** milk from a bucket may sound easy (see right), but you may need to persevere until it becomes second nature.

Slaughtering and butchering beef

As with all livestock, before you kill an animal ensure you have somwhere to store the carcass. Unless you're having a feast, you will need to keep cuts of beef in the freezer or salt them until you're ready to eat them.

The slaughtering method for cattle is the same as for pigs (see page 203). Often the abattoir will hang your beef for you, which can radically improve the texture and taste. We leave beef in a cold store at 2–5°C (35–41°F) for between two and four weeks. Everyone has their preferences, but we ask for the carcass back in quarters. This makes the meat marginally easier to handle and means we can carefully decide on the cuts we want for making mince, curing in salt, and packing away as treasured roasts in the freezer.

Invest in a large butchers' block *if you are doing your own butchering and preparing your meat. Look out for them secondhand as new ones can be expensive.*

Beef cuts of meat *are numerous and cooking times vary depending on which part of the animal they come from.*

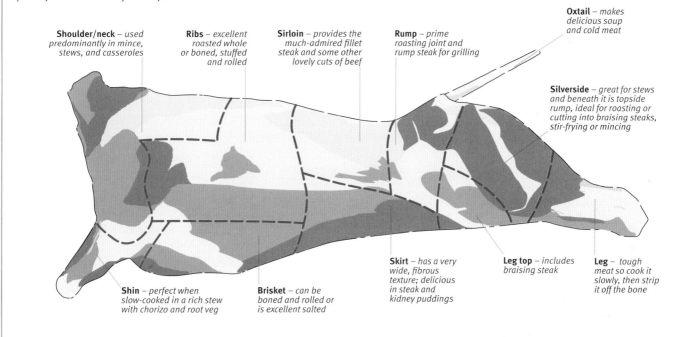

Shoulder/neck – *used predominantly in mince, stews, and casseroles*

Ribs – *excellent roasted whole or boned, stuffed and rolled*

Sirloin – *provides the much-admired fillet steak and some other lovely cuts of beef*

Rump – *prime roasting joint and rump steak for grilling*

Oxtail – *makes delicious soup and cold meat*

Silverside – *great for stews and beneath it is topside rump, ideal for roasting or cutting into braising steaks, stir-frying or mincing*

Shin – *perfect when slow-cooked in a rich stew with chorizo and root veg*

Brisket – *can be boned and rolled or is excellent salted*

Skirt – *has a very wide, fibrous texture; delicious in steak and kidney puddings*

Leg top – *includes braising steak*

Leg – *tough meat so cook it slowly, then strip it off the bone*

Teaching a calf to suck

If you want to feed the calf from a bucket you will need to teach it to suck. To do this, try putting two fingers in its mouth and getting it to suck them. Then tease its head down into the bucket of milk, still sucking on your fingers, and once it starts sucking the milk, remove your hands. Feed a calf twice daily on one part warm water to three parts milk. After two weeks, introduce good quality hay and after four months wean it off milk and put it out on good pasture.

Keeping cattle for beef

Herds of cattle that are primarily kept for beef are likely to be successful if you allow the calves to remain with their mothers to suckle. These are often referred to as "suckler-herds", and remain in family groups. They take less effort to keep and, if you opt for a traditional hardy breed, they have a greater tendency to put on fat and produce marbling in the meat. Suckler-herds also seem to do much better than other cattle when the weather is changeable.

POTENTIAL PROBLEMS

■ **Mastitis** is a common complaint among cows where one or more teat becomes blocked and the resulting milk is useless.

■ **Other problems** include lameness, worms, foot-and-mouth disease, and milk fever. If your cattle suffer from any these, call your vet!

■ **Ask your vet** for information on the recommended vaccines in your area. Keep your cattle well fed, with a clean water supply. Fortunately, cattle that are reared outdoors and kept naturally rarely get sick.

Keeping bees

Honey is the food bees produce for themselves from nectar. We started keeping bees 15 years ago in the garden of our suburban home because the honey we produce is far superior to anything from the supermarket, and the majority of imported honey. However, be wary of taking up beekeeping if you suffer from anaphylactic reactions to stings or have extreme allergic reactions.

Establishing your colony

To get started, you can: order "package bees", essentially a swarm in a box – queen included – that arrives without brood or frames; establish a colony from a nucleus or small hive of about five frames that includes a laying queen; or you can buy yourself a colony that is already up and running, which is what we did.

Secondhand hives regularly come up for sale and your local beekeeping association will know what equipment is available. If you have never kept bees before, it is essential to spend time with a beekeepers' group, where you can get advice and share tips.

The elements of a hive

There are several styles of hive, but they all have the same main parts.

The brood box is located at the base and is where the queen lives and new bees are hatched and tended. The queen lays eggs in the brood nest and, once hatched, the larvae are fed with pollen and honey stored around the nest.

The supers stand above the brood and this is where the honey is stored. Some honey is stored in the brood, but a beekeeper takes the harvest of surplus honey from the supers. Make sure that there is a 6mm (¼in) gap, also known as "beespace", between each frame in the super so the bees can move through the hive. Spacers are needed between some types of frame to maintain good "beespace". Smaller spacers are used in the brood box and larger spacers in the gaps of the supers.

The queen excluder is a grill between the brood and supers and does just what it says: it prevents the queen from going up to the supers. It has holes wide enough for the worker bees to travel up and down but, due to her larger abdomen, the queen can't pass through the narrow gaps.

Frames sit inside the brood and supers, and are the building blocks that enable your bees to start the honey-storing process. They normally have wooden sides enclosing a sheet of wax in hexagonal cell shapes to give the bees a head start.

Siting your hive

The position of your hive is of prime importance. Point it away from the prevailing wind and, if possible, facing east or southeast to catch the early morning sun.

If you live in an urban area, put a barrier made out of a willow hurdle in front of the entrance to your hives. This will help to force the bees' flight

1. **Bees leave and enter** the hive through small "beespaces" in the sides of the super. **2. An open hive** exposes the frames that stand upright within the super as it rests on the brood below. **3. Wear a bee suit** with everything tucked in, as bees tend to crawl upwards. Wear boots and gloves too. Hives are best positioned at least 1m (3ft) apart.

Gather honey

Harvest your honey in late August or September, but seek advice from a local beekeeper before you enter a hive. A smoker and centrifugal extractor are essential pieces of equipment. The smoker simulates a forest fire and encourages the bees to eat honey, making them nice and docile. The centrifugal extractor can be expensive to buy, but often you can borrow one from a beekeepers' association.

YOU WILL NEED
- Smoker
- Sharp knife
- Centrifugal honey extractor
- Glass jars

1. Fill your smoker with a fuel that smokes for a long time. We use dried, rotted wood and rolled-up corrugated cardboard.
2. Blow a few wisps into the front of the hive and leave it for a few minutes while word spreads through the colony that it's time to get eating.   **3. Take out the heavy frames** and start scraping out the honey as quickly as possible – before the bees find out what you're up to!   **4. Use a sharp knife** heated in boiling water to cut just under the surface of the capping on each cell. This will allow the honey to ooze out.   **5. Secure four frames** that have had the caps cut off into a centrifugal honey extractor. Gently spin the handle until all the honey is flung onto the edges of the tub and drips down the sides to a sump with a tap.   **6. Filter the honey** through a sieve to remove waxy bits and store in sealed glass jars in a dark place.

path upwards into the air when they exit the hive, rather than straight across your neighbours' gardens. Provide a source of water near the hive so the bees don't become a nuisance around someone else's pond.

Maintaining the colony

Regularly check on the health and progress of your bees. The best time to inspect your hives is on warm afternoons when most of the colony is out gathering nectar and pollen. Make a routine inspection every week from April to mid-October, checking:
- **the queen** is still laying.
- **the brood** look healthy and disease-free.
- **the bees** have enough space for their honey – be prepared to add an extra super.

If you don't visit your hive regularly, you may find your bees have produced queen cells (by feeding selected larvae royal jelly) and they

may swarm, which means you will lose a large portion of your honey-producing worker bees. In addition, your bees will have glued everything together with layers of propolis. Moving them then jolts the other frames and you are likely to disturb your bees.

In years when the weather has been bad or the bees have suffered from disease, we don't harvest honey as it is the best food to give your colony. When you do harvest or when your bees are short of honey you will need to feed them so they survive the winter. Fill a small plastic container with cold syrup made from 1kg (2¼lb) sugar heated in 1 litre (1¾ pints) water. Cover the container with fine gauze and then pop on a lid with a small hole in it. Turn it upside down and place on the crown board on top of the uppermost super. The vacuum formed by the syrup in the container stops it dribbling onto the hive.

POTENTIAL PROBLEMS

Stay up-to-date with information issued by beekeeping groups and DEFRA (www.defra.gov.uk).
- **Varroa mite** This tiny parasite rides on a worker bee's body, enters a brood cell, and feeds on the larvae. Check for infestation by inspecting brood cells and counting dead mites that have dropped out the bottom of a hive. Control with pyrethroid-based chemicals on slow-release plastic strips.
- **European foulbrood** This disease creates malformed larvae, but can be treated with a technique called "shook swarm"; literally shaking bees into a new brood chamber.
- **Swarming** Hives containing an older queen are more prone to swarming. A colony about to swarm can be distracted by moving the hive 2m (6½ft) and turning it through 180°. Place an empty hive in the original position and the bees should fill up the new hive. Feed both until the colonies re-establish themselves.

Game, fish, and vermin

Many city and town dwellers struggle to come to terms with hunting for their food, while those of us brought up in the country take for granted that some animals are "fair game" when it comes to filling the pot. That said, gone are the days when anyone could have a gun or rod and help themselves to the bounty of the countryside. Licences and permits are required.

SHOOTING TIPS

To become proficient, you need plenty of practice and attention to safety. Use these tips as a guide to key safety practices, controlling your pests, and becoming a better shot.

Safety
■ **NEVER** point your gun at a person.
■ **Do not** climb over fences or gates with a loaded weapon.
■ **Never fire** at animals on the horizon.
■ **Clean your gun** regularly and take it to a firearms dealer if there is a problem rather than risk using it.
■ **If in doubt** – don't!

Practice
■ **Always** zero your weapon before going shooting.
■ **Buy plenty** of paper targets and practise on your groupings, so that when you do go out you achieve a clean kill.
■ **Keep practising** until you are consistently accurate.
■ **Try to lie down** or adopt a kneeling position.
■ **Always aim** for head shots or shoot through the shoulder to hit the heart.
■ **Control** your breathing and squeeze the trigger when you have half-exhausted your out-breath.

Stealth
■ **Wear** warm, camouflaged clothing.
■ **Stick to** the hedgerows when moving around.
■ **Remain quiet** and try to avoid strong smells – which means no smoking, after shave, or perfume.
■ **Be patient** and don't rush a shot.
■ **Take** your time.
■ **Take a sharp knife** to swiftly dispatch an injured animal.
■ **Invest in a night vision** sight if you go hunting regularly at dawn or dusk when light levels are low.

Hunting

Whatever your stance is on hunting it is worth noting that a great deal of effort goes into maintaining habitats for species of game that may not otherwise have been invested if there was not a sporting tradition.

A certain amount of knowledge and skill is required before you start hunting. You can, of course, read about the subject, but there is no substitute for experience. If you wish to shoot with shotguns, most clay pigeon clubs welcome novices and will take the time to teach you from first principles. Until you are proficient and understand how to handle a weapon and traverse obstacles you should not even contemplate going shooting. Even then it is best to go out initially as an observer, so you can learn from those with more experience.

Tools and equipment
■ **If you are beginner**, buy an under-lever or break barrel .177 calibre or .20 air rifle, which have a straight trajectory and a knock-down power capable of killing rats, rabbits, and squirrels. For foxes you would need a shot gun or a more powerful .22 rifle.
■ **If using** more than a standard air rifle you must have an appropriate

1. **We have years of experience** fishing rivers for trout and, since coming to Cornwall, salmon. If we were to be very honest, the time spent fishing compared to the catch we achieve is far from productive, but it is very relaxing.
2. **Rabbits** may be vermin, and cause untold damage to the vegetable patch, but they make fair game and are extremely tasty once skinned, jointed, and stewed (see page 217).

licence for your gun – ask at your local police station for more details.

■ **Different weights** of air pellet suit different guns. We use dome head pellets for their greater accuracy.

Types of shoot

The two types of shoot that you may like to explore are:

■ **Driven shoots**, where a team of beaters walk through an area of land driving the game in front of them towards the guns (who are static, standing at allotted pegs).

■ **Rough shoots**, where there is the opportunity to walk the land and to take whatever comes within range and is in season. This is always more of a lottery than driven shoots, but therein lies the excitement. And, of course, any vermin that present themselves can also be shot.

What to hunt and when

A certain amount of protection given to game species and to some fish to allow them an undisturbed breeding season. Both the Game Act 1831 and Game Licences Act 1860 cover taking and trading in game without an appropriate licence.

There are four types of game licence and you can purchase them at the post office. Each applies to different periods of the year, taking into account the open seasons for various game birds, so ensure you buy the correct one for your needs. A list of game and fish species and their open season for hunting is provided in the box above.

Local knowledge and contacts are invaluable, so we recommend asking at your agricultural merchants or gun shop for some good leads.

Fishing

As we live on an island and are also lucky enough to have masses of rivers, lakes, and lochs, a fishing opportunity is never far away. There

GAME SEASONS *

Game	Season
■ Blackgrouse	20 Aug–10 Dec (1 Sep–31 Jan NI)
■ Coot/moorhen	1 Sep–31 Jan (Protected in NI)
■ Curlew	(1 Sep–31 Jan NI)
■ Duck and goose (inland)	1 Sep–31 Jan
■ Duck and goose (foreshore)	1 Sep–20 Feb (1 Sep–31 Jan NI)
■ Fallow bucks	1 Aug–30 Apr
■ Fallow does	1 Nov–28/29 Feb (21 Oct–15 Feb Scot)
■ Golden plover	1 Sep–31 Jan
■ Grouse	12 Aug–10 Dec (30 Nov NI)
■ Hare	Cannot be sold Mar–Jul (12 Aug–31 Jan NI)
■ Jack snipe	Protected in England, Scotland, and Wales (1 Sept–31 Jan NI)
■ Partridge	1 Sep–31 Feb (31 Jan NI)
■ Pheasant	1 Oct–1 Feb (31 Jan NI)
■ Ptarmigan	12 Aug–10 Dec
■ Red/sika hybrids stags	1 Aug–30 Apr (NI)
■ Red/sika hybrids hinds	1 Nov–28/29 Feb (NI)
■ Red stags	1 Aug–30 Apr (1 Jul–20 Oct Scot)
■ Red hinds	1 Nov–28/29 Feb (21 Oct–15 Feb Scot)
■ Roe bucks	1 Apr–30 Oct (to 20 Oct Scot)
■ Roe does	1 Nov–28/29 Feb (21 Oct–31 Mar Scot)
■ Sika stags	1 Aug–30 Apr (1 Jul–20 Oct Scot)
■ Sika hinds	1 Nov–28/29 Feb (21 Oct–15 Feb Scot)
■ Snipe	12 Aug–31 Jan (1 Sep–31 Jan NI)
■ Woodcock	1 Oct–31 Jan (1 Sep–31 Jan Scot)
■ Salmon	1 Feb–31 Oct (1 Feb–30 Nov, no fishing Sundays Scot)
■ Trout	22 Mar–30 Sept (15 Mar–6 Oct Scot)

* *variations for Northern Ireland (NI) and Scotland (Scot) are given in brackets*

are laws and regulations governing freshwater fishing, but shore fishing is free to all.

Freshwater fishing

Most freshwater fishing is for trout or salmon, which are classed as game fish, but that is only because we have forgotten that other types of fish are edible. British stock ponds used to be filled with species that are now only caught for sport and seem to have gained the reputation of being inedible. But eels, pike, carp, and perch – to name but a few – are eaten in many parts of the world today, and are still classed as good food.

If you do decide to splash out on a rod licence, you also have to buy a permit to fish your chosen waters,

and it will have to be in season. There are some local variations to fishing seasons, but for the most usual dates, see the table above. All you will then need is the correct tackle and some skill and luck – easy really.

Sea fishing

Our local fishmonger stocks fish that have been caught within a radius of 64 kilometres (40 miles), so we are spoilt for choice for fresh local fish. However, every once in a while we pop over the hill for a bit of fishing. We have a selection of rods, reels, and tackle that we have picked up from the classified ads or car boot sales, so we have not spent much money on our equipment. That said, it's more than good enough.

When fishing, we divide into groups, as follows:

Those who wish to stay active will either use spinners or mackerel feathers and cast and retrieve to their hearts' content. When there are mackerel around this is a very successful method, and they make great fish for a barbecue or to stock the freezer. Truly fresh mackerel, simply filleted, seasoned, and popped onto the grill, are usually tasty enough to convert even the most sceptical of fish eaters.

The less active group bait fish, either on a float rig or ledgering on the bottom. This would appear to be the simpler option, but it does involve a little organizing of the bait. We keep some sand eels, squid, and mackerel in the freezer so we can go out fishing at anytime.

Vermin

It is worth establishing the difference between game and vermin: game are animals that are hunted for food or sport (sometimes both), or for profit, whereas vermin are animals that spread disease or are unwelcome because they prey, or have a detrimental effect, on game animals. Of course, let's not forget that some vermin, like rabbits, squirrels, and pigeons, taste great too.

These small mammals, birds, and rodents can cause real problems around your plot. From eating your much-loved crops to killing all of your chickens, vermin can really ruin your day. You can control them, however, as long as you keep within the boundaries of the law. Responsibility for controlling animal pests normally rests with you, the occupier of the land, and we have tried most of the methods below, normally with excellent results. We've even had a go at the theory that meat-eating men should pee around the perimeter of the plot to deter foxes.

Rabbit populations can be controlled in various ways (see box below). If your plot is under siege and your vegetables or grazing pastures are suffering, get a longdog, buy an air rifle, and consider raising some ferrets. If you are shooting at a group of rabbits, start with the one furthest away, and then work your way back until they scatter. We would also suggest investing in an electronic "shot detector" to avoid breaking a tooth if you are planning on eating them. Common signs of rabbit activity in your area, as well as actual sightings, include closely grazed grass, fresh droppings, warrens, and rabbit-sized holes in fencing.

Rats and mice are all around us. Although they deserve to be seen as a threat to productivity and a health hazard, we also accept that they are simply competing for space and don't need to be eradicated, just kept in check. For us, "rat warfare" on the farm involves setting a series of traps and sometimes putting poison down on their known routes.

Foxes have had a huge amount of press coverage in recent years with the abolition of fox hunting. Indeed, they have been given more attention than many other political issues. Our stance is that prevention is better than cure. We prevent foxes from becoming a problem by ensuring our animals are protected by well-maintained electric fences, putting our poultry away every night, and owning two big dogs. If this doesn't work for you, consider setting snares or shooting them (see below).

1 & 2. The normal balance of cat and dog control seems to work for us; a longdog is a particularly good rabbit chaser, while cats are, of course, superlative mousers. **3. To protect our geese and ducks** from foxes, we ensure they are safely behind a wire fence by day and in their houses by night.

216

TRY THIS

Keeping ferrets can be fun and functional. There is plenty of literature on the subject and we think it is a fairly natural way to reduce the rabbit populations over the winter months.

Setting snares can be effective, but it could also be considered cruel and is subject to legal restrictions. When properly practised it can quickly sort out a pest problem. We recommend talking to local pest control experts and checking with Defra (www.defra.gov.uk) first.

Shooting vermin is our preferred method for dealing with rabbit and rat problems.

Poisoning rats and mice is only used as a last resort.

PROJECT **Skin, draw, and joint a rabbit**

If you have been out controlling your rabbits and intend to eat them, the first thing to do with your dead animal is to hold it up by its front legs and stroke firmly down its abdomen a couple of times to empty the bladder. To allow them to cool, keep your rabbits separate rather than piled up or bundled into a bag.

YOU WILL NEED
- Sharp knife
- Chopping board, if you intend to joint it

1. Place the rabbit on its back and pinch a bit of the belly skin to pull it away from the body cavity. Nick it with the knife, without sticking it into the belly.   **2. Carefully cut** the skin along the belly and, if you wish, cut down to the feet, without damaging the internal organs (or it can get messy).   **3. Pull back** the skin to expose the intestines.   **4. Turn the rabbit** belly-side down and shake out the innards.

5. Cut around its "vent" and remove all droppings and lower intestines.   **6. Ease the skin** from its back and, holding the carcass in one hand and the skin in the other, pull them apart like a set of chest expanders.   **7. The skin** will roll down over the legs and come off, leaving fur on only its feet and tail. Chop off the head and trim off the feet and tail.   **8. Joint the rabbit** with a sharp knife: back bones and hips for stock (left), rear legs (top), front legs (middle), and loin (right).

Squirrels can do some serious damage in areas where their numbers get out of control. If you need to cull the local population, we suggest setting up live traps, shooting them, and raking the dreys with a long pole before they nest. You can eat them, but they are fiddly to skin. Never kill a red squirrel, though, as they are an endangered species.

Prevention is better than cure

Dealing with vermin can be a complex process, but the best thing to do is to keep your plot as tidy and well maintained as possible. It is good practice to keep your feed stored in sealed bins or containers with lids, and suspend feeders for poultry slightly above the ground. Other forms of prevention include:

Fencing If you have a vegetable garden that is being ravaged daily by rabbits, you could try putting up fencing to deter them. Buy fine metal mesh about 1.2m (4ft) wide. Bury at least 20cm (8in) below the ground in a trench, with 1m (3ft) above the ground. This option works for some people, but we would be wary of spending lots of money on fencing that is unlikely to completely prevent rabbits getting to your carrots.

Instead we perceive a small-scale rabbit problem as a delicious source of free food waiting to make the journey from your garden to the kitchen. On the other hand, electric fencing offers good protection for poultry from foxes (see page 175).

Dogs and cats We keep cats here at Newhouse Farm primarily as a form of vermin control. We always make sure that our cats are spayed to avoid fulfilling that farmyard stereotype with hundreds of cats and kittens hiding in every barn! The cats keep down the numbers of rats and mice, as well as being lovely pets. Our dogs are useful for deterring foxes, rabbits, and sometimes rats. The ideal breed of dog for catching rats is definitely a terrier, particularly a Jack Russell or other small terrier. Our two dogs are a pleasure to have as pets, but it's also great that they earn their keep by patrolling the plot.

TRADITIONAL KNOWLEDGE

IN THE KITCHEN We practically live in our kitchen. Eating freshly cooked, high-quality food is a real pleasure and we love to pop out into the garden, see what is ready, and plan supper around the best produce. Even if you don't have enough space for a kitchen garden, you can still enjoy food at its best by buying fresh, local, seasonal produce. In this chapter, you'll learn about lots of traditional kitchen crafts and may even discover that you're a natural cheese maker or artisan baker. With a larder full of home-made chutneys and colourful jams, you'll find yourself smiling every time you open the cupboard.

Eco-kitchens

The kitchen is the heart of many homes – it's where we have our morning cup of coffee, preserve garden produce, enjoy family meals, and entertain guests. But the kitchen is also where we use the most energy, and conserving it by preparing and cooking food with care is one of the easiest ways to reduce the bills. We also minimize food waste and ensure none ends up in landfill.

Avoiding food waste

The first step to creating an eco-friendly kitchen is to avoid any food waste and prevent any from reaching a landfill site. This means eating products before their sell-by dates and buying in bulk, which reduces packaging and transport costs to and from the shops.

Sort the contents of your pantry by food type and arrange products like the aisle of a supermarket so that you can easily see what you have and what needs replacing. In our pantry we have one clearly labelled shelf for open condiments and another marked 'Closed for storage', which prevents us from opening too many jars at the same time and any going off. You may also find that pull-out baskets are useful for fresh produce.

We have invested in sealed plastic containers to store bulk buys, such as sugar, flour, and oats. If you don't have space to store large amounts of food, then you can try to set up a share scheme with friends or family, which allows you to save money on bulk deliveries but have smaller quantities to store.

Remember, too, that "best before" dates on products simply refer to the time when food is at its best, so it will be okay to eat after that date. The only foods you should avoid after their best before date has expired are eggs. If more perishable food is close to its "use by" date and you are going away for a few days, or you have other meal plans, then freeze it.

Another great way to reduce food waste is to be creative and make meals with leftover food. Try turning to established leftover recipes or experiment with your own. You could try throwing old apples into a pan with sausages or using some stale biscuits as a crumble topping. The possibilities are endless.

Low energy cooking

Most ovens are powered by gas or electricity. Electricity is the most inefficient option, as energy is converted from fossil fuels to electricity and then back to heat; taking energy directly from gas to heat is more efficient. However, the most sustainable choice is an electric oven that is powered by renewables on a green tariff.

Another green fuel option is wood. Wood is a carbon neutral fuel and modern woodburners are highly efficient (see pages 82–83). Although we find that using a woodburner for cooking only makes sense on colder days, it is at these times when a warm hot pot is just what we want. When cooking on a woodburner make sure that you use a pan or pot with a thick base, and start nice and early as cooking times are much longer. When the woodburner is fired up we also use it to boil a kettle, and to heat water for the washing up.

Earth ovens also burn wood as fuel. However, we only really use our outside oven in the warmer months.

USING A HAY BOX

One way to save energy while cooking is to turn off the oven or burner just before your food is completely cooked, and allow the heat in the pan to continue the process for you using a traditional method called a hay box.

■ **You will need** a box made from plastic or metal. Then fill it with dry hay.
■ **Cook your food** in the usual way until it is hot but not completely cooked.
■ **Turn off the heat**, then quickly place the pot or pan into the hay box on a layer of straw. Make sure that you cover the pot with more hay and seal the box lid.
■ **Leave for a few hours** while your food continues to cook in your insulated home-made oven. Plan well ahead, as the normal cooking time for this method is about 4–5 hours, but it varies greatly depending on what you're cooking. Experiment but ensure any meat is fully cooked through.

Best for liquid-based food, *hay boxes use the heat energy already in the pan to finish the cooking process. Line the box with hay and cover the pan with plenty more. Ensure the box lid fits tightly to keep the heat in.*

1. **Slow cooking** on a woodburner is perfect for a warming stew and to boil a kettle for tea. **2. Shallow shelves** allow us to see all our produce and none festers at the back of the cupboard. **3. Buy flour in bulk**; it has less packaging and you will always have some to hand to make fresh bread.

Pressure cookers

Old-fashioned pressure cookers used to be a bit scary, but modern versions are absolutely safe and very easy to use. They are far more energy efficient than conventional pots and pans because the higher internal temperature and pressure they exert cooks food in a third of the time. In addition, more of the vitamins and minerals in foods are retained when cooked in a pressure cooker. If you want to live a greener life and save a bit of money at the same time, then a pressure cooker is a must-have eco-gadget for the kitchen.

Engine cooking

When travelling by road, food that is available at service stations can be a real disappointment. It often has lots of packaging and the only choice available is unhealthy fast food. The eco answer is "engine cooking", after which road trips will never be the same again. Simply find a spot under the hood of your car with no moving parts that heats up while driving. Then before you set off wrap the meal you wish to cook in two or three layers of foil and start your journey. By the end of your trip your meal on wheels should be ready.

Kelly kettles

Ideal for a quick cuppa while you are working outside, a kelly, or volcano, kettle has a double-walled chimney that you fill with water. Then fill the fire base with twigs and dry grass, and light. Heat goes up the chimney, and the good surface contact area with the water leads to a quick thermal transfer and faster boiling.

QUICK TIPS

Try these simple tips to reduce food waste, transport costs, and your energy consumption.

Shopping

■ **Order food in bulk**; we order ours from an organic wholesaler, allowing us to enjoy the benefits of organic produce at a cheaper rate. The food also has far less packaging.

■ **Buy from local shops** rather than supermarkets. This reduces your transport costs and the food may also contain fewer preservatives. We are lucky to have local butchers, greengrocers, and a man who brings fresh local fish to the village.

■ **Buy a good variety of food** to make cooking more exciting and create different menus every day.

■ **Make a shopping list**; check your pantry before you go, and only replace items that are finished. Stick firmly to your list.

■ **Opt for recyclable packaging** by choosing juice and condiments in glass rather than plastic bottles. Glass can be recycled infinitely and you can reuse jars at home to make more preserves or chutney.

■ **Choose long-life products** like tinned beans, dried fruit, nuts, pasta, noodles, rice, and grains, which are unlikely to go off before you use them.

Cooking

■ **Just cover veg with water**; the less water you use the quicker it will boil. Don't throw excess water away after cooking; allow it to cool and use it to make stock, or feed it to your plants.

■ **Cover pans** as the lids prevent heat loss. Also ensure pots and pans cover the stove's coil or gas rings to maximize their efficiency.

■ **Try using a solar dryer** for cooking in the summer (see pages 244–245).

■ **Try one-pot cooking** like stews and soups that take one burner to cook and produce less washing up.

■ **Allow food to cool** before freezing or refrigerating, as previously cooled food won't need as much energy.

■ **Don't fill kettles** and only use as much water as you need.

■ **Keep ovens door closed** – opening them to check on food wastes energy. In winter leave the oven door open after cooking to heat the room, or use the heat to dry mushrooms or herbs.

Preserving the harvest

Certain times of the year bring with them a bountiful supply of produce, but the harvesting season is often short and sweet. However, you can make the most of these seasonal gluts by storing and preserving your produce, allowing you to enjoy it all year round. Some preserving methods also intensify flavours and make tasty treats to cheer you up on cold winter days.

Filling the larder

If you are living and eating in tune with the seasons, you will notice a change in the types of food available locally at different times of the year. Yet by eating purely seasonal produce you could find yourself with a vitamin deficiency in the cold dark days of winter, which a supply of stored summer crops can help to remedy. Besides, there comes a time in the depths of winter when all you really want is a tasty fruit pudding or fresh tomato sauce with pasta. To achieve this, you need to look ahead in summer and early autumn, and store your produce when it is ripe. Get the technique right, too, so that you don't end up with a jar of inedible mould.

Best preserving methods

■ **Pickling and making chutney** (see pages 236–237) can actually improve the taste of your produce, as well as preserving it. The processes rely on preserving food in vinegar and flavouring it with spices and other ingredients. Both pickles and chutneys are delicious with cold meats, cheese, and curries.

■ **Making jams and jellies** (see pages 238–239) is a great way to preserve all those fruits that grow in excess during the summer and early autumn.

■ **Bottling** (see page 240–241) needs precision and attention to detail, but results in colourful jars of summery fruit to line your pantry.

■ **Drying** (see pages 242–245) is the oldest method of preserving produce, and it is also one of the cheapest and simplest. Here at Newhouse Farm we frequently dry herbs, tomatoes, seeds, chillies, salamis, and hams, and have built a solar dryer (see pages 244–245).

■ **Curing** (see pages 246–247) is a preserving technique that is normally reserved for meat and fish. It usually involves using large amounts of salt to draw the moisture out of meat or fish and so make it inhospitable to harmful microorganisms.

■ **Hot and cold smoking** (see pages 248–251) are methods to preserve food, but are more reliable if you cure or dry it first. Today, smoking is primarily used for flavouring, rather than as a preserving technique. Having said that, if you smoke something for long enough, it will also dry out enough for storage.

■ **Clamping** and using a sand box (see pages 164–165) are other traditional storage techniques that are very easy to do at home.

■ **Freezing** allows you to store a wide selection of meats, fish, fruits, and vegetables. We also often freeze soups and leftover meals once they have cooled down. The benefit of freezing fruit and vegetables is that most of the vitamins and goodness is retained, but the drawback is that the texture of foods can be lost. Make sure you label and date your bags and containers, and that you organize your freezer well, with the newest produce at the back, or you will end up losing last year's frozen peas until the next ice age.

1. Vegetables and other garden produce are best preserved as soon as possible after picking.   **2. Bottling** is a good way to preserve fruits, but it is not suitable for vegetables.   **3. Freeze berries** on trays before putting them into bags.

1 2 3 4

THE PRESERVING YEAR

January

■ **Mushrooms** Dry in a solar dryer or oven and then store in jars in a dark cupboard. They will need rehydrating before using for cooking, but they last for ages.

■ **Swede** Set up a clamp or store in a sand box.

February

■ **Leeks** Freeze them, but they are happy left in the ground – the simplest storage of all.

March

■ **Rhubarb** Stems of rhubarb bottle successfully, retaining much of their flavour.

■ **Thyme** Store stems using the traditional drying method, and make salt rubs for barbecues.

April

■ **Asparagus** If you have an abundance of spears, blanch them for 2 minutes and then freeze them.

■ **Spinach** You could freeze it, but do so as soon as possible after harvesting.

■ **Sage and rosemary** Drying is the quickest and most effective method for most herbs.

May

■ **Beetroot** Either pickle them or place in sand trays ready for roasting or turning into mash.

■ **Radish** Slice and pickle them in vinegar.

■ **Gooseberries** Frozen berries retain their original taste.

■ **Dill** We store dill alongside salmon when we make our own gravadlax. This involves placing salt, dill, and salmon under pressure in a small press.

■ **Mint** Consider drying it to make a tin of tea leaves for a refreshing cuppa.

June

■ **Broad beans** These are best blanched and then thrown into the freezer.

■ **Carrots** You could place them in a sand box or a clamp – or freeze them.

■ **Onions** Dry on a wire tray and then plait to hang up and dry. Don't leave them in the dark or they will start to sprout.

■ **Peas** No contest: freeze them if you have a glut.

■ **Redcurrants** Freeze redcurrants or turn them into a deliciously sweet jelly.

■ **Strawberries** Making strawberry leather is a nice way to preserve strawberries for a little longer. Pulp the fruit, mix with sugar, and then roll it into thin strips and lay them on muslin to dry in the sun. The result is a chewy fruit snack.

July

■ **Cucumber** Cucumber pickle is very tasty and worth a try.

■ **Chillies** We either preserve our fiery chillies in spicy chutneys or dry them on lengths of string and then store in sealed jars.

■ **Potatoes** These are best stored in a clamp or in a big paper sack in a dark and dry place (**1**).

■ **Runner beans** Top and tail them, slice diagonally into thin strips, blanch for 2 minutes and when they have been drained and cooled, freeze them.

■ **Tomatoes** We add them to chutneys and bottled sauces, and sun-dry them.

■ **Blueberries** These freeze particularly well.

■ **Raspberries** Turn them into jam or store in the freezer if you have a glut (**2**).

■ **Chives** Chopping them up and freezing in ice-cube trays works really well.

■ **Lemon verbena** Dry some of this aromatic herb and use it to make a relaxing tea.

August

■ **Garlic** Heads of garlic are stored at Newhouse Farm in plaits that hang just outside the kitchen for easy use. We also pickle some cloves.

■ **Globe artichokes** We like to cook them with herbs and other delicious flavourings and then store in oil.

■ **Blackberries** An amazing crop to forage for around your hedgerows; they freeze well.

■ **Coriander seed** Simple to dry and they add huge amounts of flavour to curries, dressings, and oils.

September

■ **Horseradish** Around this time of year we make jars of horseradish sauce.

■ **Marrows** Using marrow for chutney is a good way to add flavour to and preserve these overgrown beasts!

■ **Apples** Cider is one way to preserve apples (see pages 260–261) (**3**). Or wrap them in newspaper and keep in the store room, or slice and make sun-dried apple rings.

■ **Grapes** The only methods of preserving grapes that we are prepared to consider are adding them to chutney, or using them to make our own wine (see pages 256–257).

October

■ **Squash** Just before or straight after the first frost, cut the squashes and store them in nets or on shelves in a dark place; they should last until the following year.

■ **Cranberries** We are traditionalists when it comes to cranberries. We try to make our own cranberry sauce and keep it untouched until Christmas day to enjoy with our home-reared turkey.

■ **Sweet chestnuts and walnuts** These nuts are very easy to freeze.

November

■ **Cauliflowers** Make your own piccalilli year on year (**4**).

■ **Parsnips** Best stored in clamps or in sand boxes.

December

■ **Brussels sprouts** These can be blanched and frozen, but we try to time the growing season so they are harvested fresh on Christmas morning.

■ **Cabbages** Pickling is an effective preserving method, especially for red cabbage.

Making cream, butter, and yogurt

If you have a cow or goat, then making cream, butter and yogurt is a great way to make the most of their milk. It's also enormously satisfying to make your own dairy products, even if you live in the city with no animals and have to go out and buy the milk. We often whisk up a batch of butter to go with some home-baked bread, and always make enough to freeze some for later.

Skimming milk for cream

If you milk a cow or goat and then leave a bowl of the milk to stand at room temperature, the cream will separate naturally and rise to the surface. You can then skim it off with a skimmer – a flat, saucer-shaped utensil about 20cm (8in) across, traditionally made out of wood or tin, and perforated with small holes to allow the excess milk to drain away.

The alternative way to separate cream from milk is to use a specially designed shallow trough, often made of slate, with a plughole in the base. Pour the milk in and wait for the cream to rise. Once the cream is almost solid, pull the plug and the milk runs away into a vessel below, leaving you with a trough of cream.

If you are buying milk to make cream, you need non-homogenized whole milk, such as Gold Top. Some supermarkets, farm shops, and home-delivery dairies sell it. You can't use homogenized milk, as the homogenization process stops the fat, or cream, from separating out.

Souring milk for yogurt

Yogurt is milk that has been soured, or cultured, with lactic-acid bacteria. Simply stir around 30ml (2 tbsp) of shop-bought live yogurt into about 1.2 litres (2 pints) of whole or semi-skimmed milk that's been sterilized, then cooled to blood temperature. Cover the container and leave in a warm environment to work overnight. We recommend using a hay box (see pages 222–223). The yogurt is ready to eat when it has a thick consistency, at which point it's probably best to move it to the fridge. If you want to keep your yogurt culture alive to make more than one batch, keep it in the hay box and every time you take out some yogurt to eat, replace it with the same quantity of fresh milk.

Souring cream for butter

To turn cream into butter you first need to sour, or ripen, it by encouraging bacteria to turn some of the lactose into lactic acid. In warm weather this will happen naturally; for a quicker result and on cooler days, add a few teaspoons of already soured cream or yogurt to the cream and stir to mix.

Clotted cream

Clotted cream is made by heating unpasteurized or non-homogenized milk so that the cream becomes very thick and gains a yellow crust. Leave the fresh milk for 12 hours at room temperature, then heat it to 92°C (197°F). Cool it immediately by pouring it into a bowl. Once cool, leave it in the fridge for a further 24 hours, then skim off the delicious home-made clotted cream.

FLAVOURED BUTTER

Freeze flavoured butter for up to three months. Add slices to fish or steak for an instant sauce. Try:
- Dried thyme and salt
- Chopped chives
- Chopped parsley and lemon zest
- Sage and wholegrain mustard

Add salt and herbs *to fresh butter and roll up in greaseproof paper.*

1. Fresh home-made butter that was made in a traditional wooden mould.
2. Thick clotted cream is great with strawberries and shortbread.

RECIPE **Home-made butter**

Shaking soured cream (see opposite) turns it into butter. You can simply use an electric whisk to do this – you don't need a butter churn. If the cream is at a temperature of about 20°C (68°F) then the butter will "come" (change from cream to butter) in a matter of minutes.

YOU WILL NEED
- 1.2 litres (2 pints) double cream
- 15ml (3 tsp) live natural yogurt
- Salt
- Electric whisk
- Draining board
- Butter pats and stamp
- Mould or greaseproof paper

1. Pour the cream into a clean sterilized bowl. **2. Add the live yogurt** and whisk for a few minutes. **3. The consistency** starts to change to make soft peaks **4. Continue whisking** until the cream looks like scrambled eggs and turns pale yellow. After 2–3 minutes more, small globules of butter form. Add a little cold, clean water when the mixture looks like a firm mass of butter globules and carry on whisking for 1 minute on a low speed. Pour off the milky by-product (buttermilk) and keep it for making pancakes (see box below).

5. Use butter pats or wooden spatulas to transfer the butter to a wooden chopping board for washing. (Butter pats are grooved paddles.) **6. Mix and squeeze** the butter with the pats. Keep adding more water to wash the butter – this prevents it turning rancid later on. **7. Collect the buttermilk** as it washes off. Continue rinsing the butter with water and collecting buttermilk until the liquid runs clear.

IRISH BUTTERMILK PANCAKES

Soda flour mix
- 500g (1lb) plain flour
- 5ml (1 tsp) cream of tartar
- 5ml (1 tsp) bicarbonate of soda
- 2.5ml (½ tsp) salt
- 2.5ml (½ tsp) sugar

For the pancakes
- 500g (½lb) soda flour
- 300ml (10fl oz) buttermilk
- 2 small eggs

Make a well in the flour and crack the eggs into it. Whisk together with a fork, gradually adding the buttermilk to make a batter. Oil and heat a griddle or frying pan and drop in spoonfuls of the batter. Cook for 2–3 minutes on each side.

8. Layer the butter in a mould, salting it with at least 2 per cent of its weight in salt.
9. Push the layers down to drive out air bubbles. **10. Stamp** the butter to decorate. If you don't have a mould, roll up the butter in greaseproof paper instead.

Making your own cheese

Making cheese originally began as a way of using up surplus milk and it's a useful technique to learn if you keep cows or goats. Even if you don't produce your own milk, making cheese is still extremely creative and gives you the chance to experiment by adding home-grown herbs to flavour your own delicious soft and hard cheeses.

What is cheese?

Milk that has been left in a warm place, or has had additives mixed with it, increases its acidity and causes curds and whey to form. Cheese is made from the curds.

Delicious and a great source of protein, cheese is also very high in calories, even more so than some cuts of meat, although soft cheese made from semi-skimmed milk is a less fattening option.

What milk to use

If you don't own milking animals, buy whole or semi-skimmed milk to make cheese (avoid skimmed milk). Unlike making cream (see pages 226–227), you can use homogenized milk.

Pasteurised milk is fine for cheese-making, as long as you use an effective starter (see right) and allow the lactic-acid bacteria to develop overnight before you begin.

Making soft cheese

You can make soft cheese by allowing some milk to curdle naturally on warm days in summer, or by adding a coagulant. It is fairly tasteless, which gives you the opportunity to be adventurous with flavourings (see recipe opposite). Cream cheese is a soft cheese made with curdled cream instead of milk. It has a smoother texture and more buttery taste.

Making hard cheese

A great way to preserve the summer glut of fresh milk into winter, hard cheese was traditionally made from the milk from more than one cow, and from an evening and a morning's milking. The process was started off with evening milk and morning milk added next day. But don't worry if you have no cows – we get great results using organic supermarket milk (see pages 230–231).

Using a starter

"Starters" are batches of milk that are very high in lactic-acid bacteria, which speeds up the cheese-making process. You can buy milk-based starters or make your own. We make ours by leaving a litre (2 pints) of semi-skimmed milk at 27–30°C (81–86°F) for 24 hours to go sour – this is known as the "mother culture". Then skim off the top layer of the starter and add it to another pint of semi-skimmed milk. Cover this with a cloth and leave for another 24 hours at 21°C (70°F) to create the working culture.

Using a coagulant

Rennet is a key ingredient in cheese-making. It comes from the stomach of a calf, goat or lamb, and is the enzyme that causes milk to coagulate into curds and whey. Milk that is curdled with rennet without further processing is known as junket.

For vegetarian cheese, buy rennet made from fermented microorganisms, plant extracts, or synthetic animal rennet – or use lemon juice.

1. Soft cheese doesn't need rennet to help the milk curdle – lemon juice will do the job – making it an ideal vegetarian option. Serve it with rustic slices of hot buttered toast. **2. Home-made hard cheese** will keep for months if stored correctly, but in practice it gets eaten all too quickly. This version has been rolled in finely chopped fresh chives for a mild oniony flavour. Serve with a stack of traditional oatcakes.

RECIPE **Soft cheese**

Soft cheese is quick and easy to make, and is ready to eat in less than 24 hours. It doesn't keep for long and needs to be eaten up quickly. Its mild taste gives you the chance to jazz it up with different flavourings, from classic crushed garlic and chopped fresh herbs, to coarsely crushed peppercorns.

YOU WILL NEED
- Large pan
- Slotted spoon
- Muslin bag
- String
- 1 litre (2 pints) milk
- Juice from a lemon
- Chopped herbs
- Chopped garlic
- Salt and pepper

1. Bring a pan of milk to a gentle simmer. Take off the heat immediately and add the lemon juice. Stir the milk, which will start to curdle. **2. Use a slotted spoon** to put the curds into a muslin bag. Tie up the bag with string. **3. Hang the curds** above a bowl or sink overnight, to allow the whey to drip out.

4. Unwrap the curds and you'll see they have turned into a home-made soft cheese. **5. Spread the cheese** out on a work top and mix in some flavourings. We used chopped fresh chives, crushed garlic, salt, and pepper. The soft cheese lasts a few days when stored in the fridge.

CREAM CHEESE

Warm some cream slowly until it is curdled. Leave the curds in the whey overnight. Then drain the whey off and cut up the curd with a long-bladed knife. Add some salt and some butter if you want it to taste a bit richer, and tie it up in a muslin bag. Hang the bag for a day to drip. The following day, tighten the bag up and leave it to hang for a month. You can leave it for up to four months to mature, but we are never that patient!

BUY LOCAL

We don't have time to make as much cheese as we would like, so we buy a selection of local cheeses. There has been a revival in small-scale dairies who take pride in producing truly delicious cheese. Look around and do some research into which regional specialities are available in your area, instead of opting for a bland block of Cheddar from some distant factory. Another option when choice is limited is to buy ordinary, uninspiring cheese and smoke it at home to add another rich, exciting flavour (see pages 250–251).

Hard cheese

We used to think that making cheese was only possible if you had all sorts of hi-tech equipment and scientific knowledge, but in fact cheese can be made in the comfort of your kitchen. Clean all equipment thoroughly with scalding hot water before starting. If you've got enough self-restraint, you'll find the taste of cheese greatly improves with age.

YOU WILL NEED

- Large settling pan to hold 9 litres (2 gallons)
- Cooking thermometer
- Muslin, calico
- Long-bladed knife
- Sieve, ladle, slotted spoon
- Mould, heavy weight

- 9 litres (2 gallons) whole milk
- 1 heaped tablespoon of starter
- Small tub of live yogurt
- 5ml (1 tsp) rennet
- Salt
- Chopped chives or other fresh herbs

SEPARATING THE CURDS AND WHEY

1. Pour about 4.5 litres (8 pints) whole milk into a settling pan. Heat it to 20°C (68°F). Take off the heat, add the starter and half a cup of live yogurt, cover the pan with muslin, and leave it overnight.   **2. Skim off the cream** with a sieve and heat it in a separate pan to about 30°C (86°F). Stir this back into the first pan of milk.   **3. Add another** 4.5 litres (8 pints) of milk. Heat gently to 32°C (90°F).   **4. Mix a teaspoon of rennet** with a cup of cold water. Remove pan from heat and pour in the rennet.

5 & 6. Stir the milk for 5 minutes using your hands. Stop stirring when the mixture starts to stick to your fingers as it separates into curds and whey.   **7. Stroke the surface** of the mixture with the rounded bottom of a sieve to stop any cream rising to the surface. Do this for a good 5 minutes so that the cream gets trapped in the curds. Leave the curds and whey to stand for an hour.   **8. Ladle off the whey** into another pan and reserve a little of it for step 10.   **9. Dice the curds** into 5mm (¼ in) cubes using a long-bladed knife, to release more whey. Ladle off the whey.

PITCHING THE CURDS

10. Heat the curds with a little whey to 39°C (97°F), stirring with your hands, to cook the mixture. It should look like scrambled eggs. **11. Test the acidity** of the curds with the pitching test. Stretch a small amount between your fingers: if it doesn't snap before it reaches 5cm (½ in), it's ready. If it fails the test, leave it for a bit longer. **12. Let the curds settle** into small pieces about the size of a walnut. You can do this using your fingers. This stage is known as "milling". Add herbs and spices and other flavourings at this point if you want to.

MOULDING, PRESSING, AND SALTING

13. Lift the curds into a muslin-lined mould using a slotted spoon. Use a knife to slide off the curds. We used a clean tin can as a mould. You should be able to make 2 small cheeses. **14 & 15. Press the curds** into the mould in layers (we used a wooden garlic crusher) and add salt between layers – 25g (1oz) for every 500g (1lb) of curds. **16. Bring in the ends** of

18. Unwrap the cheese and wash in warm water. Turn it upside down, rewrap and weigh it down again for another day. **19. Unwrap the cheese** and roll it in chopped chives or any fresh herbs. **20. Wrap it back up** in the muslin and weigh down for another two days. Remove the muslin and wrap the cheese in calico. Store on a shelf at about 13–16°C (55–61°F). Turn the cheese daily for the first week and then weekly after that.

Baking bread

Even if you're a long way from the self-sufficient life, the smell of freshly made bread is reason enough for baking it regularly at home instead of buying it. There is an amazing number of breads you can make in the comfort of your kitchen, and whatever sort you decide on, and whichever type of grain you use, the process is simple. So experiment, be inventive, and have fun.

Variety is the spice of life

Bread can be broadly divided into two types plus sourdough:

▪ **Leavened breads,** such as white or wholemeal bread, rye bread, and bagels, each of which use yeast as a rising agent.

▪ **Unleavened breads,** such as pitta breads, chappatis, and rotis.

▪ **Sourdough** (see pages 234–235) is a rising bread that doesn't use yeast.

Yeasts

The most commonly found breads are those leavened by yeasts; they rise when the yeast converts the sugars in the flour into alcohol and gases. After the alcohol has evaporated, carbon dioxide makes bubbles in the dough giving it an unmistakable fluffy texture. Yeast is a temperamental ingredient that needs a warm environment to flourish, but make sure it doesn't get higher than 35°C, or you'll kill it.

Fresh yeast looks like soft putty with a strong yeasty smell. Keep it in the fridge or freeze it in 2.5cm (1in) cubes. We prefer it to dried yeast, but if you are using dried, use half the weight stated for fresh in the recipe.

Kneading

Pummelling your dough is not only a very important part of the bread-making process, it is also a superb stress-buster. While you're dissolving any pent-up anger or tension, you are distributing the yeasts evenly through the dough and developing the gluten strands, without which the bread simply wouldn't have the elasticity and strength to be able to rise properly. It can be treated harshly and will love you for it. Push and pull the dough until it becomes silky and elastic. After a while, do the window pane test: stretch a portion of dough between your hands until it forms a thin sheet that you can see light through. (If it tears, it's not ready.)

Now put the dough aside until it has doubled in size. You'll know the bread is fully risen if it springs back to its original size when you stick your finger in it.

Experiment with flours

Try traditional breads from your local bakery and a variety of flours in your baking instead of buying cotton wool loaves from a supermarket. Here are some of our favourite flours:

▪ **Wheat flour,** which is a rich source of fibre as well as protein and vitamins B and E. It is also rich in gluten, rises very well, and produces a workable, stretchy dough.

▪ **Rye flour,** a traditionally dark, heavy bread with a slightly sour taste and an excellent chewy texture. It's a favourite in much of eastern Europe. It is low in gluten and a popular choice for people with wheat intolerance.

▪ **Barley flour** is extra delicious if you toast the barley flour first. It makes a lovely, sweet-tasting bread. We mix one-third barley flour with two-thirds wheat flour for a good loaf. Barley is also low in gluten.

▪ **Spelt flour** is made from the earliest known grain and is especially high in protein, vitamins, and minerals as well as being naturally low in gluten. The loaf can be fairly dry so add some wheat flour if you want it to rise well.

WHOLEMEAL BREAD

▪ 600g (1lb 5oz) spelt or wholemeal flour
▪ 2 tsp yeast
▪ 400ml (¾ pint) water
▪ 100g (3½oz) mixed seeds
▪ 2 tsp salt

▪ **Mix the flour and yeast** in a bowl and add the water (in cold weather use tepid water to activate the yeast).

▪ **Work the mixture into a dough,** spread it on the work surface, and knead it thoroughly until it is elastic. Sprinkle the salt over it and most of the seeds.

▪ **Use a scraper** to bring in the edges of dough. Consolidate it into a neat shape.

▪ **Put the dough in an oiled bowl,** spray with oil, cover with a damp tea towel, and leave it in a warm place to rise.

▪ **Knock back the dough,** divide it into halves, and put them in oiled loaf tins.

▪ **Spray with water** to make a sticky surface, and sprinkle with seeds. Cover with cling film and leave for 2 hours.

▪ **Bake at 200°C (400°F/Gas 6)** for 20 minutes. Knock it out of the tin and bake on a tray for 10 minutes to form a crust.

RECIPE **Herby white rolls**

There will be bread-baking purists wondering why we have included white rolls here, but we have never found another sort of bread that toasts quite so well. Use the herbs listed, or forage for others, such as wild garlic, or add seeds or honey.

YOU WILL NEED
- 1kg (2¼lb) strong white flour
- 600ml (1 pint) warm water
- 30g (1oz) fresh yeast
- 3 tbsp olive oil or rapeseed oil
- 20g (¾oz) salt
- Handful of mixed herbs, such as sage, rosemary, and thyme
- Oil spray and bowl

1. Mix together all the ingredients except for the salt and herbs. Turn onto a work surface, flatten the dough, then knead it well and flatten again. Sprinkle on the salt. **2. Chop the herbs** and sprinkle them on. Work the dough again twice, doing the window pane test each time. Consolidate the dough by folding it into a smaller, neater mushroom shape. Put the dough in an oiled bowl and spray it with oil. Cover the bowl with a warm damp tea towel and leave the dough to prove. **3. Turn the dough** onto a work surface and pull off pieces to make rolls. **4. Flour them** or wet them and sprinkle with seeds and leave them to rise. Cook in a preheated oven at 200°C (400°F/Gas 6), for about 20 minutes until golden.

RECIPE **Soda bread**

Soda bread is easy to make because it doesn't need to be left to rise. In Northern Ireland we eat flattened triangles of soda bread called soda farls. They are delicious toasted and extra special when fried in bacon fat and served with an Ulster fry-up.

YOU WILL NEED
- 450g (1lb) strong white flour
- 1 tsp cream of tartar
- 1 tsp bicarbonate of soda
- ½ tsp salt
- 350ml (12fl oz) buttermilk
- Mixing bowl
- Griddle, palette knife
- Loaf tin

1. Put the dry ingredients into a mixing bowl, then whisk in the buttermilk. **2. It will be crumbly** at this stage, so work it together with a palette knife. **3. Turn the dough** onto a work surface and divide into two. Flour your hands and firm up each half, then roll one half into a rough circle. Cut into four to make triangular soda farls. **4. Flour a hot griddle,** lay on the farls, and let them cook for about 10 minutes until they are golden. **5. Turn them over** and cook for a further 10 minutes. **6. Shape the other half of the mixture,** put it in an oiled loaf tin, and cut a cross on top. Bake in a preheated oven at 200°C (400°F/Gas 6) for about 30 minutes, until golden.

RECIPE **Sourdough bread**

Sourdough is a half-way house between unleavened bread with no yeast, such as roti and chapattis, and yeast-based bread. It's made using a natural fermenting process so you don't need to add yeast. However, you do need to make a "starter" 2–3 weeks ahead of when you plan to start baking sourdough for the first time. A plastic scraper is a versatile little tool to use when making bread. It is great for getting dough out of bowl, for cutting and dividing it, and for cleaning hands and work surfaces.

YOU WILL NEED
- 500g (1lb 2oz) strong white flour
- 400g (14oz) sourdough starter (see below left)
- 250ml (8fl oz) water
- 3 tsp salt
- 1 tsp brown sugar
- Mixing bowl
- Plastic scraper
- Oil spray
- Couche cloths
- Lame (razor)

MAKING THE STARTER

- **Mix equal quantities** of strong white flour and water, say 500g (1lb 2oz) of flour and 500ml (16fl oz) of water in an open container. Cover with a cloth and leave somewhere out of harm's way at room temperature.
- **After 2–3 weeks** the starter will start to ferment and increase in volume. You will also see air pockets in it. A wild yeast culture has been formed and is ready to use.
- **After using** some of the starter, you have to replace it – called "feeding" it. If you use 400g (14oz) of starter in your recipe, replace it with 200g (7oz) of flour plus 200ml (7fl oz) of water, whisked in to the original starter.
- **If you are not** baking every day, keep your starter in the fridge and take it out 24 hours before you need to use it. This will bring it back to room temperature and kick-start it back into action.
- **You can also freeze** the starter, which puts it into a suspended state. To bring it back to life again, let the liquid defrost and then leave it at room temperature for a day before topping it up to feed it.

1. Put the flour and starter into a bowl. There's no need to sieve the flour.
2. Work the flour into the starter with your hands, using the plastic scraper to remove the sticky stuff off your hands every now and then.

3. Turn the dough onto a lightly floured work surface. **4. Flour your hands** and work the dough thoroughly by stretching it with the heel of your palm. Be brutal with it and don't be afraid – you won't hurt it. The dough will feel wet but don't be tempted to add more flour. Flatten the dough once again and sprinkle with the sugar and then the salt, which will absorb any excess moisture.

5. Fold the dough in with the scraper and start working it again. You will feel it starting to dry up. **6. To test** whether the dough is ready to be left to rise, apply the windowpane test. Stretch a portion of the dough between your hands. If it tears, the dough is not yet elastic enough and you should continue kneading. **7. If it stretches** to form a thin sheet that you can see the light through, then it is ready. This test is much more accurate than any instruction on exactly how long to knead for.
8. Consolidate the dough by folding it into a mushroom shape to make it smaller and neater.

9. **Oil a large bowl** and pop the dough into it. Spray the dough with oil to stop it forming a skin, then cover with a warm wet cloth (or cling film or carrier bag) to stop the dough drying out. Put it somewhere warm but not hot, to prove for at least 2 hours. Unlike most breads, sourdough won't double in size, but you should see some movement.   10. **When the sourdough has risen**, prepare the couche cloths. These are made of tightly woven, unbleached cotton or hemp. Work flour into them with your hands.   11. **Turn out the dough** onto a floured surface and consolidate it by folding in the edges.

12. **Halve the dough** using your scraper.   13. **Then pull in the edges** of each piece of dough to form a ball.   14. **Put the prepared couche cloths** into bowls and drop each ball of dough into the cloth. Leave the "untidy" seam side of the dough uppermost.   15. **Loosely fold** over the edges of the cloth and leave to rise again in a warm place for 2 more hours.

16. **Peel off the couche cloth,** putting the loaves onto floured baking trays, seam-side down. (Never wash your couche cloths; just leave them to dry and then put away.)   17. **Make several slashes** across with the lame – this will encourage the sourdough to burst open in the steam when being cooked. We use an old cut-throat razor; a knife is not sharp enough.   18. **Then flour the sourdough loaves** and put in a preheated oven at 180°C (350°F/Gas 4). Chuck a small bowl of water directly onto the oven floor and shut the door quickly before any steam escapes. Bake for about 15 minutes, or until golden.

Making pickles and chutneys

The difference between pickle and chutney is quite simple: pickles are pieces of vegetable or fruit preserved in vinegar, whereas chutneys are made from fruit or vegetables cooked in vinegar. Vinegar is used because its high acidity inhibits the actions of harmful microorganisms that cause foods to go bad, and it adds a tangy flavour to your preserves.

Pickles

Generally, pickling is quicker and easier than making chutney, and makes use of young, undamaged, fresh fruit or vegetables. When pickling vegetables, it is important to first ensure that they are moist, and to then soak them in brine or pack them in salt for 24 hours to draw out some of the water in them. To make brine, mix 100g (3½oz) of salt with 1 litre (1¾ pints) of water.

Then place the vegetables into sterilized jars (see step 4 opposite) and completely cover them with vinegar. Distilled vinegar is the strongest preservative, but also one of the most expensive; the more you pay for your vinegar, the tastier your pickles and chutneys will tend to be. However, you can always take the home-made option and make your own vinegar (see page 260); flavour it with your chosen herbs and spices.

■ **Pickled eggs** If you find yourself with more eggs than your family or friends can eat, pickling them is a great option. Hard boil the eggs, then shell them and pack into large jars with about 1 litre (1¾ pints) of spiced vinegar to every dozen eggs. Close the lids tightly. The eggs should be ready to eat after about one month.

■ **Pickled onions** To achieve a sweet pickled onion, we add a little sugar to the vinegar (we use white sugar to keep the pickle clear and light). Before peeling the onions, soak them in a brine solution for 12 hours, then skin them and submerge in fresh brine for another two days before packing them into a jar. Cover them with spiced, sweet vinegar and seal the jar. Resist eating the onions for at least two months after pickling them.

Chutney

The chutneyfication process is one of the most satisfying and exciting aspects of growing your own food. We turn huge volumes of our produce into chutney and they can be made from almost any fruit or vegetable. We've used marrows, apples, grapes, radishes, rhubarb, red and green tomatoes, chillies, aubergines, pears, squashes, and turnips – to name but a few. Then there are all the various spices that add those distinctive chutney flavours: cumin, coriander, allspice, cloves, ginger, peppercorns, paprika, mustard seed, and garlic are some of our first-rate selections.

1

2

3

BRINING OLIVES

We grow our own olives in the polytunnel, but raw olives need to be pickled to make them palatable. To remove any impurities, cut each olive to the stone, place in sterilized jars, and cover with water. To keep the olives submerged, place a small plastic bag filled with water on top. Change the water every day for a week and then pickle them in brine – 75g (2½oz) salt to 1 litre (1¾ pints) of water – for five weeks. Add a thin layer of olive oil for an airtight seal.

1. The perfect pickled onion should be both sharp and sweet. **2. Spooning chutney** into sterilized jars is a good deal easier with the aid of an old-fashion funnel. **3. Crunchy vegetables** like cucumbers and cabbage can be pickled directly in cold vinegar; they don't need soaking in brine first.

RECIPE **Spiced pickling vinegar**

There is a wide variety of vinegars suitable for pickling, such as malt, wine, or cider vinegar. You can also add your own spices and herbs to clear distilled vinegar. For the contents to remain recognisable and look attractive, use whole spices, as ground spices make the vinegar go cloudy.

YOU WILL NEED
- Dried chillies
- Juniper and sumac berries
- Cinnamon sticks
- Star anise
- Muslin squares
- Bottle of distilled vinegar

1. Lay two squares of muslin on top of each other on a work surface. Crush the chillies and berries, and then put the spices in the centre of the fabric. Gather up the corners and tie with string to form a spice bag. Ensure the string is long enough to loop over and hang from the handle of the saucepan. **2. Put the bag** and vinegar in the saucepan and bring it to the boil. Remove from the heat and leave the vinegar and spices to cool for a couple of hours. Take out the spice bag. The flavoured vinegar is now ready to use. **3. Use the vinegar** to pickle garlic, onions, cabbage, or eggs, for example.

RECIPE **Newhouse Farm chutney**

The key to making chutney is to cook the fruit and vegetables for a long time, so that most of the moisture evaporates and it has a thick, jam-like consistency. The colours will change and the flavours intensify in the process. A good chutney also benefits from bold and contrasting flavours, so be experimental and don't be afraid to mix together fruits and vegetables.

YOU WILL NEED
- 2 large pumpkins
- 6 large cooking apples
- 1.5kg (3lb 3oz) tomatoes
- 5 onions
- 1 tsp chilli
- 1 tsp allspice
- 1 tsp mustard seeds
- 1 tsp red peppercorns
- 1 tsp paprika
- 1 small bowl of sultanas
- 1kg (2¼lb) demerara sugar
- 4 litres (7 pints) red wine vinegar
- Muslin
- Pestle and mortar

1. Peel and roughly chop the pumpkins, apples, tomatoes, and onions. **2. Crush the spices** with a pestle and mortar. **3. Place all the ingredients** in a large pan, mix, and bring to the boil. Then turn down the heat and leave to simmer for 3 hours or until the contents take on a jam-like consistency and a wooden spoon drawn across the base of the pan leaves a trail. **4. Spoon into** sterilized jars, seal, and label. To sterilize a jar, wash in hot water and put in a cool oven at 140°C (284°F/Gas 1) for 15 minutes, or in a dishwasher on the hottest setting, or microwave for 2 minutes with 4 tbsp of water.

Making jam and jelly

Jam-making is really enjoyable and captures those delicious fruity summer flavours for use all year round. Our pantry is lined with rows of gleaming jars and top quality condiments that are expensive to buy in shops, but are made from fruits like greengage or quince that are easy to grow or forage for. Jams and syrups also make use of your surplus crops, ensuring that nothing goes to waste.

Jam-making ingredients

Good jam-making relies on three key ingredients: good-quality fruit, pectin, and sugar.

■ **Prime quality fruit** is better for jam than over-ripe fruit. If you don't have your own fruit trees or soft fruit canes, visit a local "pick your own", or forage the hedgerows for a bumper crop of fresh blackberries.

■ **For jam and jelly** to set properly you need the correct balance of pectin, acid, and sugar. Fruits that are rich in pectin (see the table, opposite) set well without any added ingredients, but those with medium to low pectin levels will need some

pectin stock (see box below, right). Alternatively, you can add granulated or liquid pectin, or use jam sugar, which has pectin included in it. Lemon peel contains pectin, offering another option, but be wary of adding too much as this can affect the final flavour of the jam or jelly.

■ **Sugar preserves** the fruit by inhibiting the growth of yeasts. The sugar content must be more than 60 per cent to stop the jam from fermenting. A rough guide is to add 550g (1¼lb) of caster sugar to every 450g (1lb) of any fruit that you know is rich in pectin; 450g (1lb) sugar to 450g (1lb) fruit that is fairly rich in

pectin; and only 350g (12oz) sugar to 450g (1lb) of fruit that is low in pectin.

■ **Any sugar** can be used to make jam. Preserving sugar is more expensive, but very easy to use as it dissolves quicker and needs less stirring. Brown sugar produces darker jams with a slightly different flavour.

Making jelly

Jellies are made using a similar process to jam, but you don't need to throw away all skins, stones, and pips before heating the fruit. This is because they are removed, along with any pulp, when you strain the mixture to obtain the juice.

RECIPE **Plum and cinnamon jam**

Plums contain particularly high pectin levels (see box opposite), especially when they are not quite ripe, so there is no need to add a setting agent to this recipe.

YOU WILL NEED
■ 2.5kg (5½lb) dark plums or damsons, halved and stoned
■ 2 cinnamon sticks
■ 3kg (6½lb) granulated sugar
■ Preserving pan

1. Put the plums, cinnamon sticks, and 1 litre (1¾ pints) of water into a preserving pan and heat gently for about 20 minutes until the fruit is really soft and the syrup is reduced. **2. Remove the pan** from the heat, add the sugar, and stir until dissolved. Bring back to a rapid boil for about 10 minutes, stirring occasionally, until the setting point is reached. Test as described (see box, right). **3. Spoon the jam** into sterilized jars (see page 237). Seal and label.

ACHIEVING A SET

■ **Test for the setting point** When you think your jam is ready, test it to see if it will set. Spoon a little jam onto a cold plate and allow it to cool. Push your finger across the surface of the jam and if it wrinkles, then remove the jam pan from the heat. Alternatively, remove some jam from the pan on a wooden spoon. If, after cooling, the jam sets in the spoon and any drops on the edge form into flakes, it is ready.

■ **Make pectin stock** This helps to set fruits that have a medium or low pectin content (see the table opposite). Put 1kg (2¼lb) chopped, unpeeled (the peel contains the pectin) cooking apples into a preserving pan and just cover with water. Cover the pan, bring to the boil, then simmer for 20 minutes or until soft. Remove the pulp by straining the apples over a clean pan. Simmer the juice gently once again until reduced by half. Pour into small freezer pots. Generally 150ml (5fl oz) of pectin stock is sufficient to set 2kg (4½lb) of fruit.

RECIPE **Apple and blackberry jelly**

Try this easy jelly recipe – you don't need to add pectin, as the apples contain enough to make it set. Remember when making jams and jellies to always remove the pan from the heat before adding the sugar, and warm the sugar before mixing it with the fruit so that it dissolves more quickly. Take care when boiling your jam too. Boil it for too long and it will set rock hard; boil it too little, and it will be a runny mess.

YOU WILL NEED
- Equal quantities of cooking apples and blackberries
- 450g (1lb) golden caster sugar for each 600ml (1 pint) of jelly liquid
- Preserving pan, Jelly bag, funnel

REDUCING THE FRUIT

1. Core and chop the apples but leave unpeeled. Place in a large pan with the blackberries and 1.5 litres (2¾ pints) of water.
2. Bring to the boil, turn down the heat, and leave to simmer for about an hour. **3. Remove any scum** and then test the jelly consistency on a plate. It should be a pulpy mass. If not, simmer for another 10 minutes and re-test. **4. Ladle the liquid** into a jelly bag suspended over a pan. Leave to drip overnight. Resist squeezing the bag or the jelly will turn cloudy.

MAKING THE JELLY

5. In the morning, remove and compost the pulp. Measure the juice and weigh the correct amount of sugar for the volume of liquid. Gently heat the syrup. Remove from the heat, and stir in the sugar until it has dissolved. **6. Boil the jelly** for about 10 minutes, stirring occasionally. Turn down the heat and skim off any further scum that rises to the top.
7. Test the jelly for a set (see box). **8. Ladle into sterilized jars** (see page 237), filling them to the top, as the jam will shrink when cool. When the jelly is hot, seal the jars with cling film and a rubber band. Screw the lids on tightly, and label.

PECTIN LEVELS

Fruits high in pectin	Fruits with medium pectin levels	Fruits low in pectin
Blackcurrants	Apricots	Blackberries
Citrus fruits (mainly in the peel)	Cranberries (ripe)	Blueberries
Cooking apples	Grapes (unripe)	Cherries (dessert)
Crab apples	Loganberries	Figs
Cranberries (unripe)	Medlars	Grapes (ripe)
Gooseberries	Morello (cooking) cherries	Melons
Plums (unripe), damsons	Plums (ripe)	Nectarines
Quinces	Raspberries	Peaches
Red- and white- currants		Rhubarb
		Strawberries

Bottling fruit and vegetables

Bottling was invented in 1809 by Nicholas Appert, who won the prize offered by Napoleon Bonaparte to anyone who could invent a method for preserving food to provide his troops with rations while marching. Since then, bottling has enabled people to store their produce easily and safely, and to make winter meals tastier and more nutritious with summer and autumn fruits.

Bottling fruit

You can use one of three ingredients – alcohol, brine, or syrup – to bottle all the lovely excess fruit from your garden. Each of these ingredients will kill all bacteria, mould, fungi, and viruses, but when preserving with brine or syrup, you need to heat the fruit in the bottles, too, since the high temperature destroys harmful microorganisms. The jars must also be sealed immediately after bottling to prevent any other bacteria or pathogens from tainting the food.

Heat preservation

The heat produced when food is cooked destroys enzyme activity and almost all harmful microorganisms. In addition, the air in the jars expands when filled with hot food, and tightens the seals, forming a partial vacuum, when it cools.

■ **The pan method** involves washing your jars and sterilizing them by submerging them in boiling water for five minutes. Then fill the jars with fruit. Wet the rubber seals in boiling water and put them on the lids. Fix the lids loosely on the jars and put them in a deep pan on a wooden rack or a folded tea towel (or a sterilizing pan with a false bottom). Cover the jars with hot water and simmer for the recommended time and temperature (see table, below left).

■ **The oven method** involves preheating your oven (see table, left) and putting the fruit into jars without adding the syrup or brine. Fit the lids loosely to the top of the jars, as for the pan method, and place them in the oven on a pad of newspaper or a tray. After cooking for the allocated time, fill the jars with boiling syrup or brine, seal tightly, and allow to cool.

When it comes to eating your produce, if the lid comes off too easily, or there are bubbles in the jar, or if the fruit smells wrong or has gone mouldy – don't eat the contents. In fact, if there is any doubt, throw the fruit away.

PROCESSING TIMES

Fruit	Pan method	Oven method
Soft fruit e.g. raspberries, blackberries, apple rings, currants	Raise the temperature over 1 hour to 60°C (140°F), then simmer at 80°C (176°F) for a further 10 minutes	Preheat the oven to 120°C (250°F/Gas ½) and cook the jars for 45–55 minutes
Stone fruit e.g. plums, greengages, cherries	Raise the temperature over 1 hour to 60°C (140°F), then simmer at 85°C (185°F) for a further 15 minutes	Preheat the oven to 150°C (300°F/Gas 2) and cook the jars for 40–50 minutes

1. Buy strong specialist jars with screw tops or use clip jars with rubber seals. Metal must not come into contact with the contents. **2. Rubber ring seals** should only be used once.

Bottling vegetables

Preserving vegetables at home by bottling is not advisable since the jars have to be heated to a very high temperature to make the contents safe. This is because bottling is only appropriate for foods with a high acid content, since the acid prevents the *botulinum* bacteria, which can be lethal, from ruining your produce. Vegetables contain very little acid, and to avoid all risks you would need to heat the jars beyond the boiling point of water using a specialist pressure canner, which is like a large pressure cooker. So our advice is to only bottle fruit, and preserve your vegetables by freezing them.

RECIPE Raspberries in sugar and alcohol

When bottling fruit in alcohol you don't need to cook the contents in a pan or oven; simply let the alcohol do the preserving for you. Use equal measures of raspberries and caster sugar, and an alcoholic beverage of your choice, but remember that the higher the alcohol content, the longer the fruits will last.

YOU WILL NEED
- Raspberries
- Caster sugar
- 1 tsp juniper berries
- Muslin square
- Sterilized jars (see page 237)
- Alcohol (we used brandy here)

1. Put the raspberries and caster sugar in a bowl and mix. **2. Make a spice bag** from the juniper berries (see page 237) and pop it into a jar of alcohol. **3. Add** the sugared raspberries. **4. Ensure the fruit** is fully covered by the alcohol. Seal and store in a dark place; gently shake the jar daily for the first week.

RECIPE Tomatoes in brine

Tomatoes are delicious when used in a winter meal, as they provide a rich summery taste and plenty of vitamins. Bottling tomatoes is also an excellent way to store any surplus produce you may have.

YOU WILL NEED
- Tomatoes
- Brine made of 15g (½oz) salt for each 1 litre (1¾ pints) boiling water
- Sterilized jars (see page 237)
- Thermometer

1. Remove any green stalks from the tomatoes and score the skins in a few places.
2. Put the tomatoes in a bowl and pour boiling water over them. Leave until the skins have loosened, but not for so long that they go soggy. Drain, rinse with cold water, and peel the skins carefully so the tomatoes keep their shape.

3. Pack your jars tightly with tomatoes and fill with boiling brine. Put on the lids loosely. **4. Using the pan method** (see opposite), place the bottles in water and simmer at 90°C (194°F) for 30 minutes. Leave to cool. Loosen each jar's clip; lift the jar by the lid. If the seal doesn't hold, eat or freeze the contents immediately.

BOTTLING PEACHES IN SUGAR SYRUP

- **Add 400g (14oz) granulated sugar** to 1 litre (1¾ pints) of water in a pan. Bring gently to the boil, and simmer for 1–2 minutes at 60°C (140°F).
- **Skin 4–5 peaches,** cut in half and remove the stones.
- **Place warm,** sterilized preserving jars (see page 237) in a deep roasting tray or pan, pack them with fruit, and fill to the brim with hot syrup.
- **Tap the jars** to encourage any air bubbles to rise to the surface, then top up with syrup once again.
- **Cover the fruit** loosely with the lids and use the pan method and processing times given opposite.
- **Leave to cool** and test the seal as described in step 4 (see left).

Drying fruit, herbs, and vegetables

Sun-dried tomatoes and dried mushrooms and strawberries are sold at a premium as luxury foods, but drying food is a traditional way of preserving produce for winter use that's easy to do at home with little effort or cost. The drying process also often intensifies the flavour of the food, and apple slices and vegetable crisps make delicious healthy snacks.

How it works

Drying is a really effective way to preserve food. It prevents the development of unwanted enzymes, bacteria, yeasts, and fungi by removing the moisture they thrive on. There are various ways of doing this, from using the sun's heat or an oven on a low setting, to mixing food with desiccants such as salt and sugar.

Air drying

Air drying is one of the oldest and simplest ways to preserve produce. All you need is a dry, dark, well-ventilated place to hang herbs, fruit and vegetables – an airing cupboard is ideal – and food will dry quickly and efficiently. Avoid hanging food where humidity levels are high as it will go mouldy and rot.

Leave herbs to hang for a week or so, then crumble the leaves in your fingers to remove them from the stems. Hang the stems upside down in a paper bag to collect herb seeds.

Sun drying and solar dryers

Laying out food on racks to dry in the sun is an effective preserving method, but it is more difficult in temperate regions where a few days of back-to-back sunshine without rain are rarely guaranteed. You also need to bring racks under cover every evening to prevent the produce from rehydrating. A solar dryer can simplify the process (see box opposite).

Oven drying

You can dry sliced vegetables and fruit in a fan-assisted oven at about 45–55°C (113–131°F). (To make sure air is circulating in a conventional oven, prop the door open fractionally by slipping a skewer between the door and frame.) To dry mushrooms, brush off any dirt first, but do not

DRYING TIPS

■ **The freshest, top-quality** fruit and vegetables are best for drying.
■ **Use sharp tools** when harvesting and slicing produce.
■ **Always harvest produce** in the afternoon. Produce covered in morning dew takes longer to dry and could go mouldy.
■ **Test food frequently.** Bend herbs or chillies in your hand: if they snap they're ready; if they are bendy, leave them for a little longer. Squeeze fruit and veg – no juice should come out.
■ **Store dried foods** in airtight containers in a cool, dark place. We take eco-pride in saving every glass jar that comes into the house and reusing them for storing our dried produce.

1. Hang herbs in an airy place to dry. Suspend chillies by their stems, tying them to a length of string at 5cm (2in) intervals. **2. Salt** draws out moisture from fresh herbs and helps preserve them. **3. Dry borlotti beans** in their pods until brittle, then shell and dry the beans.

wash them. They take between 4–6 hours to dry and are ready when they shrink to half their size and are still be pliable. Tomatoes take longer as they are fleshier – between 8–12 hours. Apples and pears may take up to 24 hours. If you want to save fuel, use an earth oven (see pages 252–253). Leave all oven-dried foods to cool before storing in airtight jars.

Using a microwave

You can also use a microwave to dry produce. Slice fruit and vegetables, wrap them in a paper towel and cook for a minute at a time on a high temperature setting. Test between each session. Use the microwave to dry herbs too; wrap them in paper, and make sure you place a small cup of water in the microwave at the same time – herbs (and some vegetables) don't contain much moisture and could damage your microwave.

Electric dehydrator

Electric food dehydrators are table-top units with a heating element, a fan, and a series of trays or racks that stack on top. They are efficient but expensive – the perfect present for an enthusiast who likes gadgets.

Desiccants

These draw the moisture out of produce while preserving colour and flavour. Salt and sugar are the most commonly used. This is a more expensive method, as you need enough salt or sugar to fill a container and completely cover the food.

We use the technique to make aromatic herb "rubs" for cooking joints of meat. Layer rosemary, marjoram, oregano, and salt in a container, and leave the herbs to dry. Then crumble them up with the salt and store in an airtight jar for a very tasty herb mix.

DRY THIS

■ **Apple and pear rings** Use a solar dryer or thread them on a length of string and hang above the stove.
■ **Peas and beans** Air dry ripe pods until brittle to touch, then shell the beans or peas. Finish drying in a solar dryer. Rehydrate before cooking, or save and sow in spring.
■ **Beetroot, carrot, and parsnip crisps** Slice thinly and dry in the oven or in a solar dryer.
■ **Herbs** Air dry bunches of herbs, such as rosemary and sage, before they flower, when aromatic oil levels are highest.
■ **Strawberries** Try this Native American technique. Mash ripe berries and add 2 tbsp sugar. Roll the mixture out to a depth of 2–3mm (0.08–0.12in) on a piece of muslin. Air dry on a rack for a few hours to a couple of days, then slice into tasty snack-sized pieces.
■ **Chillies** Hang up to air dry.
■ **Mushrooms** Slice large ones, leave small ones whole. Dry in the oven or a solar dryer.

DRYING FRUIT, HERBS, AND VEGETABLES

IN THE KITCHEN

PROJECT Use a solar dryer

A solar dryer needs no fuel and costs nothing to run. Place it in direct sunlight, facing south, and move it every couple of hours to track the sun. If you know you're not going to be able to do this, position it to face the sun when it's at its highest point. See pages 244–245 for how to make a dryer.

YOU WILL NEED
■ Sharp knife
■ Chopping board
■ Apple peeler, corer, and slicer

1. An apple peeler, corer, and slicer is a handy gadget that does all the functions at the turn of a handle. It works on pears too. **2. The apple** comes off in a continuous spiral. Cut into rings and dip in a solution of water, lemon juice, and a teaspoon of sugar. Pat slices dry before putting in the dryer. **3. Cherry tomatoes** are simply cut in half. **4. Arrange food** on wire shelves, which allows air to circulate. Poppy seedheads don't need any preparation. Close the door, position the dryer, and leave for a few days. Test produce regularly (see box opposite). **6. Store dried foods** in airtight jars.

PROJECT **Make a solar dryer**

Solar drying is an ancient cooking method. Sunlight is converted to heat in the solar collector – an insulating box with a glass front – and the hot air rises into the dryer or cooking chamber. A solar dryer is not nearly as powerful as a conventional oven. We use ours for drying fruit and vegetables (see pages 242–243), rather than cooking a full meal – you would need a very sunny day for that.

YOU WILL NEED

- Glass-fronted cabinet
- Plywood, spare timber, battens
- Drill and various size bits
- Ruler
- Saw and hacksaw
- Corrugated iron
- Black paint, white paint
- Mesh – metal, plastic, or muslin
- Spirit level
- Door knob, hinges, catch

Adjustable vent controls air circulation

Tightly fitting door

White walls reflect heat back into dryer

Wire racks allow air to circulate round food

Angle of collector means it gets maximum sunlight

Holes in the dryer base allow the hot air to enter

Air is heated as it passes along the hot black metal

Solar collector

Cool air enters through holes in the base of the solar collector

MAKING THE SOLAR COLLECTOR AND STAND

1. Reuse an old cabinet. The glass door will form the top of the solar collector and the cabinet the dryer. Drill a hole at one end of the cabinet using an 25mm (1in) hole saw, to form the air vent (see step 16).   **2. To find the best angle** for the solar collector prop it against a wall at midday. Adjust the angle of the glass door until a small notebook held upright on the frame casts virtually no shadow. At this point the collector will be at the optimum angle to receive the maximum amount of sunlight all day.   **3. Measure the height** of the door against the wall; this will be the height of the dryer base.   **4. Cut a piece** of 50 x 25mm (2 x 1in) batten to the same width as the cabinet and drill a row of holes using a 25mm (1in) spade drill bit.

5. Measure the glass door and make a shallow 3-sided box from plywood to the same width but longer, to fit beneath the dryer, and just deep enough to hold some corrugated iron. Use the drilled wood for the end and 50 x 25mm (2 x 1in) for the sides.   **6. Paint** the inside white. **7. Tack mesh** across the holes to keep insects out.   **8. Add wooden spacers** for the iron to rest on, to let air circulate.   **9. With a hacksaw** cut some metal to fit inside the box. Paint it black.

10. Screw the glass door to the top of the box. **11. Hold the box** at the correct height for the optimum angle, as calculated in steps 2 and 3. Use a spirit level to mark a horizontal edge along each side of the box at the open end. Cut along the lines with a saw. These form the edges where the dryer cabinet is fixed on top, and determine the size of the stand. **12. Slide** the black iron inside the collector. **13. Build a stand**. Use two square frames for the ends, and screw them to two side pieces of 50 x 25mm (2 x 1in) wood. The stand should be the same width as the dryer, and the height as calculated in steps 2 and 3 at the back, and the height less the depth of the collector at the front. Attach the collector using timber side braces.

MAKING THE DRYER

14. Mark two staggered rows of holes in the base of the dryer to allow air to enter from the solar collector. **15. Drill** the holes using an 8mm (⅓in) drill bit. **16. Stand the dryer** on top of the collector, with the air vent at the top, to check the fit, but don't join them together yet. **17. Cut a door** for the dryer from a piece of plywood and attach it with hinges. Nail equally spaced runners made from thin wooden battens to the sides of the dryer, to hold wire shelves for drying the food.

18. Add a catch to keep the door securely shut. **19. Paint the inside** of the dryer white. **20. Attach a door knob** to a square piece of wood big enough to cover the vent hole, then screw the wood in one corner so that it can be swivelled open to let air out or closed to stop rain getting in. Screw collector and dryer together tightly, with no gaps. **21. Add wire shelves**. For food preparation tips, see pages 242–243.

Curing meat and fish

Preserving food with salt used to be an essential method for storing meat over the winter in pre-refrigeration days. Today, it's a traditional skill worth learning for the delicious flavour it gives both meat and fish. By experimenting with spices and herbs, which you can add to a basic salt cure, you can create your own secret recipe for hams, bacon, and fish.

How it works

Salt is an effective preservative because it inhibits the growth of microbes and bacteria. It does this by removing moisture in a process known as "osmosis", where water moves from an area of low salt concentration – the food being preserved – to an area of high salt concentration – the curing mix.

There are two ways to cure food with salt. You can either cover it completely in dry salt, or immerse it in brine. Both methods also create an air-free environment, which prevents the growth of microorganisms. Keep your food in a cool place while you're curing as low temperatures inhibit microorganisms. Salting or brining is also the essential first stage when smoking food (see pages 248–249).

Brining

An 80 per cent solution of salt is the most effective way to preserve food by brining (see box opposite). This means dissolving a staggering 1.3kg (2lb 10oz) of salt in every 4.5 litres (1 gallon) of water. You can also add extra ingredients for flavour, including brown sugar, cloves, white pepper, molasses, and even rum. Don't rinse after brining: pat with kitchen roll, then air dry.

Dry curing

This is a more popular method for beginners, and removes more water from food than brining – worth knowing if you plan to smoke your meat or fish afterwards, as you won't need to smoke it for so long. Buy more salt than you think you'll need,

as you have to add extra while curing to replace the brine by-product that's drawn out of the food. Table salt is cheap and efficient, but for specialist recipes, such as gravadlax (see box below), try coarse sea salt flakes.

When curing for the first time, start with small fish. Lay fillets side-by-side on a bed of salt and cover them with a 1cm (½in) layer of salt. Repeat the layers, finishing with salt, and leave for 1–2 days. Then wash the fish to remove the salt, and hang the fillets to dry for 24 hours.

Air-dried ham (see box opposite) is more of a challenge. When you unwrap it every bone in your body will be telling you that the meat has gone off. Trust us: cured properly and air dried for long enough, the meat inside will be safe and delicious.

1. **Salt and sugar** in roughly equal proportions, plus a teaspoon of ascorbic acid, make an ideal cure for breakfast bacon. **2. Cured bacon** is pink all the way through. Soak in cold water for a day if a test slice tastes too salty when fried. **3. Sliced cured bacon** can be frozen. Eat within two to three months.

GRAVADLAX

Mix 75g (3oz) sugar, 2 handfuls of chopped dill, 15ml (1 tbsp) lemon juice, 50g (2oz) sea salt flakes, and 5ml (1 tsp) black pepper. Lay a fillet of skinless salmon in a dish. Spread with cure and place the other fillet on top. Wrap in cling film and weigh down. Turn after 12 hours, pouring off any brine. Leave for 1–2 days then rinse, dry, and cover with fresh dill.

Serve gravadlax finely sliced after it has cured for 1–2 days in the fridge.

RECIPE **Air-dried leg of pork**

This is our version of Parma ham, one of Italy's most famous exports. We like the chillies' kick, but you can vary the mix to your taste. Other ingredients to try are cardamom pods, cumin, coriander seeds, rosemary, star anise, thyme, mustard and caraway seeds, bay, and nutmeg.

YOU WILL NEED
- Leg of pork (5–8kg/11–18lb)
- 3 dried chillies
- 6 star anise
- handful black peppercorns
- 12 cardamom pods
- 3kg (6lb 8oz) salt
- A plastic container large enough to hold the leg of pork, plus a lid
- Spice grinder or pestle and mortar
- Muslin and string
- Stiff brush

1. Grind the spices into a coarse powder. Pour the salt into a large plastic container. Add the spices. **2. Rub the spices and salt** evenly into the meat, working the cure into the skin, especially around the ball joint of the bone. **3. Bury the meat** in the cure, add the lid and leave in a cold place – ideally in a fridge – for 10–14 days, depending on the saltiness you prefer. Every few days, pour out brine that has formed. Add more salt, if required, and rub it in. **4. Lift out the ham**, and remove the cure using a stiff brush. **5. Wrap the ham** in muslin and tie securely with string.

6. Hang the ham outside in a dry but well-ventilated area, such as a lean-to shed, for 18 weeks minimum; we hang for 18–24 months. **7. Unwrap** the meat. **8. Scrub off** any surface mould with cider vinegar. Trim off any yellow (tainted) fat and some of the excess white fat. Pat dry with kitchen roll. **9. The cured ham** is a pinky-red colour in the middle with no grey patches in the flesh.

USING A BRINING AND SALTING TUB

Wooden tubs were originally used for brining and salting, but plastic containers work just as well. Never use metal vessels as these taint food, and always cure fish and meat separately.

For best results
Ensure there is space in the tub between pieces of meat or fish so that the brine can reach every part, and weight the lid. To just flavour meat or fish, rather than preserving it, leave in the brine for 2–3 hours; to cure a ham, leave for 3–4 days. Stir occasionally. After curing, pat with a clean cloth and air dry. Use fresh brine for new batches of food.

Heavy weight on wooden lid

Cuts of meat or fish

Add a drainer if using the tub for salting instead

Smoking your own food

If you like the taste of smoked food then why pay a premium for it when you can smoke your own at home, with little effort and hardly any cost? So-called smoked food that you buy in the shops has often had no contact with real smoke and has been artificially flavoured. With these techniques you can smoke everything from a wedge of cheese to a whole chicken just the way you like them.

The principles of smoking

Smoking started out as a way of preserving food in the days before refrigeration. Like brining, it works by drawing moisture out of food so bacteria can't survive. Smoking works by coating food with antibacterial and antioxidant compounds found in the wood smoke, while at the same time adding a delicious, smoky flavour.

Smoking only penetrates the surface of the food – the centre won't benefit from the preserving effect –so it is essential to start off by salting or brining food (see pages 246–247). This does most of the preserving; smoking helps and adds more flavour.

Cold smoking

This is our preferred method of smoking food. It's an outdoor activity and to do it successfully you need a slow-burning fuel and an enclosed heatproof container of some sort, with enough space for the smoke to circulate around the food. The fire smoulders rather than burns fiercely and produces clouds of aromatic wood smoke. The heat from the fuel doesn't actually reach the food, so the food doesn't cook; instead, it absorbs all of the flavour from the smoke.

Food that has been cold smoked needs to be left for a minimum of 24 hours before eating for the flavour to develop fully. After that, it will normally keep for at least a week in the refrigerator but this all depends on the type of food and the extent to which it has been cured before smoking – if in any doubt, don't eat it! Cold-smoked salmon can be eaten raw, but other smoked foods such as bacon, kippers, cod, and haddock will require cooking afterwards.

Hot smoking

This method is really more of a cooking technique that gives food a smoky flavour. You can do it in a wok on the hob (see opposite) or special stove-top smoker, basically a metal box with racks. Hot smoking uses very hot smoke, and the heat cooks the food while simultaneously smoking it. Hot smoked food doesn't store for long – just a few days in the fridge – but, unlike cold smoking, it's ready to eat straight away.

Fuel for the smoker

We believe that choosing your own favourite fuel is a journey of personal taste. However, let's start you off by saying that only hardwoods are good for smoking food. Americans swear by hickory; the British adore oak. Other woods to try are beech, maple, birch, chestnut, and apple. We have even heard of dried corncobs used as fuel. We always use shavings or sawdust as they don't flare up, smoulder steadily for hours, and generate a consistent column of smoke. Never use kerosene or petrol to light the fuel, as they contaminate food and spoil the taste.

1. **Hang fish** from the bars of a smoker on old coat hangers. **2. Cut cheese** into wedges and blocks to maximize surface area for smoke to penetrate. **3. Home-smoked cheese** develops an appealing, speckled, golden rind; spicy smoked chorizos don't need further cooking.

DIY cold smokehouse

In a permanent cold smokehouse, the smoke is produced by a fire in a pit. It passes through a flue and into the smoke chamber, where the food is arranged on shelves or hanging in the space. To build a moveable cold smoker see pages 250–251.

The smoke chamber

Almost anything large enough, made of fireproof material, and with no paint or enamel that could burn off and contaminate food, will do – an old refrigerator is ideal. Cold smoking won't damage the plastic lining, which is easy to clean. Do not use galvanized metal, copper, or brass oxides for shelves as they taint the food and are a serious health hazard.

WHAT TO SMOKE

It takes a minimum of five to six hours to smoke small items of food. A large ham, on the other hand, can take weeks.

- Cheese
- Fish
- Chicken
- Ham
- Bacon
- Sausages
- Hard-boiled eggs

Insect-proof mesh on top of flue

Smoke circulates around the food as it is drawn up through the flue at the top of the chamber.

There's plenty of space for smoke to circulate round items of food.

Removable open shelves: use stainless steel ones that won't taint the food

The draught passing through the smoke chamber is regulated by adjusting the metal lid over the burning sawdust.

Perforated metal baffle

Rising smoke drifts through the holes in the baffle and disperses evenly around the food.

Metal sheet lid

Smoke enters via the stovepipe and a hole in the bottom of the fridge

Stovepipe runs at a slight incline to improve the draw

Pit is 60cm (2ft) deep

Pit lined with stones

Smouldering sawdust

Getting the temperature right

In cold smoking the temperature should be around 32°C (89.6°F) and should never go higher than 50°C (122°F). Use an oven thermometer to check the temperature in the smoke chamber.

HOT SMOKING ON A HOB

Line a wok with foil and place 110g (4oz) tea leaves, 250g (8oz) rice, and 2 teaspoons of sugar in the bottom. Add a rack and lay fish on top. Fold the foil over the lid to seal. Cook on high for 5 minutes and a further 10 on a lower heat. Never leave wok unattended and eat the cooked food straight away.

Lid

Foil folded over lid

Fresh fish

Metal rack

Rice, tea, and sugar mixture

Make a cold smoker

Building a smoker is surprisingly easy, cheap, and quick – it can be done in an hour. Find a spot for it in the garden on a heatproof base, such as bricks or concrete, but store it under cover when not in use. Experiment with what you put in your smoker. We have tried our own chorizo sausages, eggs, fish, even entire legs of ham. The time it takes to smoke the food to your taste may vary, but the amazing smoky undertones are consistently gorgeous.

In a cold smoker, gently smouldering sawdust produces clouds of smoke to flavour and preserve food.

Loose-fitting wooden lid

Wire rack to hold food

Space to hang fish or sausages from metal bars

Perforated baffle to distribute smoke evenly

Door for lighting sawdust

Mound of sawdust

YOU WILL NEED

- Empty oil drum
- Flexible metal ruler, pencil, scribe, punch
- Power drill, protective goggles
- Hinges and door knob
- Electric jigsaw with a metal cutting blade
- Hammer, leather gloves
- Nuts and bolts, threaded metal bars, wire rack, piece of ply

CUTTING OUT THE DOOR

1. Mark the door of the smoker by drawing a small rectangle at the base of the drum with a metal rule. It should be at least 15cm x 25cm (6in x 10in).   **2. Score the shape** using a metal scribe.   **3. Mark the position** of the holes for the hinges on one side of the door using the scribe   **4. Dent the hinge holes** with a punch to stop the drill from sliding around on the metal.

5. Drill holes for the hinge through the drum. The hinge will be fixed in place later, but it is good to drill at this stage while the door is still joined to the drum and the surface is solid. Remove any burrs with a small file. Next, drill a hole at each corner of the door that is large enough to fit the jigsaw blade.   **6. Jigsaw out the door** and keep to one side.   **7. Drill four holes** above the door, two on each side of the barrel, all level with one another. (Use a punch first, as in step 4.) These will hold the two threaded bars that feed through the drum for the baffle to rest on. Make four more holes higher up which will hold two more threaded bars to rest the grill or wire rack on for cooking – or you can hang food from them.

ASSEMBLING THE SMOKER

8. Perforate the top of the barrel with lots of holes spread evenly around. This will form the baffle, which sits just above the smouldering sawdust and distributes the smoke more evenly around the food. **9. Cut around the top** of the drum with a jigsaw and place your newly made baffle inside the drum. Throw the door into the drum as well. **10. Burn off** any unwanted residue or contaminants with a large wood fire. Feed the fire for half an hour or so until the smoke is burning more cleanly. Please be considerate and warn your neighbours before you start this!

11. Saw a circular plywood lid for your smoker using the jigsaw. This will sit on top of the drum and shouldn't be airtight.
12. Hammer flat the sharp inside rim of metal on the lid, so you don't cut yourself reaching in and out. **13. Attach the door** with the set of hinges using nuts and bolts. **14. Screw a door knob** onto the door to make opening and closing easier and reduce the chance of injury on sharp metal edges. **15. Feed the metal bars** through the two sets of holes you made earlier.

USING THE SMOKER

16. Pour the sawdust into the smoker. **17. Brush it** so that the sawdust curves up and around the edges in a crescent shape, for a slower, more gradual burn. **18. Position** the baffle. **19. Use a tin can** with top and bottom cut off, and push it into the sawdust.
20. Light the sawdust inside the tin can so that the burning starts right within the mound. We use a little gas bottle lighter. Do not use kerosene or other fuels that will affect the taste.
21. Place food on the wire rack and put the wooden lid on top. Leave to smoke overnight.

PROJECT **Make an earth oven**

Few tastes compare to the stone-baked flavour you get from cooking in a traditional earth oven. They can be used for everything from bread and pizzas to fish pies. On an environmental front, the simple clay structure and use of carbon-neutral wood fuel makes cooking in an earth oven a low-impact option. The cost of building one is next to nothing and the process, while a bit messy, is a lot of fun.

YOU WILL NEED

- Tape measure
- Pen
- Garden riddle
- Rolling pin
- Knife
- Trowel
- Clay – dig your own if possible
- Sand
- Newspaper
- Bricks or breeze blocks
- Stone slabs
- Wood

- 60cm (2ft)
- To heat the oven, light a small fire in the centre and rake out the embers before cooking
- Thick walls retain heat
- Height of door is 63 per cent of internal height
- Width of the door is half the internal diameter
- 24cm (9½in)
- 25 cm (10 in)
- Build the oven at waist height so it is easy to use
- Soak the wooden door in water to stop it charring

Each oven has its own unique cooking temperature. Light the fire inside the oven, leave the door open, and wait a few hours. When the soot goes from the inside, remove the cinders with a shovel and start cooking.

BUILDING THE STAND

1. Build a firm support. We used some spare breeze blocks. Keep it level and build the structure up to a comfortable working height for cooking.   **2. Prepare a solid floor** for your oven. It must have a smooth surface. We used a couple of paving slabs.
3. Mark the centre of the oven. Make it as large as possible. Ours is about 60cm (2ft) in diameter.   **4. Draw two circles**, one 7.5–10cm (3–4in) inside the first, to show the thickness of the walls. Note down the radius of the inner circle.

PREPARING THE CLAY

5. Riddle the clay to remove pebbles and debris if you dug your clay from the ground.   **6. Lay a big tarp** on the ground and mix your clay – best done with bare feet.   **7. Add sharp sand** (about a bucketful) and some water if the clay is very dry. Mixing takes time and effort. Don't slip over!

8. Keep turning and mixing the clay.
9. Test the clay to see whether it is ready to work with. Make a clay sausage.   **10. Hold it** with half in your palm and the other half dangling over your hand. If the clay bends but does not break, it's ready to use.

MAKING THE OVEN BASE AND WALLS

11. Roll out a circular layer 1cm (½in) thick on the internal circle of the base. Trim the edges with a trowel. **12. Wet the clay**, then smooth it with your hands. This will serve as a smooth base for sliding whatever's being cooked in and out of the oven. **13. Cover the circle** with a layer of moist newspaper to stop any sand sticking to it. **14. Pile on moist sand** and sculpt the shape of the earth oven, making a dome that is 5–7.5cm (2–3in) taller than the internal radius of the oven. **15. Measure the height** of the sand dome, which will be the interior height of your oven. Multiply this by 0.63 to get the height of the door.

16. Cover the sand dome with wet newspaper to stop the clay sticking to it. **17. Shape the clay** into small briquettes, then flatten and squash them into place. Start at the base and work round and up, to cover the dome. **18. Use the width** of your hand as a rough measurement: the layer of clay should be around 7.5–10cm (3–4in) thick. **19. Try to push** the clay against itself, not against the mound of sand, as you join each briquette. Cover the entire dome with clay, making sure it is still the same thickness at the top as the bottom. Wet your hands and smooth the surface of the finished dome.

MAKING THE DOOR ·

20. Mark out the height of the door using measurements you made earlier. Our sand dome is 38cm (15in) tall so the door is just under 24cm (9½in) in height. Mark the width of the door. Ours measures 25cm (10in). **21. Draw the shape** of the door freehand with a pen. Use a sharp knife to cut it out in two sections, cutting down the midline of the door. **22. Slide the knife** under one half of the door. Slide the excess clay out. Repeat for the other half of the door. **23. Cut away the** excess clay on the inside of the door to enlarge it slightly. Leave the oven for a few days to a week. **24. Remove the sand** when the walls resist denting when you poke them. The oven will dry and harden over time, or you can "fire" it by lighting a small fire using kindling – build up the heat slowly.

FINISHING TOUCHES

Repair any cracks that emerge on the oven as it dries, and fit a door.

■ **Wet the surface** and gently score it with a cross-hatch pattern (left). Apply more clay to the cracked area (right). Repeat if cracks appear after the oven is used.

■ **Make a wooden door.** Use a paper template to get the shape right. However, it doesn't need to be a perfect fit.

Brewing beer and mead

Over the years we have made and consumed large quantities of our own beer. You can brew beer just about anywhere, and the resulting drink can be strong and delicious. Make your own beer to save money and have fun experimenting, but on the whole we'd recommend brewing more unusual beers or traditional mead – drinks that test your taste buds yet are not available in the pub.

Beer and ale

Ale was traditionally made with water, malt, and yeast, while beer was produced using a malt brew, with the magic of hops adding bitterness. Over time, this became the accepted brewing method.

Brewing kits are probably the simplest way to attempt your own home brew for the first time. Simply mix together sugar, dried yeast, and water, plus other chosen ingredients (see recipes opposite), to enjoy your very own refreshing beer. On the other hand, you may want to go down the traditional route, as follows:

■ **Make "wort"** by using a rolling pin to crush malted grain wrapped in a cloth. Mix the husks with the required amount of hops. Transfer the mix into a muslin bag and place it in a saucepan, cover with water, and simmer for 45 minutes.

■ **Strain the contents** into a vessel for fermenting, such as a demijohn or a clean bucket with a lid. Add cool water to top it up – make it up to 4.5 litres (1 gallon) in a demijohn.

■ **When the wort cools** to 15°C (59°F), stir 1 tsp yeast into each 4.5 litres (1 gallon) of liquid. Cover and keep in a warm place for a week.

■ **When fermentation** has ceased (the bubbles are no longer rising to the top), leave the brew for a further day to cool down and for the sediment to settle.

■ **Siphon the beer** into sterilized bottles and add ½ tsp of sugar to each one to give the beer extra fizz when you open it. Label the bottles and start drinking after 2 weeks.

BREWING TIPS

■ **Use brewer's yeast** rather than baking or wine-making varieties for a better quality beer.
■ **Invest in a "hand crowner"** to close the corks on the bottles.
■ **Try bottles at intervals** when waiting for your home brew to mature to ensure you don't get a secondary fermentation. And don't leave them for so long that they explode.
■ **Test your brew** with a hydrometer, which gauges the fermentation progress, showing you when the beer is ready to siphon into bottles. It also indicates the alcohol content.
■ **To sell home-made beer** and wine in Britain the maker must have a license from HM Revenue & Customs. Any breach of these laws can lead to fines and/or imprisonment. Of course, that doesn't mean you can't share your home brew with friends and family for free.

RECIPE Honey mead

Mead is one of the oldest drinks known to man, and was especially popular in northern Europe where grapes didn't grow well. It was drunk after Norse weddings on a holiday known as a "honeymoon". Every year we make our own mead using honey from our beehives and it's as good a reason as any to become a beekeeper (see pages 212–213).

YOU WILL NEED
■ 2kg (4½lb) honey
■ Juice of 2 lemons
■ Juice of 2 oranges
■ 1 heaped tsp yeast

1. Mix the honey with 4.5 litres (1 gallon) of water in a large pan and warm it until the honey has dissolved. **2. Add the fruit juices** to the honey mixture and leave to cool. **3. Add the yeast** and mix it in. **4. Strain** the golden liquid into a demijohn and leave the mead to ferment with an airlock seal attached to it (see page 257). When fermentation stops, siphon off the mead into sterilized bottles (see pages 256–257) and "lay down" for 6 months to mature.

RECIPE **Nettle beer**

Nettles make surprisingly delicious beer. Generally, we are not too keen on nettle soup or nettle tea, despite the health benefits, but nettle beer is on a whole other level. It is easy to make and tastes great. Use the fresh green tops of the nettles, as they make the best beer, and ensure all your equipment is scrupulously clean (see page 256).

YOU WILL NEED
- 1kg (2¼lb) young nettles
- 2 lemons, rind and juice
- 500g (1lb) demerara sugar
- 25g (1oz) cream of tartar
- 1 tsp brewer's yeast
- Large pan
- Plastic funnel
- Bottles

1. Cut off the tops of the nettles and throw away any roots. Rinse them briefly to get remove any bugs.   **2. Boil the nettles** in about 4.5 litres (1 gallon) of water.   **3. Strain the liquid** into a large container and add the lemon rind and juice, sugar, and cream of tartar. Make up to a volume of 4.5 litres (1 gallon) with water and then stir vigorously.   **4. Transfer** to a demijohn. Then, when the brew is cool, add the yeast. Allow 3–4 days for fermentation to take place and then strain the beer into clean, sterilized bottles (see page 256).

RECIPE **Ginger beer**

Ginger beer has always been a great favourite of ours and ever since we discovered that we can grow ginger at Newhouse Farm, the beverage has become a seasonal treat. To grow ginger, in spring plant a sprouting section of root into a pot of good compost and wait for the rhizome to develop. Ginger must be brought inside over winter to avoid the cold, and we harvest ours when the tall stalk withers in winter, saving a bit to replant ready for next year.

YOU WILL NEED
- 25g (scant 1oz) root ginger
- 15g (½oz) cream of tartar
- 1 lemon, rind and juice
- 500g (1lb 2oz) white sugar
- 1 tsp brewer's yeast

1. Pick your ginger and scrub it clean before peeling it.   **2. Crush the ginger** in a pestle and mortar and then mix it with the cream of tartar and some grated lemon rind in a bowl. Add to a bowl of boiling water and then mix in the sugar. Stir until the sugar has fully dissolved and allow to cool. Add the yeast and the lemon juice and make the mixture up to 4.5 litres (1 gallon) with water.   **3. Cover with a tea towel** and leave in a warm position until fermentation starts. Remove the surface scum.   **4. Transfer** to a demijohn. Bottle and cork after 2 days and drink within a few days after that.

Making wine

Pursuing the self-sufficient dream can be a lot of hard work. Indeed, sometimes getting out of bed early in the morning to feed your animals or braving the cold weather to weed the vegetable beds can feel monotonous or deflating. However, on a cold day after labouring outside, what could be better than relaxing in front of a roaring wood fire with a glass of aromatic, home-made wine?

Successful wine making

When you make a good bottle of wine there is not much in the world that can beat the feeling of satisfaction, pride, and, after a glass or two, relaxation. For a small investment it is easy to make lots of drinkable wine, and you also get the chance to try some exotic recipes that are not available at any wine merchants we know of. To make a fine wine, however, requires good ingredients, overall cleanliness, and loads of patience.

Wine making can be approached as a scientific experiment with accurate measurements and meticulous preparations, or treated as a vibrant and fun activity, as we do. We are not too bound by a strict regime and prefer to let the process evolve naturally. Having said that, there are a few basic rules.

Essential tips

All wines consist of water, flavourings, sugar, acid, tannin, and yeast. The quantity of each ingredient varies greatly and the wine improves or degrades accordingly. Time is another key component and the need to exercise patience during the process cannot be over emphasized.

Keep your bottles and all other apparatus scrupulously clean. Warm bottles in the oven, and then fill with boiling water. Leave for a few minutes, pour out the water, and hang them upside down to dry. Or use a sterilizing solution. Campden tablets clean all types of equipment. Read the instructions and always leave for the fully designated time so they can do their job properly.

1. Use secateurs to cut bunches of grapes from vines. **2. The traditional way** of making wine is excellent fun. Get your socks off and give your feet a very good clean. Then squish the grapes under your feet and between your toes until they are reduced to pulp and swills of grape juice.

Our quantities of sugar for making wine come from old-fashioned advice. We use 1kg (2¼lb) of sugar "in the gallon" (4.5 litres) to make dry table wine ("in the gallon" means you put the sugar in the container and add wine up to the volume of a gallon). Use 1.25kg (2¾lb) of sugar for a medium wine; anything over 1.35kg (3lb) makes a very sweet wine.

Use good-quality wine yeast, granulated or liquid, available from wine-making shops or online. You can use baker's yeast, but it often makes a poorer quality frothy wine. For a good strong wine you can also add yeast nutrients available from most wine-making shops.

More acid may be needed for wine that you make from flowers or grain. Buy citric acid from a wine shop, or use lemon juice, which works well.

Two fermenting stages. The first is the frothy active stage where the yeasts are multiplying and need some air around them. Leave the jar or demijohn three-quarters full during this stage. For the second stage, top up the jar with water and place a fermentation lock on the top. This allows the gases that have been produced by the wine to escape, while simultaneously keeping the air out. The lock also prevents the bacteria that turn wine into vinegar from forming, and stops any fruit flies that carry vinegar bacillus from entering the jar and contaminating your precious wine.

Temperature is all-important, and you must try to keep your wine at temperatures favourable to the vital yeasts. During the first fermentation, aim for 24°C (75°F). Do not allow the temperature to rise over 27°C (81°F) or the yeast will start to die; allow it fall below 21°C (70°F) and it will be too cold for the yeast to work.

RECIPE **Wine from grapes**

You can make wine out of just about anything! Some of our more unconventional favourites are pea pod, blackberry, nettle, parsnip, and rosehip. We have tried and enjoyed all of them, but in our opinion it's hard to beat the taste of a traditional grape wine. We have struggled to make a heavy-bodied red wine, but have been very successful using our own grapes to make rosé, as shown here. Grape vines can thrive even in our colder climate (see page 149). Try growing them against south-facing walls, under cover in a greenhouse, or outside on a warm, south-facing slope.

YOU WILL NEED
- Red and white grapes
- Sugar (for quantities, see opposite)
- Wine yeast
- Citric acid
- Wine press
- Mesh cloth
- Campden tablets
- Demijohn, funnel, and fermentation lock
- Sieve
- Bottling and racking equipment

1. Place a mesh cloth on the press within a stainless steel frame and cover it with a layer of grapes; they can stay in bunches. Add the sugar and yeast to a demijohn (see opposite for quantities). Then fit a funnel on top and place beneath the press ready to catch the juice. **2. Wrap the mesh cloth** around the grapes, ensuring none can fall out. **3. Remove** the stainless steel frame **4. Repeat** for up to three layers, separating each layer with a sheet of wood. **5. Squeeze the grapes**.

6. Don't fill the demijohn right up to the top or it may explode during the first fermentation stage; the yeasts also need air to multiply. Leave it about three-quarters full. **7. When the wine is no longer frothy**, indicating that it is in the second stage of fermentation, top up the jar with water and place a fermentation lock on top. When the wine is six months old, it will be time to rack it and bottle it (see right). **8. The by-product** from the pressing stage of wine-making is a flat, fairly dry cake of grape skins and pips. We feed this to our pigs as a little treat.

RACKING AND BOTTLING

To "rack" means to siphon your wine off from the yeast (or "lees") that has settled at the bottom, so it doesn't spoil the flavour. We use a short plastic tube to siphon the wine into a clean container. Repeat a month later and, if you have the patience, do it again three weeks after that. Some people leave their wine in a cold place to hasten the settling of any sediment. After six months the wine should be ready to seal in sterilized bottles without risk of exploding. Leave about 2.5cm (1in) at the top for the cork. A corking gun is a good investment, or use a wooden mallet. Cork and label the bottles and leave them for a year, stored on their sides in a dark place at about 13°C (55°F).

Flower, vegetable, and hedgerow wines

Country wines are fermented drinks made out of all sorts of different ingredients other than grapes. Vegetables also make interesting country wines, but need extra table sugar or honey added to them. Not everyone lives in a location suited to growing grapes, but everyone can make some type of country wine. The only disadvantage is that these wines don't store for long, and are best consumed within a year of bottling.

Flower wines

Flower wines are extremely easy to make, tasty, and beautifully aromatic. Simply pour 4.5 litres (1 gallon) of boiling water into a large fermenting vessel, preferably made of metal, and add the flowers (see below). Bring the water and the flowers to the boil and simmer on a low heat for 15 minutes, stirring occasionally. Once the mixture has cooled, add 1.8kg (4lb) of caster sugar and the juice of 3 lemons. When it has cooled to about 24°C (75°F), add 1 teaspoon of yeast. Strain and pour the wine into a demijohn, and put a fermentation lock on top. Leave it to ferment and bottle when ready (as described on page 257). Leave for a few months, then drink.

Some of our traditional flower wine favourites are:

■ **Gorse** Never go and collect gorse flowers in a T-shirt! The fragrant flowers are protected by hundreds of prickly spines, so wear long sleeves and gloves to grab them. It's worth the effort, though, as they make amazing gorse wine, which smells a bit like coconuts and is very sweet. You will need at least 1.7 litres (3 pints) of gorse flowers for every 4.5 litres (1 gallon) of water.

■ **Dandelion** This is a lovely light wine that is fun to make. Collect the dandelion flowers from mid to late morning and then pick the petals off the flower heads. You will need 1.2 litres (2 pints) of petals. Wash them in running water to remove any bugs or unwanted residue. Then leave in 4.5 litres (1 gallon) of water to infuse overnight. The next day, make the wine as described (see left).

Other traditional favourites

■ **Pea pod** This wine is particularly remarkable because it is made from the bit you normally throw into the compost bin. You can use any sort of pea pods, or even bean pods, as long as they are still greenish. Add 1.8kg (4lb) of empty pea pods, plus the rind of an orange and a lemon, to 4.5 litres (1 gallon) of water. Bring to the boil and simmer for at least 30 minutes, then allow to cool. Strain the liquid over 900g (2lb) of sugar, 1 teaspoon of yeast and the juice of the lemon and orange, and then stir until everything is dissolved and mixed. Ferment and bottle, and leave for 6 months before indulging in one of the great mysteries of the vegetable plot.

■ **Parsnip** These vegetables produce a very pleasant, light white wine. Pick and scrub 1.8kg (4lb) of parsnips. Then slice them, without peeling them, and place in a large pan with 4.5 litres (1 gallon) of water. Cook until tender and strain the liquid into another vessel. Remove the parsnips and make a warming winter soup with them. For the wine, reheat the infused liquid with 1.35kg (3lb) of sugar, plus the juice of a lemon, its rind, and 1 teaspoon of yeast. Ferment and bottle (see page 257), and drink within 6 months.

Pick elderflowers on a hot day while they are in full bloom and strongly scented. It is worth using a ladder to get the best ones, which always seem to be just out of arms' reach. Remember not to strip a tree bare, otherwise there will be no elderberries to use later in the season!

BIRCH SAP WINE

If you like German dry white wine, find some mature birch trees to make a country alternative. Tap the sap in midspring from a few trees with trunks at least 30cm (12in) in diameter, so that no tree gets over-tapped. Use a battery drill to make a 2.5cm (1in) diameter hole in the trunk. Insert a short off-cut of pipe into the hole, hang a bucket beneath it, and wait for the rising sap to flow out. Make wine as for pea pods, boiling 4.5 litres (1 gallon) of sap (adding water if you don't have quite enough) with 900g (2lb) of sugar. Drink after a month.

You can collect *about 4.5 litres (1 gallon) of sap in a day from a mature tree.*

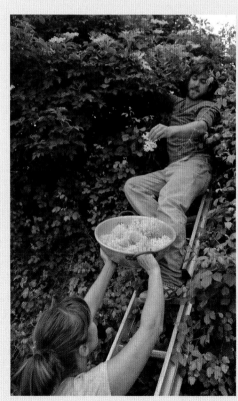

RECIPE **Elderflower champagne**

Elderflower champagne is definitely at the glamorous end of self-sufficiency. It is made simply by fermenting the natural yeasts in the flowers, which then turn into a refreshing bubbly drink that is only mildly alcoholic. The good things about elderflower champagne are that it is cheap, delicious, incredibly fragrant, and quick to make. The main problem with this bubbly stuff, however, is that it if you leave it to ferment for too long, the bottles will start exploding, spraying sticky floral liquid all over the place. Luckily, this can be easily avoided by slowly releasing some of the gases when the plastic bottles start to bulge and look ready to burst.

YOU WILL NEED
- About 600ml (1 pint) compressed elderflowers
- 675g (1½lb) white sugar
- 2 lemons
- 2 tbsp wine vinegar
- Large metal container that holds 4.5 litres (1 gallon) water
- Zester
- Jug
- Sieve
- Funnel
- Plastic pop bottles

BREWING

1. Once you have collected enough flowers, mix them together with 4.5 litres (1 gallon) of water and stir thoroughly.   **2. Add the sugar** and continue stirring until most of the sugar has dissolved.   **3. Remove the zest** from the lemons with a zester.   **4. Cut the lemons** in half and squeeze out the juice.   **5. Add the zest** to the elderflowers and water, then add the lemon juice and white wine vinegar.

BOTTLING

6. Cover the container and leave in a warm place for 24 hours.   **7. The next day**, strain the liquid into a clean jug.   **8. Then pour** into sterilized bottles. We like to use 2 litre (3½ pint) plastic pop bottles as they allow you to release the explosive gas by turning the screw top a little. Sterilize using Campden tablets rather than boiling water, which could melt the plastic bottles (see page 256). Leave the bottles capped for a fortnight and drink before the bubbly is a month old.

ELDERBERRY WINE

- **Make elderberry wine** in late summer or early autumn. With a fork, strip 1.8kg (4lb) berries from their stalks. Crush in a large bowl with the end of a rolling pin.
- **Add 4.5 litres** (1 gallon) boiling water, stir and, once it has cooled to 20°C (68°F), add 1 tsp yeast and the juice of 2 lemons. Cover the mixture and leave in a warm place for a few days, stirring daily.
- **Strain the liquid** through a sieve into a pan with 1.35kg (3lb) sugar and stir until it has dissolved. Pour from the pan into a large demijohn. After the first ferment has finished, put on a fermentation lock and leave to continue fermenting.
- **Transfer to dark bottles** and wait at least 6 months before opening.

Making cider

Cider making is a really social activity. Every year we collect apples from our orchard, but we also do a bit of scrumping. This which involves making the most of any under-appreciated fruit trees in the area and going around the village with a trailer attached to a mountain bike – of course, we ask permission first. We then make the cider from the fermented juice of our apple collection.

Know your apples

Any variety of apple can be used to make cider, and even dodgy-looking windfalls can be turned into good 'scrumpy', as cider is known in the West Country. Some varieties of apple store well, like Cox's for example, but on the whole apples don't last too long unless they are picked when ripe and are not bruised or damaged in any way. So, the advantage of cider is that you can successfully preserve huge quantities of fruit and save lots of money on alcohol by doing so.

Unless you are growing specific cider-making apples, such as Langworthy, Foxwhelp, or Crimson King, which can be brewed on their own, the trick to making a truly tasty cider is to use a mixture of different varieties. Combine about one-third each of bitter-sweet, sweet, and sharp apples for a good brew. Try the following:

▪ **Bitter-sweet apples** are low in acid but high in tannins, such as Dabinett, Somerset Red, and Yarlington Mill.

▪ **Sweet dessert apples** that have a medium acidity and are low in tannin, such as Cox's Orange Pippin, Golden Delicious, and Worcester Pearmain.

▪ **Sharper apples** include Royal Russets and Hereforshire Costards.

We have planted all sorts of traditional apple trees for eating, cooking, and for making cider, but until the trees are mature and fruiting well, we tend to use whatever apples we can lay our hands on, and the resulting cider always does the job.

Fermenting

Once you have your fresh apple juice stored in demijohns or a larger fermenting bin, it's time for the natural yeasts to work their magic. We allow the yeasts from the apple skins and surrounding orchard to do the fermenting, but if you want to guarantee success, add a few teaspoons of yeast to the mix.

Many people dislike roughly-made scrumpy and add sugar or syrup to their cider to make it taste sweeter.

We don't mind the dryness of pure cider and find that it is also great to use in cooking, particularly with rabbit loin, mustard, and some root vegetables. Yummy...

Once fermentation has ceased (anytime from ten days to a month), you can rack off the cider straight into bottles for storage, using a plastic tube to siphon (see page 257). You'll often find a secondary fermentation takes place in the bottle. We once bottled some apple juice after trying to pasteurize it and were surprised to find it had turned into a bubbly cider similar to the fizzy drinks of Normandy. Of course, we didn't reveal the mistake to our guests, who loved it.

There is a stage in the fermentation process of cider when it is described as being "hungry". We have heard countless stories from locals about cider makers throwing in bits of beef and even the odd rat to add strength to the brew. Undoubtedly, most of this will just be hearsay, but it pays to be wary of unknown scrumpy.

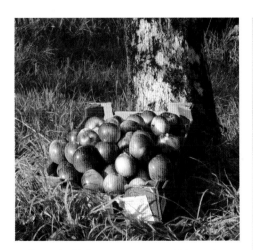

Collect windfalls *as soon as possible or they will start to ferment naturally on the ground. Don't worry if they are a little bruised.*

MAKE CIDER VINEGAR

When cider turns into vinegar by mistake it's a disaster, but when made specially it is great for cooking, and in chutneys and pickles. To make vinegar, soak some wood shavings in a vinegar you like the flavour of, then place them in a large barrel or plastic bin with a tap at the bottom. Put a wooden or plastic plate, drilled with pin-sized holes, on top of the shavings, and pour over your cider so it drains slowly though the holes. Cover the top of the barrel with muslin. As the cider drips down, it is exposed to air and the active bacteria *Acetobacter*. Drain off the liquid and leave in an open container; it will turn into vinegar in a week.

Muslin covering to protect from insects

Pin-sized holes in a perforated wooden plate

Beech wood shavings

RECIPE **Apple cider**

Before you crush your ripe apples, leave them in a heap for 2–3 days to soften, or pick up your windfalls, which will already be very juicy. Try to avoid using apples that have serious pest problems – feed them to the pigs if they are maggoty. Generally, most apples will be usable and even if they don't look perfect they can still be turned into cider. The quantity of juice apples produce in the press varies greatly, but on average we'd expect about 4.5kg (10lb) of apples to make just under 4.5 litres (1 gallon) of cider. Make sure all of your equipment is scrupulously clean and sterilized (see page 256). As with many seasonal jobs, it can be almost a whole year since you last used your tools so a good cleaning is essential. Use this same method for making perry – a sweeter drink than cider and made from pears.

YOU WILL NEED
- Apples (or pears if making perry)
- Apple crusher
- Apple press
- Mesh fabric or muslin
- Sterilized demijohn or fermenting bin

1. Pour your apples into the crusher, keeping your hands away from the rotating blades, having first positioned a container to catch the apples. A less hi-tech means is to chop the apples in a wooden box using a spade, described below.
2. The crushed apples will appear, as if by magic, in the container at the foot of the machine.   **3. Place the mesh fabric** over the apple press base, leaving plenty of spare fabric around the edges. Spread a layer of crushed apples.

4. Cover the apples with the mesh fabric and place the demijohn under the press.
5. Wind down the pressing mechanism until all the juice has run into the demijohn. Unwrap the leftover pulp and feed it to the pigs or put it in the compost bin. Then refill your press with more crushed apples and repeat the steps until you have pressed them all.   **6. The juice looks cloudy** initially, but it clears throughout the fermenting process. Leave to ferment in the demijohn and then bottle.

CRUSHING BY HAND

We have invested in an electric apple crusher that's quick and easy to use, and allows us to make large volumes of cider. But you can crush the apples with just a strong wooden box and a spade. Fill the box almost to the top with apples. Make sure that they are closely packed together so that they can't move easily, but don't overfill the box or the fruit will jump out and spill onto the floor. Use a sharp clean spade to chop the apples into small pieces before laying them on the fruit press.

NATURAL REMEDIES With an ever growing awareness of the impact harmful chemicals can have on our bodies, people are returning to more natural ways of treating everyday ailments. We tend to use quite a lot of complementary remedies and have suggested some of our favourites that you might like to try. Our bodies and homes have become battlefields and we are encouraged to use more and more chemical-based products to kill all the germs. We feel that there is a need for balance, and some of the ideas in this chapter may help you think a little differently about the job of cleaning.

Herbal tinctures

Tinctures are an efficient and simple way to preserve herbs. Alcohol, or a mixture of alcohol and water, is used to dissolve and extract the active substances from the herbs at the same time as preserving them. On pressing, fresh herbs yield more tincture than dried herbs, so if you want to make your own at home, consider growing your own medicinal herbs.

The ingredients

Tinctures can be made from all sorts of herbs and flowers. Some plants that make effective tinctures include echinacea for immunity boosting; nettle leaves for arthritis and rheumatism; dandelion to help with indigestion or loss of appetite; and hawthorn to help with high blood pressure. However, we would recommend that you always seek expert advice from a qualified herbalist before making and using your own tinctures, especially for more serious medical complaints.

The simplest way to make a tincture is by maceration (soaking the herbs in a solvent). Clear alcohol is the most commonly used preserving solvent in tincture making. The minimum proof required to inhibit the growth of unwanted organisms is 25 per cent. Qualified herbalists have access to ethanol, which is 96 per cent alcohol, but for home-made tinctures, 40 per cent vodka is more than adequate.

The weight of herbs to volume of alcohol used indicates the potency of the tincture: the greater the proportion of herbs, the higher the potency.

Taking a tincture

Consuming your tincture is as easy as making it. All you need to do is add a few drops to a glass of water once a day or as prescribed by a herbalist. Tinctures are stronger than infusions (see pages 266–267), so the required dosage can be much smaller.

RECIPE **Digestive tincture**

This tincture is ideal for those who suffer from burping, bloating, or indigestion. If you have wolfed down a meal too quickly and regretted it, the time spent making this remedy will be more than worthwhile. Take it before or after eating to stimulate your digestive enzymes. Do not use it during pregnancy.

YOU WILL NEED
- 100g (3½oz) rosemary
- 85g (3oz) bay leaves
- 10g (¼oz) wormwood
- 400ml (14fl oz) vodka
- Kilner jar
- Press
- Muslin
- Dark-coloured bottle

1. Pick your herbs and remove any insects. Chop the herbs into 2cm (¾in) pieces and place in a large jar. Pour the vodka over them, close the lid tightly and shake the jar well. Continue to shake the jar daily for at least 2 weeks. **2. Strain the contents** into a jug using the cheese cloth or muslin and squeeze as much of the liquid out of the herbs as possible with your hands or with a small press, if you have one. **3. Transfer the tincture** into a dark glass bottle, label it with the contents and date, and store in a cool, dark place. Take 1 tsp in a small cup of water up to three times a day.

Plant your own medicinal garden

It's easy to create a medicinal bed or border in the smallest garden. At our farm we have a medicinal garden of herbs, which we use in tinctures and infusions to help treat common minor ailments. Medicinal plants not only look attractive, they also tend to attract bees and smell gorgeous. Although many of the plants overlap in their healing properties, together they make a dazzling display.

KEY

Bites and bruises
1 Calendula
2 Comfrey
3 Lavender

Sleep
4 Chamomile
5 Passionflower
6 Valerian
7 Hops

Hangover and fatigue
8 Echinacea
9 Dandelion
10 Mint
11 Chillies

Headache
12 Rosemary
13 Feverfew
14 Mint

Coughs and colds
15 Lemon balm
16 Garlic
17 Sage
18 Thyme

Indigestion
19 Senna
20 Mint
21 Fig

QUICK STING RELIEF

If you are plagued by bites and nettle stings in the garden, find the nearest bunch of plantain and pick a handful of leaves. The juice from the leaves is more soothing than the traditional remedy of dock leaves.

Rub the plantain leaves firmly *between your hands until they start to produce some juice. Keep going and then squeeze the cooling green liquid on to the sore area.*

Revitalizing infusions

For a refreshing pick-me-up, cover the leaves and flowers from herbal plants with boiling water to make an infusion. Your choice of herbs will depend on taste and dedication to good health: some are delicious while others are an acquired taste and can be very bitter. Over the years we have tried out various combinations and, as well as those described here, particularly enjoy mint and lemon verbena as an everyday cup of tea. Experiment with different herbs to discover your favourites.

Making an infusion

Infusions are relatively easy to make from leaves and flowers. Place a heaped teaspoon of each herb in a mug of boiling water and allow the leaves and flowers to infuse. Or to be more scientific about it, add 30g (1oz) dried herbs or 60g (2oz) fresh herbs to 600ml (1 pint) boiling water. Cover and leave the herbs to infuse for about 10 minutes. We like to use a tea pot with a central strainer. Alternatively, you can use an old-fashioned tea strainer that infuses in the mug and is then removed when the drink is to your taste.

Using infusions

You can drink these herbal teas either hot or cold and also use infusions topically as a wash or in a bath, as a douche or enema, or use them as a mouthwash or gargle – mint is especially effective here.

■ **Drink 200ml** (7fl oz) three times a day if you are a bit under the weather or 150ml (5fl oz) every 2 hours to relieve particular symptoms.

■ **Infusions keep** in the fridge for 24 hours and can be taken cold, but be aware that cool infusions can stimulate urination.

Great healers

As well as our favourite healing herbs listed to the right, try drinking ginger infusion for travel sickness; feverfew for reducing the intensity of a migraine; elderflowers for helping ease cold symptoms; and nettle leaves – wear your gloves when picking them – to reduce stress.

CALMING HERBS

■ **Chamomile** makes a great lawn and has the reputation of soothing the central nervous system, leaving you super calm. It also combines well with mint. As well as drinking the flowers as an infusion, place dried chamomile in a muslin bag in the bath for extra relaxation. Mix it with any of these calming herbs: comfrey, hyssop, lemon balm, passionflower, and valerian.

■ **Lavender** flowers are highly attractive to bees and as a bedtime drink will encourage a good night's sleep. It is also especially soothing for a headache: use 2 tsp of fresh flowers or 1 tsp dried and infuse.

Beautiful flowers *Chamomile and lavender are, of course, also very attractive additions to the garden – and bees love them, too.*

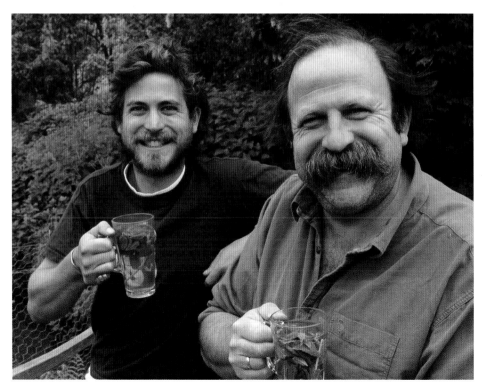

Take time out to chill *After an afternoon's hard work in the veg patch, you can't beat a refreshing glass of mint tea, with leaves freshly plucked from the medicinal garden.*

Spiced propolis infusion

RECIPE

We've been making this drink to soothe sore throats since we started keeping bees. Propolis is a fantastic bee product used in the hive as a sort of glue, but it has great antiseptic properties. To collect it, install a propolis net above a super or brood box (see pages 212–213). The bees don't like the holes and will start to fill them with propolis. To harvest it, remove the net and place in the freezer for a few hours. Scrunch it up and collect all those valuable pieces. You will need at least a 60 per cent proof alcohol, such as Stroh rum, to dissolve the propolis. For smaller amounts of propolis, use 2 tbsp alcohol to each 10g (¼oz).

YOU WILL NEED
- 100g (3½oz) propolis
- 400ml (14fl oz) 60%+ alcohol
- Fresh ginger
- 1 lemon
- Cloves
- 1–2 tsp honey
- Glass jar
- Coffee filter

1. Harvest the propolis as described.   **2. For the tincture,** put the propolis and alcohol in a jar and shake every day for 6–8 days until the propolis has dissolved. Strain the liquid through a coffee filter to remove bits of bee that may be mixed in with it.   **3. To make the drink,** squeeze the juice from half the lemon and slice the rest, studding each slice with cloves. Cut some slices of ginger.
4. Squirt a few drops of propolis into a mug and add boiling water with the honey, lemon juice, and slices of ginger and lemon.

OTHER FAVOURITE INFUSIONS

Some of our favourite infusions are (from left to right): lavender and chamomile, the perfect calming drink before bedtime; sage and thyme, for relief from a sore throat; lemon balm, for days when you are feeling stressed out and need to relax; and peppermint and elderflower to ease cold symptoms.

Immunity-boosting syrups

Our mindset with illness is that prevention is considerably better than a cure. Generally, we try to stay healthy by eating plenty of fresh fruit and vegetables full of vitamins and minerals, but sometimes a quick fix is needed when a cold appears on the horizon or if we start to feel under the weather. This is where health-giving syrups come to the fore.

Preserving in sugar

Using plenty of sugar in syrups is a common preserving technique that was widely used when refrigeration was not available. Saturating herbs and berries with sugar means there is not enough water for microorganisms to multiply and yeasts to develop.

Some good health-stimulating syrups to make at home are thyme and liquorice; rosehip; garlic and honey; and burdock. Always make sure you track down recipes from a trusted source before you start consuming home-made concoctions.

Healing combination

Elderberry syrup, described below, is rich in vitamin C. To make a more intensely soothing concoction, mix equal quantities of the syrup with an elderberry tincture, which is made as the digestive tincture on page 264, mixing together 200g (7oz) berries and 400ml (14fl oz) vodka. Take 1 tsp of the remedy every few hours.

Elderberries *Elder has been called "the medicine chest of the people", as it provides so many remedies for common complaints. The berries follow the flowers.*

RECIPE **Elderberry syrup**

Elderberry syrup is an excellent remedy for boosting your immune system because it has high levels of vitamin C and anti-viral properties, making it effective against colds, sore throats, and even flu. Always use plenty of sugar in syrups, but not so much that the mixture crystallizes when it cools. Elderberry syrup has a high sugar content, so it can be easily stored over the winter months and is pleasant and convenient to take.

YOU WILL NEED
- 200g (7oz) elderberries
- 400g (14oz) sugar
- 12 cloves
- 2.5cm (1in) sliced fresh ginger
- Funnel
- Glass bottles

1. Collect ripe stalks of elderberries and strip the berries from the stems with a fork. Put them in a pan and add 250ml (8fl oz) water. Bring to the boil, reduce the heat, and simmer for about 30 minutes, until the berries yield their juice. Remove from the heat and mash the berries. Then strain the contents of the pan through a sieve and return the juice to the pan. **2. Add the sugar**, cloves, and ginger. Return the pan to the heat and stir until the sugar dissolves. Bring to the boil for a further 5 minutes. **3. Pour the liquid** into a bottle, seal and store in the fridge. Take 1 tbsp in a mug of boiling water every 2 hours when cold symptoms start and then three times a day until you feel better.

Healing beauty

Working outside on the farm we suffer from our fair share of scratches, grazes, bites, and chapped skin – but we still like to look beautiful! We don't spend the day itching and complaining, we just apply some home-made salve. A few years ago we started using dried calendula flowers in oil to soothe rashes and scratches, but now we make a salve using plants from our medicinal garden.

Be kind to your skin

Most skincare items are made with 90 per cent water, some petroleum derivatives, and a concoction of chemicals to add fragrance and that bubbly lather. We strongly believe that these products carry much of the blame for exacerbating skin problems, such as eczema, and are not the best beauty option. So try making your own natural beauty products instead; they can save you money and they smell wonderful.

"Natural" products

There are many green and gorgeous skincare products that profess to be natural, but check their ingredients. The words "organic" and "natural" on the label needn't mean they are certified organic. Beware, too, of "green" claims on packaging and in the marketing campaigns of some skincare giants. They are often misleading and may only mean the contents were derived from nature at some stage in their production.

Calendula is one of our favourite flowers. It grows easily in a temperate climate, works well for companion planting (see page 101), and self-seeds, so requires little attention.

RECIPE Calendula salve

Salves are similar to tinctures in that they are made by extracting the active properties of plants and preserving them to be used medicinally. However, salves are made with pure vegetable oil rather than alcohol or vinegar, and combining the oil with wax produces a soothing ointment that can be applied directly to the skin. Calendula has wonderful healing properties and works brilliantly as an antiseptic. It makes a great lip balm too.

YOU WILL NEED
- Enough dried calendula flowers to fill a tall jar
- Sunflower oil
- Bees wax
- Sieve
- Small glass jars

1. Collect the flowers and dry them (a solar dryer is good way to do this, see pages 243–245). When they are dry, fill a jar with as many of the flowers as are needed and then cover with sunflower oil. Leave them to infuse for at least 2 weeks or until the oil has become a warm, orange colour. **2. Strain the oil** into a measuring jug and pour it into a pan. **3. Add beeswax** to the pan, a little at a time (approximately 5g (¼oz) wax to every 2 tbsp of oil), and heat gently until the wax has melted. Test the setting point of the salve by dipping a cold spoon into the pan and removing it; it should set on the spoon fairly quickly. If it doesn't set, add some more wax. To finish, pour your mixture into the jars, leave to set, then seal and label. Use within one year.

Greener cleaners

Surprisingly, the most environmentally damaging objects in our houses tend to be found hiding under the kitchen sink or lurking in the cleaning cupboard. Among all those bottles and cans there are all sorts of harmful combinations of toxic bleaches and chemical-based polishes and disinfectants that can be seriously damaging to us and the environment.

Eco-alternatives

A few years ago we switched from using artificially produced cleaning products to eco-alternatives. Many of the cleaners we now use are made from simple home-made recipes that originate from old-fashioned cleaning techniques. As well as being less harmful to humans, animals, and the environment, they are also cheaper. We are reducing packaging waste as we've stopped buying new bottles and packets over and over again.

We also find that, having stopped using conventional products that always seem to promise to "kill 110 per cent of all germs", we have become noticeably more sensitive to the noxious smell of commercial cleaners. These days we much prefer the aroma of our natural alternatives, many of which are outlined here for you to make and enjoy yourself.

Bicarbonate of soda

Also known as sodium bicarbonate, baking soda, or simply bicarb, this naturally occurring substance is extremely cheap and will not harm you or the environment.

■ **Dealing with a smelly carpet** Sprinkle baking soda over the carpet. Add dried crushed lavender or basil leaves and leave for 30 minutes. Vacuum thoroughly afterwards.

■ **Cleaning work surfaces** Apply baking soda and scrub with a damp cloth or sponge. For ingrained dirt and stains, use a brush.

■ **Oven cleaning** Sprinkle the mess with some salt and then mix 2 tbsp of baking soda with water in a cup to make a thin paste and apply to the oven surface. Use an old toothbrush or bristle brush to scrub it off.

■ **Clogged sinks and shower drains** Try to avoid using conventional drain cleaners in your home because they contain particularly nasty ingredients. If you have a blocked drain, pour in a cup of white vinegar plus one cup of baking soda. Let that sit for a few minutes (don't panic – it's normal for it to bubble like Vesuvius). Then flush the mixture down with a kettle of boiling water.

Distilled vinegar

Also known as clear or white vinegar, distilled vinegar is another great cleaner for the home as well as an effective disinfectant and deodorizer. Any kind of vinegar will do, but we recommend distilled as its smell is less likely to linger than other types. This the only issue that we have with vinegar – the smell reminds us of being in a fish and chip shop. However, mixing in lavender essential oil and/or lemon juice is a very effective way to mask the smell.

If you are using a vinegar cleaner on tiles or marble, always be sure to rinse the cleaned area well because it can continue to react with any lime-based product.

■ **Window cleaner** Mix 120ml (4fl oz) vinegar with 4 litres (1 gallon) of water and use to wipe down your

1. Bicarbonate of soda is a very efficient cleaner. Sprinkled it over a surface and then wipe it off with a damp cloth. **2. For a blocked drain,** combine bicarbonate of soda with distilled vinegar in the proportions described above. **3. To clean windows,** mix equal parts of vinegar and water and put in an old spray bottle. **4. Wipe half a lemon** over your chopping block to disinfect and deodorize it.

windows. For extra shine, try rubbing the window glass dry with sheets of screwed up newspaper.

Replacement for fabric conditioner You will find a splash of white vinegar in the final rinse leaves your clothes, sheets, and towels soft and absorbent. It has the added benefit of breaking down the washing detergent more effectively, thus keeping the washing machine drum clean. It is especially useful for family members who have sensitive skin or allergies. Don't worry – any smell of the vinegar goes when the clothes are dry.

Basic furniture polish To bring a shine to wood, mix 60ml (2fl oz) vinegar with 175ml (6fl oz) olive oil. Alternatively, mix 60ml (2fl oz) lemon juice with 120ml (4fl oz) olive oil. Wipe down your furniture with a soft cloth soaked in the solution for excellent eco-cleaning results.

Lemon juice

This everyday liquid is a mild, yet very effective, green cleaner. You can use lemon juice as a non-toxic way of removing grease and also as an effective antibacterial in many parts of your home.

Disinfectant Squeeze some neat lemon juice over any tough stains on your chopping board, let the juice sit there for about 10 minutes, then wipe it away.

Freshen and deodorize your microwave Place a few slices of lemon in a small bowl of water and heat it for 30–45 seconds. Use the hot liquid to wipe down all the surfaces in the microwave.

Everyday toilet cleaning Sprinkle some lemon juice and baking soda into your toilet and leave it to fizz for a few minutes. Then scrub it clean with a toilet brush.

HERBAL DISINFECTANT

Choose one fresh herb, such as lavender, juniper, or thyme. Simmer a handful of the leaves and stems in a pan of water for about 30 minutes. Add water – the less you add, the stronger the solution and the more useful its disinfectant properties. Strain the liquid and pour it into a bottle with a dash of natural soap. This herbal disinfectant cuts through grease and smells good too.

Sage leaves *steeped in water also work well as a disinfectant. The resulting liquid cleans any surface except glass.*

RECIPE **Natural hand scrub**

Keeping your hands clean can be expensive, especially using squirty hand cleaners, so we started making our own scrub to keep next to the washroom sink. Our recipe is basically a salt and oil scrub, infused with soothing calendula, which we have found to be excellent at removing garden grime. Use it regularly and you'll find that it is also a great moisturizer for the skin.

YOU WILL NEED
- Rock salt
- Calendula flowers
- Calendula oil
- Small jar

1. To make the scrub, put a 5cm (2in) layer of rock salt in the bottom of a small jar. **2. Mix the salt** with some dried calendula flowers and then cover with infused calendula oil (see page 269). **3. To use,** scoop a small amount of the scrub, mix it between your fingers, then use like normal hand soap. Wash off with warm water.

CRAFT SKILLS In our consumer driven society nearly everything is disposable, probably because we mass produce things so that objects begin to lose their value. When you make something yourself, from scratch, you will find that you look after it in a different way because of all the effort you have invested in it. We have forgotten many craft skills and our lifestyles mean that we do not have time to do everything ourselves. Hopefully, this chapter will persuade you to have a go and, who knows, you may end up with a productive new hobby.

Working with wood

You can approach working with wood as science, using a carpenter's discipline. Now that we have learned the basics, we prefer to experiment with this amazing material, for pleasure and to save money. We found that being a perfectionist doesn't always get the job done. Instead we employ a very liberal attitude to woodworking – also known as "near as dammit"!

Choosing wood

Buying wood can be confusing, but it's worth knowing what to look for, as bad wood can lead to all sorts of problems later. Keep an eye open for defects and try to buy wood that is straight. These guidelines will help:

■ If wood is **warped or bowing** it has probably been badly stacked for some time. This may have introduced stresses into the wood that make it harder to cut.

■ Look for wood where the **grain runs straight** through the wood, rather than diagonally across it. This reduces the chances of it warping as it shrinks and seasons.

■ Avoid buying wood with any **"shakes" or splits**. End splits often occur when the wood is dried too quickly, making it difficult to work – dimensions can shrink and joints may open up. Sealing the ends of timber with waterproof paint can prevent splitting.

■ **Ingrown bark** can ruin the appearance and reduce structural strength. **Knots** in the wrong places make wood harder to work.

Plywood

This is not good-looking wood but it is cheaper than solid timber and is less prone to shrinking or warping. It's made from sheets of wood laid so that the grain runs in opposite directions in each sheet, then bonded with adhesive.

Marine plywood is a much more expensive version, but has proved its worth to us in both durability and convenience. It's made with stronger waterproof glue and was developed for use with boats, so is ideal for outdoor projects. It's easy to cut and can be varnished or painted.

Hand tools

A properly equipped tool box or, even better, workshop (see pages 52–53) is essential for woodworking. Here are our recommendations for tools you can't do without and some advice on how touse them.

Saws

You want a hand saw to be straight but flexible – it should spring back into place quickly. A taper-ground blade won't stick in the wood. For greater control, hold a hand saw so that your forefinger is extended down towards its "toe". Use the knuckle

---

TYPES OF WOOD

Softwoods come from coniferous trees and hardwoods from deciduous trees – the definition has nothing to do with their relative strength. Each wood has its own particular applications.

Softwoods
■ **Cedar** A good, relatively light wood for furniture, and for building greenhouses and sheds.
■ **Larch** Tougher than many other conifers, with a straight-grained timber. Ideal for joinery and fencing.
■ **Pine** For light construction work and to make housing for livestock.
■ **Spruce** A lovely pale wood for interior joinery and making boxes.

Cedar   Larch   Pine

Spruce   Ash   Beech

Cherry   Oak   Walnut

Hardwoods
■ **Ash** Excellent for replacement handles for tools or for green woodworking (see pages 282–283).
■ **Beech** Close-grained, hard, and strong; used for cabinet-making and finer indoor furniture, and for chopping boards.
■ **Cherry** Our old cherry tree blew down in a gale and we intend to turn its lovely wood to make bowls (see pages 282–283). Often used in furniture making and for tobacco pipes.
■ **Oak** Durable and strong, with a lovely grain – we use it for flooring and furniture. It would be our top choice for an outdoor building project.
■ **Walnut** Fairly hard to come by, this is a beautiful wood for carving. Its colour ranges from golden brown to mud red. Ideal for furniture and, due to its often wavy grain, for making gun stocks.

of your thumb to align the saw against your mark and gently make a few short strokes, gliding past your thumb until you establish a "kerf". Once the cut is made, use the full length of the blade with slow, steady strokes. Near the end of the cut, support the off-cut to avoid splintering the wood.

Planes

Being able to use a plane means you can take salvaged or reclaimed wood and turn it into something smart enough to make indoor furniture. It takes more effort but saves money on buying expensive prepared timber.

To use a bench plane, hold the handle with your forefinger extended in the direction you are going to plane. Place your other hand on the round knob to provide downwards pressure. Stand beside the work bench with your rear foot pointing towards it and your front foot parallel to it. As you start planing, put some pressure on the toe of the plane and, as you finish the length of the stroke, transfer the pressure back to the heel. This avoids rounding off the ends. Plane a flat surface in two different directions, finishing with the grain along its length.

Chisels

Different gouge types suit different jobs. Most chisels have a bevelled edge. Respect the sharp edge. We store our chisels in a wall-mounted rack rather than loose in a tool box as it keeps the tools sharp and our fingers safe.

Using a chisel is a matter of allowing the sharp edge to do the hard work for you. With very little pressure and at the right angle, a chisel can slice through wood like a warm knife through butter. Use your body weight to drive it forwards. If you need some extra force, use the ball of your hand on the end of the

1. **Use your thumb knuckle** to align a saw as you start to cut.   **2. A bench plane** smooths rough surfaces. Check your progress by laying the plane on its side to see how flat the wood is.   **3. A sharp chisel** makes neat work of a tenon (see page 277).
4. **Mark wood accurately** with a steel rule.

handle. For deep cuts, for example a mortice joint, use a wooden mallet. For really delicate work, use the side of the mallet to tap the chisel.

Tape measure and spirit level

A phrase that has stood the test of time with us is: "Measure twice, cut once". Checking your measurements a second time before you cut a piece of wood can save hours of work. Having said that, we are by no means slaves to the spirit level. Often when you are simply knocking something together outside, these tools are just something else to tidy away at the end.

Set squares

These will improve your accuracy and overall carpentry skills. Use one to ensure a joint meets perfectly at 90°,

to mark a right angle on a piece of wood, and even to work out a line at 45° without any fuss. A 45° angle line is also known as a mitre.

Hammers

One of our mottos is: "If in doubt, get a bigger hammer!" We have the largest selection of hammers that we know of and we use every single one.

■ **Cross-peen hammers** help when you're holding nails between your finger and thumb and starting them off. Then swivelling and using the striking face to drive them in.

■ **Pin hammers** are for small staples, tacks, and oddly enough, pins.

■ **Claw hammers** come in different shapes and sizes. Our favourite is a steel-shafted claw hammer with a non-slip handgrip. The head is moulded onto the shaft. The hammer's unbreakable and comfortable to use.

▧ **Sledge hammer** Good for both fine adjustments and gentle persuasion.

Power drills and screwdrivers

Cordless electric screwdrivers have revolutionized woodwork. However, there are still some basic guidelines. Most important of all is to always match the screwdriver tip to the slot in the screw. If you don't you will damage your screwdriver or the slot, score the surrounding wood, or get really annoyed. Always screw or unscrew in line with the screw – imagine an invisible line that goes through the screwdriver and aligns with the screw itself.

With power tools and cordless drills use your battery responsibly if you want it to last a long time. We use ours until they are completely flat and sound like a gramophone playing at slow speed. Then we charge them up for the full amount of time required.

It's worth having more than one battery so that you can use and charge them on a rotational cycle. Some key drill bits worth buying are:

▧ **Dowel bit** with a central lead-point and two spurs either side prevent the bit from sliding or being deflected by wood grain.

▧ **Countersink tip** cuts a tapered recess into wood so you can hide the head of a screw below or flush with the wood's surface.

▧ **Flat bit** is for boring larger holes.

PROJECT **Make a window box**

Making a window box is a great way to practise the basics of woodworking. You can make it out of almost any durable wood and design it to fit a sloping windowsill exactly. Decorate the front with driftwood for a bit of fun.

> **YOU WILL NEED**
> ▧ Ruler and pencil
> ▧ Saw, hammer
> ▧ Spirit level
> ▧ Drill plus bits
> ▧ Durable wood or plywood
> ▧ Brass or galvanized screws, plus glue (optional)
> ▧ Driftwood plus tacks

1. Measure your sill. Deduct twice the thickness of the wood from the length and cut two pieces of wood to this length to form the front and back. Make them around 13cm (5in) high to hide plant pots inside the box, without stopping too much light entering the window. **2. Lay a spirit level** on the windowsill from the inner to the outer edge. Raise it until it is level, then measure the height from sill to spirit level. **3. Cut each end piece** deeper by this amount at the front, to match the sloping sill. **4. Measure the base** and cut a piece of wood to fit inside the sides, front, and back pieces. **5. Drill 13mm (½in) holes** for drainage along the base at intervals of about 10cm (4in) before screwing the window box together. **6. Drill pilot holes** and screw all of the joints together. Use wood glue as well if you want to. **7. Tack driftwood** to the front of the box. **8. Secure** window box firmly in place with an angle bracket fixing.

Make the box deep enough to disguise plant pots

Base cut to fit within other pieces of wood

Drainage holes

Driftwood for rustic decoration

Use brass or galvanized screws

Sloping sides match the slope of the windowsill and allow it to support weight of window box.

Window box base line is horizontal to keep plant pots level

Screws and nails

Label boxes or keep fixings in clear jars. Always have a large supply.

■ **Countersunk woodscrews** are for strength and they also look good. Make a pilot hole before screwing in, to avoid splitting the wood. Countersink to recess the head.

■ **Roundhead screws** need pilot holes before drilling. We keep a supply of these in stock to replace screws on old household fixings so that we preserve the original look.

■ **Coach screws** are excellent for outdoors. Galvanized ones last longer. Make small pilot holes and tighten with a spanner.

■ **Posidrive screws** are one of the inventions that has most enhanced our ability to build things. They don't need pilot holes. Use for all projects.

■ **Staples** are indispensable if you keep poultry. Use them to fix wire netting on to chicken runs.

■ **Roofing nails** are twisted and won't pull out, even in a gale.

■ **Flat-head wire nails** are standard nails for fixing wood together. Use galvanized ones for outdoor work.

■ **Masonry nails** are made of toughened steel. Be careful of sparks and splinters when hitting them.

■ **Lost-head nails** are so-called because you can bury the head of the nail into the wood. Ideal for floors.

■ **Clout galvanized nails** are for fixing battens and slates to roofing.

■ **Wallbolt** are for when you want a really strong, load-bearing fixing.

PROJECT Basic joints

Use these two techniques to make a neat, strong joint between two bits of wood. Dowel kits from hardware shops include the lengths of dowel plus the right size drill bits. Make sure that your pieces of wood are cut exactly with a set square so that they will fit flush together. The next stage in joinery for beginners is making mortice and tenon joints. The mortice is a slot in one piece of wood and the tenon on the other piece fits neatly into it. Use this joint for more professional-looking projects.

YOU WILL NEED
- Metal ruler and pencil
- Clamp
- Drill plus bits
- Set square
- Wood glue
- Chisel and mallet
- Saw

DOWEL JOINT

1. Measure and mark the centre of the end of the wood with a metal ruler and a pencil.   **2. Mark half the depth of the dowel** on the drill bit with tape as a guide. Drill holes for the dowels. Insert dowels and marry them up with the end grain of the other piece of wood, marking the centres. Drill holes for the dowels.

3. Brush dowels and joint with wood glue, and fit the dowels into the holes in the opposite piece of wood. Clamp until the glue sets.   **4. The finished joint**.

MORTICE AND TENON JOINT

1. Mark out the shape of the mortice. Lay the other piece of wood across and draw either side. Then draw a second set of lines inside: the slot needs to be smaller than the width of the second piece of wood.   **2. Chisel out** the mortice bit by bit, using a mallet. Mark out the length of the tenon and run the lines over the end of the wood using a set square.

3. Cut out the tenon with a sharp saw. Tidy it up with a chisel.   **4. Insert the tenon** into the mortice. Adjust the fit with a chisel if necessary. Add glue for extra strength.

Working with willow

Willow is an amazing plant that can grow at a phenomenal rate – more than 2.5cm (1in) a day in summer. We harvest its long straight shoots, or "withies", annually and use them around the farm to make fencing and wigwams for climbing plants, as well as weaving them into baskets and hurdles. Nothing is wasted – even the scraps are turned into broom heads.

Growing willow

The roots of willows (*Salix* species) are renowned for absorbing moisture, which is why they are often planted beside streams or rivers to help stabilize banks and keep them intact, or on waterlogged ground where little else will grow. But willow's tendency to draw moisture from the soil also means that you should not grow it, or construct a living willow structure, too close to vegetable plots, drains, or buildings. We planted our willow in a marshy valley and around the edge of the duck pond.

Different species have different coloured stems, from yellow to black. We've mixed in some dogwood (*Cornus* species) too, adding reds and greens to the colour spectrum, and we use the cut stems in the same way as willow.

We increase our stocks every year by replanting some of the withies when we pollard (see box opposite). Planting them close together encourages new growth to compete and stretch upwards to the light to produce more withies to work with.

When planting willow withies bury at least a third of the stem in the ground. We made our own Derby dipper (a old fork with a 30cm (12in) spike welded to the bottom) to make perfectly sized planting holes. Once in ground, your job is done – the willow will sprout roots, even if you plant it upside down!

Willow crafts

Living willow rods planted into the ground can be shaped and woven into domes, tunnels, and sculptures. We have great fun creating our own structures and weaving baskets (see pages 280–281).

Living boundaries

To make a willow hoop fence, take straight withies and rub off any side shoots. Then push one end in the ground at an angle, bend the willow over into a hoop, and stick the other end into the ground. Overlap them and tie the hoops together at the top with soft twine if you want the stems to graft together. Each winter take the new vertical shoots and bend them down and back into the ground to continue the hoop pattern. This fence needs very little maintenance, but in

1. **A living willow fence** grows thicker and bushier each year. If you bind stems together, eventually they will fuse.
2. **Wigwams** are perfect for beans and other climbing plants. **3. Weave willow** into baskets and decorative items, and turn shorter off-cuts into brooms.

PROJECT **Pollard and plant willow**

Pollarding is an agricultural method that has been practised for centuries. It is a form of pruning that increases a tree's productivity. New shoots grow into straight lengths, known as "withies", which can be used for weaving baskets and hurdles, or to make living structures. Another key reason to pollard willow is to keep it under control and prevent it from growing into a massive tree. Pollard in the winter, between November and March, when the tree is dormant.

YOU WILL NEED
- Pruning saw
- Loppers
- Buckets
- Derby dipper for planting
- String

1. Allow the tree to grow and then cut the trunk off at a height of 1m (3ft) or 2.2.m (7ft) with a pruning saw. This shows the new stems that have sprouted from the cut in one year. **2. Remove any damaged**, diseased, crossing, or dead stems first and put aside for burning. Use loppers to remove any thin withies too. **3. Use a sharp pruning saw** to cut thicker branches. Remove all the current year's growth from the pollarding point. Rub off any thin shoots that are sprouting lower down. The finished tree should have a flat top – it could be dangerous to fall on to sharp spikes. **4. Plant some long straight withies** to make more trees. **5. Soak the withies** in 15cm (6in) of water in a bucket and store in a sheltered spot outdoors until you're ready to plant them.

the early stages remove any grass and weeds around the base, as they will compete for water and nutrients. Use the fence to make a decorative edging, as it takes several years before it is stock-proof.

We have found that planting willow alongside conventional wire fencing is a great overlap system. Eventually, the willow will outgrow and can replace the wire fencing. (See page 174 for making woven willow hurdles.)

Wigwams for climbing plants

Push several lengths of tall dry withies into the ground in a circle and tie the top tightly; you can use willow for this too but we tend to cheat and use a bit of wire. Weave around the base with flexible withies to bind the uprights together. Once you've woven to a

depth of about 15cm (6in) around the bottom, start to spiral upwards to strengthen the wigwam (see wigwams opposite). Lift the structure out of the ground and dry it out before you use it or it will start to sprout roots and turn into a living willow wigwam – not ideal for crops.

Using up off-cuts

The by-products of working with willow are twiggy little branches and off-cuts. But, you guessed it, all of these have uses too. You can make a useful brush. All you need is a broom handle sharpened into a point at one end and a large jubilee clip. Bundle a selection of twiggy off-cuts together and use the jubilee clip to fasten them tightly around the broom handle. We find that dogwood off-

cuts make extra colourful brushes. Alternatively, use your dry willow twigs as pea sticks to support your crops (see page 142), and to make charcoal for drawing.

Make a rooting compound

Willow bark contains auxins, a type of plant growth hormone. You can make your own rooting compound from willow off-cuts and use it to encourage cuttings of other plants to send out roots. Chop thin stems into 8cm (3in) lengths and place in a pan. Pour 4.5 litres (1 gallon) of warm water over the willow, cover and leave overnight. In the morning, strain and bottle the rooting extract; seal it and store in a cool place. When you take cuttings (see page 135), dip them in a cup of the extract before potting up.

PROJECT **Make a willow basket**

We think everyone should have a go at making a basket.
Book yourself on a course, or try this basket made from buff
willow, which has been stripped of its outer bark. Soak stems
in water for 20 minutes, then wrap in a damp cloth overnight.
Keep them pliable by spraying with water as you weave.

YOU WILL NEED
- Willow ring (1)
- Weight (2)
- Block of wood (3)
- Rapping iron (4); bodkin (5)
- Sharp curved knife (6)
- Straight knife (7)
- Secateurs (8)
- 1.2m (4ft) willow bundle sorted into 6 thick base stakes, 42 thin weavers, 24 thicker rods

MAKING THE BASE

1. Skewer through 3 of the base stakes with a bodkin, protecting the surface with some wood.   **2. Insert the other 3** in the gap.   **3. Weave around the centre** of the stakes with 2 thin weavers. Insert the thin tips into the split stakes, then use a pairing weave (see step 5). Weave twice around the centre.   **4. Pull the stakes apart** on the third round and weave them.

5. Use the pairing weave, take one weaver behind one stake and over the next. Then bring the other weaver in front of the first stake and behind the next, and so on.   **6. Join in 2 more weavers** when the first pair run out. This time start with the thick butt ends. Continue pairing.   **7. Trim the butt ends** when the weavers run out. Tuck in the tip ends.   **8. Cut 8 thin weavers** to the same length at the butt end and insert 2 pairs of 2 weavers, tips first, opposite each other on the base. Work with one pair until it reaches the opposite pair; drop them and start weaving with the other pair – the chasing technique.

9. The pairs finish opposite each other.   **10. Add the remaining 2 pairs** of weavers – this time starting with the butt ends. Continue pairing. Tuck in the tip ends.   **11. Cut off** the base stakes using secateurs.   **12. The completed base**.

MAKING THE SIDES

13. Select 24 thick rods. Make a sloping cut on the butt ends. **14. Insert the rods,** one beside each of the base stakes. Add a band of waling (see box). **15. Use a heavy weight** to steady the base. Use the back of a knife to kink each rod up at 45°. To do this, bring the rod upwards while pressing on the base of the stem with the knife. Let the rod drop back.

16. Gather the kinked rods and secure with a willow ring. Trim 12 weavers to length. **17. Insert the tip ends** of 3 weavers and work a wale around half of the basket. Insert the tips of another 3 weavers and use the chasing technique (see step 8). **18. Join in** the remaining 2 sets of 3 weavers when the first set run out. Continue waling. Repeat with another set of 12 weavers.

19. Tap down the sides evenly using a rapping iron. **20. Make a simple border.** Soak the basket in water first. Use a straight knife to kink each upright down to the right. Take it over the next two uprights, weave it behind the third upright, and trim it between the third and fourth upright, so that it lies against the third one. Thread the last few uprights into the first ones. **21. The finished basket.**

WALING

Waling is a strong weave, often used at the bottom and top of the basket to make it sturdy.

▪ Take 3 weavers and insert tips into 3 consecutive spaces.

▪ Take the left-hand weaver in front of 2 uprights and behind the third, working anti-clockwise.

▪ Take the weaver that is now on the left and work in the same way – in front of 2 uprights, behind the next one.

▪ Carry on in this way, always using the weaver on the left.

▪ Using the chasing technique in waling (see step 8), ensures the basket is an even height.

Waling *is used to strengthen a basket.*

Green woodworking

Using traditional skills that are not a million miles away from modern carpentry, green woodworking produces products with a more rustic feel. As managed woodlands are increasing in number (see pages 182–183), we are seeing a resurgence of the skills needed to turn the freshly felled green timber. Everyone can try their hand at it, and we recommend novices start by carving a spoon.

What is green wood?

Fresh and filled with moisture, green wood is much easier to cut and carve than seasoned timber, which has an average moisture content of just 20 per cent. Our favourite green wood is wild cherry because it is both strong and not too hard to cut, and comes in a surprising range of beautiful colours. Other woods suitable for green woodworking include alder, English pine, elm, and willow. The best introduction to this type of woodworking for a beginner is to make a spoon (see opposite), which allows you to try your hand at the basic techniques before investing in specialist tools.

Using a pole lathe

The real magic of green woodwork lies in the pole lathe, a simple, efficient tool that has a timeless charm. It may be an old technology but at one point in history it was responsible for the mass production of a whole range of timber goods, such as tools and kitchenware.

A pole lathe is used for "turning" wood. The wood to be worked on, known as the stock, is held firmly between two points. You then use a foot pedal to rotate the wood while you shape it using a blade resting on a wooden tool rest. Using a pole lathe is like hopping on one leg uphill. It takes skill and practice but once you've got the knack you can turn out anything cylindrical.

Preparing the wood

Choose your wood carefully, and check that the shape lends itself to the object you are planning to make. The next stage is to remove the bark using a knife and shave horse, which is essentially a large clamp that holds the wood firmly while you work. You can make one from scrap wood; look up instructions on the internet. Pull a draw knife along the wood to shave off the bark. It will glide through the wood like a knife through cheese. The shavings are great for kindling, and because the wood is so moist, you won't get sawdust in your eyes.

Split green wood with a froe (see opposite), and wiggle it as you ease it down the wood. It will cut with the grain, thereby retaining the inherent strength in the fibres.

Finishing touches

Sand items with some shavings. Dry for a couple of weeks, then coat in a mixture of beeswax and oil warmed together in a pan. Once the mixture has soaked into your items, wash them in warm soapy water and dry.

1. **A traditional pole lathe** doesn't need an electrical power supply and can be set up anywhere, even in the woods. **2. A pine bowl** and green wood goblet turned on a pole lathe, with a hand-carved cherrywood spoon. **3. Green woodworking tools**, including a froe (top left) for splitting wood and various sharp knives.

PROJECT **Make a spoon**

Michelangelo believed that every stone contained a sculpture. Green woodworkers know that within every length of wood lies a perfect spoon. Making a wooden spoon is a fun way to try out some of the easier green woodworking skills.

YOU WILL NEED
- Short-handled axe
- Shave horse
- Draw knife
- Froe or saw
- Sharp knife and hook knife
- Piece of green wood, e.g. cherry

PREPARING THE WOOD

1. Cut off any off-shoots from the wood using a short-handled axe.   **2. Remove the bark** by holding the wood in a shave horse and pulling a draw knife along it to shave off the bark. **3. Saw the wood** roughly to length.   **4. Split the wood** to make a flat block to work with. Use a froe if you have one, and hit it with a lump of wood or a mallet. Otherwise use a saw.

CUTTING AND SHAPING THE SPOON

5. Draw the shape of your spoon onto the wood. We use a template so that our spoons look similar each time we make one – we didn't say identical, only similar.   **6. Make some cuts** from one side of the wood, towards the outline of the spoon. Repeat on the other side. This makes it easier to cut out the shape.

7. Use a small axe or a sharp knife to carve the handle.   **8. Pare shavings** away from the spoon using a sharp straight knife. Be careful not to cut the spoon too thin near the neck. Try to cut over the edges of the grain, not up into them. Leave a bit of a rib on the back of the neck to give it some strength.   **9. Use the hook knife** to shape the bowl. Leave to dry for a couple of days, then use it.

SHARPENING TOOLS

Sharp tools are actually safer as you don't exert undue pressure when using them, and so they are less likely to slip. Store tools safely when not in use.

Use a mini carbon steel *to sharpen the tip of a knife blade. Draw the steel across the blade a few times.*

Sharpen both cutting edges *of the hook knife with a mini steel. Draw a knife blade back and forth over a large steel to sharpen it.*

Working with metal

Man has been using metal for millennia, yet to many of us it is a mystery how to fashion it into tools or how to mend it. There are a surprising number of small engineering shops around the country where you can pop in and ask for something to be fixed, but we decided many years ago that it was worth learning a little about metalwork so we could be more self-reliant.

Blacksmithing

To become a competent blacksmith is a long, challenging apprenticeship. It is great to see a significant number of people practising this skill, though many have become mainly artists to ensure an income.

The basic equipment for setting up a blacksmith shop is not complicated: a forge and bellows, anvil, hammer and tongs, swage and cutter, chisel and punch, and file and drill.

There is no longer the same market for shoes for horses and oxen, or for latches, hinges, farm tools, nails, hammers, axes, chisels, and carving tools. But when you discover that you need some blacksmithing done, you'll discover that the principles have not changed over hundreds of years (see box below).

You don't need to spend a fortune on tools. We have found them in classified ads, on the internet, and at car boot sales. Keep your eyes open and you may even find an anvil locally. Your anvil serves as a work bench as this is where the metal is beaten. The holes in it allow you to punch through your hot metal.

When we're working with small pieces of metal, we just use a gas blowtorch to heat metal up in a vice and bend it with a hammer.

Preparing metal

When you work with metal, it is important to remove any areas of oxidation – on mild steel, this is otherwise known as rust! You cannot expect your work to survive unless you prepare the metal sufficiently. We use an old leather apron when doing metalwork as metal tends to be quite unforgiving.

Welding

Welding is the process where two metals are fused together when they are molten. Welding is a very wide subject, but we just think of it as gluing metal together with metal. Using welding equipment requires a basic amount of knowledge so that the tool can be operated safely, correctly, and efficiently. Get expert advice until you are confident and safe. There are four main types of welding that are regularly used:

▪ **Metal inert gas (MIG) welding** is probably the easiest welding to learn (see box opposite).

▪ **Arc (or stick) welding** is similar to MIG welding. A relatively large current is passed through a welding rod (or filler rod) of the appropriate metal and a circuit is completed through it when it comes into contact with the earthed metal being welded. Enough heat is produced to melt the rod. By moving the rod along the piece to be welded, molten metal is laid down that solidifies to create a strong bond between the two items.

To stop oxidation, the filler rod is coated in flux, which produces a shielding gas that protects the metal from the oxygen in the air. The

---

How a forge works

The forge is the heart of the blacksmith's shop. Here, metal is heated up in a hearth to make it malleable enough to work. The hearth is most commonly fired by charcoal or coke. Although forges have become more sophisticated, in essence the way they work is very simple. For example, early, hand-operated bellows have been replaced in modern forges by high-power fans or blowers.

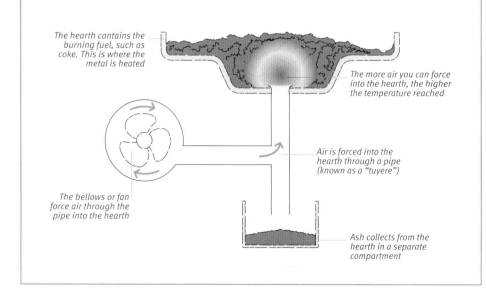

The hearth contains the burning fuel, such as coke. This is where the metal is heated

The more air you can force into the hearth, the higher the temperature reached

Air is forced into the hearth through a pipe (known as a "tuyere")

The bellows or fan force air through the pipe into the hearth

Ash collects from the hearth in a separate compartment

remains of the flux solidify on the metal, which has to be tapped off with a hammer when the work is cool.

■ **Oxy-acetylene welding** uses an oxy-acetylene torch to heat up the work. Usually, a filler rod of the same metal is also heated to its melting point. This is fed into the heated area so it runs onto and fills the area being welded. The metal solidifies and forms a bond of similar strength to the parent metal.

When using oxy-acetylene make sure the pressure of the oxygen and acetylene are set correctly (around 2 and 5 bar respectively), and that the valves on the torch are set correctly to give the desired flame. The acetylene is always lit first, and then the oxygen added to turn the sooty flame into the high temperature blue flame required for welding.

■ **Tungsten inert gas (TIG) welding** uses a fixed tungsten bit, which does not come into contact with the work. It is drawn across the metal at a short distance above the surface, melting the metal below as it does so. A filler rod can be fed into the weld with the user's free hand as with oxy-acetylene welding.

SAFETY TIPS

■ **It may sound silly**, but remember that fires are hot. You must also be very aware that metal holds its heat for a long time.

■ **Eye protection**, such as welding masks, and gloves are essential when grinding and welding. Welding masks protect the eyes from the intense light given off by the arc, but also protect the face from hot sparks and arc burn.

■ **Watch carefully** where your sparks are going because they can easily cause fires and even burn through your clothing.

■ **Do not use galvanized steel** under any circumstances because it gives off poisonous fumes when it's heated up. So don't weld galvanized sheet metal, nails, or rods.

1. The essential MIG welding kit doesn't require a huge number of items. Above left, there is the shield gas (**1**), welding gun (**2**), welder power supply (**3**), heavyweight welding gloves (**4**), grinder (**5**), and welding mask (**6**). **2. Learn the basic skills** of welding and they can be put to use surprisingly frequently. This wheelbarrow has been a trusty friend over the years, so when its bottom fell away, a bit of tender loving care with the welder meant that all was well again.

How MIG welding works

Metal inert gas (MIG) welding involves the use of a welding gun, a power supply, and a roll of filler wire. A large current in an electrical circuit melts the filler wire, which becomes the "glue" that welds the metal pieces you are working. Inert gas expelled from the nozzle of the gun creates a shield around the area of the weld to keep oxygen away and to prevent oxidation of the metal.

When the trigger is pulled, the filler wire melts and feeds into the weld pool.

Speed of the wire feed and amount of current can be adjusted on the welder

Shield gas helps to prevent oxidation

Welder power supply

A metal clamp joins the MIG welder to the work piece, so making a circuit

Roll of filler wire, which is fed through a "gun"

Mending

We firmly believe in the philosophy "make do and mend" and only throw things away as a last resort. Fixing everyday objects, like clothing and gadgets, will save you lots of money and reduce the polluting waste in landfill. Also remember the old saying, "a stitch in time saves nine", which means that if you repair an item as soon as you notice it's broken, you'll save time mending it later.

Buying goods that can be fixed

Our throw-away culture and high levels of consumption are made worse by small, plastic, breakable components and over-technical parts in products, which the average person cannot fix. Our advice is to buy good quality products and then take care of them. If something breaks, attempt to repair it instead of throwing it away, or find clever ways to recycle or reuse it, giving it a new lease of life.

Although not everyone can fix a computer or car, there are still lots of things that anyone can mend.

Reheeling stilettos

Breaking the heel on your favourite pair of shoes doesn't mean the death of them, and most can be repaired in in minutes. If you find that the rubber piece of your heel is wearing down, pull it out with a good set of pliers. Stilettos are sometimes provided with spare heel pieces, but if yours aren't, they're really cheap to buy. Place a piece of wood inside the shoe at the heel end to reinforce it while you hammer a replacement rubber piece onto the heel. Wrap your shoe in fabric to prevent it from getting scuffed, and secure it in a vice if you have one, or hold it steady on a table. Then, with the heel pointing upwards, hammer the small replacement down into the heel until it is secure.

PROJECT Basic clothes mending

Mending a tear and darning a hole are both easy and take no time at all once you have the knack. If you have worn through some socks or knitwear, or have a tear in jeans or a shirt, then have a go.

MENDING A TEAR

Tack a piece of stiff paper to the underside of the tear with small pins, so that it is temporarily held back together. Using small slanting stitches, push the needle down through one side of the tear and the paper and then bring back up through the paper and material on the other side of the tear. When you have completely sewn the tear neatly back together, remove the paper.

BASIC SEWING KIT

- **A fine sewing needle** that has a small eye and is sharp.
- **Small sewing scissors** are useful for snipping off the ends of thread.
- **Different-sized safety pins**.
- **Soft fabric tape measure**.
- **Pins** to fix everything in the right place before sewing.
- **Large pair of fabric scissors** that are sharp and cut clean, straight lines. Keep them just for fabric or they will quickly go blunt.
- **A darning mushroom** enables you to stretch a worn sock over the mushroom-shaped wood and gather it tightly at the neck, making it easier to work on a hole in the toe or heel.

DARNING A SOCK

1   2

1. Use thick thread or thin wool in a matching colour to darn a sock or sweater. First sew around the edge of the hole using a running stitch; the stitches on the back should be equal lengths and half the length of those on the front. Next, sew vertical lines up and down the hole. **2. Fill the hole** in by sewing horizontal lines, weaving the thread from side to side, over and under the vertical lines. Keep darning until the hole is no longer visible.

Saving electronic gadgets

The number of mobile phones and small electronic gadgets that are thrown away every year is quite astonishing. Many are difficult to fix, but sometimes quick reactions and common sense can save them. And if not, remember that broken phones and MP3 players can be recycled.

If you drop a gadget in water by mistake then fish it out as quickly as possible and remove the battery immediately. Then take out the sim card, storage device, or precious data, and allow them to dry. These can often be saved, even if it's too late for the rest of the device.

If any of the components are covered in wine, sugary drinks, or milk, it's important to clean them as the residue can corrode the circuitry. Carefully clean them with cotton buds dipped in methylated spirits, nail polish remover, or some very strong alcohol, and dry with a hairdryer set to cold, or a can of compressed air. More moisture can be removed by submerging the phone, battery, or other gadgetry in a bowl of uncooked rice grains. Leave for 24 hours and with luck you will have saved your gadget from a watery grave.

Remove scratches from DVDs and CDs

It's frustrating when your favourite DVD or music CD gets scratched, but you can remove the problem with toothpaste or metal polish. First, clean off any dirt and dust with a damp cloth and a drop of washing-up liquid. Then place your scratched disc on a flat clean surface with the label-side facing downwards. Rub a little white toothpaste or metal polish along the scratch, from the centre of the disc outwards. Repeat this a second time and then wash your disc with warm water if you used toothpaste, or a soft, lint-free cloth if you used metal polish.

PROJECT Repair a bicycle puncture

This is a very simple repair and you can save quite a lot of money if you take five minutes to fix a tyre yourself rather than take the bike to a repair shop. You will need a puncture repair kit and, ideally, a bucket of water, which makes the whole process much easier – a deep puddle at the side of the road will do in an emergency.

1. Remove the inner tube using levers. Then pump it up and listen for any hissing noise, or place the tyre near your face and rotate it until you feel the air escaping.   **2. Alternatively, dunk the tube in a bucket of water** and find the puncture quickly by locating the area from which bubbles are escaping.

3. Mark the hole with chalk from your repair kit. Sand the area with sand paper, and dry the tube.   **4. Apply a thin layer of glue** and wait until it starts to dry, then place a suitable patch of rubber over the puncture. Press down firmly.   **5. Check the inside rim** of the tyre to make sure there are no thorns or glass that will puncture it again. Fit the inner tube when it is slightly inflated.

Resources

We have always found thorough research to be the key to success in any new project. On these pages we list some useful websites, organizations, and books that have helped us to achieve a greater degree of self-sufficiency here at Newhouse Farm. Word-of-mouth, the internet, and your local library are vital resources to draw upon to find the information required to live a more sustainable life, and we hope these contacts and suggested reading will give you a head start.

www.newhousefarm.tv
We run courses from our home here in Cornwall on a range of sustainable living, eco-engineering, and green technologies. Our website also has information on the projects that have helped us to lower our bills and live the good life.

www.practicalselfsufficiency.co.uk
Our website dedicated to all things practical and following new projects as they happen.

www.dickstrawbridge.com
More information about Dick and his TV career as well as details of his talking engagements and contact details.

www.jamesstrawbridge.com
Information following James' TV exploits, plus contact details, and workshop opportunities.

THE HOME

The Big Green Idea
thebiggreenidea.org
A dynamic grass-roots charity dedicated to showing people how sustainable living can be easy, healthy, inexpensive, and fun.

Centre for Alternative Technology
01654 705950; cat.org.uk
Information and courses on all aspects of renewable energy, environmental building, energy efficiency, organic growing, and alternative sewage systems, plus online shop, and displays and demonstrations at the Visitor Centre in Powys, Wales.

Low-Impact Living Initiaitve (LILI)
01296 714184; lowimpact.org
Non-profit organization helping people to reduce their impact on the environment, improve their quality of life, and gain new skills, with factsheets, online shop, and courses.

The Magdalen Project
01460 30144; themagdalenproject.org.uk
Education and sustainable living centre in Somerset, showcasing organic farming techniques and traditional rural crafts.

Amazon Nails
0845 4582173; amazonnails.org.uk
Strawbale building courses and advice.

The British Earth Sheltering Association
besa-uk.org
Non-profit organization that aims to encourage the design and construction of earth-sheltered buildings.

The Cornish Lime Company
01208 79779; cornishlime.co.uk
For eco-paints and lime plaster for building and restoration.

The Sustainable Building Association
0845 4569773; aecb.net
Non-profit organization promoting excellence in sustainable design and construction methods, offering information, advice and courses.

Compost Toilets
composttoilet.org.uk
Blog posts, articles, and videos about building compost loos around the world, plus lots of useful links.

Ecofan
01691 772922; ecofan.co.uk
For information on ecofans and local stockists.

Ecotricity
08000 302302; ecotricity.co.uk
Electricity company that uses and invests in clean forms of power like wind energy.

Energy Development Co-operative Limited
01502 589407; solar-wind.co.uk
Specialist supplier of wind and solar energy systems.

The Energy Saving Trust
0800 512012; energysavingtrust.org.uk
Non-profit organization that provides free and impartial advice on how to save energy.

Futurenergy
01789 451235; futurenergy.co.uk
For wind turbines and photovoltaic panels, and courses on installation.

Good Energy
0845 4561640; goodenergy.co.uk
Renewable electricity supplier.

Heat Project
0800 0934050; heatproject.co.uk
Britain's largest and most established energy efficiency insulation schemes, offering grant assistance for loft and cavity wall insulation.

Kindle woodburning stoves
0845 5050085; kindlestoves.co.uk
For Clearview and other types of woodburning stoves.

NIRBC Ltd
028 93344055; nireedbeds.co.uk
Specialists in sustainable water treatment using reed beds, including domestic set-ups.

Proven Energy
01355 597004; provenenergy.co.uk
Leading supplier of small wind turbines.

The Renewable Energy Centre
therenewableenergycentre.co.uk
Website devoted to all forms of renewable technologies, with advice on installation, a directory of contractors and suppliers, and links to sources of funding and further information.

Renewable Energy UK
reuk.co.uk
For information on wind and solar power for the home, as well as biodiesel recipes, plus products via mail order.

RenewableUK
020 79013000; bwea.com
Professional body offering advice and information for those wanting to generate power from wind and other renewables.

The UK Rainwater Harvesting Association
ukrha.org
Industry association with useful links and downloads.

Ebay
ebay.co.uk
Online marketplace for new and second-hand renewable energy products and suppliers.

Freecycle
uk.freecycle.org
Organization that matches people with items they want to dispose of with people who can use them.

Green Fibres
0845 3303440; greenfibres.com
For eco-friendly goods and clothing.

Greenshop
01452 770629; greenshop.co.uk
Sustainable products for the home and organic clothing.

Howies
01239 614122; howies.co.uk
Organic clothes company.

Natural Collection
0845 3677001; naturalcollection.com
For Fairtrade and organic food, clothing, and homeware.

THE PLOT

Allotment Growing
allotment.org.uk
For advice on obtaining an allotment and growing on one.

Department for Environment, Food and Rural Affairs (DEFRA)
08459 335577; defra.gov.uk
Check the website or call for regulations on keeping and moving livestock, as well as information on recycling and climate change.

Federation of City Farms and Community Gardens
0117 9231800; farmgarden.org.uk
Supports, represents, and promotes community-managed farms and gardens in the UK.

Garden Organic
024 76303517; gardenorganic.org.uk
Organic charity providing help and advice on all aspects of growing food organically. Also contact the charity for information on the Heritage Seed Library, which works to safeguard rare vegetable varieties; members receive free seeds every year.

Landshare
landshare.net
Scheme connecting people with land to share with people who have no land but want to grow their own food.

National Farmers' Retail and Markets Association
0845 4588420; farmersmarkets.net
Directory of inspected and genuine farmers' markets in the UK.

Scottish Association of Farmers' Markets
scottishfarmersmarkets.co.uk
Listing of markets in Scotland, and information on how to set one up in your local area.

Soil Association
0117 3145000; soilassociation.org
Promoting organic cultivation and certification to farms and businesses that meet their standards.

Bubblehouse Worms
01886 832559; bubblehouseworms.com
The best wormery available in the world and bokashi suppliers.

Edwin Tucker
01364 652233; tuckers-seeds.co.uk
Organic seed suppliers.

Geo-dome
07833 791997; geo-dome.co.uk
For geodesic domes and greenhouses.

Gourmet Woodland Mushrooms
0560 2122543; gourmetmushrooms.co.uk
For logs and kits to grow your own mushrooms.

The Organic Gardening Catalogue
01932 253666; organiccatalog.com
The official catalogue of Garden Organic (see above), selling organic seeds, pest control, and other garden supplies.

Tamar Organics
01579 371087; tamarorganics.co.uk
Organic seed and garden supplies.

Walcot Organic Nursery
01905 841587; walcotnursery.co.uk
For a wide range of organic fruit trees.

Wiggly Wigglers
01981 500391; wigglywigglers.co.uk
Information and supplies on everything from worm composting to encouraging wildlife and eco-living.

Community Woodland Network
01476 581111; yourwoods.org.uk
Set up by The Woodland Trust, offers help and advice in managing your own woods.

Dry Stone Walling Association of Great Britain
01539 567953; dswa.org.uk
Charitable organization promoting the craft of dry-stone walling.

National Hedgelaying Society
01525 873795; hedgelaying.org.uk
Committed to conserving hedgerows through traditional skills.

Alpaca Spinner
0775 4497004; alpacaspinner.com
For hand-spun alpaca wool, spinning wheels, and tuition.

The Battery Hen Welfare Trust
01769 580310; bhwt.org.uk
Non-profit making organization that rehomes battery hens.

Best of Breeds
bestofbreeds.com
Internet directory of sheep, goats, poultry, and pigs for sale.

The British Association for Shooting and Conservation
01244 573000; basc.org.uk
National representative body for sporting shooting.

The British Beekeepers' Association
02476 696 679; britishbee.org.uk
For advice and courses on beekeeping and bee health.

The British Goat Society
01434 240 866; allgoats.com
For advice on choosing and keeping goats.

The British Pig Association
01223 845100; britishpigs.org.uk
For information on breeds and certification if you are planning to sell your pigs for meat.

The British Waterfowl Association
01892 740212; waterfowl.org.uk
For advice on choosing and keeping ducks and geese.

Poultry Club of Great Britain
02820 741056; poultryclub.org
For information on choosing and keeping poultry.

Rare Breed Survival Trust
024 76696551; rbst.org.uk
Information on the conservation and welfare of rare breeds.

Twist Fibre Craft
01337 842843; twistfibrecraft.co.uk
For spinning wheels, wool, courses, and information on spinning, weaving, dyeing wool, and felt making.

The Woolly Shepherd
01404 892862; woollyshepherd.co.uk
Sheep wool insulation and natural wool for knitting and weaving; products from a sustainable source.

TRADITIONAL KNOWLEDGE

Home Brew Centre
0117 9868568; homebrewcentre.co.uk
Large range of wine and beer making products and equipment.

The Thoughtful Bread Company
01761 239074; thethoughtfulbreadcompany.com
Much more than a bakery, with specialist baking kit available from their shop in Bath as well as online.

Ethicalsuperstore.com Ltd
0845 0099016; ethicalsuperstore.com
For a huge range of eco-friendly household products online.

Faith in Nature
0161 7244016; faithinnature.co.uk
For organic beauty and household cleaning products.

Lavera
01557 870567; lavera.co.uk
Organic natural cosmetics.

Love Lula
01829 742946; lovelula.com
Online organic skincare and beauty products.

National Institute of Medicinal Herbalists (NIMH)
01392 426022; nimh.org.uk
For information on medicinal herbs and a list of medical herbalists in your area.

Simply Washing
0800 1073454; simplywashing.com
For eco-friendly dishwashing and laundry cleaning products.

Spiezia Organics
01326 221797; spieziaorganics.com
For organic beauty products made in Cornwall.

Weleda
0115 9448222; weleda.co.uk
Organic beauty and healthcare products.

Zoe Hawes
01761 439920; zoehawes.co.uk
Bristol-based medical herbalist offering workshops and walks learning about medicinal plants.

The Cherry Wood Project
07921 361484; cherrywoodproject.co.uk
For courses on green woodwork and woodland craft skills.

Cornish Willow
01566 782626; cornishwillow.co.uk
Rustic garden furniture and traditional willow products, plus weaving courses.

Water Willows
0845 0204225; waterwillows.com
Suppliers of organic live willow cuttings and willow products.

West Dean College
01243 811301; westdean.org.uk
For a range of short courses on craft skills, including horticulture, blacksmithing, pottery, and basket weaving.

Woodsmith's Store
0191 2524064; woodsmithstore.co.uk
For green woodworking tools and accessories.

Further reading

Green Building Bible
by Keith Hall,
published by Green Building Press

How to Make Biodiesel
by Jon Hallé and Dan Carter,
published by Low-Impact Living Initiative

It's a Breeze!: A Guide to Choosing Windpower
by Hugh Piggott and Dave Thorpe,
published by The Centre for Alternative Technology

Lifting the Lid: An Ecological Approach to Toilet Systems
by Peter Harper,
published by The Centre for Alternative Technology

The New Complete Book of Self-Sufficiency
by John Seymour,
published by Dorling Kindersley

Saving the Planet Without Costing the Earth: 500 Simple Steps to a Greener Lifestyle
by Donnachadh McCarthy,
published by Fusion Press

Solar Electricity Basics: A Green Energy Guide
by Dan Chiras,
published by New Society Publishers

The Solar House
by Dan Chiras,
published by Chelsea Green Publishing Company

Sustainable Energy – Without the Hot Air
by David J C MacKay,
published by UIT

The Allotment Book
by Andi Clevely,
published by Collins

Allotment Month by Month
by Alan Buckingham,
published by Dorling Kindersley

The Complete Gardener
by Monty Don,
published by Dorling Kindersley

Compost
by Ken Thompson,
published by Dorling Kindersley

The Earth Care Manual: A Permaculture Handbook for Britain and Other Temperate Countries
by Patrick Whitefield,
published by Permanent Publications

Food For Free
by Richard Mabey,
published by Collins

The Forager Handbook
by Miles Irving,
published by Ebury Press

Garden Organic's Encyclopedia of Organic Gardening
published by Dorling Kindersley

Goat Keeping Manual
by Alan Mowlem,
published by The Crowood Press

Grow Organic
published by Dorling Kindersley

A Guide to Traditional Pig Keeping
by Carol Harris,
published by The Good Life Press

How to Make a Wildlife Garden
by Chris Baines,
published by Frances Lincoln

Keeping Chickens: The Essential Guide to Enjoying and Getting the Best from Chickens
by Jeremy Hobson and Celia Lewis,
published by David & Charles

Keeping Ducks and Geese
by Chris and Mike Ashton,
published by David & Charles

Organic Gardening
by Geoff Hamilton,
published by Dorling Kindersley

A Practical Manual of Beekeeping
by David Cramp,
published by Spring Hill

Practical Sheep Keeping
by Kim Cardell,
published by The Crowood Press

Bread: Baking by Hand or Bread Machine
by Eric Treuille,
published by Dorling Kindersley

Brew Your Own British Real Ale
by Graham Wheeler,
published by CAMRA

Cheesemaking and Dairying: Making Cheese, Yoghurt, Butter and Ice Cream on a Small Scale
by Katie Thear,
published by Broad Leys

Craft Cider Making
by Andrew Lea,
published by The Good Life Press

The Encyclopedia of Green Woodworking
by Raymond Tabor,
published by Eco-Logic Books

Home Smoking and Curing
by Keith Erlandson,
published by Ebury Press

Jams and Chutneys: Preserving the Harvest
by Thane Prince,
published by Dorling Kindersley

Hand Mending Made Easy: Save Time and Money Repairing Your Own Clothes
by Nan L. Ides,
published by Palmer-Pletsch

Making Country Wines, Ales and Cordials
by Brian Tucker,
published by The Good Life Press

Mastercrafts: Rediscover British Craftsmanship
by Tom Quinn,
published by David & Charles

Pickles, Relishes and Chutneys: Step-by-step Recipes for Home Preserving
by Catherine Atkinson,
published by Apple

Wild Drugs: A Forager's Guide to Healing Plants
by Zoe Hawes,
published by Gaia Books

Woodwork: The Complete Step-by-step Manual
published by Dorling Kindersley

Index

Acknowledgements

Our thanks

The knowledge we have collected in this book comes from years of experimenting and playing outside. We have to thank everyone who has given their time to teach us, and those who have allowed us to watch and learn. More specifically, this book is dedicated to the ladies – mothers, "loves of our lives", and sisters – who have supported us over the years and allowed us to be the little boys we are.

Dick's personal thanks

I'm not sure that I should be thanking my co-author, but James has been my conscience, personal organizer, and artistic director. While I have been off gallivanting, he has kept the project on schedule and it has been a privilege working with him. It's not often a father gets a chance to spend such quality time with his son; I'm a very lucky man.

James's personal thanks

I would like to thank my Mum for inspiring me and providing useful advice on all things green; my little sister Charlotte for taking so many of the amazing photographs that have been included in this book and for her encouragement; Holly my fiancée for her loving support and all her hard work to help make Newhouse Farm so productive – she is a true "Land Girl"; Sophie for introducing us; my Dad for trying to teach me about electricity and allowing me to invite DK down for more and more photoshoots; my Granny in Ireland for teaching me how to pluck turkeys and make pancakes; my Granny in Dorset for instilling in me the ambition to be a writer; my Grandpa for revealing how many beans make five; and Steve, Duncan, Kev, Zoe, Carol, Dave, and Val for helping with their respective areas of expertise. Thanks also to everyone who has ever helped dig the ground, weed, plant, or harvest produce here at NHF over the last few years. Finally, a big thanks to all the editing and design team from Dorling Kindersley who have made creating this book such an enjoyable experience.

Dorling Kindersley would like to thank

James Strawbridge for the artwork concepts; Stephanie Jackson for commissioning; Kat Mead, Adèle Hayward, and Helen Spencer for the set-up; Zia Allaway, Pip Morgan, and Diana Vowles for editorial assistance; Sue Bosanko for indexing; and Lucy Claxton at DK images.

Picture credits

The publisher would like to thank the following for their kind permission to reproduce their photographs:
(key: b-bottom; c-centre; l-left; r-right; t-top)

39 Energy Star: (cr). **NAEEEC:** (tr). **Siemens Home Appliances www.siemens-home.co.uk:** (br). **41 Photolibrary:** Johnny Bouchier (tr). **44 Alamy Images:** Paul Glendell (tl). **45 Alamy Images:** Peter Barritt (bl); maurice joseph (tl); Christian Klein (br); Yadid Levy (tr). **46 Photoshot:** David Wimsett (tr). **Science Photo Library:** Alex Bartel (tl). **Still Pictures:** Martin Bond (b). **47 Alamy Images:** The Garden Picture Library (t). **48 Science Photo Library:** David Hay Jones. **49 Corbis:** Dietrich Rose (b). **Still Pictures:** Martin Bond (t). **50 Alamy Images:** Jeff Morgan 05 (t); Steven Poe (b). **51 Alamy Images:** camera lucida environment (b); Steven Poe (t). **54 Marianne Majerus Garden Images:** Caroline Holmes (cl). **68 Science Photo Library:** Martin Bond (l). **80 Science Photo Library:** Simon Fraser (tl). **81 Alamy Images:** Wolfgang Polzer (bl). **88 Photolibrary:** Banana Stock (bl). **89 Alamy Images:** Doug Houghton (tr). **99 GAP Photos:** Jerry Harpur (tr). **121 Getty Images:** Lawrence Lawry (tr); Andrew Parkinson (tl). **122 Getty Images:** Dianna Jazwinski (bl). **123 Getty Images:** Frederic Pacorel (br). **143 Getty Images:** Will Heap (cr). **144 GAP Photos:** Christina Bollen (cr). **145 Getty Images:** Wally Eberhart (cl). **149 Getty Images:** Martyn Chillmaid (r). **150 Getty Images:** Taesam Do (l). **151 Corbis:** Radius Images (r). **Getty Images:** Ina Peters (cr). **152 Getty Images:** Travel Ink (r). **153 Alamy Images:** Goss Images (r). **Getty Images:** De Agostini (cr). **163 Alamy Images:** blickwinkel (cr). **Photolibrary:** Vidal (r). **176 GAP Photos:** Howard Rice (cr). **Garden World Images:** Flowerphotos / Carol Sharp (l); MAP / Alain Guerrier (cl). **Getty Images:** Marc O'Finley (r). **177 Alamy Images:** Nigel Cattlin (l). **GAP Photos:** S&O (cr). **178 GAP Photos:** Howard Rice (r). **Getty Images:** Willard Clay (cr). **179 Corbis:** Mike Grandmaison / AgStock Images (l). **Getty Images:** De Agostini (cl). **Jennifer MacKenzie:** (r). **181 Getty Images:** Thomas Kitchin & Victoria Hurst. **182 Alamy Images:** Christine Whitehead (bl). **211 Alamy Images:** David Page (tr). **248 Getty Images:** Ashok Sinha (bl).

The following images are from the personal archive of Dick and James Strawbridge and are used with permission:
12 (ct); **13** (c, tr); **15** (tl, cl, bl); **16** (c, tr); **17** (r); **19** (cl); **26** (t, bl); **27** (l, tr, cr); **29** (bl, br); **31** (tl); **34** (cl, cr); **37** (tl, bl); **58**; **60** (tl); **65** (l); **78** (tl); **83** (tl); **101**; **108** (tr); **112** (tl, tc, bl, br) **115** (bl, cr); **118**; **123** (cr); **140** (cl); **142** (cr); **145** (cr, r); **147** (r); **152** (l); **157** (cl); **159** (br); **170–171**; **178** (cl); **191** (b); **194** (r); **196** (bl, br); **200** (tl, bl); **202** (bl); **203**; **214** (b); **216** (l, tr); **262** (c); **266** (l).

All other images © Dorling Kindersley. For further information, see www.dkimages.com